A TO Z OF
AMERICAN WOMEN
LEADERS AND
ACTIVISTS

A TO Z OF
AMERICAN WOMEN
LEADERS AND
ACTIVISTS

WITHDRAWN

DONNA LANGSTON

Facts On File, Inc.

A to Z of American Women Leaders and Activists

Facts On File, Inc.
132 West 31st Street
New York NY 10001

Library of Congress Cataloging-in-Publication Data

Langston, Donna.
   A to Z of American women leaders and activists/Donna Langston.
      p. cm.
   Includes bibliographical references and index.
   ISBN 0-8160-4468-6 (alk. paper)
   1. Women social reformers—United States—Biography—Dictionaries. 2. Women civic leaders—United States—Biography—Dictionaries. 3. Women political activists—United States—Biography—Dictionaries. I. Title.

   HQ1412 .L36 2002
   303.48′4′092273—dc21   2001046014

Facts On File books are available at special discounts when purchased in bulk quantities for businesses, associations, institutions, or sales promotions. Please call our Special Sales Department in New York at (212) 967-8800 or (800) 322-8755.

You can find Facts On File on the World Wide Web at http://www.factsonfile.com

Text and cover design by Cathy Rincon

Printed in the United States of America

VB Hermitage 10 9 8 7 6 5 4 3 2 1

This book is printed on acid-free paper.

CONTENTS

AUTHOR'S NOTE

Selections for entries in this volume were made with two guiding principles in mind: to define the term *American women* and to define *activists* and *leaders*.

First, this volume considered how to define *American women*. The women selected for inclusion represent a cross section of American women in terms of race, class, ethnicity, age, and regional background. As a group they reflect the reality of a multicultural American society as well as the contributions made by all women in shaping America's history. This volume illustrates that women have been activists and leaders at all ages and time periods. The reality of women's activism and leadership is found in the variety of their differing stories and backgrounds.

Second, this volume considered how to define *activists* and *leaders*. The women selected for this work represent a broad spectrum of approaches to activism and leadership. An examination of social change movements reveals that activists employ a number of varied strategies and tactics. Among the most prominent are education, legal change, nonviolent direct action, the vote, and self-help efforts. Some activists focused their efforts on a single strategy, but many combined several strategies at the same time, employed different tactics over a lifetime, or employed different tactics as situations changed.

Many groups sought to educate both themselves and members outside their group. Women have been involved in educating the public through speaking, writing, and teaching. During the 1800s, few occupations other than teaching were open to women. Many 19th-century activists worked as teachers before becoming full-time social activists. They were the vanguard who changed educational systems and started autonomous schooling when formal institutions were reluctant to change. This volume includes activists who worked as educators and who addressed the general public to create change in educational institutions.

American women have also employed legal strategies to create change. Changing the status quo often requires legal challenges. Women's legal activities have included pressing cases through the courts and lobbying for legislative changes. This volume includes activists and leaders who worked to create legal and legislative changes from inside or outside formal systems.

Another core strategy in creating social change is the use of nonviolent direct action. Nonviolent direct action includes boycotts, arrests, mass marches, and sit-ins, strategies that are often used when legal changes have been created but not enforced. This volume includes activists and leaders who engaged in direct action strategies.

The right to vote is considered a primary tenet of democracy. Yet, the United States Constitution originally excluded all citizens except propertied white males from exercising this privilege. Many groups struggled for the right to vote, and lives were sometimes lost in these endeavors. This volume includes activists and leaders who worked to extend suffrage to all American adults.

Various social groups employed self-help efforts. Through persistent and earnest efforts, women organized their own newspapers, clinics, colleges, churches, and social service organizations. Battered women's shelters and rape crisis centers exist today due to the efforts of community activists and leaders. Today, some may assume that these organizations have always existed, but many women struggled to make such institutions a part of the American fabric. This volume includes activists and leaders who initiated change through self-help efforts.

Many people were instrumental in supporting this project. First, I must thank the best literary agent a girl could have, Elizabeth Frost-Knappman. She encouraged me to undertake this project and remained a cheerful adviser who lent much-needed encouragement and advice. I am indebted to her generous spirit. My friend Marge Freking assumed the painstaking task of proofreading the manuscript and went beyond the call of duty in her efforts. I am indebted to her dedication. Only a true friend would take on such an onerous task. My editor at Facts On File, Nicole Bowen, offered much-needed criticism and guidance, which resulted in a better manuscript. Victoria Harlow researched photographs. Her visual selections strengthened the impact of the text. Our department administrative assistant, Cindy Veldhuisen, gave support in compiling two computer-generated lists, and graduate student Sharon Van Natta performed the tedious task of copying needed references. I was assisted by independent researchers Adrienne Baker, Laura Fulton, Michelle Grace, Lydia Graecyn, Alana Kohmann, and Maureen McDowel.

Most important, I thank my family. My sons, Dimitri and Alexi; grandfather, Cornell Langston; brother, Tony Langston; uncle, David Langston; and father, Donald Langston, provided me with emotional substance and living examples of the way I hope all men will be in the future.

The inspiration for this book came from the women in my family. They served as role models of unparalleled strength and human possibility. I remain impressed by the wit and warmth of my mother, Verna Allen Langston Simonian; my grandmother, Christine Redman Hightower Langston; my aunt, Venita Langston Norman; my aunt, Hazel Allen Ayers; my sisters, Julie Langston Armstrong and Jill Langston Brown; and my nieces, Misty, Darcy, Calie, Katie, Jamie, and Jenny.

Finally, I dedicate this work to my mother. Her survival as a woman who dealt successfully with teen pregnancy, poverty, and underpaid work allowed me to pursue dreams that had been unattainable for her. Her exceptional intelligence and remarkable perseverance inspired me to always do my best. After a lifetime of hard work she died of ovarian cancer at age 59. She remains the most extraordinary "ordinary" woman I have ever known.

INTRODUCTION

The very definition of *leaders* and *activists* often favors public acts and figures over private ones. However, most women are "ordinary" women who lead extraordinary lives, whose contributions never gain public acknowledgment. A common dilemma in traditional accounts of prominent women is the bias that favors women privileged by their race and class. Privileged women often receive more resources and opportunities than other women. Suffragist Alice Paul, for example, never had to work for wages. Hull House founder Jane Addams used part of her inheritance to start the settlement house. Republican governor Christine Todd Whitman and Senator Nancy Kassebaum were born into wealthy, politically influential families. Privileged women are often among the public "firsts," the first elected to political office and the first admitted to universities and professions.

In attempting to provide an accurate representation of the past, there is an apparent shortage of written materials by or about women who lack race or class privilege. However, many women from humble beginnings manage to achieve monumental results despite the odds against them. Cherokee chief Wilma Mankiller rose from a childhood of rural poverty in Oklahoma and urban poverty in California to become chief of the largest American Indian nation in the United States. Former slave Bridget Mason became one of Los Angeles's first millionaires and used her for-

tune for philanthropic purposes. The parents of Senator Margaret Chase Smith worked as a waitress and a barber. The parents of Congresswoman Barbara Jordan worked as a truck driver and a clerk in segregated Texas. Congresswoman Barbara Mikulski's parents ran a bakery. Representative Geraldine Ferraro, raised by her widowed mother, became the first female vice-presidential candidate on a major party ticket in 1984.

Labor and civil rights movements often afford some leadership opportunities for nonprivileged female participants, though usually not at the top ranks. Rosa Parks sparked the modern civil rights movement by her refusal to move to segregated seating on a city bus. During the 1964 Democratic Party national convention, the head of the Mississippi Freedom Party, Fannie Lou Hamer, galvanized the nation with her testimony on voting rights in the South. Her leadership contributed to the end of all-white primaries and delegations. Fishing rights activist Janet McCloud used direct action protests that eventually led to a court decision supporting the treaty rights of Northwest tribes.

Many women who became leaders never married or had children, including Jane Addams, Susan B. Anthony, Clara Barton, Dorothea Dix, Jeannette Rankin, and Dixy Lee Ray. Some women did not find their true vocation until after their children were raised. Abolitionist and women's rights activists Elizabeth Cady Stanton and Angelina

Grimké both had their work interrupted by child-rearing. Ella Baker took a few years off from her work as an organizer in the civil rights movement to raise her niece. The time-intensive demands of child-rearing are often in conflict with the time-intensive demands of leadership.

Many women's rights advocates led emotional lives that centered on other women. Many suffragists, such as Susan B. Anthony and Anna Howard Shaw, and settlement-movement leaders, such as Jane Addams, led lives in which their significant partners in professional or private life were other females. Traditional historical accounts have often ignored sexual identities outside the heterosexual world, yet historians have found evidence of romantic friendships or lifelong companionship in the lives of Jane Addams, Judi Bari, Rachel Carson, Dorothea Dix, Helen Keller, Alice Paul, and Eleanor Roosevelt. In more recent decades, some women, such as Joan Baez and Kate Millett, have publicly claimed a bisexual identity or a lesbian identity, as Urvashi Vaid has.

In the United States, radical political identities have also often been downplayed or ignored. Although the names of a few politically radical women, such as Emma Goldman, "Mother" Mary Harris Jones, Lucy Parsons, Elizabeth Gurley Flynn, Emma Tenayuca, and Angela Davis, are prominent in American history, the radical identities of other popular public figures, such as Helen Keller, Frances Willard, Charlotte Perkins Gilman, Florence Kelley, and Margaret Sanger, who were all socialists, seldom appear in traditional historical accounts.

Also often overlooked is the racially mixed identity of some American women leaders. Ignoring the racially mixed identity of American leaders supports the myth that the United States is racially "pure." Activists with racially mixed identities include Ada Deer, Frances Harper, Winona LaDuke, Wilma Mankiller, Bridget Mason, Janet McCloud, Pauli Murray, Lucy Parsons, Linda Chavez, and Josephine Ruffin.

The lives of the women in this volume resonate with the experiences of many. It is empowering to learn that others have struggled and failed, some-

times failing several times before achieving their goals, or that their goals changed as they strove to achieve them. For example, Clara Barton lost several jobs because of the sexism she encountered before she established the American Red Cross while she was in her 50s.

Although some women acquired leadership positions late in their lives, Others, such as civil rights activist Ruby Doris Smith Robinson, Secretary of Health, Education and Welfare Oveta Culp Hobby, Planned Parenthood president Faye Wattleton, and *Roe v. Wade* attorney Sarah Weddington, achieved great results from their efforts at an early age. Some women remained activists into old age. Mary Church Terrell participated in a sit-in to desegregate public accommodations in Washington, D.C., when she was in her 80s. Grace Thorpe began organizing against nuclear waste storage on her reservation, funded only with her social security checks. Senator Margaret Chase Smith served until age 74. Former governor Nellie Ross served as director of the United States Mint until age 77. Some women were spurred into activism late in life, while others, such as Ruby Doris Smith Robinson, became activists before they reached adulthood.

Several women struggled with visible and not-so-visible disabilities. Abolitionist Harriet Tubman suffered from sudden spells of narcolepsy following a head injury she received while enslaved. Wilma Mankiller dealt with kidney disease; Girl Scout founder Juliet Low was deaf; U.S. Surgeon General Antonia Novello underwent multiple surgeries for a congenital colon condition; and environmentalist Judi Bari experienced permanent injuries after her car was bombed. Many women fought periods of severe depression, among them Jane Addams, Joan Baez, Dorothea Dix, Charlotte Perkins Gilman, Kate Millett, Eleanor Roosevelt, and Clara Barton.

Some women found that their religious background compelled their activism. Among abolitionist and early women's rights advocates, Quakers and Unitarians were represented in higher numbers, including Susan B. Anthony, the Grimké sisters, and Lucretia Mott. Quakers and

Unitarians traditionally sought gender equality in their practices. A number of civil rights activists found the foundation for their work in African-American churches, while some Catholics felt that liberation theology urged them to action.

The stories of the women in this volume, their setbacks and triumphs as well as their battles against gender, race, and class injustice, offer inspiring examples to us and to future generations. The following historical overview presents an outline of broad historical movements that underlay and in many cases spurred women to activism and leadership.

1. *Pre-Conquest America.* Historians argue that for the last 1,300 years Europe has been more uniformly patrilineal and patriarchal than many American Indian cultures. Gender relations varied greatly among the nations in preconquest America. Some American Indian nations were every bit as oppressive to women as were European cultures. However, other American Indian cultures were matrilineal and, some argue, matriarchal. Women held elevated positions, both formally and informally, in the largest of the contemporary American Indian nations, the Cherokee and Navajo. The Beloved Woman of the Cherokee Nation, Nancy Ward, held office on the tribal council. Other nations that have been noted for the high status of women included those of the Iroquois, Hopi, Zuni, Northern Paiute (Numu), Mandan, and the groups of the eastern Pueblo. European emigrants wrote extensively, and most often with disapproval, of the greater freedom women and children enjoyed in some American Indian societies.

The 1848 Seneca Falls women's rights convention sought many of the same rights that some American Indian women already had, including the right to own property, divorce, retain custody of children, relax restrictive clothing, vote, hold political offices, serve in the ministry, practice medicine, and pursue other professions.

2. *The Colonial Years: 1607–1775.* In European societies, women's public roles were often limited. In the rapidly growing American colonies, however, roles were less rigid, and many female emigrants from Europe took advantage of managerial and entrepreneurial opportunities. Women such as First Lady Abigail Adams ran both the family farm and business enterprises during their husbands' long absences. European emigrant and author Fanny Wright wrote of the freedom women had in America compared to that in Europe. Starting with religious leader Anne Hutchinson, women in America rebelled against the restrictions placed on them by religious orthodoxy and other institutions.

3. *The Early Republic: 1775–1825.* Female intellectuals were influenced by the egalitarian philosophy of the French Revolution and by their own observations of some American Indian societies, including the Iroquois. The voluminous letters of Abigail Adams recorded the public and private relations that women endured during this time period. Some of the first women's organizations were formed as charities for poor women and children in an increasingly urban society.

4. *The Age of Colonization: 1825–1860.* The U.S. government policy of Manifest Destiny (which held that the United States had the right to expand west across the continent to the Pacific Ocean) led to dire consequences in the lives of American Indian women. Disease, massacre, and displacement decimated Indian nations. Some Indian societies were exterminated entirely. Others faced great pressure to assimilate to European-American ways. One of the largest and most "civilized" nations, the Cherokee, was marched by force from their already reduced lands in Georgia to what they were told would be Indian territory forever. Today that Indian territory is the state of Oklahoma. One in four Cherokee died on the Trail of Tears. The annexation of northern Mexico in the Treaty of Guadalupe-Hildalgo in 1848 also dispossessed many Latinos of their property.

European-American families of the time were moving, both westward to more rural settings and into the paid workforce of factories in urban areas. The earliest American factories initially employed young farm girls in New England textile mills.

Employed women began to organize groups such as the Lowell Female Labor Reform Association to gain better wages and working conditions. These groups articulated clear understandings of gender and class dynamics. They are among the earliest feminist groups in America.

Public schooling was expanding at this time. Some female seminaries began to offer secondary schooling to women. One of the first colleges for women was established at Mount Holyoke in Massachusetts. Such women's colleges were established in increasing numbers because most universities at the time did not admit women.

Some religious groups, such as the Quakers and Unitarians, taught and emphasized gender equity. Consequently, many early feminists and abolitionists were Quakers and Unitarians, such as Lucretia Mott, Angelina Grimké, Susan B. Anthony, Jane Addams, and Alice Paul. Members of these denominations were involved in women's rights causes in larger numbers than their actual proportion in society.

African-American women often became involved in feminist causes after first being active in the abolitionist movement. Women such as Sojourner Truth and Harriet Tubman were active in both movements, though they often faced racism in groups dominated by white women and sexism from male abolitionists.

5. *The Civil War and Industrial Society: 1860–1890.* Women's public activities often expanded during wartime, when the number of men at the battlefront created labor shortages at home. Women also contributed to military projects during wartime. During the Civil War, women carried the major load of hospital and relief work. Dorothea Dix, who advocated better care for the mentally ill, served in the army as superintendent of female nurses. Clara Barton organized the collection of medical supplies for the Union army and served as a nurse on the battlefield. Schools for nurses opened at the end of the Civil War and professionalized this work, though most schools were racially segregated. A few women, such as abolitionist Harriet Tub-

man, were involved in military maneuvers and served as scouts and spies.

At the end of the Civil War, many women worked for freedmen's aid societies, which offered assistance and schooling to those who were formerly enslaved. Female abolitionists, among them Sojourner Truth became involved in this work.

By the 1870s, campaigns to reform prisons and charitable institutions were coalescing. Women visited institutions, wrote reports, and lectured publicly on these issues. Dorothea Dix published reports, testified before legislative bodies, and campaigned publicly to improve the treatment of the mentally ill in institutions and society.

The depression of 1873 and the growth of poverty induced women such as "Mother" Mary Harris Jones to become involved in early labor groups including the Knights of Labor and the coal miners' union. Leftist Lucy Parsons and socialist Kate Richards O'Hare sought answers to economic inequity in radical left political groups.

Other women were drawn to missionary work and moral issues dealing with temperance and prostitution. The Woman's Christian Temperance Union (WCTU) was formed in 1875. President Frances Willard joined the movement after serving as an administrator of a women's college. She moved the WCTU toward support of suffrage.

The women's rights movement after the Civil War focused increasingly on suffrage. Early organizing had been achieved through petitions and lectures. Two large-scale suffrage organizations were both founded in 1869: the American Woman Suffrage Association, headed by Lucy Stone, and the National Woman Suffrage Association, headed by Elizabeth Cady Stanton and Susan B. Anthony. Twenty years later the two organizations merged and began a united battle for suffrage.

In the 1870s Paiute activist Sarah Winnemucca lectured nationally on the plight of American Indians. Among the white reformers drawn to her message was Helen Hunt Jackson, who indicted the federal government for its mistreatment of American Indians in her book *A Century of Dishonor.*

6. *The Progressive Era: 1890–1920.* The idea of settlement houses, which served the poor, began in England but was quickly adapted by women in the United States. Single women with college educations from women's colleges, such as Vassar and Bryn Mawr, were particularly drawn to this work. Jane Addams established Hull-House, one of the most famous settlement houses in the United States. Many talented women, including children's bureau director Julia Lathrop, came to live and work at Hull-House. Another resident of Hull-House, Dr. Alice Hamilton, was a pioneer in the field of industrial diseases.

Many settlement house workers supported unions. The National Consumers' League, led by Hull-House veteran Florence Kelley, inspected factories and issued reports on wages and working conditions of the largely female workforce. They boycotted businesses that were particularly problematic in their treatment of workers. Women began to receive appointments to state boards and institutions in recognition of their work experience and expertise. Many women who would become prominent in the New Deal era of the 1930s began their careers in settlement houses, including Secretary of Labor Frances Perkins and First Lady Eleanor Roosevelt.

Jane Addams, Emily Greene Balch, and Congresswoman Jeanette Rankin were also prominent in the peace movement that grew with World War I. They organized the Woman's Peace Party in 1915, hoping to find alternatives to war in international relations.

By the 1890s the suffrage movement was headed by Anna Howard Shaw and Carrie Chapman Catt. They sought to bring women's homemaking skills into the public realm and "clean house" on political corruption. Others sought recognition for women's work in the home. Traditional female skills used to manage households were professionalized into the home economics movement, headed by chemist Ellen Richards, the first female faculty member at the Massachusetts Institute of Technology (MIT). She founded the American Home Economics Association in 1908.

African-American women organized the woman's club movement, which was composed largely of middle-class women working to benefit the African-American community. Segregation existed in the club movement. In 1900 the General Federation of Women's Clubs refused to seat Josephine Ruffin, who was representing an African-American club. Suffrage clubs were often segregated as well. The Young Women's Christian Association (YWCA), founded in 1890, was the only integrated women's group.

Discrimination in white women's groups did not deter women of color, however. Journalist Ida Wells-Barnett spearheaded an active antilynching campaign and worked on behalf of suffrage. In the 1920s Selena Sloan Butler founded the first African-American parent-teacher association (PTA), which later merged with the segregated white groups.

7. *1920s to World War II.* In August 1920, shortly after the end of World War I, women won suffrage. Some women were elected to Congress based on their own merits, such as Jeannette Rankin of Montana, who became the first female congressional representative. More often, however, widows of elected officials who died in office assumed the positions vacated by their husbands' deaths. Senator Margaret Chase Smith and Governor Nellie Tayloe Davis Ross attained office in this way.

After women won the vote, the suffrage movement split into two groups. The more moderate branch formed the League of Women Voters to promote political education, and the radical National Woman's Party, headed by Alice Paul, pushed for passage of an equal rights amendment to the Constitution.

The rising acceptance of psychoanalysis and the economic boom of the Roaring Twenties brought a focus on individual issues and new freedom, although women's romantic friendships were frowned upon. One of the most difficult public policy battles, for birth control, was led by nurse Margaret Sanger. Birth control devices—condoms, for example—could prevent disabling and deadly venereal diseases for which there were no cures at the time, but birth control was considered both immoral and illegal. Abortion had been made illegal in 1873, and approximately 10,000 women died each year in illegal abortions. Many children were orphaned as a result. The Great Depression led to a decrease in marriage and birth rates, since large families were not affordable. Subsequently, support for birth control increased. Gallup polls in the 1930s showed that the majority of Americans—63 percent—favored birth control education and practices.

8. *World War II: 1941–1945.* During World War II a shortage of males at home meant increased employment opportunities for women. With only brief training, women performed 80 percent of all jobs previously held by men. Federal funding for day care was made available as women's labor was indispensable to the war effort. While men were fighting the war, women provided support services in the military, building the planes, ships, and weapons used to win the war. The Women's Army Corps (WAC) and Women Appointed for Voluntary Emergency Service (WAVES) were created in 1942 to enlist women in noncombatant duties. Women were integrated into the armed forces when the Women's Armed Services Integration Act was passed in 1948. Women of color were able to find employment outside of domestic and agricultural labor. Not all American women were able to enjoy expanded job opportunities however. During World War II one of the most shameful episodes in American history occurred when Japanese-American citizens were incarcerated in camps.

9. *1950s.* After the war women were laid off from their jobs en masse so returning male veterans might find employment. This occurred although many women were the sole support of their families. The media supported the idea that women belonged at home after the war ended. Some advancements for women were made during this decade, however. Women were finally admitted to Harvard Medical School and allowed to work as interns in hospitals. Symphony orchestras also began to accept female musicians.

Scientist Alfred Kinsey conducted a study which found that one in 10 Americans was homosexual.

This was a startling statistic, as it made clear that variety in sexual identity was much more common than previously thought. The 1950s were a time of repressive politics symbolized by Senator Joseph McCarthy's "witch hunt" for people he believed to be homosexuals and communists. More alleged homosexuals were fired from government jobs than were reputed communists. Most homosexuals remained "in the closet" until the gay liberation movement of the late 1960s and 1970s.

10. *1960s.* By the 1960s, increasingly reliable methods of birth control, specifically the development of the birth control pill, led to smaller families. Birth control was legalized by a 1965 Supreme Court ruling, although marriage was a prerequisite to get a prescription for birth control. Many churches continued to proselytize against the use of birth control. By the beginning of the 21st century, 97 percent of women of childbearing age use contraceptives, a right that is often taken for granted.

Reduced demands in child rearing allowed women to seek employment opportunities. In 1963 former first lady Eleanor Roosevelt chaired President John F. Kennedy's Commission on the Status of Women. One of the recommendations of that commission resulted in the Equal Pay Act of 1963, mandating that women and men must receive the same wages for doing the same jobs. Because of segregation in the job market, however, most men and women were not employed in the same jobs. Further protection against gender discrimination was enacted in the 1964 Civil Rights Act, which was shepherded through the legislative process by Congresswoman Martha Griffiths.

The largest feminist organization in the nation is the National Organization for Women (NOW), founded in 1966. One of the issues concerning feminists at that time was that advanced math and science classes in many public schools were closed to girls. Additionally, many high school shop and cooking classes were segregated by gender. Women were not allowed to wear slacks in schools and many workplaces. Some colleges exercised admission quotas of 5 percent or less for women students, and women had to achieve better scores than men in order to be accepted into a college. Women's athletics received only 1 to 2 percent of athletic budgets. Pregnant students or teachers could be expelled from colleges. Married women were routinely denied promotions and credit.

One of the first issues that NOW activists addressed was the practice of gender-segregated want ads in newspapers. NOW also lent early support to the plight of airline stewardesses who were fired if they married. Stewardesses were routinely fired at age 32 since at that age they were deemed too old to be attractive to customers. Businesses routinely asserted that they had the right to regulate the appearance of female employees. While liberal organizations like NOW pushed for legal and legislative reforms, the more radical branch of the women's movement used more militant direct action. Many younger radical feminists, or women's liberationists, as they were called, had been influenced by the African-American civil rights movement. The leadership of Ella Baker, adviser of the Student Nonviolent Coordinating Committee (SNCC), led to the adoption of more democratic processes in civil rights, student, and women's groups. Unlike the large national and hierarchical structure of NOW, radical feminists operated from small collectives like the symbolic WITCH group. (The acronym stood for Women's International Terrorist Conspiracy from Hell, and they participated in such ad hoc actions as the hexing of Wall Street.) Radical feminists raised public awareness of issues that had traditionally been considered private, such as battering, sexual assault, incest, and the effects of pornography on society. Many women liberationists were involved in starting the first sexual assault crisis centers and battered women's shelters.

11. *1970s.* By the early 1970s lesbian feminists began to challenge the homophobia they confronted in women's groups. NOW president Betty Friedan urged lesbians to stay in the closet so that they would not damage the movement, but they were increasingly unwilling to do so and found support among heterosexual allies.

Although socialist feminism was never as influential in the United States as in Europe, Latin America, and other regions in the world, by the late 1970s several groups and publications advocated that class differences among women should be recognized. Leftist activist Angela Davis was one national figure in this movement. Socialist feminists supported welfare rights and unionization efforts among women workers. Many activists lent their energies to economic issues such as comparable worth.

12. *1980s to Present.* While middle-class settlement workers had gone into poor immigrant communities in their work, in the 1980s and 1990s many women returned to their own communities to create social change. Women of color had been involved in feminist groups from the beginning. NOW was originally the idea of civil rights attorney Pauli Murray, who proposed that an organization similar to the National Association for the Advancement of Colored People (NAACP) was needed for women. In the early 1970s, many women of color had formed groups separate from white feminists as they felt their concerns were not fully supported in mainstream groups. The 1983 publication of *This Bridge Called My Back,* an anthology of writings by women of color, edited by Cherríe Moraga and Gloria Anzaldúa, vocalized many of their concerns

During this time, Wilma Mankiller returned to work in the Cherokee Nation, Winona LaDuke returned to the White Earth Reservation to start a land recovery project, vice president of the United Farm Workers (UFW) Dolores Huerta continued to lead the farmworkers movement, and Linda Chavez-Thompson became vice president of the largest labor organization in the country, the AFL-CIO.

A great deal of change has occurred as a result of the activism and leadership offered by American women from all walks of life. Women gained the right to attend colleges, to practice in professions, to vote, and to use birth control. Women activists broke the silence concerning violence against women and children. They established institutions now taken for granted, such as shelters for battered women shelters and sexual-assault crisis centers. Women athletes have excelled in a broad range of sports at all levels including the Olympics.

Women who engaged in various forms of activism and who led groups and movements in every generation created enormous social change, though it often fell short of their vision of what they hoped to accomplish.

At the beginning of the 21st century, women are blessed with the broadest range of choices ever, thanks to the work of women throughout U.S. history. It is necessary to remain mindful of their sacrifices and pioneering spirit as women today travel in their footsteps on a path many hope will lead to a more just world for future generations—both daughters and sons.

A

 ABZUG, BELLA SAVITSKY
(1920–1998) *Congressional Representative, Women's Rights Leader*

Bella Abzug was the first woman elected to the House of Representatives on a women's rights platform. Her campaign slogan was "This woman's place is in the House—the House of Representatives." Bella Savitsky Abzug was born on July 24, 1920, the year women gained suffrage, to Emanuel and Esther Savitsky. Her father was a Russian-Jewish immigrant butcher who died when Abzug was 13. After her father's death, Abzug recited Kaddish in the synagogue every day for a year, a Jewish prayer ritual traditionally performed only by males. She was elected student body president at Hunter College and completed her bachelor of arts degree in 1942. She married stockbroker Martin Abzug in 1944 and had two daughters.

Abzug's application to Harvard Law School was rejected due to the school's male-only policy at that time. She became one of six women admitted to Columbia University's School of Law in a class of 120. Abzug graduated from law school in 1947 after serving as editor of the *Columbia Law Review.*

She defended unions, civil rights clients, and those prosecuted by McCarthyism, a "witch hunt" of leftists and others during the 1950s led by Senator Joseph McCarthy. In 1961, Abzug was a founder of Women's Strike for Peace and served as its executive director from 1961 to 1970.

When she was 50, in 1970, Abzug was elected to Congress from New York City's 19th District. She was one of only nine women in the House of Representatives and the only Jewish woman. Abzug served three terms in Congress, starting in 1971. On her first day in Congress she made a resolution calling for the immediate withdrawal of troops from Vietnam. Abzug was also the first person to call for President Nixon's impeachment and was a founder of the Congressional Caucus on women's issues.

In the 92nd Congress, along with Representative MARTHA GRIFFITHS of Michigan, Abzug introduced 20 bills pertaining to women, on such issues as abortion rights, social security, credit for women, extension of the minimum wage to domestic workers, and more comprehensive child care. Abzug authored the first law banning the discrimination women then faced in obtaining credit.

Member of Congress Bella Abzug in one of
her trademark hats
(Prints and Photographs Division,
Library of Congress, Washington, D.C.)

While in Congress she worked on behalf of the
Equal Rights Amendment, which was never
enacted. In 1971, with representatives SHIRLEY
CHISHOLM and PATSY MINK and women's rights
activists BETTY FRIEDAN and GLORIA STEINEM, she
founded the National Women's Political Caucus
with the goal of getting more women into public
office. In 1977, Abzug and Mink were successful in
gaining funds for the first and thus far only federally funded national women's conference. Held in
Houston, Texas, the conference drew 15,000 participants. In 1970 Abzug authored the Freedom of
Information Act (which allowed citizens access to

unclassified government documents). In 1971 she
was unable to secure passage of the first gay rights
bill. Her colleagues named her one of the three
most influential members of Congress in a 1976
U.S. News and World Report poll. A 1977 Gallup
poll rated her as one of the 20 most influential
women in the world.

Abzug's diary-type account of her first two years
in Congress, *Bella! Ms. Abzug Goes to Washington,*
was published in 1972. In 1976, Abzug ran for the
U.S. Senate but lost the New York State Democratic primary to Patrick Moynihan by only one percentage point. Abzug also ran for mayor of New
York City in 1977, but lost to Ed Koch. She was
the first woman candidate for both positions. Her
last national position was as cochair of President
Jimmy Carter's National Advisory Council on
Women.

In 1984, with her congressional aide Mim Kelber,
Abzug coauthored *Gender Gap: Bella Abzug's Guide
to Political Power for American Women.* Her husband
died two years later, in 1986. Her last book, *Women
Looking Beyond 2000,* published in 1995, examined
how closely women in the developing world were
tied to environmental issues. Abzug used a wheelchair for mobility during her last few years, and died
at age 77 on March 31, 1998, following heart surgery. Gloria Steinem said of Abzug, "In a just country, she would have been president."

Further Reading

Abzug, Bella, with Mim Kelber. *Gender Gap: Bella Abzug's
Guide to Political Power for Women.* Boston: Houghton
Mifflin, 1984.
Abzug, Bella. *Bella! Ms. Abzug Goes to Washington.* New
York: Saturday Review Press, 1972.
———. *Women: Looking Beyond 2000.* New York: United
Nations, 1995.
Education Development Center. "Bella Abzug." Available
online. URL: http://www.edc.org/WomensEquity/
WOW/abzug.html. Downloaded on December 15,
2000.
Rodgers, Kathy. "In Memoriam—Bella Abzug." *Columbia
Law Review* 98, no. 5 (June 1998): 1145.
Steinem, Gloria. "Born To Be a World Leader." *Ms.* 9, no.
1 (July/August, 1998): 62–63.

ADAMS, ABIGAIL SMITH
(1744–1818)   *First Lady*

Abigail Adams was a prolific writer, patriot, abolitionist, and feminist, the wife of the second president of the United States and mother of the sixth president. Abigail Smith was born on November 11, 1744, in Weymouth, Massachusetts, a coastal town south of Boston. She was the second child of Elizabeth Quincy Smith and Congregational minister Reverend William Smith. Her mother was descended from notable Puritan clerics. Her father was a large landholder and political leader.

Like most girls of her time, Adams was educated at home. Most New England schools admitted only boys; girls were taught within the family household. Generally, girls were taught only enough reading so they could read their Bibles and write letters. They also learned basic arithmetic to be able to help balance their family budgets. Adams read much more than the Bible in her family's library and she took an avid interest in political events.

When she was 14 she met John Adams, a former schoolteacher and Harvard graduate. They were married on October 25, 1764, and John Adams began a career in law. The couple lived on his small farm at Braintree, Massachusetts. His practice soon expanded to Boston.

Adams had six children in seven years, three sons and two daughters; a sixth child was stillborn. Early in their marriage, her husband traveled as a circuit judge; later he moved into politics. She wrote him daily letters that detailed life in the colonies as the American Revolution loomed, struggles with wartime shortages, and inflation.

Adams bought land, managed the family farm and its tenants and employees, raised her children, and served as "deputy husband." Even when living abroad, she made the decisions regarding the farm and dairies. Her skillful management allowed the family to become modestly prosperous. During the Revolutionary War she became a merchant by selling items her husband sent her as gifts. From this modest start, Adams expanded her business by importing and retailing tea, china, handkerchiefs, ribbons, and fabrics. She made purchases in her husband's name, since married women could not own property. Because she raised her children alone, due to her husband's long periods of absence, she sometimes referred to herself as a "nun" or a "widow."

In 1784, she joined her husband at his diplomatic post in Paris. The following year, she accompanied him to Great Britain in his role as the first U.S. minister to that country. They returned to Massachusetts in 1788 and John served under President George Washington as the first vice president of the nation. In 1796, Adams was elected the second president of the United States.

First Lady Abigail Adams, from an original painting by Gilbert Stuart, circa 1830
(Prints and Photographs Division,
Library of Congress, Washington, D.C.)

Adams pursued an active self-education throughout her lifetime. She read numerous newspapers, a broad range of literature, and a little French, and attended lectures on science at the Royal Academy while she was in England. Adams often regretted her lack of formal education. She believed women were the intellectual equals of men and should have equal rights to education. As she stated to her husband, "It is really mortifying Sir, when a woman possessed of a common share of understanding considers the difference of Education between the male and female Sex, even in those families where Education is attended too." She was one of the most well-read women in America, and the thousands of letters she wrote recorded the details of life during times of revolution and reflected the history of the young country.

She was an influential adviser to her husband and son and held many progressive ideas. As a believer in equal education for men and women, she made certain that her own daughter received a good education. The rhetoric of liberty and freedom influenced her ideas regarding slavery, which she opposed, and she defended her right to teach a black servant to read. As Adams stated, "I have sometimes been ready to think that the passion for Liberty cannot be Eaquelly Strong in the Breasts of those who have been accustomed to deprive their fellow Creature of theirs." One of the most famous passages from her letters was written to her husband in 1776, regarding the formation of the U.S. Congress. She told him: "Remember the ladies, and be more generous and favorable to them than your ancestors. Do not put such unlimited power into the hands of the husbands—If particular care and attention is not paid to the ladies, we are determined to foment a rebellion, and will not hold ourselves bound by any laws in which we have no voice or representation."

Like the early feminist theorist Mary Wollstonecraft, Adams applied the ideals of late-18th-century democratic revolutions to the status of women. Suffrage leader ELIZABETH CADY STANTON later called Adams "the first American woman who threatened rebellion unless the rights of her sex were secured."

The Adams family retired to Quincy, Massachusetts, in 1801 after John was defeated in his reelection bid by Thomas Jefferson. Their daughter Abigail had a mastectomy in 1811 and died two years later in 1813. Abigail Adams died October 28, 1818, at age 74. Her son John Quincy Adams became president less than a decade after her death. In 1840, her grandson Charles Francis Adams edited two small volumes of the *Letters of Mrs. Adams* and her literary contribution in capturing the nation's history became clear. The edition went through four printings in the 1840s alone. Charles Adams also published *The Familiar Letters of John Adams and His Wife* in 1876. Her letters offered a glimpse into the life of a president's family and the personal side of the American Revolution. Letters were one of the few respectable outlets for women's writing at the time since they were expected to be read privately, and women writing for publication were still frowned upon. (They were also an efficient way to communicate; by the 17th century the postal system had been developed to the point that letters could be delivered within the same city on the day they had been written.)

In 1952, the family donated Abigail Adams's letters to the Massachusetts Historical Society. Harvard University Press currently publishes her letters in six volumes. Adams declined the suggestion to have her letters published during her lifetime, perhaps out of a desire to maintain her privacy, but they remain one of the best accounts of an American woman's life in the revolutionary period.

Further Reading

Akers, Charles. *Abigail Adams: An American Woman.* Menlo Park, Calif.: Addison-Wesley, 1999.

Gale Group. "Abigail Adams." Available online. URL: http://www.gale.com/freresrc/womenhst/adamsab.html. Downloaded on December 16, 2000.

Gelles, Edith. *First Thoughts: Abigail Adams.* Old Tappan, N.J.: Macmillan, 1998.

———. *Portia: The World of Abigail Adams.* Bloomington: Indiana University Press, 1995.

Instructional Materials Center, School of Education at the University of Missouri at Kansas City. "Abigail Smith Adams." Available online. URL: http://cctr.umkc.edu/user/breese/adamsa.htm. Downloaded on December 16, 2000.

Nagel, Paul. *The Adams Women*. Cambridge, Mass.: Harvard University Press, 1999.

White House. "Abigail Smith Adams." Available online. URL: http://www.whitehouse.gov/WH/glimpse/firstladies/html/aa2.html. Downloaded on December 16, 2000.

Jane Addams as a young woman
(University of Illinois at Chicago, the University Library, Jane Addams Memorial Collection)

 ## ADDAMS, LAURA JANE
(1860–1935)   *Founder of Hull-House, Nobel Peace Prize Winner*

Jane Addams was the founder of Hull-House in Chicago, one of the first settlement houses in the United States, and she also won a Nobel Peace Prize.

Laura Jane Addams was born on September 6, 1860, in rural Cedarville, Illinois, the youngest of five children. Her parents, Sarah Weber Addams and John Huy Addams, were Quakers. Her mother died in childbirth when Jane was two. Her father, an abolitionist and state senator for eight terms, remarried five years later.

Young Jane was a good student and wished to pursue a college education at Smith College, recently opened in Northampton, Massachusetts. Her ambition was unusual; at that time the general opinion held that higher education for women was unnecessary and even dangerous. Harvard Medical School professors published books claiming to prove that higher education damaged women's reproductive systems. Though her father supported the concept of women's education, he would not allow her to attend Smith, which he considered too distant; he wanted her closer to home. In 1877, Adams enrolled in the Rockford Female Seminary in Illinois from which she graduated as valedictorian.

The summer following her graduation, her father died suddenly from appendicitis. Addams inherited part of his considerable fortune. In the fall she enrolled in the Woman's Medical College of Pennsylvania, but she had to quit medical school after one semester, as she required a spinal operation. She struggled with depression for several years. During this time she traveled abroad. While in England in 1887, she visited a settlement house called Toynbee Hall. That visit set her life on a different path.

The settlement movement had started in 1884 in England and represented an entirely new method of bringing middle-class charity to the poor. Toynbee Hall was the first settlement house where volunteers with university backgrounds lived with the poor rather than just working in poor neighborhoods during the day and returning to their middle-class neighborhoods in the evening. Previous organized charities had stressed moral virtue as the cure for poverty. However, settlement house workers labored for social change, believing that people were poor not due to personal defects but because of social dynamics. Between 1890 and 1910, about 400 settlement houses were founded. Hull-House was among the first in the United States.

In 1889, Addams used her inheritance to found Hull-House in Chicago with her college companion, Ellen Gates Starr, to serve the poor, largely immigrant urban population. (Addams never married, but in 1890, at age 30, she met Mary Rozet Smith, a benefactor of Hull-House, who became her lifelong companion.) Volunteers resided at Hull-House and did their own laundry, cooking, and cleaning. In the first year of operation, Hull-House volunteers served nearly 50,000 neighborhood residents. Addams wrote, "The relationship of the settlement to its neighborhood resembles that of the big brother whose mere presence on the playground protects the little ones from bullies." Female settlement workers in the United States had a long-term influence on the development of social work and the development of the welfare state, although Addams always remained somewhat critical of the social work profession, because it "spoke of 'clients' rather than of 'neighbors in need.'"

One of Hull-House's first projects was a day care center. Parents normally worked 12- to 16-hour days, leaving their children unsupervised, and settlement workers wanted to help members of the neighborhood with, as Addams recalled, "the humblest neighborhood services. We were asked to wash the newborn babies, to prepare the dead for burial, to nurse the sick, and to mind the children." Hull-House offered vocational training, citizenship and literacy classes, child and medical care, a meeting place for labor unions and cultural groups, music and art classes, an art gallery, and leisure activities.

Hull-House volunteers helped pass legislation to improve the conditions of workers, especially women and children, including the first state protective legislation for women and children, compulsory education laws, and in 1903, state child labor laws, so strong that they would not be matched by federal legislation until 1916. They also reformed the juvenile justice system, establishing the first juvenile court in the nation.

Addams hired only union labor for all Hull-House construction projects. Some wealthy Chicago residents thought she was a socialist. Although some later critics have critiqued Hull-House for its commitment to the assimilation of immigrants into American culture, Addams stated repeatedly that the diverse community surrounding Hull-House provided a model for respecting cultural differences, given the range of ethnicities, and further believed, "Internationalism engendered in the immigrant quarters of American cities might be recognized as an effective instrument in the cause of peace."

Addams became the vice president of the National Woman's Trade Union League in 1903 and was a founder and an executive committee member of the National Association for the Advancement of Colored People (NAACP). She joined the National American Woman Suffrage Association in 1906, serving as its vice president from 1911 to 1914. In 1910, she became the first woman granted an honorary doctorate from Yale University.

Jane Addams's reputation as a writer made her the country's best-known settlement worker and Hull-House the country's most famous settlement house. She wrote more than 450 articles and 12 books, including the best-seller *Twenty Years at Hull-House,* published in 1910. Addams had all her books printed only in union shops.

In 1915, she was elected chair of the Woman's Peace Party and served as the first president of the Women's International League for Peace and Freedom from 1919 to 1929. She was one of the founders of the American Civil Liberties Union (ACLU) in 1920.

Addams's popularity declined during the Red Scare, a wave of hysterical fear of communism that swept the United States after the 1917 Russian Revolution. The Red Scare led to the Palmer Raids of 1919–21, during which thousands of innocent people were arrested as radicals. Addams defended those arrested. The Daughters of the American Revolution (DAR) of which Addams was a member, denounced her as procommunist, and later expelled her. Her advocacy of labor unions and her pacifist values also caused her to lose some supporters. In particular, her pacifist stance during World War I was widely criticized. By 1919 her name appeared on a "traitor list" presented to the Senate Judiciary Committee.

In 1931, Addams became the first American woman awarded the Nobel Peace Prize and remains the only social worker to receive such recognition. She donated the prize money to the Women's International League for Peace and Freedom. Addams died of colon cancer in a Chicago hospital four years later at age 74, on May 21, 1935, and was buried in Cedarville, Illinois. Her funeral, held at Hull-House, was attended by thousands. As she had requested, her work for the Women's International League for Peace and Freedom, as well as for Hull-House, were listed on her tombstone. Hull-House continued to operate into the 1960s.

Further Reading

Addams, Jane. *Democracy and Social Ethics: And Other Essays.* 1902. Reprint, New York: Scholarly Press, 2000.
———. *Newer Ideals of Peace.* 1907. Reprint, Peace Movement in America Series. New York: J. S. Ozer, 1972.
———. *Twenty Years at Hull-House.* 1910. Reprint, New York: Signet, 1999.
Diliberto, Gioia. *A Useful Woman: The Early Life of Jane Addams.* New York: Scribner, 1999.
Sklar, Kathryn Kish. "The Jane Addams Papers, 1860–1960." *The Journal of American History* 76, no. 4 (March 1990): 1337.
Stebner, Eleanor. *The Women of Hull House: A Study in Spirituality, Vocation, and Friendship.* Albany: State University of New York Press, 1997.
University of Illinois at Chicago. "Hull-House Museum." Available online. URL: http://www.uic.edu/jaddams/hull/. Downloaded August 8, 2000.

 ## ALBRIGHT, MADELEINE KORBEL
(1937–) *Secretary of State, UN Ambassador*

Madeleine Albright was the 64th U.S. secretary of state and the first woman to fill this post. Madeleine Korbel was born on May 15, 1937, in Prague, Czechoslovakia. Her father, Josef Korbel, was from Moravia, which is now part of the Czech Republic. His family moved to Prague in 1928, and he married his high school sweetheart, Mandula Spieglova. Madeleine was the first of their three children. When she was an infant, her family moved to Belgrade, Yugoslavia. Her family was forced to flee their home twice. First, when Madeleine was two, they went to London to escape the Nazis. After the war the family returned to Czechoslovakia and in 1947, Madeleine was sent to boarding school in Switzerland, where she learned to speak French. But the Korbels fled Czechoslovakia again in 1948, this time driven out by Stalinism. Her father, a Czechoslovakian diplomat, was able to bring his family to America when Madeleine was 11 years old. They settled temporarily in New York City, then moved to Colorado, where Josef Korbel taught international relations at the University of Denver.

She completed high school in 1955 and received a scholarship to attend Wellesley College in Massachusetts, where she studied politics and journalism. She graduated with honors in 1959 with a degree in political science. During a summer job at the *Denver Post,* she met her future husband, Joseph Albright, whose family owned a number of newspapers, including the *Denver Post.* Three days after graduation they married and moved to Chicago, where her husband worked as a reporter for the *Sun-Times.* An editor at the *Sun-Times* told Albright that he would not hire her because her husband worked there. No other local newspaper would hire her either, so for a time she worked for the *Encyclopedia Britannica.* The family moved to Long Island, New York, in 1961 when her husband went to work for *Newsday.* Albright gave birth that year to twin daughters; a third daughter was born six years later.

Albright enrolled in the graduate program in public law and government at Columbia University, earning a master's degree and a certificate in Russian studies in 1968. The family then moved to Washington, D.C., where her husband was transferred.

During this time she studied international relations at Johns Hopkins University. In 1976,

Albright became the chief legislative assistant for Democratic Senator Edmund Muskie. Also in 1976, Albright earned her Ph.D. at Columbia University's Department of Public Law and Government. Her doctoral dissertation focused on the role of the press in the 1968 reform movement in Czechoslovakia.

Albright served on President Jimmy Carter's National Security Council from 1978 to 1981 through the mentorship of one of her Columbia professors, Zbigniew Brzezinski. The next year, after 23 years of marriage, Albright's husband left her for a younger woman.

After leaving government, Albright wrote *Poland: The Role of the Press in Political Change* (1983), which won an award from the Smithsonian Institution's Woodrow Wilson Center for Scholars. She taught at Georgetown University from 1982 to 1993 and served as director of the Women in Foreign Service program. Albright took pride in winning Best Teacher awards four years in a row while at Georgetown.

In 1992, under President Bill Clinton, Albright served as ambassador to the United Nations and as a member of Clinton's National Security Council. She was the second woman to hold the position at the United Nations. (The first was JEANNE KIRKPATRICK, appointed by President Ronald Reagan in 1981.) In 1996, the Senate unanimously confirmed Albright's historic nomination for secretary of state. Shortly after her confirmation, a Czech cousin revealed to the press that Albright's family were not Catholics, as Albright believed, but Jews, and that three of her grandparents had died in concentration camps. A *Washington Post* reporter found the evidence in documents that had just recently been made available by the Czech Republic. Some suspected that Albright had kept her family history a secret, but Albright said that her parents had practiced "historical amnesia" with the hope of protecting their children from anti-Semitism. In January 1997, when she took office as secretary of state, Albright became the highest-ranking woman in the history of the fed-

eral government, and the third-highest-ranking official in the Clinton administration.

Albright served as secretary of state during a period of rebuilding in post–cold war Europe. She negotiated the expansion of NATO and peace accords in Bosnia and the Middle East. She resigned with the election of President George W. Bush in 2000. As of 2001 Albright remained the only woman to be secretary of state, and she was the last to serve in this position at the close of the 20th century.

Further Reading

Albright, Madeleine. *Poland: The Role of the Press in Political Change.* New York: CBS Educational and Professional Publishing, 1983.

Blackman, Ann. *Seasons of Her Life: A Biography of Madeleine Korbel Albright.* New York: Scribner, 1998.

Blood, Thomas. *Madam Secretary: A Biography of Madeleine Albright.* New York: St. Martin's, 1999.

Borrelli, Mary Anne. "Gender, Politics and Change in the United States Cabinet: The Madeleine Korbel Albright and Janet Reno Appointments." In Sue Tolleson-Rinehart and J. Josephson eds. *Gender and American Political Women, Men and the Political Process.* Armonk, N.Y.: M.E. Sharpe 2000.

Dobbs, Michael. *Madeleine Albright: A Twentieth-Century Odyssey.* New York: Holt, 1999.

Hirsh, Michael. "Sweet Victory for Albright." *Newsweek* 136, no. 16 (October 16, 2000): 34–35.

Lippman, Thomas. *Madeleine Albright and the New American Diplomacy.* Boulder, Color.: Westview Press, 2000.

Public Broadcasting Service. "Newsmaker: Madeleine Albright." Available online. URL: http://www.pbs.org/newshour/bb/white_house/jan-june00/albright_2-7.html. Downloaded on February 7, 2000.

 ## ANTHONY, SUSAN BROWNELL
(1820–1906) *Suffrage Leader*

Susan B. Anthony was the most prominent women's suffrage organizer and activist of the 19th century. Born on February 15, 1820, in Adams, Massachusetts, to Quakers Lucy Read Anthony and Daniel Anthony, Susan B. Anthony was second of seven children. Because of the economic

Susan B. Anthony, 19th-century suffragist
(Still Picture Branch, National Archives, College Park, MD)

depression of 1837, her family was forced to declare bankruptcy. They moved to Rochester, New York, where their home became a meeting place for antislavery activists, who included their neighbor, the great African-American antislavery orator Frederick Douglass. Quakers were against slavery and believed in equality between men and women. When a male schoolteacher refused to teach Anthony long division, a subject he viewed as only fitting for boys, her father started a home school and employed a female teacher. Anthony completed her formal education at a Quaker seminary for women in Philadelphia.

Teaching was one of the few professions open to women at that time. Anthony became a teacher in 1839 and helped support her family with her wages, which were one-fifth of what her male colleagues made. At a state teacher's convention she offered resolutions against racial segregation in schools, which read in part: "Resolved: That the exclusion of colored youth from our public schools, academies, colleges, and universities is the result of wicked prejudice." In 1846, she became headmistress of Canajoharie Academy in Rochester, New York. However, Anthony protested the inequity in her wages as a woman and resigned after three years.

Anthony joined the Daughters of Temperance in 1848, and in 1852 she founded the Woman's New York State Temperance Society. The leaders of the temperance movement, which advocated against the use of alcohol, were concerned mainly with the abuses women and children suffered at the hands of alcoholic males. But Anthony encountered sexism even in the temperance movement and was refused permission to speak or even be seated at conventions. When she attended a state convention of the Sons of Temperance in 1852, she was told that, as a woman, she should listen and not speak. Shortly thereafter, Anthony attended her first women's rights convention. She became a representative for the American Anti-Slavery Society in New York in 1856. Rioters burned her effigy and chased after her during her antislavery speaking engagements.

Anthony met women's rights leader ELIZABETH CADY STANTON in 1851 when she traveled to Syracuse, New York, for an antislavery convention. The two became prominent women's rights advocates and formed a 50-year friendship. When she first met Stanton, Anthony was a 31-year-old retired teacher. Because Anthony and Stanton were criticized for talking too much about women's rights, they resigned from the Woman's New York State Temperance Society. By 1854, Anthony had circulated petitions for married women's property rights and women's suffrage and begun a New York State campaign for women's suffrage. At a New York State Teachers Convention in 1857, Anthony called for the education of women and African Americans. An expanded Women's Property Act that allowed women to control their own wages, children, and inheritance, was passed in 1860, but suffrage was a more prolonged battle.

For a brief period Anthony wore bloomers, a style composed of a skirt that fell slightly below the knees and loose trousers gathered at the ankles. The new design challenged the fashion of tightly laced waists, which constricted women's bodies. Elizabeth Miller, a cousin of Stanton's, had designed the dress and named it after Amelia Bloomer, who publicized it in a paper she edited. Women who wore bloomers were accused by the press of advocating an end to marriage and the family because of their masculine attire. Women who sported the modified dress were harassed in public. Anthony stopped wearing the garment and noted, "The attention of my audiences was fixed upon my clothes instead of my words."

In one of their first joint actions, Anthony and Stanton formed the National Woman's Loyal League in 1861, which demanded the emancipation of all slaves in the United States. In the same year they collected 400,000 signatures on an anti-slavery petition, the largest number ever collected.

After the Civil War, Anthony and Stanton opposed ratification of the Fourteenth and Fifteenth Amendments to the U.S. Constitution, which extended suffrage to black males but excluded women. As Anthony stated, "I would sooner cut off my right hand than ask the ballot for the black man and not for woman." In her view, "My work will not be done until the power of the ballot is in the hands of all women black and white." Some historians would later surmise that part of her reaction may have been elitist and racist, since she opposed giving the vote to "illiterate males before educated women."

Debate over the proposed Fifteenth Amendment divided the suffrage movement into two organizations in 1869: the National Woman Suffrage Association (NWSA), led by Anthony and Stanton, and the American Woman Suffrage Association (AWSA) led by Lucy Stone. Anthony was the founder and an officer of the NWSA from 1869 to 1890.

Men could become members of, but not hold office in, the NWSA. (Men headed many women's organizations at this time.) As the radical branch of the women's rights movement, Stanton and Anthony's NWSA had a broader agenda than just suffrage, as indicated in its statement of purpose: "The woman question is more than a demand for suffrage—It is a question covering a whole range of women's needs and demands—including her work, her wages, her property, her education, her physical training, her social status, her political equalization, her marriage and her divorce." Divorce was an unpopular issue due to the influence of churches.

Anthony voted in the 1872 presidential election in Rochester, New York. She was quoted in the press as saying that the framers of the Constitution said, "We, the people, not we, the white male citizens." She was arrested for voting and stood trial, but as a woman, was prohibited by law from testifying. The judge wrote his opinion and the all-male jury's verdict before the trial had even started and fined Anthony $100 for illegal voting, a fine she never paid.

During the nation's centennial Fourth of July celebration at Independence Hall in 1876, Anthony gained access to the event by using a reporter's pass, and after the Declaration of Independence was read she disrupted the proceedings by reading the Declaration of Rights for Women.

Anthony was owner and editor of the women's rights newspaper the *Revolution,* published from 1868 to 1870. This short-lived NWSA journal had 3,000 subscribers. Its motto was, "Men, their rights, and nothing more; women, their rights, and nothing less!" The paper investigated employment discrimination, scrutinized divorce law changes, examined the organization of female laundry workers, tailors, and typesetters, and endorsed equal pay for women. Similar to the stance *Ms.* magazine would take a century later in declining what it saw as unethical advertising, Stanton refused to accept advertising for quack medical cures.

During the years that the *Revolution* was published, Anthony formed the Working Women's Association (WWA). Anthony served as president for this organization of women in the publishing and garment trades who were excluded from all-male trade unions. The WWA was one of the first unions in the country for women.

In response, the men's typographical union accused her of running a nonunion shop at the *Revolution* offices and presses. When the paper ceased operations in 1870, Anthony assumed responsibility for $10,000 worth of debts owed by the *Revolution.* She went on the lecture circuit for six years, earning $75 per lecture in order to repay the debt with interest.

Anthony organized the first Woman Suffrage Convention in Washington, D.C., after the NWSA and the AWSA, the two branches of the suffrage movement, merged in 1890. Once again she created a unified group, the National American Woman Suffrage Association (NAWSA). Anthony served as vice president (1890–92) and then president (1892–1900) of the NAWSA.

In later years the differences between Anthony and Stanton became more apparent. Stanton viewed Anthony's suffrage-first strategy as conservative compared to her own larger perspective of social reform. But the two worked together to document the history of the women's rights movement. Anthony, Stanton, and two other women's rights activists, Matilda Joslin Gage and Ida Harper, edited four volumes from 1882 to 1902. Two more volumes were published after Anthony's death. The six volumes of the *History of Woman Suffrage 1881–1922* were the official records of the NAWSA. In the 1890s, Anthony raised $50,000 for the University of Rochester in exchange for their admitting women for the first time, in 1900. During this same time period, Anthony also worked on her autobiography, *Life of Susan Anthony.*

In 1900, at age 80, Anthony retired as president of NAWSA. At a Baltimore conference in 1906, which celebrated her 86th birthday, she gave one of her most famous speeches regarding suffrage, "Failure is Impossible." Susan B. Anthony died shortly afterward, in Rochester, New York, on March 13, 1906. Stamps with Anthony's portrait were issued in 1936 and 1955. In 1979, she became the first woman to appear on U.S. currency when her image appeared on the dollar coin.

Anthony appeared before Congress every year from 1869 to 1906 to petition for suffrage. Fourteen years after her death, suffrage for women was attained in the Nineteenth Amendment, passed in 1920—often known as the Susan B. Anthony Amendment. It had taken 144 years for women to gain full citizenship.

Further Reading

Banner, Lois. "The Selected Papers of Elizabeth Cady Stanton and Susan B. Anthony." *Journal of American History* 85, no. 1 (1998): 229–30.

DuBois, Ellen Carol. *The Elizabeth Cady Stanton—Susan B. Anthony Reader: Correspondence, Writings, Speeches.* Boston: Northeastern University Press, 1992.

Library of Congress. "Susan B. Anthony, Defendant." Available online. URL: http://lcweb.loc.gov/exhibits/treasures/trr005.html. Downloaded on December 19, 2000.

Public Broadcasting Service. "Not for Ourselves Alone: The Story of Elizabeth Cady Stanton and Susan B. Anthony." Available online. URL: http://www.pbs.org/stantonanthony/html. Downloaded on December 19, 2000.

Rutgers University. "Susan B. Anthony Papers Online." Available online. URL: http://ecssba.rutgers.edu/. Posted on October 21, 1999.

Ward, Geoffrey, and Ken Burns. *Not for Ourselves Alone: The Story of Elizabeth Cady Stanton and Susan B. Anthony.* New York: Knopf, 1999.

B

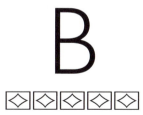

 ## BAEZ, JOAN CHANDOS
(1941–)   *Peace Advocate, Singer*

Joan Baez became the first famous female folksinger and used her name recognition for peace advocacy. Joan Chandos Baez was born on January 9, 1941, in Staten Island, New York, the second of three daughters. Her mother, Joan Bridge, was an immigrant from Edinburgh, Scotland, and her father, Albert Baez, was an immigrant from Puebla, Mexico. Her father grew up in Brooklyn, New York. His father, a Methodist minister, worked with Brooklyn's Hispanic community. Albert Baez completed a degree in physics at Drew University in Madison, New Jersey, then moved the family to California when he entered a master's program in mathematics at Stanford University. The family moved back to the East Coast after Joan's father completed his Ph.D. Hired as a research physicist at Cornell University in Ithaca, New York, her father worked on secret military projects there. Because he and his wife had become Quakers and were opposed to war, he left the university position for a lower-paying career as a college professor at a number of schools.

Joan Baez attended junior high school in Redlands, California, where a color line existed between Anglos and Mexicans, which left her excluded from both groups. She suspected she was not accepted into the girls' glee club because of her skin color. She completed high school in Palo Alto and joined the Quakers' social action wing, the American Friends Service Committee.

While still in high school, Baez committed her first act of civil disobedience by not participating in practice air raid drills. Her photo appeared on the local newspaper's front page. In 1956, she first heard Martin Luther King Jr. speak about civil rights. She also bought her first guitar, and during periods of depression, taught herself how to play music.

In 1958, the Baez family moved to Belmont, Massachusetts, when her father accepted a post at the Massachusetts Institute of Technology. Baez enrolled in Boston University but ended up spending most of her time singing in local coffeehouses. At 18, she was discovered by a talent scout while performing at a Boston coffeehouse in 1959. Baez became well known after her appearance at the Newport Folk Festival in

Folksinger Joan Baez on National Educational
Television folk music special, 1967
(Prints & Photographs Division,
Library of Congress, Washington, D.C.)

1959. In 1960, her first album was third on the list of 100 best-selling albums. She was briefly involved romantically with Bob Dylan and admitted to the public that she had had at least one affair with a woman.

In 1962, she conducted the first of three concert tours to southern college campuses—playing for integrated audiences only. In 1963, she sang the unofficial civil rights anthem "We Shall Overcome" at the famous civil rights March on Washington. She joined Martin Luther King Jr. on several civil rights marches, including the Selma-to-Montgomery march in 1963.

Beginning in 1964, Baez refused to pay federal taxes to support U.S. military involvement in the Vietnam War. She withheld 60 percent of her income—the amount of the federal budget that the government devoted to military expenditures—and the Internal Revenue Service responded by placing liens on her house and cars. She continued to with-

hold her taxes for a decade. In 1964, she played at a benefit concert to oppose Proposition Fourteen, which would have allowed segregated housing in California. When she showed up at the Free Speech Movement protest at the University of California, Berkeley, the police waited until she left the occupied building before arresting 800 students. In 1965, she began protesting against the Vietnam War outside the White House. That same year she founded the Institute for the Study of Nonviolence in Carmel, California, which remained there for more than a decade before moving to Santa Cruz, where the name changed to the Resource Center for Nonviolence.

In 1966, Baez gave a benefit concert for farmworkers in California. The following year, she was denied permission to perform at Constitution Hall in Washington, D.C., by the Daughters of the American Revolution because of her antiwar activism. Instead, Baez gave a free concert at the base of the Washington Monument. She also appeared at the Women Strike for Peace benefit. In October of that year, she was among 119 people arrested for blockading the induction center, where young men were drafted for military service in Vietnam, in Oakland, California. For this action, she was sentenced to serve 10 days in jail. Martin Luther King Jr. visited her in jail during her confinement. Two months later, Baez was arrested again with a group of 49 demonstrators at the same induction center. For the second offense, she was given a 90-day sentence.

She published her first autobiography, *Daybreak,* in 1968, and the book became a best-seller. In March 1968, she married David Harris, the leader of an antidraft organization called the Resistance. They had one son and divorced after a few years.

Baez remained a strong antiwar, antinuclear, and peace advocate. In 1972, she helped organize an antiwar demonstration for women and children called Ring Around the Congress. She then spent a year on the West Coast establishing Amnesty International, an organization that drew attention to human rights abuses throughout the world. Baez protested the 1973 military coup in

Chile whereby the dictatorship of General Augusto Pinochet replaced the democraticaly elected government of Salvador Allende. In 1976, she marched with the Irish Peace People in Northern Ireland. In 1977, she appeared at a protest at Kent State University organized in response to official plans to build a gymnasium over the site where four students protesting the Vietnam War were shot by National Guardsmen in 1970. Throughout the 1970s and 1980s, Baez remained active in the nuclear freeze movement. In 1978, she gave several benefit concerts in California to defeat Proposition Six, which would have prevented openly gay people from teaching in public schools. Baez founded Humanitas International Human Rights Committee in 1979 and headed the group for more than a decade. In 1987, her second autobiography, *And A Voice to Sing With,* became a *New York Times* best-seller. She remains on the board of Amnesty International.

Further Reading

Bernikow, Louise. "The Ballad of Joan Baez." *Lear's* 6, no. 2 (April 1993): 72–75.

Chonin, Neva. "Joan Baez." *Rolling Stone* no. 773 (November 13, 1997): 155.

FolkLib. "Index for Joan Baez." Available online. URL: http://www.execpc.com/~henkle/ftindex/b/baez_joan. html. Downloaded on December 20, 2000.

Fuss, Charles. *Joan Baez: A Bio-Bibliography.* New York: Greenwood, 1996.

Kerstetter, Rich. "Joan Baez: From Folk Madonna to Folk Matriarch." *Sing Out* 41, no. 2 (August 1, 1996): 36.

 BAKER, ELLA JOSEPHINE
(1903–1986) *Civil Rights Leader*

Ella Baker was a prominent leader in the movement for African-American civil rights, and she founded many of the most important civil rights organizations of the 20th century. She organized African-American cooperative campaigns in Harlem during the Great Depression; became a leader of the National Association for the Advancement of Colored People (NAACP) in the

1940s; served as the first interim director of the Southern Christian Leadership Conference (SCLC) in the 1950s; helped found the Student Nonviolent Coordinating Committee (SNCC) in 1960; and helped found the Mississippi Freedom Democratic Party in 1964.

Ella Baker was born in Norfolk, Virginia, on December 13, 1903, to Georgianna Ross Baker and Blake Baker, the children of former slaves. Ella Baker was the second of three children. Her family moved to Littleton, North Carolina, when she was eight, to land her maternal grandparents had purchased from their former master. Her grandfather was pastor at the local church. Her father worked as a waiter on a ferry between Norfolk, Virginia, and Washington, D.C., and her mother had worked as a schoolteacher before having children. Because there was no local secondary school, when Baker was 15 she was sent to the high school academy of Shaw University, Shaw boarding school in Raleigh, North Carolina. After completing high school, she attended college classes at Shaw. Baker graduated from college in 1927 as valedictorian of her class. Although Baker wanted to be a medical missionary or social worker, she could not afford the extended education these professions required. She was also unable to afford graduate work in the sociology department at the University of Chicago, although she had been accepted there. At the start of the Great Depression, Baker moved to New York City, where, despite her college diploma, she initially waitressed and worked in factories. The first political group she joined in Harlem was the Young Negroes Cooperative League, a consumer cooperative. Baker became the group's first national director in 1931, overseeing a network of buying clubs and cooperative grocery stores. She taught literacy classes for the Workers Education Project, part of the New Deal Works Progress Administration (WPA) programs. As Baker later recalled, "New York was the hotbed of let's-call-it radical thinking. You had every spectrum of radical thinking on the WPA."

She married longtime friend T. J. Robert in the late 1930s but never used her husband's name. Baker worked as a reporter and editor for a variety of African-American publications, including the *American West Indian News* and the *Negro National News.* A 1935 investigation that she conducted on African-American domestic workers was published in *The Crisis,* the magazine of the NAACP.

She began working for the NAACP in 1938, first as a field secretary, then as its director of branches from 1943 to 1946. As a field secretary, she traveled six months of every year to branches in the South to raise money and membership. Her work was dangerous, because NAACP members in the South risked being beaten or killed by people opposed to its mission. In 1944, she organized a series of regional leadership conferences to help develop local leaders. Baker was critical of what she saw as the NAACP's top-heavy hierarchy and agitated constantly for local empowerment. (The NAACP's primary focus had been on increasing its membership, and thereby its dues, not on increasing the participation of its members.) She resigned from her paid position in 1946 when she assumed custody of her nine-year-old niece. In 1951, Baker made an unsuccessful bid for a New York City Council seat, running on the Liberal Party ticket. She continued to act as a volunteer for the NAACP and became the first woman president of the New York branch in 1954.

In 1956, she cofounded and served as executive secretary of a northern organization, In Friendship, which helped raise funds for the southern civil rights struggle occurring around the Montgomery, Alabama, bus boycott. Baker was centrally involved in integrating New York City schools in 1957. That same year, the SCLC was formed, and Baker moved to Atlanta in January 1958 to serve as its executive secretary and to coordinate its citizenship campaign.

One of her first tasks for SCLC in 1958 was to organize meetings throughout the South on Lincoln's birthday. The purpose of the meetings was to announce SCLC's plans to increase the number of black registered voters in the South in one year. Ultimately, Baker would organize more than 65 SCLC branches in the South. Although she organized the entire operation, she was not made a director of SCLC—because she was not a minister and was not a man. As Baker later recalled, "I knew from the beginning that having a woman be an executive of SCLC was not something that would go over with the male-dominated leadership. And then of course, my personality wasn't right. . . . I was not afraid to disagree with the higher authorities."

She was a critic of the male ministers who led SCLC, including civil rights leader Martin Luther King Jr. Baker criticized both the NAACP and SCLC for their entrenched hierarchy and exclusion of women. She was 54 when she started to work at SCLC and had considerably more experience in organizing on behalf of civil rights than did the ministers for whom she worked. She was especially critical of overreliance on one leader, no matter how charismatic. As Baker perceived it: "In government service and political life I have always felt it was a handicap for oppressed peoples to depend so largely upon a leader, because unfortunately in our culture, the charismatic leader usually becomes a leader because he has found a spot in the public limelight. It usually means he has been touted through the public media, which means that the media made him, and the media may undo him."

A strong proponent of participatory democracy, Baker stated, "You didn't see me on television, you didn't see news stories about me. The kind of role that I tried to play was to pick up pieces or put together pieces out of which I hoped organization might come. My theory is, strong people don't need strong leaders."

When student-led sit-ins began in Greensboro, North Carolina, in February 1960, Baker helped found an independent student organization. (Sit-ins protested public segregation at restaurants and other establishments.) Baker organized a conference for students in April 1960 at Shaw University that led to the formation of SNCC. The student organization challenged the more moderate and hierarchical SCLC.

In 1964, Baker helped found and served as chief adviser to another cutting-edge civil rights group, the Mississippi Freedom Democratic Party (MFDP), which challenged the all-white Mississippi delegation to the Democratic National Convention. (FANNIE LOU HAMER served as vice president of the MFDP.) The grassroots, participatory model, which Baker struggled to achieve in every organization she was involved in, served as a role model to numerous groups outside the civil rights movement, including Students for a Democratic Society and the women's liberation movement of the 1970s.

Ella Baker died in New York on December 18, 1986, at age 83. Her funeral was held in Harlem. Pallbearers included major civil rights leaders such as Stokely Carmichael, H. Rap Brown, Julian Bond, James Forman, and Bayard Rustin. According to Forman, "She has served black people without fanfare, publicity, or concern for personal credit." During her lifetime, historian Howard Zinn acknowledged Baker as "the most tireless, the most modest, and the wisest activist I know." Her life was the subject of a 1983 documentary, *Fundi: The Ella Baker Story.* Her legacy continues, for as Baker stated, "I believe that the struggle is eternal. Somebody else carries on."

Further Reading

Baker, Richard. "Ella's First Year." *Life* 21 no. 7 (June 1998): 114–115.

Elliott, Aprele. "Ella Baker: Free Agent in the Civil Rights Movement." *Journal of Black Studies* 26 (May 1996): 593–603.

Grant, Joanne. *Ella Baker: Freedom Bound.* New York: Wiley, 1998.

First Run/Icarus Films. "Fundi: The Story of Ella Baker." Available online. URL: http://www.frif.com/cat97/f-j/fundi.html. Downloaded on December 21, 2000.

National Women's Hall of Fame. "Ella Baker." Available online. URL: http://www.greatwomen.org/baker.htm. Downloaded on December 21, 2000.

 BALCH, EMILY GREENE
(1867–1961)   *Nobel Peace Prize Winner*

Emily Greene Balch, an economist and peace advocate, was awarded the Nobel Peace Prize in 1946. She was born on January 8, 1867, near Boston, Massachusetts, to Ellen Noyes Balch and Francis Vergnies Balch. Her father, a graduate of Harvard University who volunteered to fight in the Civil War, became a successful attorney. Her mother worked as a teacher before her marriage and died when Balch was 17. Balch was the third child in a family of six girls and one boy. She attended private schools and graduated in 1889 from the first class at Bryn Mawr College, a women's educational institution founded by Quakers. A fellowship from Bryn Mawr allowed her to study economics in Paris for a year and to write *Public Assistance of the Poor in France,* which was published in 1893. She cofounded the Denison Settlement House in Boston. She then studied at Radcliffe College and the University of Chicago and spent a year at the University of Berlin (1895–96).

Balch began teaching social economics at Wellesley College in 1896. In 1906, she publicly declared herself a socialist. In 1910, she authored a classic work in sociology, *Our Slavic Fellow Citizens.* By 1913, she had been promoted to the rank of full professor and chair of the sociology department. She participated in movements for child labor laws, women's suffrage, and racial justice issues. She became the first president of the Boston Women's Trade Union League, and in 1915 she was among 42 women who served as delegates to the International Congress of Women at The Hague. This international gathering of prominent women leaders attempted to prevent World War I by persuading representatives of both the directly involved states and the neutral states to engage in a mediation process. After the congress, she coauthored, with Hull House founder JANE ADDAMS and industrial health pioneer ALICE HAMILTON, a summary of the delegation's attempts to mediate World War I entitled *Women at The Hague: The International Congress of Women and Its Results* (1915). Balch next went to work on the editorial staff of the progressive weekly, *The Nation*.

In 1918, in a response to her pacifist activities during World War I, Balch was dismissed from Wellesley College. At age 52, she lost both her position and her pension. Nevertheless, Balch upheld an outspoken internationalist position when most Americans still maintained an isolationist view. She served as secretary-treasurer of the Women's International League for Peace and Freedom (WILPF) for three years, from 1919 to 1922, and would work for WILPF for the rest of her life. During this period Balch, who was raised as a Unitarian, became a Quaker.

Balch advocated withdrawal of U.S. troops from Haiti in 1926 after an 11-year U.S. occupation, and she published her views in 1927 in the book *Occupied Haiti*. Largely as a result, troops were withdrawn in 1934. Balch, ever active in the WILPF, again served as its secretary-treasurer in 1934.

Nazi persecutions of Jews, the disabled, the left, and "racially impure" groups led her to change her strong pacifist views during World War II, for she believed that neutrality in the face of Nazism was "impractical, amoral, and selfish." She spoke out against U.S. internment of Japanese-American citizens and advocated monetary compensation for their losses. She also lobbied the U.S. government to accept Jewish refugees.

Balch was awarded the Nobel Peace Prize in 1946 at age 79. Only two other women had previously received that prize: Jane Addams in 1931 for her work in the settlement housing movement, and Austrian writer Baroness Bertha von Suttner in 1901 for her poetry. Balch donated her 1946 Nobel Peace Prize money to the WILPF. She spent her last four years in a Cambridge nursing home. Emily Greene Balch died just one day after her 94th birthday on January 9, 1961. She had devoted her life to the pursuit of peace.

Further Reading

Alonso, Harriet Hyman. "Nobel Peace Laureates." *Journal of Women's History* 7 (summer 1995): 6–26.

Balch, Emily Greene. *The Miracle of Living*. New York: Island Press, 1941.

———. *Occupied Haiti*. 1927. Reprint, New York: Garland, 1972.

———. *Our Slavic Fellow-Citizens*. 1910. Reprint, New York: Arno, 1969.

Randall, John. *Emily Greene Balch of New England: Citizen of the World*. Washington, D.C.: Women's International League for Peace and Freedom, 1946.

Randall, Mercedes. *Improper Bostonian: Emily Greene Balch*. New York: Twayne, 1964.

 BARI, JUDITH BEATRICE
(1949–1997)   *Earth First! Environmental Activist*

Judi Bari, the leader of the Earth First! movement in northern California, was born in Baltimore, Maryland, on November 7, 1949. Her Italian-American father was a diamond setter; her Jewish mother, a teacher. Bari was the second of three daughters and grew up in a middle-class suburb in Maryland. She entered the University of Maryland in 1967 and protested against the Vietnam War while she was a student there. After leaving school she worked for the U.S. Postal Service in Washington, D.C., where she organized a strike of postal workers and wrote a newsletter about the strike. She moved to Sonoma County, California, with her husband in 1979. While there, she was involved in protests for peace in Central America and remained active in labor issues, including the organization of sawmill workers into an International Workers of the World local.

While working as a carpenter, she learned that the wood she used was coming from old-growth redwood trees. Some of those redwood trees were at least 1,000 years old and 97 percent of old-growth redwoods had already been cut. The environmentalist group Earth First! used rallies, demonstration blockades, and tree sittings to protest the continued cutting. Bari began to get involved by organizing blockades of logging trucks for Earth First! She guided Earth First! to reject tree spiking, a method of protest that involved driving metal spikes into trees to damage logging, a tactic that could cause injuries to workers. She began to build alliances between timber workers and environmentalists. As Bari later recalled, "When I got involved with Earth First! I liked the direct action, the spirit, the music; but I was appalled at the anti-working-class attitude that says loggers are the enemy—the lack of distinctions between the loggers and the corporations and the owners." Bari worked as a laborer, and in her opinion the companies did not treat the workers any better than they treated the trees.

In 1989, her car was wrecked when a logging truck, which had been brought to a standstill the previous day by an Earth First! blockade, rammed it from behind. In the spring of 1990 Bari organized Redwood Summer, a campaign that sought national attention for the Earth First! cause. The campaign brought 3,000 college students from around the country to northern California in an effort that was modeled on the Mississippi Freedom Summer campaigns of the 1960s civil rights movement. In May 1990, a bomb exploded under the driver's seat of Bari's car, nearly killing her and leaving her permanently disabled. When the FBI accused her of planting the bomb herself, she filed suit against the FBI and continued to organize for Earth First! as she slowly recovered from her injuries. When someone remarked on her ability to organize strategic campaigns after the bombing, Bari stated, "They bombed the wrong end of me."

Bari hosted a popular weekly public-affairs radio show on Mendocino County (California) public radio station KZYX. She chronicled her experiences as an activist in her 1994 book, *Timber Wars,* published by Common Courage Press.

Judi Bari died on March 22, 1997, of breast cancer that had spread to her liver. She refused hospitalization, choosing instead to die at home in her mountain cabin near Willits, California, with her daughters, companion, family, and friends nearby. She requested that her obituary list her occupation as "revolutionary."

Further Reading

Bari, Judi. *Timber Wars.* Monroe, Maine: Common Courage Press, 1994.

Dowie, Mark. "The Redwood Warrior." *Utne Reader* no. 81 (May/June 1997): 22.

Kohl, Judith. "Environmental Justice." *Social Policy* 21, no. 3 (winter 1991): 71–76.

Redwood Summer Justice Project. "Redwood Summer Justice Project Official Judi Bari Web Page." Available online. URL: http://www.monitor.net/~bari. Updated on May 30, 2000.

Talbot, Stephen. "Earth First! What Next?" *Mother Jones* 15, no. 7 (November 1990): 46–51.

BARTON, CLARISSA HARLOWE
(Clara Barton)
(1821–1912) *Founder of the American Red Cross*

Clara Barton founded the American Red Cross and served as its first president for nearly 20 years. Born on December 25, 1821, in Oxford, Massachusetts, she was the last child in a family of five. Her mother, Sarah Stone, believed slavery was wrong and that women should have the same rights as men. Her father, Captain Stephen Barton, was a prosperous farmer, miller, and state legislator who had served in the American Revolution.

Teaching was one of the few jobs open to women at that time, so in 1839 Barton became a teacher in a one-room school in her hometown. She protested the lower pay women were routinely offered. She left teaching for a year to attend the Liberal Institute of Clinton, New York, in 1850, a school open to both men and women. Later, she moved to Bordentown, New Jersey, where she taught in a private school. Despite opposition, Barton worked in 1852 to establish the first free school in New Jersey. Her project was so successful

Clara Barton, founder of the American Red Cross
(Still Picture Branch, National Archives, College Park, MD)

that enrollment at the school increased from six students to 600. When a male principal was appointed to the position that she believed should have been hers, she resigned and suffered severe depression afterward.

In 1854, Barton became one of the first female civil servants in the federal government when she went to work for the Patent Office in Washington, D.C. A year later, Secretary of the Interior Robert McClelland raised opposition to women working in government. Barton's position as a clerk was reduced to that of a copyist. She was paid 10 cents for each 100 words copied, yet she still managed to earn $70 to $80 a month. The administration of President James Buchanan eliminated her position at the Patent Office after the 1856 election, and suffered another period of depression. She later returned

to the Patent Office when President Abraham Lincoln was elected, in 1860.

During the Civil War Barton raised money for medical supplies and later established a federal office for missing soldiers. Her talent lay in gathering and distributing supplies to the Union army. Operating outside of official bureaucracy, she privately advertised in newspapers for donations of food and clothing, then delivered those items to battlefronts. Quitting her job at the Patent Office, Barton turned her home into a warehouse and learned to garner publicity from the media in order to increase donations of much-needed supplies.

When Barton first requested permission from an official at the War Department to go to the battlefields to help the wounded, she was told that single women should not even suggest such a thing. She persisted and began her work. Barton helped both Confederate and Union soldiers. She found soldiers lying in blood and filth, many suffering sunstroke and lack of water. Hospital floors were slimy with blood and body waste. She would recall, "I never realized until that day how little a human being could be grateful for." She wrote to a friend during this time that "I am a U.S. soldier." She discarded her bulky hoopskirt for a plain one, so she could move more easily among the injured. She wrote, "I wrung blood from the bottom of my clothing before I could step, for the weight about my feet."

When Barton lashed out at army personnel over the insufficient food and water the soldiers received, military authorities declared her to be a troublemaker, refused to give her access to army supplies, and took her tent away. Sanitary Commission nurses did exist, but Barton did not work with them because she did not want to be concerned with regulations regarding uniforms, supplies, and procedures. She wanted to go to the battlefield rather than wait for days until soldiers were finally brought to hospitals and the infections that would claim their lives had already set in. Soldiers referred to her as the

"Angel of the Battlefield." Barton appealed to the War Department to force private homeowners to open their houses to the wounded. She became the unofficial head of the 10th corps hospital, still without government pay.

At the close of the war in 1865 she requested permission from President Lincoln to identify missing soldiers. She set up an office in Annapolis, Maryland, and used the title General Correspondent for the Friends of Missing Prisoners. When someone inquired about a soldier, she put the soldier's name on a master list, which she then had published in newspapers. Again she spent her personal funds and lectured in order to fund the project.

Secretary of War Edwin Stanton asked her to travel to the Andersonville prisoner-of-war camp in Georgia in order to identify unmarked graves and notify family members. That summer she identified 13,000 of the dead. By 1868, she had identified 22,000 missing men. That fall, she hoped the War Department would give her funds to continue her work, but they did not, and when her work came to an end, she suffered another bout of depression. She went abroad, hoping to alleviate the symptoms.

While in Geneva, Switzerland, in 1869, she had the opportunity to work for the Red Cross, which had been established in 1864 when 11 countries signed the Geneva Treaty. The treaty was intended to establish rules of treatment for wounded soldiers and prisoners of war. The U.S. government had declined an invitation to sign the treaty because of governmental policy against making treaties with European countries. Many Americans were isolationists who had no interest in belonging to international organizations. The United States did not become a member of the Red Cross until 1882.

On her return to America in 1876, Barton spent a year in Dansville, New York, in a sanitarium well known for treating nervous disorders. In 1877, she wrote to the Red Cross in Geneva, asking permission to promote their organization in the United States. Appointed as their representa-tive, she worked to convince Congress to accept the Treaty of Geneva and recognize the Red Cross. A group of 22 supporters established the first branch of the American Association of the Red Cross on May 21, 1881, with Barton elected as president. Auxiliaries opened in Rochester, Syracuse, and Onondaga, New York. Finally, in March 1882, Congress ratified the Treaty of Geneva. Barton received a charter in 1900 and at age 79, began another new career.

Barton served as president of the American Red Cross until 1904, when she was 82 years old. Her style was sometimes viewed as autocratic, and some coworkers called her the "Great I Am."

After stepping down as president of the Red Cross, Barton served briefly as superintendent of a prison for women in Sherborn, Masschusetts, at half the salary of her male predecessor. Once again she suffered a period of depression. She then organized and served as president of the National First Aid Association, which developed the original first-aid kits. The Red Cross later incorporated first-aid training into its work.

Barton wrote her autobiography, *Story of My Childhood,* in 1907. An attack of bronchitis led to pneumonia, and Clara Barton died on April 12, 1912, in Glen Echo, Maryland. She is buried in her hometown of North Oxford, Massachusetts. Thirty-five volumes of her diaries are housed in the Library of Congress. The American Red Cross, which Barton founded, continues to serve people in need of assistance.

Further Reading

Burnett, William. *Clara Barton at Andersonville.* Conshohocken, Pa.: Eastern National Park and Monument Association, 1995.

Burton, David Henry. *Clara Barton: In the Service of Humanity.* Westport, Conn.: Greenwood, 1995.

IncWell DMG, Ltd. "Clara Barton." Available online. URL: http://www.incwell.com/Biographies/Barton.html. Downloaded on December 21, 2000.

Marko, Eve. *Clara Barton and the American Red Cross.* New York: Baronet Books, 1996.

National Association for Home Care. "Profiles in Caring: Clara Barton." Available online. URL: http://www.nahc.org/NAHC/Val/Columns/SC10-1.html. Downloaded on December 21, 2000.

Oates, Stephen. *A Woman of Valor: Clara Baron and the Civil War.* New York: Free Press, 1994.

 ## BATES, DAISY LEE GATSON
(1914–1999)   *Civil Rights Leader*

Daisy Lee Gatson Bates advised and guided a courageous group of African-American students who desegregated a Little Rock, Arkansas, high school in 1957. The confrontation garnered national and international media coverage and secured her a place in civil rights history.

Daisy Lee Gatson was born in Hutting, a small sawmill town in southeast Arkansas, on November 11, 1914. Her father, Orlee Gatson, worked in the lumber mill. When Daisy was an infant, her mother was murdered while resisting the sexual assault of three local white men. Her father left immediately after the incident, and friends of the family reared Daisy. When she was in elementary school, she learned the story of her mother's brutal murder, and she followed the guilty man and glared at him in public, a daring approach for a young African-American girl. Her behavior led the man to plead, "In the name of God, leave me alone."

She married Lucius Christopher Bates in 1942, and together they published the weekly *Arkansas State Press* from Little Rock. It became the largest black-interest paper in the state and during its 18-year history was a leading voice in the civil rights movement. The paper criticized police brutality, segregation, and racism in the criminal justice system. It was the only African-American newspaper in Arkansas for more than 30 years. Bates was the only woman pilot in the Arkansas Civil Air Patrol in World War II.

In 1952, Bates was elected president of the National Association for the Advancement of Colored People (NAACP) for the state of Arkansas and served from 1953 to 1961. While president, she became the adviser to nine African-American students, six girls and three boys. In 1957, these students became the first African-American students to attend Central High School in Little Rock. In the 1954 *Brown v. Board of Education* case, the Supreme Court had ruled that segregated public schools were illegal, overturning the 1896 *Plessy v. Ferguson* decision. Three years later, school districts throughout the South still had not desegregated. African-American students throughout the South attended separate and unequal schools. Often the only textbooks they had were worn-out, outdated, hand-me-down books that had been discarded by white schools.

In the wake of *Brown v. Board of Education,* the decision to desegregate local schools was made by the Little Rock school board during the 1955 Arkansas gubernatorial campaign, however, it was almost two years before it was implemented. The winner of the 1955 election, Governor Orval Faubus, had declared, "It is evident to me that Arkansas is not ready for a complete and sudden mixing of the races in the public school." In the interim, between the decision to desegregate and its implementation, Bates developed a plan in which the Little Rock Nine, as the press dubbed the student group, were to be accompanied into the school by a group of local white and black ministers. On the first morning the nine African-American students were to attend the new school, plans changed because of so many threats to the lives of all involved. Bates reached all the students and their families to notify them of the change, except for Elizabeth Eckford, whose family did not have a phone. The Arkansas National Guard, following the orders of Governor Faubus, would not allow the African-American students to enter the school, and Elizabeth, surrounded by a white mob, faced a life-threatening situation. However, a white woman stepped forward from the crowd and escorted Elizabeth safely to a bus. President Eisenhower sent army troops into Little Rock to enforce the *Brown v. Board of Education* court decision and escort the

African-American students to class. The confrontation garnered national and international attention. Violence continued to be directed at the Little Rock Nine once they entered the school, and also at Bates for years afterward. Her home was bombed and shot at, and she was hanged in effigy. Her newspaper was boycotted by local businesses. Community volunteers guarded her home around-the-clock. In 1957, the Associated Press named her one of the top nine news personalities in the world.

In 1960, Bates moved to New York City and spent two years writing her memoirs, *The Long Shadow of Little Rock,* which were published in 1962. ELEANOR ROOSEVELT wrote the book's introduction. Bates worked in Washington, D.C., for the Democratic National Committee and later for antipoverty programs in the administration of President Lyndon B. Johnson. During the landmark 1963 March on Washington for civil rights, women were originally excluded from the three-hour schedule of speakers. When criticized by women, the committee asked Bates to say a few words.

Bates suffered a stroke in 1965. In 1968, she returned to Arkansas and directed a self-help project in Mitchellville for six years. Under her guidance, residents were able to secure a new water system in 1970, a sewer system in 1971, and paved streets and a community center in 1972. Bates retired in 1974.

Bates was widowed in 1980. In 1984, the University of Arkansas awarded her an honorary doctor of laws degree. She briefly revived the *Arkansas State Press* in 1984, then sold the paper in 1987. She donated her personal papers to the University of Arkansas in 1986. A reprint of her memoirs by the University of Arkansas Press in 1988 won the American Book Award, the first time a reprint had received this recognition. Bates died November 4, 1999, at age 84. The year following her death, the state of Arkansas commended her for her outstanding service to the state. In 1999 her home was approved as a national landmark. In March 2001, the state of Arkansas signed legislation to create a Daisy Bates annual holiday to be celebrated on the third Monday in February, the same day as President's Day. Daisy Bates successfully challenged southern racism and offered a role model of leadership to the rest of the nation.

Further Reading

"Arkansas Civil Rights Heroine Daisy Bates, 84, Succumbs in Little Rock." *Jet* 96, no. 25 (November 22, 1999): 58–59.

Bates, Daisy. *The Long Shadow of Little Rock: A Memoir.* 1962. Reprint, Fayetteville: University of Arkansas Press, 1987.

Bennett, Lerone. "Daisy Bates and Nine Students Helped Change History." *Ebony* 53, no. 2 (December 1997): 132.

Blackburn, Julia. *Daisy Bates in the Desert.* New York: Vintage Books, 1995.

Calloway-Thomas, C. "Daisy Bates and the Little Rock School Crisis: Forging the Way." *Journal of Black Studies* 26, no. 5 (1996): 616.

 BERRY, MARY FRANCES
(1938–) *Chair of the U.S. Civil Rights Commission*

Mary Frances Berry was the first African-American woman to serve as assistant secretary for education in the Department of Health, Education and Welfare (HEW). She was born on February 17, 1938, in Nashville, Tennessee, to Frances Southall Berry and George Ford Berry. Her childhood was marked by poverty and racial discrimination. She graduated with honors from Pearl High School in 1956 then worked her way through college as a laboratory technician. She earned a bachelor of arts and a master's degree at Howard University in Washington, D.C., then entered a Ph.D. program at the University of Michigan in Ann Arbor, where she studied constitutional history and completed a law degree.

After completing her doctorate in 1966, she taught at Central Michigan University in Mt. Pleasant, first as an assistant and then an associate professor of history. In 1970, she became the director of Afro-American Studies at the University of Maryland in College Park. Within a few years she rose to the position of provost of the university and became the highest-ranking African-American woman on campus. Her distinguished record of publications included the 1971 book *Black Resistance/White Law: A History of Constitutional Racism.* In 1976, she became chancellor of the University of Colorado at Boulder, the first African-American woman to head a major research university, presiding over a student body of 21,000. President Jimmy Carter appointed her assistant secretary of education in HEW, and she served from 1977 to 1980.

After leaving her position at HEW she returned to Howard University in 1980 to teach legal history as the senior fellow at the Institute for the Study of Educational Policy. In 1980, President Carter appointed her to the U.S. Commission on Civil Rights, and she served as the vice-chair until 1982. In her role on the commission she entered into public conflicts with Presidents Ronald Reagan and George H. W. Bush over their administrations' policies. Her next book, *Long Memory,* was a history of African Americans published in 1982. A cofounder of the Free South Africa movement, she was arrested in 1984 in a sit-in at the South African embassy, part of nationwide protests against Reagan's policies on South Africa. President Reagan tried to remove her from the civil rights commission in 1984, but she successfully sued to remain. In 1986, she published *Why the ERA Failed: Politics, Women's Rights, and the Amending Process.*

In 1987, she received the University of Pennsylvania's distinguished Geraldine R. Segal Professorship in Social Thought. She also served as vice president of the American Historical Association. In 1993, President Bill Clinton appointed her as chair of the U.S. Commission on Civil Rights.

Berry holds honorary doctorates from a number of universities and has been recognized with honors and awards from the National Association for the Advancement of Colored People (NAACP), the Southern Christian Leadership Conference (SCLC), the Congressional Black Caucus, and *Ms.* magazine. Her contributions as a scholar trained in history, law, public service, and political activism have left a legacy that benefits future generations at home and abroad.

Further Reading

Barthel, Joan. "Mary Frances Berry." *Ms.* 15 (January 1987): 68–70.

Berry, Mary Frances. *Black Resistance/White Law: A History of Constitutional Racism in America.* 1971. Reprint, New York: Penguin, 1995.

———. *Long Memory: The Black Experience in America.* New York: Oxford University Press, 1986.

———. *The Pig Farmer's Daughter and Other Tales of American Justice: Episodes of Racism and Sexism in the Courts from 1865 to the Present.* New York: Vintage Books, 2000.

Matthews, Frank. "Civil Rights Voice and Conscience." *Black Issues in Higher Education* (March 10, 1994): 8–17.

 BETHUNE, MARY McLEOD
(1875–1955)   *Educational Leader*

Mary McLeod Bethune was both a civil rights and education activist who established educational institutions for African-American youth. Born 10 years after the Civil War ended and two years before the end of Reconstruction, on July 10, 1875, in Mayesville, South Carolina, to former slaves Patsy McIntosh McLeod and Sam McLeod, she was the 15th of their 17 children, and the first to be freeborn. Her mother continued to work for her former owner, and Mary herself worked in his fields as a child. She walked 10 miles a day to attend school. After completing a rudimentary elementary education, Mary expected to return to work in the fields. However, a young Quaker teacher volunteered her earnings from dressmaking to provide Mary with a scholarship. Her Quaker mentor accepted this responsibility through the missionary outreach efforts of her church. This teacher continued to support Bethune for the next 50 years, though they didn't meet until 1930. When she was 12, Mary attended Scotia Seminary in Concord, North Carolina, on her mentor's scholarship so she could complete her secondary education. Scotia Seminary had an integrated faculty, unusual for that time. Wanting to become a missionary in Africa, Mary used her scholarship money to attend Chicago's Moody Bible Institute, where she was the only black student. She graduated in 1895, but no church was willing to sponsor her as a missionary, so she returned to the South to teach, recognizing that "Africans in America needed Christ and school just as much as Negroes in Africa. . . . My life work lay not in Africa but in my own country."

In 1898, she married former-schoolteacher-turned-haberdasher Albertus Bethune. They had one son. Her husband was interested in making money, while Bethune was more interested in her mission work. After separating from her husband after less than a decade, at age 29 she moved with her son to Florida in 1904.

Bethune opened a boarding school for African-American girls in Daytona Beach, Florida, in 1904. Like most southern cities, Daytona Beach excluded minorities from its public schools. Bethune sold homemade potato pies to raise the money—five dollars—for a down payment on a four-room cottage that she opened as Dayton Normal and Industrial Institute, a private school for African-American girls. Many African-American mothers in the area were maids who traveled north with their vacationing employers during the summer and needed boarding schools for their daughters. Tuition was 50 cents a week, but no student was turned away for lack of funds. The school started with six students. By using wooden crates for desks and ink made from elderberries, Bethune's thrift and fund-raising skills helped the school grow rapidly. Bethune trained a school choir that raised money for the school through concert tours. Because African Americans were refused admittance to white hospitals, Bethune added a hospital for African Americans to her school in 1911. Bethune also conducted voter registration drives for African-American women despite Ku Klux Klan (KKK) threats.

As public but segregated schooling became available to more southern African Americans, Bethune changed her school curriculum from elementary to college. By 1923, the school had a faculty and staff of 25 and a student body of 300. She expanded the school by merging with a boys' school, the Cookman Institute, and then incorporating it into Bethune-Cookman College in 1929. The institution ended its role as a high school in 1936. By 1941, the college had 14 buildings on 32 acres. In 1943, with 1,000 students enrolled, Bethune-Cookman College issued its first college diplomas.

Bethune served as president of the Florida Federation of Colored Women from 1917 to 1924 and of the National Association of Colored Women (NACW) from 1935 to 1949. She was the eighth president of the NACW. At the time this was the highest office an African-American woman held in a national organization of any kind. As president of the NACW, one of her first accomplishments was the establishment of a national headquarters in Washington, D.C. She also cofounded the National Council of Negro Women and headed the organization from 1935 to 1949. The National Council of Negro Women united major national African-American women's organizations. Bethune also served as director of the Florida Red Cross during World War II.

Bethune had many influential friends. Through her conversations with Vice President Thomas Marshall, she was able to convince policy makers to integrate the American Red Cross in the 1940s and allow African Americans to perform the same duties that white Americans performed. She became a close friend of ELEANOR ROOSEVELT through her work in the National Council of Negro Women. Once, while visiting the White House, a southern politician asked Bethune, "Auntie, what are you doing here?" She replied, "Which one of my sister's children are you?"

With her business skills, she established and served as president of an insurance company for African Americans, who had difficulty buying insurance from white-run companies. In 1952, she was the only female president of an insurance company. From 1940 until 1955 she was vice president of the NAACP. She was on the boards of Planned

Mary McLeod Bethune, educator, 1949
(Prints & Photographs Division,
Library of Congress, Washington, D.C.)

McLeod Bethune Foundation to support interracial research and activity and to sponsor scholarships for African Americans. She retired from public life two years before her death.

Mary McLeod Bethune died May 18, 1955, of a heart attack in Daytona Beach, Florida. She was 80 years old. One son, one grandchild, and 11 great-grandchildren survived her. She was buried on the grounds of Bethune-Cookman College. Today the college has 2,300 students. Former students remember her greeting to them, "My beautiful black boys and girls," as one that engendered pride in their heritage and identity. The first statue to honor any African-American or woman on public land was unveiled in Bethune's honor in Lincoln Park in Washington, D.C., in 1974. And in 1985 the post office issued a stamp bearing her image.

In Bethune's last will and testament she related: "Sometimes as I sit communing in my study I feel that death is not far off. I am aware that it will overtake me before the greatest of my dreams, full equality for the Negro in our time, is realized. Yet, I face that reality without fear or regrets. I am resigned to death as all humans must be at the proper time. Death neither alarms nor frightens one who has had a long career of fruitful toil. The knowledge that my work has been helpful to many fills me with joy and great satisfaction." At the end of her life Bethune pointed out, "Love thy neighbor is a precept which could transform the world if it were universally practiced. . . . Loving your neighbor means interracial, inter-religious, and international."

Parenthood and the Girl Scouts of the U.S.A. and also a member of the League of Women Voters.

By 1931, she had developed a national reputation and was number 10 on a list of 50 outstanding American women. She served as an adviser to President Franklin Delano Roosevelt and headed the Office of Minority Affairs in the National Youth Administration from 1936 to 1943, becoming the first African-American woman to head a federal agency. President Harry Truman sent Bethune to the founding conference of the United Nations in 1945. She was the only woman of color present in an official capacity.

Her awards included the Spingarn Medal from the NAACP in 1935, the Medal of Honor and Merit from Haiti in 1949, and the Star of Africa from Liberia in 1952. She received degrees from a dozen universities. In 1953, she founded the Mary

Further Reading

Bethune, Mary McLeod. *Mary McLeod Bethune: Building a Better World.* Bloomington: Indiana University Press, 2000.

Collison, Michele. "Race Women Stepping Forward." *Black Issues in Higher Education* 16, no. 7 (May 27, 1999): 24.

Greenwood, Monique. "Home: Mary McLeod Bethune Slept Here." *Essence* 28, no. 10 (February 1998): 148.

Height, Dorothy. "Remembering: Mary McLeod Bethune." *Essence* 24, no. 10 (February 1994): 102.

King, John. *Mary McLeod Bethune: A Woman of Vision and Distinction.* Madison, N.J.: General Commission on Archives, 1988.

Newsome, Clarence. "Mary McLeod Bethune and the Methodist Episcopal Church." *Journal of Religious Thought* 49, no. 1 (fall 1992): 7.

 ## BLACK, SHIRLEY JANE TEMPLE
(1928–) *Ambassador, Actress*

Shirley Temple Black, the first woman in the history of the United States to serve as chief of protocol, did so during the administration of President Gerald Ford. She also served as U.S. ambassador to Ghana from 1974 to 1976 and as the ambassador to Czechoslovakia in 1989. Shirley Jane Temple was born on April 23, 1928, in Santa Monica, California, to a mother who had ambitions for her. Her father, George Francis Temple, was a banker and her mother, Gertrude Temple, a housewife.

In 1931, her mother enrolled her in the Meglin dance studio, which trained young children for work in film and advertising. Shirley Temple made her film debut at age three and was starring in movies by age six. Of her childhood she said, "I stopped believing in Santa Claus when my mother took me to see him in a department store, and he asked for my autograph." She was the star of more than 40 films, most of them made in the 1930s before she was 12. She was Hollywood's top box office attraction for four years, from 1935 to 1938. Her films made millions for the studios, saving them from bankruptcy. The first child actress to win an Academy Award, she received a special, diminutive award in 1935 for her contributions to film. By 1938, at age 10, she was making more money than the president of General Motors.

During her film career she was not allowed to swim since it might harm her trademark curly hair—there were always exactly 56 curls—and by contract, only her mother was permitted to touch her hair. She worked daily and was not allowed to play with other children, for fear she would catch an illness. To maintain her wholesome image, the studio bosses at Twentieth Century–Fox did not want her to mix with adults unnecessarily. She was not allowed to dine in the studio commissary but took her meals in a private bungalow, where she also studied alone with her tutor. Despite her isolation, her interest in world affairs was nurtured. "Whenever an important visitor from another country would come to the studio, my tutor would assign me for one week to study about that country. And that got me interested in international relations." When she signed with the studio, her birth certificate was changed to make her one year younger. She did not find out her true age until she was 13.

Shirley and dancer Bill "Bojangles" Robinson were one of the first interracial pairs captured on film. Their partnership began in 1935 with the film *The Little Colonel.* They made three more films together, *The Littlest Rebel, Just Around the Corner,* and *Rebecca of Sunnybrook Farm.* She recalled learning her first lesson about racism when Robinson had to stay in the chauffeurs' quarters at a hotel that did not allow African Americans to stay in their guest rooms.

Temple's friendship with J. Edgar Hoover of the Federal Bureau of Investigation (FBI) began at a young age when he offered protection against kidnapping, extortion attempts, and death threats. One of the closest death threats came during a live radio broadcast when she was 10 years old. A mentally unstable woman in the front row pulled a gun out of her purse and pointed it at Temple, but FBI agents intercepted her.

Her studio dropped Temple by the time she was 12 years old, after two of her films had flopped at the box office. She was not able to make a successful transition from child star to adult actor. Temple had earned more than $3 million in her film career, but her father's bad management and her parents' lavish lifestyle left her with nothing. Her parents had homes with swimming pools, badminton courts, electric merry-go-rounds, stables with a staff of 12, and supported extended family members and friends, but her father had broken the law by not depositing any money into her trust account for the last eight years that she worked, and $1 million in securities had disappeared.

As a girl, she cited ELEANOR ROOSEVELT and Amelia Earhart as her role models. She attended an exclusive Los Angeles girls' school, Westlake. Her 1945 autobiography, *My Young Life,* was penned by a ghost writer.

At 17 she married U.S. Army Air Corps private John Agar. She quit her career in 1949, but Agar's drinking led to a divorce that same year, only one year after the birth of their daughter. Divorced by age 21, Temple left Hollywood to vacation in Hawaii, where she met her second husband, former naval officer Charles Black. Before planning to marry again, she called J. Edgar Hoover to run an FBI background check on Black so she would not be unpleasantly surprised. Apparently, Charles Black passed the test, and the two married in 1959. They moved to the San Francisco suburbs

Shirley Temple Black at United Nations press conference
(United Nations Photo Library)

and had two more children. She returned briefly to entertainment with a popular television show, *Shirley Temple's Story-book,* in 1957 to 1959, and the less successful *Shirley Temple Show* in 1960.

In 1967, while supporting war against North Vietnam, she ran as a Republican candidate for Congress, coming in second in a field of 14 candidates. That was the first and last time that she would seek elected public office. Pro-choice on abortion and a moderate on social issues, Black had a reputation as a strong anti-Communist, perhaps leading President Nixon to appoint her as a delegate to the 24th United Nations General Assembly in 1969.

In 1972, she had a modified radical mastectomy following a diagnosis of breast cancer, and discussed her breast cancer frankly and publicly at a time when it was considered a private issue and two years before First Lady Betty Ford made similar revelations. Temple recalled, "I did it because I thought it would help other women, my sisters."

She served as U.S. ambassador to Ghana from 1974 to 1976 and the first woman chief of protocol for President Gerald Ford, from 1976 to 1977. Temple found that her past career as a film star was an advantage in her diplomatic career. She noted, "When I go to a country, people there already know me. So there's a recognition that was very helpful when you want to explain your country's position on various foreign affairs." She found members of her fan club in countries throughout the world 50 years after her career had ended.

A full-size Oscar was given to her in 1985 to replace the tiny statue she had been awarded in 1935. Her best-selling autobiography, *Child Star,* was published in 1988. McGraw-Hill paid her a $300,000 advance on her autobiography. It retold many details of her film career, including a sexual advance by a Hollywood producer when she was only 12. She returned to public service in 1989 and served as ambassador to Czechoslovakia under President George H. W. Bush's administration for three years. In 1998, she was the recipient of a Kennedy Center Honor. She remains interested in serving her country with another substantive job.

In 2001, she was working on the second volume of her autobiography; this one focusing on her diplomatic career. Her early films are available on video. A made-for-TV movie based on her autobiography was aired in May 2001. Although she spent 27 years working for the U.S. government, longer than she spent in films, she is still better known to the general public for her movie career.

Further Reading

Black, Shirley Temple. *Child Star.* New York: Warner Books, 1989.

Blashfield, Jean. *Shirley Temple Black: Actor and Diplomat.* Chicago, Ill.: Ferguson, 2000.

Fiori, Carlo. *The Story of Shirley Temple Black: Hollywood's Youngest Star.* Milwaukee, Wisc.: Gareth Stevens, 1997.

Hammontree, Patsy Guy. *Shirley Temple Black.* Westport, Conn.: Greenwood, 1998.

Kennedy Center Honors. "Shirley Temple Black." Available online. URL: http://www.kennedy-center.org/honors/years/temple black.html. Downloaded on December 23, 2000.

"Shirley Temple Recalls That Bias Experienced by 'Bojangles' Robinson Taught Her About Racism." *Jet* 955, no. 4 (December 21, 1998): 37–39.

BLOCH, JULIA CHANG
(1942–) *Ambassador*

Julia Chang Bloch was named ambassador to Nepal by President George H. W. Bush in 1989, an appointment that made her the first Asian-American ambassador for the United States.

Julia Chang was born on March 2, 1942, in China to Eva Yeh Chang and Fu-yun Chang. Her father was the first Chinese director of the customs service in Shanghai during British rule. When the Communist Revolution occurred, her family left China. They came to the United States when she was nine years old. Chang earned a bachelor's degree in communications and public policy from the University of California, Berkeley, in 1964. She then joined the Peace Corps and served for two years in Malaysia, where she taught English as a second language.

She returned to the United States, and in 1967 she earned a master's degree in government and East Asian studies from Harvard University in Cambridge, Massachusetts. Chang decided to work for the U.S. government since government service in China is considered very respectable. She faced gender discrimination once she completed her schooling at Harvard and found that male Chinese classmates were given free trips to Washington, D.C., to be interviewed because they, like Chang, were fluent in Mandarin.

Chang was initially offered a secretary's job in the Peace Corps office in Washington, D.C., and was promoted to a training officer position in the Peace Corps. She based her party choice—Republican—more on pragmatics than ideology; "It's simple. The Democrats wouldn't hire me (early in her career). They wanted me to be a secretary." In 1968, she married Stuart Marshall Bloch.

In 1977, Bloch became deputy director of the Office of African Affairs of the International Communication Agency. She developed and directed U.S. public diplomacy policies for Africa with a staff of 500 and a budget of $20 million. In 1979, she received the Hubert Humphrey Award for International Service.

She received a fellowship to the Institute of Politics at the Kennedy School of Government at Harvard University in 1980. Following this she served as special assistant at the U.S. Agency for International Development (USAID), where she directed assistance programs in war-torn and famine-stricken Somalia. In 1981, she became assistant administrator of the Food for Peace and Voluntary Assistance Bureau, a division of USAID. She became the first Asian-American presidential appointee and administered the world's largest food aid program, serving 80 countries and managing a budget of more than $2 billion. Under her leadership 3 million tons of food were delivered to 40 million people throughout Africa in 1984 and 1985 alone. She was awarded an honorary doctorate from Northeastern University in 1986 and recognized as Woman of the Year by the Organization of Chinese American Women

in 1987. She also received a Leader for Peace award from the Peace Corps in 1987.

In 1987, Bloch left the Food for Peace program to become the assistant administrator of the Asia and Near East Bureau, another division of USAID. She administered the largest program in the agency, with a staff of more than 2,000 serving 26 countries. Her budget was $3.8 billion.

In 1988, she returned to academia as an associate in the U.S.–Japan Relations Program at Harvard University's Center for International Affairs. The following year President George W. Bush appointed Bloch the U.S. ambassador to Nepal, a Himalayan kingdom. During her tenure Bloch was one of only 17 female ambassadors out of a total of 130 U.S. ambassadors. During her service, a popular uprising occurred in Nepal, which resulted in the first democratically elected government in more than 30 years. In the first elections, communists won more than one-third of the legislative seats. During her three-year ambassadorial appointment, she and her husband, Washington, D.C., attorney Stuart Bloch, commuted two days to see each other just four times a year. When her service as ambassador ended, some speculated that she might return to Washington, D.C., or San Francisco and enter politics. Instead, she retired from public service in 1993 to work as a vice president of corporate relations at BankAmerica.

In reflecting on her life's work, Bloch noted, "Only in this country can a first-generation American become an ambassador and go on to a major corporate executive position in one lifetime."

Further Reading

"Bank America Corporation Who's News." *Wall Street Journal,* June 3, 1993, B7 (W), B8 (E).
"Bank of America Executive Changes." *New York Times,* June 4, 1993, C3 (N), D3 (L).
Chinese Registry. "Julia Chang Bloch." Available online. URL: http://www.chineseinc.com/32002.htm. Downloaded December 23, 2000.
Fineman, Mark. "Speaking Her Mind Diplomacy." *Los Angeles Times,* June 3, 1991, 1.

Lichtenstein, Grace. "Witness to Freedom." *Savvy Woman* 11, no. 7 (July–August 1990): 56–61.

 ## BOXER, BARBARA LEVY
(1940–   )   *Senator*

Barbara Boxer was elected to the U.S. Senate from California in 1992, becoming one of just six female senators. She was born on November 11, 1940, and raised in Brooklyn, New York, the younger of two daughters in a Jewish family. Her father, Ira Levy, was an attorney, and her mother, Sophie, a homemaker. She married Stewart Boxer, a law student, during her senior year at Brooklyn College, and they later had two children.

Boxer completed a bachelor's degree in economics at Brooklyn College in 1962. After graduation, she attempted to work on Wall Street, but because no firm was willing to enroll a woman in its stockbroker training program, she took a job as a secretary. She studied and passed the exam to become a broker on her own. She worked briefly as a broker and became an activist in the Democratic Party. In 1965, the family moved to Marin County, California, north of San Francisco, after a vacation visit there.

Boxer served six years on the Marin County Board of Supervisors and was the first female president of the board. She served as supervisor of Marin County from 1976 to 1981. Boxer was elected to the U.S. House of Representatives in 1982 and served five terms in Congress from the California's Sixth Congressional District before being elected to the U.S. Senate in 1992, winning the seat vacated by retiring Senator Alan Cranston.

Boxer, a Democrat, advocated military reform and brought overcharges by Pentagon contractors to public attention. While in the House, she successfully authored more than 20 bills, including coauthoring the Violence Against Women Act and the first antistalking federal legislation. In 1989, she authored the Boxer Amendment, which would have granted federal funding for abortions for victims of rape or incest, and was the first pro-choice legislation to pass Congress in a decade. It was ultimately vetoed by President George W. Bush.

In 1994, she wrote a book, *Stranger in the Senate.* In 1998, she was reelected to the Senate by a large margin. Her daughter married the brother of HILLARY RODHAM CLINTON, and Boxer is now a grandmother. In the Senate she serves on the Environment and Public Works Committee where she chairs the Superfund, Toxics, Risk, and Waste Management Subcommittee; the Foreign Relations Committee where she is chair of the International Operations and Terrorism Subcommittee; the Budget, Banking, Housing and Urban Affairs Committee; and the Appropriations Committee. She is also chief deputy for strategic outreach as a member of the Senate Democratic leadership, and a member of the Senate's Hispanic Caucus. Her top-priority issues have been community policing, eradication of assault weapons, health maintenance organization (HMO) patient protection, and quality education. In 2000, the Senate passed Boxer's plan to fight AIDS and tuberculosis worldwide, as well as an amendment she authored, which banned the use of toxic pesticides in areas used by children. The National Education Association and the Sierra Club have both endorsed her. Female senators remain a distinct minority, but this gender gap may be lessened by young women who are inspired by Barbara Boxer's record of service. Her current six-year Senate term ends in 2005.

Further Reading

American Civil Liberties Union. "Senator Barbara Boxer." Available online. URL: http://www.aclu.org/vote-guide/254info.html. Downloaded December 24, 2000.

League of Women Voters. "Barbara Boxer." Available online. URL: http//sunsite.berkeley.edu/smartvoter/1998nov/ca/state/vote/boxer_b/. Downloaded on December 24, 2000.

Sample, Herbert. "Barbara Boxer." *California Journal* 35 no. 6 (June 1994): 19.

U.S. Senate. "Barbara Boxer." Available online. URL: http://www.senate.gov/~boxer/home.html. Downloaded on December 24, 2000.

Victor, Kirk. "Fightin' Women." *National Journal* 29, no. 31 (1997): 1544–49.

Whitney, Catherine. *Nine and Counting: The Women of the Senate.* New York: Perennial, 2001.

 ## BRYANT, LOUISE MORAN
(1887–1936) *Journalist*

Louise Bryant was a journalist who covered wars, the Russian Revolution, and the Red Scare of the 1920s. She was born Louise Moran in San Francisco, California, on December 5, 1887. The third child of Anna Louisa and Hugh Moran, she was christened in the Roman Catholic Church. Her father was a newspaperman who had worked in the coal mines of Pennsylvania as a boy. He was a journalist for the *Irish World* and other prolabor publications. Her mother worked as a dressmaker and divorced her father when Louise was three years old. Louise, her mother, and siblings then moved to Reno, Nevada.

When Louise was six, her mother married Sheridan Daniel Bryant, who worked for the Southern Pacific railroad as a brakeman and conductor on freight trains. The young girl adopted the last name of her stepfather. She had a private Chinese tutor for her elementary education. After graduating from Wadsworth High School, Bryant attended the University of Nevada, where she was on the staff of the school paper and its journal. In 1906, at 19, she attended the University of Oregon and became an active suffragist. After graduating, she worked briefly as a schoolteacher before becoming a journalist in Portland, Oregon. In 1909, she married Paul Trullinger, a wealthy dentist, but retained her own name. She took part in the successful 1912 Oregon Crusade for Suffrage and would later picket with suffragists in front of the White House in 1919. In 1912, Bryant started writing for such radical publications as *The Masses* and *Blast,* a San Francisco anarchist weekly edited by EMMA GOLDMAN's lover, Alexander Berkman. Bryant left Trullinger and Portland for her lover, radical writer John Reed, and moved to New York on December 31, 1915, and arrived in New York on January 4, 1916.

Bryant became part of an inner circle of radicals associated with *The Masses,* which included playwright Eugene O'Neill, novelist Sherwood Anderson, journalist Max Eastman, and activist John Reed. Many of her friends were younger feminists, including CRYSTAL EASTMAN, MARGARET SANGER, and Emma Goldman. Bryant was an advocate of suffrage, labor unions, communism, and pacifism. She founded the Provincetown Players with playwright Eugene O'Neill and others and wrote several plays that the theater group produced. She married John Reed in 1916.

During World War I, Bryant covered the war as a correspondent in Europe for the Bell New Syndicate. In 1917, she took a trip to Russia with John Reed and witnessed the communist revolution in Russia firsthand. Bryant interviewed women leaders of the revolution, including Alexandra Kollontai, who was the only female in Lenin's cabinet. Bryant's articles from this period were published as a book in 1918, *Six Red Months in Russia.* (Her husband wrote *Ten Days That Shook the World* in 1919.) While Reed became engaged in the two communist parties in America, Bryant did not. (The first two communist parties in the United States were founded in 1919. They were derived from the Socialist Party. John Reed and Benjamin Gitlow cofounded the Communist Labor Party. The other organization, the Communist Party of America, included the Russian and most foreign federations of the Socialist Party.)

In 1919, Bryant appeared before a Senate committee chaired by Senator Lee Overman, a Democrat from North Carolina, who was investigating "Bolshevik [Communist] propaganda." She was interrogated on the witness stand for two days about her marriages and political activities. When asked by one senator if she belonged to "the picket squad," referring to the suffragists who had burned the U.S. president in effigy and gone on a hunger strike, Bryant replied, "I do not know what that has to do with the truth about Russia, but I did. I believe in equality . . . even in my own country." When one senator promised that they planned to treat her like a lady, Bryant responded, "I do not want to be treated as a lady, but I want to be treated as a human being." Bryant revealed her activities on behalf of Russia to the committee: "The purpose was to protest against intervention in Russia. I, as an American, believing in self-determination cannot believe in intervention. I do not see how we can fight for democracy in France and against it in Siberia. . . . I believe we ought to take our troops out of Russia . . . it would be better for both nations to have friendly relations."

In 1920, Bryant returned to Russia a second time during the height of the Red Scare in the United States. (Red scares, outbreaks of fear of communists and their influence, have a long history in the United States. Accusations of marxism, socialism, and communism have been used against abolitionists, labor organizers, and those in the civil rights movement.) While in Russia in 1920, Reed died of typhus, and Bryant returned to Europe. She continued working as a journalist, reporting for the Hearst press from Turkey and Russia. In 1923, her second book, *Mirrors of Moscow,* was published, and she married Willian Bullitt, a wealthy diplomat. In 1926, two years after Lenin's death, she revealed her misgivings about the Soviet Union as "the supreme example of dictatorship."

She and Bullitt had had a daughter, Anne, born on February 24, 1924, but Bryant lost custody of her in the 1930 divorce, where Bullit was the only witness at the divorce hearings. He claimed Bryant was an alcoholic and had a lesbian relationship with Gwendolyn Le Gallienne, daughter of the English writer Richard Le Gallienne.

Addicted to alcohol and drugs, Bryant spent her last years in poverty in Paris. Bryant died of a cerebral hemorrhage at age 49, on January 6, 1936, in Sèvres, France. After Bryant's death her husband became ambassador to France.

In 1981, Warren Beatty made *Reds,* a movie about the romance between Reed and Bryant. The film was nominated for 12 Academy Awards. Bryant's obituary in the *New York Herald Tribune* noted, "An unusually competent journalist, Miss Bryant sought to dispel many foolish legends concerning the Soviets that had gained widespread credence in the United States."

Further Reading

Bryant, Louise. *Mirrors of Moscow.* 1923. Reprint, New York: Hyperion Press, 1973. Available online. URL: http://www.marxist.org/archive/bryant.works/1923-mom/. Downloaded December 25, 2000.

———. *Six Months in Russia.* 1918. Reprint, New York: Ayer, 1970.

Dearborn, Mary. *Queen of Bohemia: The Life of Louise Bryant.* New York: Replica Books, 2000.

Spartacus Educational. "Louise Bryant." Available online. URL: http://www.spartacus.schoolnet.co.uk/lbryant.htm. Downloaded on December 25, 2000.

 BUTLER, SELENA SLOAN
(1872–1964)   *Parent-Teacher Association Cofounder*

At a time when most U.S. organizations, including parent-teacher associations, were segregated, Selena Sloan Butler founded the first African-American parent-teacher association (PTA). Selena Sloan was born on January 4, 1872, in Thomasville, Georgia. Her mother, Winnie Williams, was of African and American Indian descent, and her father, William Sloan, was white. Her father did not live with them, but took care of Selena's mother and two daughters. Butler completed elementary school, taught by missionaries in Thomas County, and then attended Spelman Seminary, later Spelman College, in Atlanta, Georgia. She spent six years at Spelman, where she worked on the school magazine and graduated second in her class in 1888, at age 16. After graduation she taught kindergarten in Atlanta, Georgia, and Florida.

As a teacher in Atlanta she met and married Henry Rutherford Butler. They moved to Boston, where her husband attended medical school at Harvard University, and she studied at the Emerson School of Oratory. They returned to Atlanta in 1895, where Selena Sloan Butler became a pioneer in teaching night school for adults at the

Yonge Street School. For several years, she served as editor and publisher of the *Woman's Advocate,* a monthly newspaper addressing an African-American female audience.

After her son's birth, she could not find a preschool teacher in her neighborhood, so she started a kindergarten in her home. When her son started public school, Butler started the first African-American PTA in the country at Yonge Street School in 1911. By 1920, she had established a state-level African-American PTA, and by 1926 she had established the National Congress of Colored Parents and Teachers.

Butler served as delegate to the founding convention of the National Association of Colored Women in Boston. Her paper on the convict lease system was published as a pamphlet. In 1930, she helped found the Southern Women for the Prevention of Lynching. Butler also worked in the Phillis Wheatley Young Women's Christian Association, named after one of the nation's first famous African-American authors, serving as chair of its board for many years.

After her husband's death in 1931, she moved to England with her son, who, like his father, also pursued a medical career. While in London, Butler worked in the Nursery School Association of Great Britain, the British equivalent of the PTA. Butler returned to Atlanta during World War II and retired in 1953 in Los Angeles to live near her son and his family. She died in Los Angeles in 1964 of congestive heart failure and is buried next to her husband in Atlanta's Oakland Cemetery. After Butler's death, the African-American PTA organization merged in 1970 with the all-white National PTA, and Butler was recognized as one of the national founders, along with Phoebe Hearst and Alice McLellan Birney from the white group.

A park in Atlanta was named in her honor in 1966. The park is located next to the Younge Street School, now the site of the Henry Rutherford Butler Elementary School, where Butler founded the first African-American PTA. In 1976, her portrait was hung in the Georgia Hall of Fame. Some of her papers are stored in the Special Collections of the Atlanta University Center's Robert W. Woodruff Library and at Spelman College Archives in Atlanta, Georgia. The PTA that Selena Sloan Butler founded continues to benefit students and parents throughout the nation.

Further Reading

Herzog, Susan. *The PTA Story: A Century of Commitment to Children.* Washington, D.C.: National PTA, 1997.
History of the Georgia Congress of Colored Parents and Teachers. Atlanta: The Congress, 1970.

C

 CARSON, RACHEL LOUISE
(1907–1964) *Environmentalist, Writer*

Rachel Carson was a biologist, conservationist, and author who sparked the modern environmental movement in America. Rachel Louise Carson was born on May 27, 1907, in Springdale, Pennsylvania, the youngest of three children of Maria McLean Carson, a former teacher, and Robert Warden Carson. Her mother had raised Rachel to respect nature. When her mother found a bug in the house she would catch it and carry it outside rather than kill it, providing Carson with an early lesson regarding humans' relationships to the world around them.

Carson spent her childhood in Pennsylvania, on a 65-acre homestead of natural beauty, next to a spreading industrial landscape of coal and steel. Carson's writing talents were evident at a young age. In fourth grade she had a story published in *St. Nicholas* magazine, a prestigious children's publication that had featured youthful writings by Edna St. Vincent Millay and Eudora Welty. As Carson recalled, "Perhaps that early experience of seeing my work in print played its part in fostering my childhood dream of becoming a writer." Two more of her stories appeared in *St. Nicholas* before she finished elementary school.

She attended the Pennsylvania College for Women, now Chatham College, on scholarship in 1925. Carson lived in the dormitory, and every weekend either she went home or her mother came to visit. Carson worked on the college newspaper and wrote stories about the sea for the college literary magazine. Her favorite author was Mark Twain. Carson started college as an English major, but she switched her major to biology after taking a biology course. Her choice was unorthodox for her era; at this time, women writers were more accepted than were female scientists. She graduated magna cum laude in 1929 and attended Johns Hopkins University on a full scholarship to study genetics. While at Johns Hopkins she also worked in the zoology department at the University of Maryland.

Carson spent her summer as an intern at Woods Hole Marine Biological Laboratory on Cape Cod, Massachusetts. Her work at this lab for oceanic research was very fulfilling, especially since she said that she had felt her destiny was somehow linked with the sea before she had ever even seen it. She completed her master's degree in marine zoology in 1932 but soon found that industry did not hire women in professional jobs, and neither did museums or research institutions. In 1935, she briefly wrote scripts for a weekly radio show about marine life called *Romance Under the Waters.* The show's producers found that professional writers did not know much about scientific subjects, and most scientists could not write informative pieces that were also entertaining. Carson's background in science and creative writing allowed her to merge the two skills.

In 1936, she took a civil service exam for a post as a junior aquatic biologist. The only woman to take the test, she earned the highest score. That year, she was one of the first two women hired by the U.S. Bureau of Fisheries in other than a secretarial capacity. She was eventually promoted from junior aquatic biologist to biologist and to chief editor of fish and wildlife publications.

Carson's father died in 1935 and her sister died the following year, and Carson became the sole support of her mother and two nieces. When United States joined World War II in 1941, government offices were briefly relocated to Chicago. Carson tried to find another position in the Washington, D.C., area so she would not have to relocate her family, but with no success. She was turned down for positions at *Reader's Digest,* the New York Zoological Society, and the National Audubon Society.

An essay she had published in 1937 in the *Atlantic Monthly* led to her first book, *Under the Sea-Wind,* published by Simon and Schuster in 1941. The book had taken her three years to write, working weekends and nights in addition to her full-time government job. Her book, which depicted ocean life as perceived by sea creatures, was a critical success but only sold 1,600 copies during its first six years in print. Her second book, *The Sea Around Us,* published in 1951, was a bestseller and contributed significantly to the new science of oceanography. It told the story of the world's oceans, from their origins billions of years ago to the modern era, weaving together the disciplines of biology, zoology, and geology and drawing on seafaring history, mythology, and folktales. Carson's book won the National Book Award and an award from the American Association for the Advancement of Science as the finest example of science writing that year. It was on the *New York Times* best-seller list for a record 86 weeks. As one critic noted, "Only once or twice in a generation does the world get a physical scientist with literary genius. Miss Carson has written a classic." She was elected to the National Institute of Arts and Letters, only the second woman to receive this prestigious literary honor. The book was translated into 30 languages. The profits allowed Carson to leave government employment on June 3, 1952 and write full time. Hollywood bought the movie rights to *The Sea Around Us,* and the film won an Oscar for best documentary in 1953. A Guggenheim grant sponsored the research for her third book, *The Edge of the Sea,* published in 1955. This book was written to help children appreciate nature, but it was her next book that would change the world around her.

Carson's niece died in 1957 and left her with another young child to raise, a five-year-old boy, whom Carson adopted when she was 50.

In July 1945, Carson had approached *Reader's Digest* with an idea for an article on the dangers of pesticides, but her idea was rejected. Originally, Carson thought of the topic when a friend mentioned to Carson that she saw birds around her die when her town was sprayed for mosquitoes. The idea stayed with Carson, and over a decade later she wrote a book—*Silent Spring*—on the topic because, she said, "Everything which meant the most to me as a naturalist was being threatened." She began research on the book in 1958 and spent four years gathering data. During World War II, a new generation of more toxic chemical pesticides had been developed and were being widely used throughout the 1950s. Carson's book predicted a "silent spring" without birds and small animals if the use of these toxic pesticides was not stopped. The appendix to *Silent Spring* contained more than 50 pages of scientific references on the effects of pesticide contamination on plants, soil, animals,

Dorothy Freeman (left) and Rachel Carson (right) at their Maine home
(Courtesy of Boothbay Register, Boothbay Harbor, Maine)

and drinking water. Carson supported the use of ladybugs and praying mantises for pest control rather than the use of chemicals, with their negative effects on human genetics and public health. While Carson was working on the book, her mother died in 1958, and in 1960 Carson herself learned that she had breast cancer. Because scientists had evidence that pesticides could cause some forms of cancer, Carson had lobbied against the spraying of pesticides near her Maryland home.

Carson's last book, *Silent Spring*, published in 1962, made a national and international impact on environmental policy. At the time her book was published, the principles of ecology were undeveloped. Her work marked the beginning of the modern environmental movement. The book

detailed the damage caused by DDT and other pesticides then in common use, and it attacked the chemical industry. The book was read millions. In response, the National Agricultural Chemicals Association spent some $250,000 on booklets and publicity that attacked Carson, claiming she was more concerned about insects than human life, among other things. The association's research scientists claimed that hordes of insects would devour crops and that "We would return to the dark ages and the insects and vermin would once again inherit the earth." Agrichemical companies launched personal attacks on Carson. They ridiculed her marital status, with one spokesperson commenting, "I thought she was a spinster so what's she so worried about genetics for?" Some

37

proposed that the book was part of a communist plot to undermine the economy of the West. *Time* magazine attacked the book as being an "emotional and inaccurate outburst and one-sided and hysterically overemphatic." When CBS aired an interview with Carson about her book, three of the five sponsors withdrew financial support.

Nevertheless, President John F. Kennedy's Science Advisory Committee accepted Carson's findings. Within a year of *Silent Spring*'s publication, 40 bills were drafted in state legislatures concerning regulation of pesticides, and Carson was testifying before Senate committees. As one newspaper stated, "A few thousand words from her, and the world took a new direction." Carson received two awards from the Audubon Society. On October 3, 1963, she received the Bortsch award for distinguished contributions to natural history, and on December 3, 1963, she received its medal for distinguished service.

Rachel Carson died on April 14, 1964, two years after the publication of *Silent Spring*, at age 56. Cancer claimed her life in Silver Spring, Maryland. Her companion, Dorothy Freeman, became the guardian of Carson's nephew. In the year of Carson's death, the U.S. government changed its policy so that federal agencies no longer had to prove to industry that certain chemicals were dangerous; manufacturers had to prove the safety of a product before it could be marketed.

In 1969, five years after her death, the federal government phased out DDT use, and the environmental movement Carson inspired grew in strength and numbers. In 1980, President Jimmy Carter posthumously awarded her the Presidential Medal of Freedom. DDT and other harmful pesticides are now banned in the United States, but regulations in many developing nations remain less rigorous. Carson's work remains an inspiration to environmentalists still working toward change.

Further Reading

Carson, Rachel. *Always, Rachel: The Letters of Rachel Carson and Dorothy Freeman, 1952–1964*. Boston: Beacon Press, 1995.

———. *The Sea Around Us*. Boston: Houghton Mifflin, 1951.
———. *Silent Spring*. Boston: Houghton Mifflin, 1962.
Hynes, Patricia. *The Recurring Silent Spring*. New York: Pergamon Press, 1989.
Lear, Linda. *Rachel Carson: Witness For Nature*. New York: Holt, 1997.
McCay, Mary. *Rachel Carson*. New York: Macmillan, 1993.

 CASTILLO, SYLVIA
(1951–)   *Founder of the National Network of Hispanic Women*

Sylvia Castillo cofounded the National Network of Hispanic Women. Castillo was born on September 2, 1951, in Los Angeles, California, to Henry and Lucille Miramontes Castillo. Castillo's parents were the children of Mexican immigrants. Her father worked as a truck driver, and her mother as a retail clerk in a pharmacy. Sylvia Castillo graduated from an all-girls' parochial school, Our Lady of Loretto High School, in Los Angeles in 1969, at which she had been student body president.

Castillo earned a B.A. degree in social psychology from the University of California, Santa Barbara, in 1973. During her master's degree program in social welfare administration at the University of California, Berkeley, she had a fellowship from the National Institute of Mental Health. She completed her master's degree in 1976 and then studied substance abuse programs with a postgraduate fellowship from the University of Southern California. She worked as a career and mental health counselor at California Polytechnic State University in San Luis Obispo from 1976 to 1979. Castillo helped found the first reentry and career mentoring programs for women and people of color. In 1979, while she was at California State University, Long Beach, she held another fellowship to study upward-mobility challenges faced by Latina college professionals. In researching upward mobility in higher education, she found that most of the human subjects she studied were very isolated and had few role models. Castillo next took a job advising students in the placement office at

Stanford University, where she served as assistant dean of student affairs for academic advising and counseling from 1980 to 1985.

After exploring the difficulties faced by Latina professional women, Castillo decided to start an English-language newsletter. The 14-page newsletter, initially called *Intercambios Femeniles* ("Interchange of Women") first appeared in December 1980. Each issue had a theme, such as careers in science, technology, or health, and included resources and networking lists, statistics, and information. The publication came out four times a year and developed into a glossy, full-color periodical. As Castillo recalled, "I wanted to develop an information clearinghouse about educational advancement, career preparation, and leadership development."

Castillo spearheaded the founding of an organization first called Hispanic Women in Higher Education and later called the National Network of Hispanic Women (NNHW). The group was oriented toward the concerns of first-generation college-educated Latinas professionals. Castillo established a national office for the organization in Los Angeles, which was run by part-time staff. A primary goal was to organize seminars for companies interested in recruiting Latinas. In 1982, she established Roundtables for Hispanic Women, working with companies such as Pacific Bell, Sears Roebuck, and Avon Products. In 1985, Castillo resigned from her position at Stanford to work full time for *Intercambios Femeniles* and for the NNHW. The first national conference she organized for the group was held in Denver, Colorado, in March 1985, and attended by 500 women. Another conference was held in 1987 in Miami, Florida, and another in 1989 in Los Angeles, California.

During a one-year break from her work in 1986 because of illness, Castillo married Steven Castillo Long, and they moved to Maui, Hawaii, where she became active in the Puerto Rican community there and in women's groups. She directed the Children's Advocacy Center in Wailuku and worked part-time as an administrative coordinator for the graduate school of social work at the University of Hawaii at Manoa. Castillo returned to Los Angeles in 1990,

but during her absence, the NNHW and *Intercambios* had ceased activity. Castillo remains interested in building a national federation of Latina groups and developing fund-raising activities.

Further Reading

Moses, Eric. "Things Improving." *Los Angeles Sentinel,* May 7, 1997, A3.

Telgen, Diane, and Jim Kamp, eds. "Sylvia Castillo." *Notable Hispanic American Women.* Detroit: Gale Research, 1993.

CATT, CARRIE CLINTON LANE CHAPMAN
(1859–1947) *Suffragist*

As president of the National American Woman Suffrage Association, Carrie Clinton Lane Chapman Catt led the last stage of the effort to secure suffrage for women, then reformatted the group into the League of Women Voters. Carrie Lane was born on February 9, 1859, in Ripon, Wisconsin, to Lucius Lane and Maria Clinton Lane. After the Civil War ended in 1865, the family moved to a farm in Iowa. Her father refused to pay for her college education because he did not think women needed college, so Catt taught school for a year in order to save money for her tuition.

After graduating from Iowa State College in 1880, she studied law for a short time and then became principal of Mason City (Iowa) High School in 1881. By 1883, she had become one of the first woman school superintendents in the nation. In 1885, at age 26, she married Leo Chapman, the publisher of the *Mason City Republican,* who died the following year of typhoid fever. She then married George Catt, an engineer, in 1890, but was widowed again five years later. Their marriage was notable for its notarized agreement that she was free to work two months in both the fall and spring for the suffrage movement, and that her husband would support her activism financially.

Her activism began in 1887 with work for the Iowa Woman Suffrage Association. She worked as an organizer for the national group from 1890

39

Carrie Chapman Catt, suffragist
(Still Picture Branch, National Archives, College Park, Md.)

until 1900, when she became its president. She led the campaign that won women's suffrage in Colorado in 1893. She was elected president of the National American Woman Suffrage Association (NAWSA) in 1900, succeeding suffrage leader SUSAN B. ANTHONY. Members expected Anthony to choose suffrage lecturer ANNA HOWARD SHAW to replace her, but she selected Catt instead. Catt shifted the organization's tactics from an emphasis on education to one of direct action. She resigned in 1904 to care for her dying husband.

She founded and served as president of the International Woman Suffrage Alliance from 1904 to 1923. She was sometimes criticized for being willing to compromise on moral issues in order to gain political support. For example, she backed the NAWSA censure of *The Woman's Bible,* by women's rights leader ELIZABETH CADY STANTON, since the book had antagonized many Christians. Beginning

in 1912, Catt organized campaigns in New York State that led to the 1914 passage of suffrage for women in New York. Catt was reelected as president of the NAWSA again in 1915, succeeding Anna Howard Shaw this time and winning support over challenges from more militant women led by radical suffrage leader ALICE PAUL. While Paul wanted to focus solely on an amendment to the U.S. Constitution, Catt supported a two-pronged approach of state-level activism accompanied by a national suffrage campaign. She developed a strategy called the Winning Plan, which focused on securing suffrage in 36 states, the number needed for ratification of a federal amendment. Starting when she was 31 years old, Catt devoted 30 years of her life, from 1890 to 1920, to unpaid, full-time work in order to attain suffrage. She held her position as president of the NAWSA until her death in 1947. At the end of her term she had built the membership of NAWSA from 100,000 to 2 million.

After attaining suffrage in 1920, Catt proposed that the NAWSA transform itself into the League of Women Voters in order to educate women about their new voting power. She became a peace advocate in her later years, working through the Woman's Peace Party and then heading the National Committee on the Cause and Cure of War from 1925 to 1932. She helped to organize some of the earliest anti-Nazi protests in the United States. She had been a reporter in her earlier years and coauthored two books: *Woman Suffrage and Politics: The Inner Story of the Suffrage Movement,* in 1923, and *Why Wars Must Cease,* in 1935. Carrie Chapman Catt died March 9, 1947, at age 88, in New Rochelle, New York. Along with Anthony, Catt was one of the most effective organizers of the suffrage movement.

Further Reading

Birdsell, David. "The Rhetoric of Carrie Chapman Catt." *Argumentation and Advocacy: The Journal of the American Forensic Association* 29, no. 4 (spring 1993): 178–85.

Fowler, Robert Booth. *Carrie Catt: Feminist Politician.* Boston: Northeastern University Press, 1988.

Van Voris, Jacqueline. *Carrie Chapman Catt: A Public Life.* New York: Feminist Press, 1996.

CERVANTES, MAGDALENA
(1958–) *President of Comision Femenil Mexicana Nacional*

Maggie Cervantes is president of the bilingual Comision Femenil Mexicana Nacional Inc. Magdalena Cervantes was born on October 27, 1958, in Los Angeles County to Dolores Barron and Albert Cervantes. Her father was an upholsterer, her mother a bank teller who was eventually promoted to escrow officer. Her parents disagreed about raising her to speak both Spanish and English, because her father had been punished in school for speaking Spanish. Nevertheless, she became fluent in Spanish and English.

Her parents divorced when she was 12, partly due to her father's alcoholism. Seeing her mother struggle financially impressed on Cervantes the need for women to attain economic independence. Many women in her family worked, so she had role models of independent working women. She grew up in East Los Angeles, in a Latino neighborhood. In high school, she was bused to a school in a middle-class suburb where the difference in social status between her family and those of most of her classmates was very apparent.

After completing high school she attended East Los Angeles Community College, where, while studying sociology, she met a Latino professor who inspired her. She completed an associate of arts degree in 1979.

In 1980, she was involved in a state redistricting movement called Californios for Fair Representation. Interested in becoming a bilingual teacher, Cervantes enrolled in a private Catholic University, Loyola Marymount. Unfortunately, she did not have the financial resources to complete her dreams. She again noticed social differences between herself and most of the other students in the private school, who came from families that could more easily afford the tuition.

At Loyola, she served as the founder and first president of the student chapter of the Comision Femenil Mexicana, a feminist organization for Latinas. She became the national corresponding secretary for the Comision Femenil Mexicana

Nacional in 1981, the same year she earned her B.A. degree.

In 1982, Cervantes was awarded the National Hispanic Fellowship in Public Administration. She graduated from the University of California, Riverside, in 1984. She then directed a senior citizen program for the East Los Angeles Health Task Force. From 1984 to 1989 she served in a number of positions on the national board of the Comision Femenil, including vice president. In 1988, she served as the southwest regional chair for the Comision Femenil.

In 1992, Cervantes took a position as executive director for New Economics for Women (NEW), a Los Angeles volunteer organization dedicated to improving the economic status of Latinas. Affordable housing was a crucial issue for low-income women, and one of her primary projects at NEW was the development of a housing project, Casa Loma, for single parents. She may have been especially effective as an advocate for low-income women because she had witnessed her own mother's struggles. Casa Loma was an $18 million, 110-unit apartment complex in downtown Los Angeles, one of the poorest sections of the city. The building's design was developed by a committee of single mothers. It included a child care center, a youth center, computer center, and children's courtyard. After the Los Angeles riots of 1992, Cervantes used her position as president of the Comision Femenil Mexicana Nacional to raise funds to assist the families who had lost their homes and possessions.

Further Reading

Cervantes, Maggie. *Casa Loma, Los Angeles, Calif.* VHS. Bruner Foundation, 1995.

 CHANG BLOCH, JULIA

See BLOCH, JULIA CHANG.

 CHAVEZ, LINDA
(1947–) *Government Official*

Linda Chavez was the highest-ranking woman in the Reagan administration. Linda Chavez was born in Albuquerque, New Mexico, in 1947 to an Anglo mother, Velma, and a conservative Spanish-American father, Rudy Chavez, a house painter, whose family had lived in the Southwest for more than 300 years. The family moved to Denver, Colorado, when Linda was nine years old. She marched against racial segregation as a teenager. Chavez completed a bachelor's degree in 1970 at the University of Colorado, then pursued graduate studies in English literature at the University of California, Los Angeles. The department wanted to offer a Chicano literature class and pressured Chavez into teaching this course. She argued with her department that there was not enough material written by Chicanos to justify a course, but was pressed into teaching the course anyway. There were very deep divisions between her and the students who enrolled in the course. Latino students in the course had a renewed sense of racial pride and were eager to learn about their previously silenced history. Chavez exhibited little interest in her racial background and history. Tensions were so high that she had to lecture to a class of students who had purposely turned their backs on her. She failed them for not completing the reading list, so they vandalized her home. Chavez left the university in 1972 to join her husband, Christopher Gersten, whom she had married in 1967, in Washington, D.C.

Chavez began her public service career by working in Washington, D.C. for liberal Democratic congressman Don Edwards of San Jose, California. Chavez was a registered Democrat at the time and considered herself a liberal. She began to differ with many in the party, however, because she supported the war in Vietnam and disagreed with pro–civil rights stances, which she criticized for what she viewed as setting quotas.

In the mid-1970s, Chavez worked with liberal organizations, including the Democratic National Committee and the National Education Association. She served briefly as a consultant on education for the Department of Health, Education, and Welfare and then was hired by the American Federation of Teachers (AFT). She served as editor of the AFT journal, *American Educator,* and wrote a series of articles that brought her to the attention of conservatives in Washington who were attracted by her arguments about the need for teachers to return to traditional values.

In 1983, she became a member of the U.S. Commission on Civil Rights and was eventually appointed director of the agency, charged with monitoring the government's progress in enforcing civil rights laws. She became the center of controversy by issuing memos that called for the reversal of affirmative action policies. Affirmative action policies had been enacted in the 1960s and 1970s to remedy racial and gender discrimination in education and employment. Some thought affirmative action was unfair, because in some cases the policies established quotas for minority employment. She authorized a study to examine the negative impact she believed affirmative action had on minorities. Civil rights activists criticized her for what they saw as changing the traditionally impartial civil rights agency into a puppet of the Reagan administration. Chavez believed she was trying to remedy the liberal bias of the agency.

In 1985, she became the director of the White House Office of Public Liaison, the highest-ranking woman in the Reagan administration. Chavez changed parties to become a Republican but lasted only 10 months in her White House position. In 1986 news stories surfaced of former coworkers who asserted that Chavez presented herself as Jewish, claiming to have converted to Judaism when she married Christopher Gersten in 1967. Chavez maintained that she had remained a practicing Catholic. After leaving the Office of Public Liaison in 1986, she sought the Maryland Republican nomination for senator. She ran against incumbent Democrat BARBARA MIKULSKI in only the second U.S. Senate race in which both candidates were female. Two-thirds of the voters in the state were Democrats, and Chavez was a very new resident of Maryland. Chavez called the unmarried Mikulski an antimale, "San Francisco–style Democrat." Chavez lost the election by more than 20 percent of the vote.

In the Reagan administration she worked to repeal an executive order that encouraged minority hiring. While serving on the U.S. Civil Rights Commission she attacked liberal commissioner MARY FRANCES BERRY. Chavez was so successful in shifting the commission's focus that by the time she left the post in 1985, even some liberals were calling for the abolishment of the once-influential body which had become consumed by internal battles and had its budget slashed by Congress.

Chavez next served as president of U.S. English, a private organization devoted to making English the official national language. She resigned from the organization in 1988 after 14 months. She resigned in protest over a memo written by the group's founder and chair, John Tanton, which could be interpreted as xenophobic. Other Latino leaders from groups such as the Mexican-American Legal Defense and Education Fund were not impressed by Chavez's resignation and publicly wondered why it had taken her 14 months to figure out that, as they saw it, the organization was based on intolerance. (At least one major contributor to U.S. English advocated forced sterilization for "undesirables.")

Chavez then became a senior fellow at the Manhattan Institute for Policy Research, a conservative think tank in Washington, D.C. She also served as director of the Center for the New American Community, which considers multiculturalism to be a threat. (Multiculturalism is a movement that calls for a curriculum more inclusive than the traditional Western canon.) Chavez expressed her political ideas in her 1991 book *Out of the Barrio: Toward a New Politics of Hispanic Assimilation.* Her basic tenet is that many Hispanics have moved into the middle class and do not face severe discrimination. Chavez also opposes comparable worth, pay equity, and bilingual education programs. She served as president of the Center for Equal Opportunity in Washington, D.C., a nonprofit public policy group that focused on issues regarding race and immigration. In 1996, a report issued by the center claimed that African-American defendants had a better chance of escaping conviction than whites. Chavez continued to challenge Latino leaders who she believed were harmfully delaying the assimilation process for recent immigrants. She served as adviser to Ron Unz, a millionaire who backed Proposition 227, a successful California ballot measure that put an end to 30 years of bilingual education in the state in 1998. Chavez publicly stated that she would like a position in the area of foreign policy or defense in the administration of President George W. Bush. In 2001, President George W. Bush nominated her as U.S. secretary of labor, a nomination that the labor movement opposed. Chavez has dismissed the idea of a minimum wage as a "marxist" concept, and called sexual harassment suits proof that the United States is "a nation of crybabies." Chavez withdrew her nomination when allegations that she had employed an undocumented illegal alien surfaced.

Harboring an illegal alien is a felony, but Chavez argued that keeping an undocumented Guatemalan in her home had been an act of charity. "I would not turn away from my door a woman who had no place to live and who had been badly mistreated and needed help," she explained. She denounced the "politics of personal destruction" that led her to withdraw her nomination. Her critics argued that a two-year illegal immigrant "houseguest," who was not her relative and performed household chores, was a maid. They also noted that her gifts of cash to the woman constituted less than minimum wage. Chavez was willing to acknowledge that she had known her guest was an illegal alien within three months of her arrival.

Chavez is working on a second book that will critically analyze the impact feminism has had on American social policy. When she appears to speak on college campuses she has been met by protestors, some armed with eggs and some who have punched her. Chavez has resumed writing her syndicated column, which appears in 50 newspapers, including *USA Today,* the *Philadelphia Inquirer,* the *Chicago Tribune,* and the *Orange County Register.* She remains active in conservative politics.

Further Reading

Chavez, Linda. "Is Bilingual Education Failing to Help America's Schoolchildren?" *Insight* 12, no. 21 (June 3, 1996): 24.

———. "Multicultural Movement Makes Immigration Tougher." *National Minority Politics* 7, no. 5 (May 31, 1995): 7.

Hernandez, Macarena. "Conservative and Hispanic, Linda Chavez Carves Out Leadership Niche." *New York Times,* August 19, 1998, A28.

Martinez, Demetria. "Chavez's Charity." *National Catholic Reporter* 37, no. 12 (January 19, 2001): 18.

"Meet Linda Chavez." *NEA Today: A Newspaper for Members of the National Education Association* 15, no. 9 (May 1, 1997): 42.

Menard, Valerie. "Lady Boss." *Hispanic* 11, no. 9 (September 1, 1998): 70.

"A Speedy Exit for Linda Chavez." *New York Times,* January 10, 2001, A18.

 CHAVEZ-THOMPSON, LINDA
(1944–)   *AFL-CIO Vice President*

Linda Chavez-Thompson is the first person of color elected to an executive office in the AFL-CIO and the highest-ranking woman in organized labor. Linda Chavez was born in 1944 in Lubbock, Texas, in a family of eight children. She is a second-generation Mexican-American. Her parents were sharecroppers, and she started working in cotton fields as a child. At age 10, she was hoeing cotton for 10 hours a day for 30 cents an hour. She dropped out of high school to help support her family. Chavez-Thompson had two children in her first marriage at age 19, and was widowed in her second marriage to Robert Thompson.

Chavez-Thompson was employed as a secretary for the Laborers' International Union from 1967 to 1971. She began to work as a union representative because no one in the office could speak Spanish to the largely Chicano membership. She was next hired as a business agent for the American Federation of State, County, and Municipal Employees (AFSCME) union in San Antonio and was promoted to the executive director of the local.

In 1988, she was elected vice president of the national AFSCME, a position she held from 1988 to 1996, directing the union in seven states: Arizona, Colorado, Nevada, New Mexico, Oklahoma, Texas, and Utah. The southwest is traditionally unfriendly to organized labor. Her successes in this position included gaining more than 5,000 new members in Texas in five years and getting a collective bargaining law for public employees passed in New Mexico.

In 1995, she became the vice president of the AFL-CIO at its national convention in New York. She was reelected in 1997. Forty percent of the 13.6 million members of the AFL-CIO are female persons of color. Chavez-Thompson was the first person of color at the executive level in the AFL-CIO and remains the highest-ranking female. In 2001, women and people of color make up nearly 30 percent of the AFL-CIO's executive council.

Chavez-Thompson also served as vice president of the Labor Council for Latin American Advancement from 1986 to 1996. She has been an active member of the Democratic National Committee and a board member of the Institute for Women's Policy Research. She was the only Latina to serve on President Bill Clinton's advisory board on race. In 1998, she was appointed vice chair of President Clinton's Committee on Employment of People with Disabilities, a small federal agency created to coordinate efforts to increase the employment of people with disabilities.

Chavez-Thompson envisions a broad goal in her role with the AFL-CIO: "It's not just the members. We're also working for those who have no representation, who have no voice." In her travels throughout the country she has noted, "I've met working people who can't make enough money to feed their families and pay the rent; or they are living scared because they have too little health insurance or none at all; or they're working two jobs and don't have the chance to be with their kids when they say their first words and take their first steps." She remains a visionary, however: "Let me suggest that in the new century, some of our biggest and most important challenges are going to be about reducing the terrible inequality in our land."

Further Reading

Kokmen, Leyla. "Bringing New Life Into AFL-CIO." *Seattle Times,* May 17, 1996. Available online. URL: http://archives.seattletimes.nwsource.com/cgi-bin/texis/web/vortex/display?slug=afl&date-19960517.html. Downloaded on December 26, 2000.

Lord, Mary. "A Sharecropper's Daughter Revives Labor's Grass Roots." *U.S. News and World Report* 119 (December 25, 1995): 95–96.

President's Committee on Employment of People with Disabilities. "President Clinton Names AFL-CIO Leader to Committee on Employment of People with Disabilities." Available online. URL: http://www.dol.gov/pcepd/press/summer98/chavez.htm. Downloaded on December 26, 2000.

President's Initiative on Race Advisory Board. "Linda Chavez-Thompson Advisory Board Member." Available online. URL: http://www.whitehouse.gov/Initiative/OneAmerica/BIO-LCT.html. Downloaded on December 26, 2000.

Women's History Month. "Linda Chavez-Thompson." Available online. URL: http://www.sunherald.com/whmod/whmod3a.htm. Downloaded on December 26, 2000.

CHISHOLM, SHIRLEY ANITA ST. HILL
(1924–   ) *Congressional Representative*

Shirley Chisholm was the first African-American woman elected to the New York State Assembly, the first African-American woman elected to the U.S. Congress, and the first African American or woman to run as a presidential candidate for a major political party. Shirley Anita St. Hill was born in Brooklyn, New York, on November 30, 1924, the first of four daughters of Ruby Seale St. Hill and Charles St. Hill. Her parents had each fled the famines of Barbados in the 1920s and met each other in Brooklyn. Her mother worked as a seamstress and domestic; her father, as a factory worker. Shirley and her sister Odessa went to live in Barbados with their maternal grandmother for seven years when Shirley was four years old. When she returned to school in Brooklyn in 1933, she knew a great deal about British history, but very little about American history or geography. She worked hard in school to overcome that deficiency and excel in all her studies.

At Girls High School in Bedford-Stuyvesant, a neighborhood in Brooklyn, Chisholm was vice president of the honor society. Chisholm's parents expected their daughter to attend college, and she received scholarship offers from Vassar and Oberlin colleges when she graduated from high school. The scholarships covered full tuition but not room and board, so due to her limited economic resources, in 1942 Chisholm enrolled at Brooklyn College, which did not then charge tuition.

At Brooklyn College, Chisholm joined the Harriet Tubman Society, which served as a discussion group on politics. She also ran an arts and crafts group in an Urban League settlement house and joined the Political Science Society. Additionally, in Bedford-Stuyvesant she began attending local neighborhood meetings, which had segregated seating for African Americans and whites.

Chisholm graduated cum laude in 1946 from Brooklyn College with a degree in sociology. She was inspired by her role model, educational leader MARY MCLEOD BETHUNE, to consider a teaching career. Chisholm began working at Mt. Calvary Child Care Center in Harlem while continuing her studies in a graduate program for early childhood education at Teachers College of Columbia University.

In 1949, she married Conrad Chisholm, who was from Jamaica. After two miscarriages, Chisholm realized that she could not have children. She completed her master of arts degree in 1951 and became the director of a large child care center on the Lower East Side of Manhattan. She remained active in local Democratic Party politics and served as vice president of the Bedford-Stuyvesant Political League. By 1962, she gained a seat on the district committee of the Unity Democratic Club, a group that worked to elect African Americans and women to political office.

Gerrymandering, or manipulating voting district boundaries, had been used to divide African-American neighborhoods, splitting them apart and assigning small areas of African-American voters to

45

Shirley Chisholm, member of the
House of Representatives
(Prints & Photographs Division,
Library of Congress, Washington, D.C.)

Chisholm served on the Education Committee in the New York Assembly. She authored a bill in 1965 that created the Search for Education, Elevation, and Knowledge (SEEK) program, which offered scholarships to minority students. She also authored a bill for domestic workers in 1965, which required employers to contribute to unemployment insurance. Chisholm also authored a 1965 bill that allowed pregnant schoolteachers to maintain their tenure during maternity leaves.

After four years in the New York State Assembly, Chisholm became a candidate in 1968 for a seat in the U.S. House of Representatives. She adopted the campaign slogan, "Vote for Chisholm for Congress—Unbought and Unbossed." The Liberal Party nominated former director of the Congress of Racial Equality (CORE) James Farmer as their candidate, and the Republicans endorsed him. Farmer, a Manhattan resident, lived outside the district but was a nationally recognized figure. Farmer emphasized the need for "A man's voice in Congress" and portrayed Chisholm as "the little schoolteacher." Chisholm won the election, gaining two-and-one-half times as many votes as Farmer, and became the first African-American female member of Congress.

Joining the 435 members of the House in 1969 were nine African-American members, three of them new, the largest number of African-Americans ever to serve. (There were no African-American senators.) The previous record of seven had been set almost one hundred years ago, during the Reconstruction Congress from 1873 to 1874. In 1969, Chisholm was the first and only African-American female ever to serve in Congress. The House's official seniority system meant that she was assigned to the House agriculture committee and the subcommittee of forestry and rural development, even though she represented the inner city district of Brooklyn. She contested her assignments and was reassigned to the veterans affairs committee, a slight improvement, as Chisholm noted: "There are a lot more veterans in my district than there are trees." By her second term, she was seated on the education and labor committee.

adjacent districts with large white populations, which resulted in a history of white representation. By 1964 this had changed, and Chisholm decided to run for an assembly seat to represent the newly recognized district of Bedford-Stuyvesant. The district had a significant Puerto Rican population, and Chisholm worked to become fluent in Spanish. In the November 1964 election she received 10 times as many votes as her Republican rival and she became the only African-American woman in the New York State Assembly. Five other African-American assemblymembers were also elected, as were two state senators.

Chisholm stood up for principles more than parties at times. She supported New York City mayor John Lindsay, a Republican, whom she viewed as sympathetic to the needs of the poor and people of color. She had also been a vocal opponent of the Vietnam War at an early date. In 1968, she served as honorary president of the National Association for the Repeal of Abortion Laws (NARAL), a brave move at a time when little support existed for reproductive rights. She was a founding member of the National Organization for Women (NOW) and a strong congressional supporter of the Equal Rights Amendment (ERA). Chisholm served as a member of the Equal Rights Amendment Ratification Council. In 1971, she was a founding member of the bipartisan National Women's Political Caucus (NWPC), which supported female candidates in local, state, and federal elections.

From 1971 to 1973, she was ranked among the Gallup poll's "Ten Most Admired Women in the World. "In January 1972, Chisholm announced her candidacy for president of the United States, stating, "I am the candidate of the people." She was the first African American as well as the first female candidate to pursue a major party nomination. Throughout her political career she believed she faced more resistance as a woman than as an African American. She was a popular political figure for many disenfranchised groups, and she noted: "I am your instrument for change . . . give your votes to me instead of one of those warmed-over gentlemen who come to you once every four years. Give me your vote. I belong to you." She chose Texas politician Cissy Farenthal as her running mate, and they put forth a strong platform on women's rights. Civil rights activist Jesse Jackson, Congressman Ronald Dellums of California, and Bobby Seale of the Black Panthers publicly endorsed Chisholm, but neither feminist groups nor African-American groups rallied to her support. They were more inclined to support mainstream "winnable" politicians. In her 1973 book, *The Good Fight,* which covers her run for the presidency, Chisholm expressed disappointment with the lack of support her candidacy received from feminist and African-American organizations. Without serious coverage from the press and without necessary funds, she was able to enter campaign primaries in only 12 states.

Chisholm received 152 votes on the first ballot of the 1972 Democratic Party National Convention, held in Miami Beach. She came in fourth, after Senators George McGovern and Henry Jackson and Governor George Wallace, and ahead of Terry Sanford of North Carolina. McGovern eventually won the Democratic nomination, but lost against President Richard Nixon in the November election, but Chisholm won reelection to the House of Representatives.

Chisholm's legislation for a minimum wage bill, which would have increased the minimum wage and covered domestic workers, passed both the House and Senate but was vetoed by President Nixon. She was instrumental in saving the Office of Equal Opportunity (OEO) from planned Republican cuts. Chisholm was repeatedly reelected between 1974 and 1980. After serving for 14 years, she was the only woman on the powerful House rules committee and one of the longest-serving members of the Congressional Black Caucus.

She ended her almost-30-year marriage in 1977 and married Arthur Hardwick, the first black assemblyman from upstate New York. A new conservative political climate, heralded by the 1980 election of Ronald Reagan, and her husband's near-fatal car accident led her to decide not to run for reelection in 1982.

After retiring from political office, Chisholm became Purington Professor at Mount Holyoke, a women's college in South Hadley, Massachusetts, where she taught courses in politics and the social roles of women. She worked on behalf of Jesse Jackson's 1984 and 1988 Democratic Party nomination campaigns. In 1985, she took a leave of absence from Mount Holyoke to teach for a year in the Scholars-in-Residence program at Spelman College, an African-American women's college in Atlanta, Georgia. Her husband died from cancer in 1986, and she retired from teaching in 1987.

After 1984 Democratic presidential nominee Walter Mondale interviewed white men, white women, and black men—but no black women—as potential vice presidential candidates, Chisholm founded and served as president of the National Political Congress of Black Women (NPCBW). The NPCBW grew to include chapters in 36 states by 1988. In 1993, President Bill Clinton appointed her U.S. ambassador to Jamaica. She retired from this position when the administration of President George W. Bush took office in January 2001. She now lives in Palm Coast, Florida. Her prominence in national politics engendered confidence and pride in groups that were traditionally disposessed.

Further Reading

Brownmiller, Susan. *Shirley Chisholm: A Biography.* New York: Doubleday, 1970.

Chisholm, Shirley. *The Good Fight.* New York: Harper and Row, 1973.

———. *Unbought and Unbossed.* Boston: Houghton Mifflin, 1970.

Duffy, Susan. *Shirley Chisholm: A Bibliography of Writings By and About Her.* Metuchen, N.J.: Scarecrow Press, 1988.

Hasking, James. *Fighting Shirley Chisholm.* New York: Dial Press, 1975.

Willis, Mary. "The Straight-Talking Optimist." *Modern Maturity* 438, no. 3 (May/June 2000): 103–5)

 CLARK, SEPTIMA POINSETTE
(1898–1987)   *Civil Rights Leader*

Civil rights leader Martin Luther King Jr. called Septima Clark the "Mother of the Movement." She was best known for her work in citizenship schools, which were founded in order to increase literacy and voter registration among African Americans. Septima Poinsette was born on May 3, 1898, in Charleston, South Carolina. Her father, Peter Poinsette, was a former slave. Her mother, Victoria Warren Anderson Poinsette, had been freeborn in Charleston but was raised in Haiti by an uncle. Referring to the influence her parents' values had on her work, Clark later stated: "My father was very gentle and my mother was very haughty. The English did a better job in Haiti teaching them to read and write, so she boasted of being a free issue. She often said, 'I never gave a white woman a drink of water.' My father was such a gentle, very wonderful guy. It was good for those two to be together because my mother, with her haughtiness, and my father, with his gentleness, I felt that I stood on a platform that was built by both. And when I went to Mississippi and Texas, and places like that, I had a feeling that his nonviolence helped me to work with people, and her haughtiness helped me to stay."

Young Septima's father worked as a caterer after the Civil War and her mother took in laundry. Septima grew up in a family of eight children and attended Avery Institute in Charleston. She completed high school in 1916 and passed the state teachers' examination, even though African Americans were not allowed to teach in the public schools in Charleston at the time.

She taught on John's Island in South Carolina until 1919. She lived in an attic room with no inside plumbing and taught in a windowless school made of logs. In addition, she was paid less than white teachers who worked in better conditions. Two African-American teachers taught 132 African-American children and were paid $30 a month. Across the road, a white teacher who taught three white students was paid $85 a month and worked in a new building.

Clark next taught at Avery Institute from 1919 to 1921. She became involved in collecting signatures to send to the South Carolina legislature petitioning for the right of African Americans to teach in Charleston's public schools.

In 1920, she married a seaman, Nerie Clark, and had two children, one of whom died in infancy. Her husband died of kidney failure in 1925. In 1935, she sent her son to live with his paternal grandparents in Hickory, North Carolina. She had difficulty finding housing and supporting him, as most boardinghouses did not accept children.

In 1937, she studied at Atlanta University with W. E. B. DuBois, cofounder of the National Association for the Advancement of Colored People (NAACP). She received her B.A. degree from Benedict College in 1942 and her M.A. degree from Hampton Institute in 1945. Equalization of teacher salaries did not become law until 1945, and Clark was involved in efforts to make that change.

In 1956, South Carolina passed a law that made it illegal for anyone to be a member of any civil rights organization. Clark refused to quit the NAACP, so she was dismissed from her teaching job at age 58 and lost her pension. Highlander Folk School, in Monteagle, Tennessee, a biracial institute dedicated to addressing social injustice, recruited her as a director of their workshops. Many civil rights leaders attended the Highlander workshops, including Martin Luther King Jr. and ROSA PARKS.

Septima Clark and hairdresser Bernice Robinson opened a night school for adults in 1956, one of the first citizenship schools in the South. Their school became the model for such schools, which spread throughout the South. The teachers taught basic literacy skills and political consciousness; for example, students learned how to write their names, write letters, balance checkbooks, and register to vote. She traveled throughout the South between 1956 and 1961 and recruited thousands of African Americans, who registered to vote through Clark's efforts.

In 1961, at age 63 she became the director of education and teaching for the Southern Christian Leadership Conference (SCLC). She was the first woman elected to the executive board of the SCLC and was challenged in this position by the male ministers because she was a woman. She later spoke of the sexism such women as Rosa Parks, ELLA BAKER, and she had faced in the civil rights movement: "The thing that I think stands out was the fact that women could never be accorded their rightful place even in the Southern Christian Leadership Conference. I can't ever forget Reverend Abernathy saying, 'Why is Mrs. Clark on the Executive Board?' And Dr. King saying, 'Why, she designed a whole program.' 'Well, I just can't see why you got to have her on the Board!' They just didn't feel as if a woman,

you know, had any sense." According to Clark, Martin Luther King Jr. was one of the few male leaders who viewed women as equals.

In 1975, Clark was elected to the Charleston School Board, the same one that had dismissed her decades earlier. In 1979, President Jimmy Carter presented her with a Living Legacy Award. A section of the Charleston Highway was named in her honor in the 1980s. Septima Clark died on December 15, 1987, at age 89, in Charleston, South Carolina. Her papers are housed at the College of Charleston Library. Thousands of African Americans were registered to vote as a result of the citizenship schools that Septima Clark founded. This expansion of voting rights strengthened the political fabric of American society.

Further Reading

Clark, Septima. *Echo in My Soul.* New York: E. P. Dutton, 1962.

Clark, Septima Poinsette, and Cynthia Stokes Brown. *Ready From Within: A First Person Narrative.* New York: Africa World Press Inc., 1990.

McFadden, Grace Jordan. "Septima P. Clark and the Struggle for Human Rights." In *Women in the Civil Rights Movement,* ed. Vicki Crawford, Jacqueline Anne Rouse, and Barbara Woods. Brooklyn, N.Y.: Carlson Publishing, 1990.

 CLINTON, HILLARY RODHAM
(1947–) *Politician, First Lady, Senator, Attorney*

Hillary Rodham Clinton was the first wife of a sitting U.S. president to be elected to the U.S. Senate. She was a career woman in her own right with a record of public service for women's and children's rights. Her father, Hugh Rodham, grew up in Scranton, Pennsylvania, the son of immigrants from England. He might have been a factory worker like his father, but he won a football scholarship to Pennsylvania State University. Hillary Rodham was born on October 26, 1947, in Park Ridge, Illinois, a middle-class suburb of Chicago. Her father worked as a curtain salesman, then ran a small drapery-making business in Chicago. Her mother, Dorothy Howell Rodham, met her husband when she applied for a secretarial job at the Lace Company in 1937. They married in 1942 and Dorothy Rodham became a full-time homemaker with three children.

Her mother hoped she would become the first woman on the Supreme Court. At age 14, Hillary wrote to the National Aeronautics and Space Administration to ask about requirements for becoming an astronaut. The written response she received told her they were not "taking any girls." Her parents were members of the Republican Party, and so she worked on Barry Goldwater's campaign during her senior year. Hillary Rodham was a National Merit Scholarship finalist and president of her senior class in high school.

She attended Wellesley, a women's college near Boston, from 1965 to 1969 and majored in political science. She served as president of the Wellesley student government, worked as an intern with the house Republicans after her junior year at Wellesley, and attended the National Republican Convention in Miami. During college, her opinions became more liberal. Before graduating she organized the first anti–Vietnam War protest at Wellesley and tried to get the college to increase enrollment of African-American students. Excerpts from her commencement speech, the first ever given by a student at Wellesley, appeared in *Life* magazine.

She rejected the idea of attending Harvard University's law school when one professor remarked during her visit to the school, "We don't need any more women." In the fall of 1969 she started at Yale Law School, in New Haven, Connecticut, one of only 30 women in her class. Of those, 10 soon dropped out. Some professors and students at Yale resented the presence of women and openly accused them of taking the places of more worthy men who were fighting in Vietnam.

During her second year at Yale she met William Jefferson Clinton. She explained her initial attraction to him: "He wasn't afraid of me." She served as editor of the Yale law review. Her attendance at a lecture by MARION WRIGHT EDELMAN, founder of the Children's Defense Fund, inspired her to enter a life of public service on behalf of children. During the summer of 1970 she worked for Edelman on a project researching the condition of migrant farmworker families. After graduating from Yale she spent a year in New Haven, working at the Yale Child Studies Center. She researched the ways the legal system handled child abuse and foster care cases. She worked on the 1972 Democratic presidential campaign of Senator George McGovern, and in 1973, she became a staff attorney for the Children's Defense Fund.

Hillary Rodham next took a job in Washington, D.C., on the team of lawyers who were developing a case on Nixon's impeachment proceeding. In 1974, before impeachment hearings began, Nixon resigned. Rodham then moved to Arkansas to join Bill Clinton. He remembers thinking, "This is a woman whose future is limitless. She could be anything she decides to be. I feel so guilty about bringing her here, because then it would be my state, my life, and my political future." She summed up her decision to move to Arkansas by saying, "Caught between my head and my heart, I followed my heart." She taught criminal law at the University of Arkansas and set up the first legal services program in the area. Rodham married Clinton in 1975, but she continued to use her maiden name.

Bill Clinton had lost a congressional campaign in 1974, but in 1976, at age 30, he was elected as the youngest attorney general in Arkansas history. The couple moved to Little Rock, where Rodham joined the most powerful law firm in the state and eventually became the first female partner in the firm's history. The *National Law Journal* twice named her one of the 100 most powerful lawyers in the nation. Bill Clinton was elected governor of Arkansas in 1978. No first lady of Arkansas had ever had a career, much less been a full partner in a law firm. She was the family's main financial support, earning three to four times more than her husband earned as governor.

Their daughter, Chelsea, was born in 1980. Bill Clinton lost his bid for reelection that year. Some thought he lost because of his wife's unconventional image. Voters were used to more "traditional" first ladies, many of whom focused on fashion, makeup, their families, and home decoration. Some voters did not like the idea of having someone they considered a radical feminist as first lady of the state. Political wives who were individualists were considered unacceptable by many.

Rodham changed her name and image when Bill Clinton was reelected in 1982. In 1983, as Hillary Rodham Clinton, she served as chair of the Education Standards Committee for the State of Arkansas.

The 1992 presidential campaign stirred additional controversy about candidates' wives. The *New York Times, Newsweek,* and *Time* dubbed it "the Hillary Problem." Former president Richard Nixon remarked about Hillary Clinton, "You want a wife who's intelligent, but not too intelligent." Previously, with the exception of ELEANOR ROOSEVELT, first ladies had acted in traditional and relatively quiet, expected ways. Martha Washington, describing her experience of the position, said, "I am more like a state prisoner than anything else." Others, including those with more liberal views, felt that Hillary Clinton symbolized the changing role of women.

After Bill Clinton's election she became the first presidential wife to occupy an office in the west wing of the White House near the president and his other senior advisers. Previous first ladies had had offices in the east wing and employed social secretaries rather than policy experts on their staff. She was appointed to chair the Task Force on National Health Care Reform, heading a staff of 500. The task force held a number of public hearings, but ultimately Congress failed to pass the health care reform it recommended.

In 1996, she wrote a best-seller called *It Takes a Village,* referring to the African saying that "It takes a village to raise a child," which asserted that an isolated family alone cannot meet all its members' needs.

In 2000, she became a candidate for the U.S. Senate from New York State. Hillary Clinton raised $29 million for her New York senatorial race. She won the 2000 election, thus making an unprecedented transition from first lady to New

Hillary Rodham Clinton, first lady and senator, 2000
(Office of the First Lady)

York's first woman senator. Before assuming her senate office she received an $8 million advance from the publishing house of Simon and Schuster to write a book about her White House years. The book is scheduled for publication in 2003.

In the Senate, she serves on the Health, Education, Labor and Pensions Committee. One of her first actions as senator was to support the call for a constitutional amendment to eliminate the electoral college, after the controversial election of President George W. Bush, who lost the popular vote but narrowly won the election through the electoral college and after much controversy over allegedly miscounted or uncounted ballots in several states. She also quietly cosponsored a bill to limit abuses of presidential pardons, following allegations regarding her husband's possible misuse of the presidential pardon.

A 2001 Gallup poll found that Clinton was the most admired woman in the United States, placing her ahead of popular television talk show host Oprah Winfrey. When asked about her future as a presidential candidate, she consistently replies that she plans to serve out her senatorial term. This comment would rule out a presidential bid in 2004, but not in 2008. Hillary Rodham Clinton remains one of the most watched and discussed contemporary politicians.

Further Reading

Hunt, Albert. "The Best and Worst of Times for Hillary." *Wall Street Journal,* April 5, 2001, 1.

Mitchell, Alison. "The Freshman: Starring Hillary Clinton." *New York Times,* January 7, 2001, 1.

National First Ladies Library. "Clinton, Hillary Diane Rodham." Available online. URL: http://www.first-ladies.org/HILLARY_CLINTON/FL.HTML. Downloaded on December 26, 2000.

Olson, Barbara. *Hell To Pay: The Unfolding Story of Hillary Rodham Clinton.* New York: Regnery, 1999.

Sheehy, Gail. *Hillary's Choice.* New York: Random House, 1999.

Warner, Judith. *Hillary Clinton: The Inside Story.* New York: Signet, 1999.

Women's International Center. "Hillary Rodham Clinton." Available online. URL: http://www.wic.org/vio/hclinton.htm. Downloaded on December 26, 2000.

 COLLINS, CARDISS ROBERTSON
(1931–   ) *Congressional Representative*

Cardiss Collins was the fourth African-American woman elected to the House of Representatives and remains the longest-serving African-American female. Cardiss Robertson was born in St. Louis, Missouri, on September 24, 1931, and her family moved to Detroit when she was 10. She was the only child of Finley and Rosia Mae Cardiss Robertson. Her mother was a nurse, and her father worked as a manual laborer. She graduated from the Detroit High School of Commerce. After completing high school she moved to Chicago to find a job. She first worked as a stenographer with the Illinois Depart-

ment of Labor. She next worked as a secretary for the Illinois Department of Revenue and was promoted first to accountant, and then to revenue auditor. While there she enrolled in night school at Northwestern University. She married George Washington Collins in 1958 and had one son.

George Collins was an alderman on the Chicago City Council before his election as a Democratic representative from Illinois in 1970. He was a founding member of the Congressional Black Caucus. Cardiss Collins filled the congressional position of her husband after he was killed in a plane crash in 1973. She won reelection for more than 20 years in her Chicago district of largely African-American constituents. She recalled her early days in office by saying, "I guess I must have been a member of Congress all of 24 hours when I realized that, as the wife of a politician, I had just been a political spectator—not really playing the game. The difference started rolling in, like a sledgehammer, believe me."

She was the first African-American woman to represent a congressional district in the Midwest. She conducted investigations of college sports and their compliance with Title IX of the Education Amendments of 1972, which mandated equal opportunities for female athletes in collegiate sports. Collins was appointed Democratic whip-at-large two years after her election to Congress, the first woman and first African American to serve in that position. She served as chair of the Congressional Black Caucus in 1979, the first woman to hold that position as well.

She authored the 1990 law that expanded Medicare coverage to include mammography, sponsored legislation to expand coverage for Pap smears (which assist in early detection of cervical cancer), and authored a resolution designating October as National Breast Cancer Awareness Month. She also conducted investigations that led to adoption of the Aviation Security Improvement Act of 1990. In 1990, Collins was awarded the William L. Dawson Award from the Congressional Black Caucus for her legislative successes. A long-time advocate of universal health care she cosponsored the Universal Health Care Act of 1991 and the Family and Medical Leave Act of 1991. Collins authored legislation to fund the Office of Minority Health in the National Institutes of Health and wrote the Child Safety Protection Act of 1993, which required warning labels on dangerous toys and federal safety standards for bicycle helmets. Her investigations into child care offered to federal employees resulted in the building of 65 new centers, a threefold increase in the number of such centers. In 1992, she was reelected to her 10th term in Congress by an 81 percent margin.

She is a member of the Coalition of One Hundred Black Women and the National Council of Negro Women, and is secretary of the Congressional Caucus on Women's Issues. Collins received a high rating for her voting record from the League of Women Voters, and a 100 percent rating from the National Organization of Senior Citizens. She has represented the seventh congressional district of Illinois for nearly 30 years. Her longevity in office and clear-thinking advocacy continue to benefit her constituency.

Further Reading

"Cardiss Collins Named to Powerful House Panel." *Jet* 67 (January 14, 1985): 4.

Collins, Cardiss. "A Plea for Respect." *Ebony* 36 (July 1981): 78.

Current Biography Yearbook. "Cardiss Collins." New York: H. W. Wilson, v. 58, 1997.

Edwards, Audrey. "Cardiss Collins: Do Your Votes Count?" *Essence* 11 (November 1980): 84–85, 102, 105, 107.

House of Representatives. "Biography of Congresswoman Cardiss Collins." Available online. URL: http://www.inform.umd.edu/EdRes/Topic/WomenStudies/Govern.htm. Downloaded on December 27, 2000.

Poinsett, Alex. "The New Cardiss Collins." *Ebony* 35 (December 1979): 63–68.

⊠ COOPER, ANNA JULIA HAYWOOD
(1858–1964) *Educator*

Anna Julia Cooper was an educator, feminist scholar, and activist in the 19th century. She was born Anna Julia Haywood to Hannah Stanley, a slave, on August 10, 1859, in Raleigh, North Carolina. George Washington Haywood, her mother's master, was probably her father. Referring to her parents, Cooper would later write, "My mother was a slave and the finest woman I have ever known. . . . Presumably my father was her master, if so I owe him not a sou and she was always too modest and shamefaced ever to mention him." Her mother worked as a nursemaid. Anna developed a love of books and learning. As a child, the Emancipation Proclamation freed her from slavery. In 1868, she entered St. Augustine's Normal School and Collegiate Institute, which was founded by the Protestant Episcopal Church to serve freed slaves.

In 1877, she married the Reverend George Cooper, an Episcopal priest 14 years her senior who was a former slave from Nassau, British West Indies. He died two years later, leaving Cooper a 21-year-old widow.

In 1881, Cooper entered Oberlin College and completed her B.A. degree in 1884. Her class included two other African-American women who later also became national leaders: MARY CHURCH TERRELL and Ida Gibbs Hunt. They became the first black women to complete a four-year college degree. In 1887, Cooper completed an M.A. degree in mathematics from Oberlin. She taught modern languages for one year at Wilberforce University and then taught mathematics, Greek, and Latin for two years at St. Augustine's. She next taught Latin at M Street High School, a college preparatory school for African Americans that offered a classical curriculum rather than the more common vocational training of other institutions. M Street was the only high school in the nation that offered a college preparatory curriculum for African-American students.

Cooper published *A Voice from the South by a Black Woman of the South* in 1892. *A Voice from the South* was a collection of essays written between 1886 and 1892 that considered questions of race, gender, and education. In the volume she addressed the problem of racism in the white women's movement and sexism in African-American groups. She wrote, "While our men seem thoroughly abreast of the times on almost every other subject, when they strike the woman question they drop back into sixteenth century logic." The volume also examined the images of people of African descent in white literature. On the topic of education, she criticized the approach of civil rights leader Booker T. Washington and his Tuskegee Institute, which focused on vocational training, for being too moderate. Cooper was the only woman elected to the American Negro Academy, a group of black scholars whose members included civil rights leader W. E. B. DuBois and historian Arthur Schomburg. She became the second female principal of the M Street High School in 1901 but was fired in 1906 due to pressure from the Tuskegee Institute. Four years later she returned to teach at M Street High School.

Cooper became the guardian to five great-nieces and nephews, aged six months to 12 years, while she was in her 50s. During this time she worked toward her doctorate at Columbia University in New York and the Sorbonne in Paris. Her thesis, written in French, was a study of the history of Haiti during and after the French Revolution and the inability of France to apply its democratic ideals to the slave colony. She was awarded her doctorate in 1925, at age 65, becoming the fourth African-American woman to earn a Ph.D.

In 1930, she retired from her teaching position at M Street High School and became the second president of the Frelinghuysen Group of Schools for Employed Colored Persons, an adult evening school for African Americans that later became Frelinghuysen University. She served as president of the university until retiring in 1942 at age 83.

In 1951, Cooper published *Personal Recollections of the Grimké Family and the Life and Writings of Charlotte Forten Grimké,* about a family who were also descendants of slaves. Several Grimké family members, including ANGELINA EMILY GRIMKÉ, were active abolitionists.

Anna Julia Haywood Cooper died on February 27, 1964, in Washington, D.C., at age 105. She was buried in Raleigh, North Carolina. Her papers are housed at the Moorland-Spingarn Research Center at Howard University. She was one of the best-educated African-American leaders of her generation. Her intellect and accomplishments serve as a beacon of hope to younger generations.

Further Reading

Alexander, Elizabeth. "We Must Be About Our Father's Business: Anna Julia Cooper and the In-Corporation of the Nineteenth-Century African-American Woman Intellectual." *Signs* 20, no. 2 (winter 1995): 336.

Baker-Fletcher, Karen. *A Singing Something: Womanist Reflections on Anna Julia Cooper.* New York: Crossroad, 1994.

Cooper, Anna Julia. *A Voice from the South.* 1892. Reprint, New York: Oxford University Press, 1990.

———. *The Voice of Anna Julia Cooper: Including a Voice from the South and Other Important Essays, Papers, and Letters.* Oxford, England: Rowman and Littlefield, 1996.

Gable, Leona. *From Slavery to the Sorbonne and Beyond: The Life and Writings of Anna J. Cooper.* Northampton, Mass.: Smith College, 1982.

 COTERA, MARTHA CASTANOS
(1938–) *Civil Rights Activist*

Martha Cotera was an organizer of the Crystal City walkout in 1969, which challenged the exclusion of Mexican Americans in U.S. politics, and is an author, educator, and activist in Mexican-American politics. Martha Castanos was born on January 17, 1938, in Nuevo Casa Grande, Chihuahua, Mexico. In 1946, her family immigrated to El Paso, Texas. Castanos earned a B.A. degree in English with a minor in history at the University of Texas, El Paso. She completed an M.A. degree in education at Antioch College and began graduate work in history at the University of Texas, Austin. She married architect Juan Estanislao Cotera in 1963.

In the late 1950s, Castanos worked as a librarian, and in 1964 she became the director of documents and information at the Texas State Library in Austin. In 1969, she organized teach-ins for the famous Crystal City walkout, in which high school students protested their exclusion by the Anglo minority in their town. Crystal City, near San Antonio, was 95 percent Mexican American, but Anglos ruled the city. At first students, and then community members, protested this condition and then began the work of forming a third political party, called Raza Unida, to run Mexican-American candidates beginning in 1972. Raza Unida sponsored voting drives and grew, eventually running a field of candidates at the state level, including governor and lieutenant governor.

In 1970, Cotera helped found Juarez Lincoln University in Mercedes, Texas, and served on its faculty until 1975. The goal of the university was to prepare teachers for bilingual education programs.

In 1972, Cotera ran for the state board of education on the Raza Unida ticket. She and her husband were active in Raza Unida politics. As Cotera recalled, "We, like a lot of Hispanics, are aware of a lot of discrimination. We experienced that when we came to Austin. That radicalized us. There was a lot of police brutality, and we were very concerned because we were starting a family. We just felt that if you wanted things to be good, you had to work for it." In 1973, she helped found the Texas Women's Political Caucus. One year later she founded the Chicana Research and Learning Center in Austin and served as executive director of the umbrella organization. She published the *Educator's Guide to Chicano Resources* and wrote on the political status of women in Chicano culture, publishing *Chicanas in Politics and Public Life* in 1975. Cotera started a publishing company in 1975 called Information Systems Development, whose publications include *Mujeres Celebre,* an encyclopedia on Latinas from pre-Columbian to present times, and a Hispanic directory.

Her writings on education include the *Handbook on Educational Strategies and Resources for Sex—Culturally Relevant Classroom Practices and Materials,* published in 1980 by the U.S. Department of Health, Education and Welfare (HEW), Women's Educational Equity Program. Also in 1980, she cofounded Mexican-American Business and Professional Women in Austin. *Dona Doormat*

No Esta Aqui: An Assertiveness and Communications Skills Manual for Hispanic Women was published in 1984. She currently teaches American history at Austin Community College. Her papers are collected by the Woman's Collection at Texas Woman's University Library in Denton, Texas, and by the Benson Latin American Collection at the University of Texas at Austin. Her civil rights leadership reshaped the face of politics in the Southwest.

Further Reading

Cotera, Martha. *Las Mujeres: Mexican American, Chicana Women.* Windsor, Calif.: National Women's History Project, 1991.

———. *Lunch and Learn: Diversity in the Workplace; Assertion by Minorities in the Workplace.* KVUE-TV, Austin, Tex., VHS, 1989.

———. *Multicultural Women's Sourcebook,* Austin, Tex.: Information Systems Development, 1982.

———. *Women in Politics.* KVUE-TV, Austin, Tex., VHS, 1978.

"New Video on History of Mexican American Women." *Metro Reporter* 20, no. 33 (August 16, 1992): 10.

Velasquez, Roberto, Maria García, and Carlos Acre. *The Austin Hispanic Chamber of Commerce.* KVUE-TV, Austin, Tex., VHS, 1981.

 ## CRAFT, ELLEN SMITH
(1826–1891) *Abolitionist*

Ellen Craft escaped from slavery and then worked in the antislavery movement, devoting her resources to assist others. Ellen Smith was born in 1826 in Clinton, Georgia, a town just a few miles east of Macon. Her mother, Maria, was a house slave, and her father, Major James Smith, was her mother's master. Ellen's skin was very light, and she was often mistaken for a member of Smith's white family. She was a playmate and slave to her father's white daughter, her half sister Eliza. At age 11, she was given as a wedding gift to her half sister, who then moved with her husband, Dr. Robert Collins, to Macon, where Ellen met and married another slave, William Craft, in 1846. Her husband's family had been broken up and sold off to various owners to pay for their master's gambling debts. Craft's master was a banker who rented him out as a carpenter and garnished his wages. After marriage, the couple were unable to live together since they belonged to different owners. They made plans to run away so they could be together, and two years later fled to freedom in the North. Craft dressed as a male slave master, and William acted as her valet. Craft wrapped her face in bandages to hide her lack of facial hair. The couple got to Savannah, Georgia, by train, took a boat to Charleston, South Carolina, and took another train to Maryland. They made contact with abolitionists and stayed with a Quaker family in Philadelphia before moving to Boston, the center of the abolitionist movement. They lived in Boston, where Craft worked as a seamstress. Both gained fame on the antislavery lecture circuit. After the Fugitive Slave Act passed in 1850, which allowed the forcible recapture of former slaves living in free states, slave catchers tried to return the couple to bondage in Georgia. Consequently, they fled to England, where they lived for the next 19 years.

In England, they attended an agricultural school founded by Lady Byron in Surrey. They served on the executive committee of the London Emancipation Committee and lectured on the antislavery circuit there. Craft raised funds for southern freedmen and for a school for girls in Sierra Leone in Africa. Their five children were all born in England. When visitors from the U.S. South spread rumors in England that Craft wanted to return to the happy life of slavery, she made the famous retort, "I had much rather starve in England, a free woman, than to be a slave for the best man that ever breathed upon the American continent."

They returned to the United States in 1869, after slavery was abolished, and started a cooperative farm for former slaves in Ways Station, Georgia. Craft established a school for children in Bryan County. The Ku Klux Klan, an organization of white supremacists, burned their farm, and their school, in which 75 children were being taught free of charge, was forced to close. Ellen Craft died in poverty in 1891.

Further Reading

Craft, William. *Running A Thousand Miles For Freedom: The Escape of William and Ellen Craft From Slavery.* New Orleans: Louisiana State University Press, 1999.

Georgia Women of Achievement. "Ellen Smith Craft." Available online. URL: http://www.gawomen.org/ honorees/long/crafte_long.htm. Downloaded on December 27, 2000.

D

 DAVIS, ANGELA
(1944–   )   *Political Activist*

Angela Davis was a militant African-American communist activist who gained an international reputation in the 1970s during her trial as an accomplice to murder. In the 1980s, she became a founder of black feminist theory, which seeks to present a view of feminism from an African-American perspective. Angela Davis was born in Birmingham, Alabama, on January 26, 1944, the youngest of three children. Her grandmother was the daughter of slaves.

Davis's family lived in a segregated neighborhood known as Dynamite Hill—so called because of the frequent bombings of the homes of civil rights supporters by local whites. In 1963, four of her childhood friends were murdered when an African-American church in Birmingham was bombed. Her father, B. Frank Davis, was a former schoolteacher who left the profession due to the low salaries and then operated a service station. Her mother, Sallye Davis, taught elementary school and completed an M.A. degree from New York University by attending summer sessions. As a child, Angela attended civil rights protests with her mother. At age 15, Davis left Birmingham to attend the progressive Elisabeth Irwin School in New York City. Her tuition was paid by a scholarship from the American Friends Service Committee.

Davis majored in French literature at Brandeis University and spent her junior year studying at the Sorbonne in Paris. In her senior year she studied philosophy with the famous marxist Herbert Marcuse. She completed her degree in French at Brandeis and graduated magna cum laude in 1965, then studied philosophy at Goethe University in Frankfurt, West Germany, but returned to the United States in 1967 for graduate work with Marcuse at the University of California, San Diego. It was news photographs of Black Panthers marching in protest with guns at the California state legislature that drew her home from Germany: as she put it, "That image affected me . . . and I said 'I'm going home.'" She was involved as an activist with both the Student Nonviolent Coordinating Committee (SNCC) and the Black Panthers. The sexism of some black power groups was a source of conflict for her and she recalled, "I was criticized very heavily, especially by male members of Ron Karenga's organization, for doing a 'man's job.' Women should not play leadership roles, they insisted." Karenga had founded US in 1965, a black cultural nationalist group that emphasized African heritage. One specific incident that she remembered involved an interchange with a black male activist who stated, "Well, sister, you must be new. You see, we have to eat first, and then after the brothers eat, the sisters eat." In 1968, she joined the Communist Party.

In 1969, Davis taught philosophy at the University of California, Los Angeles. An informer for the Federal Bureau of Investigation (FBI) published a letter in the student newspaper alleging that a communist—Davis—was teaching in the philosophy department in direct contradiction to a new state law, strongly supported by then-governor Ronald Reagan, that prevented California universities from employing known communists. Davis was fired by the California Board of Regents but reinstated by the courts. Her classes were monitored, and she was again dismissed for making "inflammatory speeches" in defense of the marxist "Soledad brothers," who were viewed by many as political prisoners. (The Soledad brothers were three African-American inmates in Soledad prison who were unjustly accused of killing a white guard.) She appealed this dismissal but lost her case in the U.S. Supreme Court.

Davis considered prison inmates to be prisoners of class warfare—political prisoners. She became close to one of the Soledad brothers, George Jackson, through their exchange of letters. Guards later killed Jackson in an alleged escape attempt, right after all pending charges against him had been dropped. In 1970, George Jackson's teenage brother, Jonathan, took a judge, prosecuting attorney, and several jurors hostage in a courtroom in San Rafael, California. Jonathan Jackson, the judge, and two black prisoners died in a shootout outside the courthouse. The weapon used by Jackson had been purchased by Davis, in response to death threats leveled against her. Jackson had taken the gun from her home. Davis fled California and went into hiding. She was put on the FBI's 10 most wanted list and

remained there for two months until she was arrested in New York in October 1970. She was charged with kidnapping a San Rafael judge, prosecuting attorneys and several jurors, conspiracy, and murder. Her trial lasted for nearly two years and garnered international attention.

She used her time in jail to research and write a pivotal piece, "Reflections on the Black Woman's Role in the Community of Slaves," that was published in the journal *Black Scholar* in 1971. She did not consider herself a feminist until the 1980s but had begun writing the piece in response to the theories of some black power advocates, including George Jackson, who argued that black women were dominating matriarchs. In 1971, her book *If They Come in the Morning* was published, and after 17 months in prison, she was brought to trial in San Jose. In 1972, after 13 hours of deliberation, an all-white jury found her innocent of all charges. After gaining her release, she transformed her defense committee into the National Alliance against Racist and Political Repression, which remains active on prisoner rights.

After the trial she resumed her teaching career at San Francisco State University in 1979, teaching women's studies and ethnic studies. She was a vice presidential candidate on the Communist Party ticket in 1980 and again in 1984. She was briefly married in the 1980s but divorced after a few years. In the 1980s, she published scholarly works including *Women, Race, and Class* in 1983 and *Women, Culture, and Politics* in 1989, along with her 1988 best-seller *Angela Davis: An Autobiography.* She joined the History of Consciousness program at the University of California, Santa Cruz.

When Angela Davis was appointed to a presidential chair position at the University of California, Santa Cruz, in 1995, several California state Republican legislators protested the decision. The second-ranking Republican, Senator Bill Leonard of San Bernardino, compared honoring Davis to celebrating a professor who was "a grand dragon of the Ku Klux Klan."

Davis is no longer a member of the Communist Party (CPUSA). She left the Communist Party because of what she felt was a lack of democracy in the organization but acknowledged, "I still hold Communist or Socialist ideals—I am just no longer a member of the party." Her 1998 book, *Blues Legacies and Black Feminism: Gertrude "Ma" Rainey, Bessie Smith, Billie Holiday,* placed the works of these women within the context of working-class black feminist consciousness. Her forthcoming book is titled *Dispossession and Punishment: Essays on the Prison Industrial Complex and the New Abolitionism.* Angela Davis retained a radical political identity and faced persecution because of it, but she continues to write and educate, remaining an activist in women's, prisoners', and African-American rights.

Further Reading

Davis, Angela. *Angela Davis: An Autobiography.* 1974. Reprint, New York: International Publishing Company, 1989.

———. "Reflections on the Black Women's Role in the Community of Slaves." *Black Scholar* (December 1971): 2–15.

Fregoso, Rosa Linda. "On the Road with Angela Davis." *Cultural Studies* 13, no. 2 (1999): 211–23.

Gordon, A. F. "Globalism and the Prison Industrial Complex: An Interview with Davis." *Race & Class* 40, no. 2/3 (1999): 145.

James, Joy. *The Angela Y. Davis Reader.* Oxford, England: Blackwell Publishing, 1998.

Weathers, Diane. "New! Essence Dialogue: Angela Davis and Kathleen Cleaver." *Essence* 27, no. 1 (May 1996): 82.

 DAY, DOROTHY
(1897–1980) *Journalist, Activist*

Journalist and activist Dorothy Day was cofounder of the Catholic Worker Movement. Dorothy Day was born on November 8, 1897, in Brooklyn, New York, to Grace Satterlee Day of New York and John Day of Tennessee. She was the third of five children and the first daughter. Her two older brothers would become conservative journalists, but Dorothy became a radical journalist. Her father's family was of Scotch and Irish descent and

had fought on the Confederate side during the Civil War. Her mother's family was of English descent from upstate New York and had fought on the Union side during the Civil War.

Her family moved to Oakland, California, when Day was seven. Her father lost his job when the San Francisco earthquake of 1906 destroyed the newspaper plant where he worked as a writer. The family then moved to Chicago, where they lived for 12 years. While her family lived on the South Side of Chicago, Day was introduced to both Catholicism and the struggle of the poor. Her Protestant parents were indifferent to religion, but Day decided to be baptized in the Episcopal church.

In 1914, a scholarship allowed her to attend the University of Illinois. While there, she became interested in socialism during the early days of World War I. She rejected religion because, in her opinion, it did little to help the poor. In 1916, she quit college after two years and went to New York, where her family had moved while she was at school.

Her sports-journalist father asked his friends who were editors at papers throughout New York City not to hire her because he felt that women should not work as reporters. Day was influenced in her pursuit of a journalistic career by her family background. Her father and two brothers were journalists. Day's first job at age 19 was working as a reporter for the *Socialist Call.* She also wrote for other radical publications such as *The Masses.* She reported on strikes, unemployment, and bread riots. She joined the Socialist Party and the Industrial Workers of the World (IWW) and became a suffragist.

In 1917, at the age of 20, she joined suffragist picketers in front of the White House and was jailed for 30 days as a result. Day went on hunger strikes while incarcerated. She became a pacifist after working as a nurse in a Brooklyn hospital at the end of World War I and seeing war casualties firsthand. She also worked at CRYSTAL EASTMAN'S newspaper, *The Liberator* in 1918.

Day had several lovers and underwent an illegal abortion at age 21. She had the abortion for fear that her lover, a tough ex-newspaperman named

59

Lionel Moise, would leave her if she had a child, but he left her anyway. After returning from a one-year stay in Europe, Day went to Chicago, where she was jailed with IWW activists during the free speech movement and red raids. The free speech movement was based on the harassment and prosecution by local officials when radicals attempted to speak in public. The red raids, also known as the Palmer raids after Attorney General A. Mitchell Palmer, who instigated them, rounded up suspected leftists in 33 cities in 1920. Civil liberties were disregarded. Many people were detained without charges for long periods and deported.

Day continued working as an investigative journalist in Chicago, examining court treatment of juveniles and prostitutes. While in Chicago she wrote an autobiographical novel, *The Eleventh Virgin.* Published in 1924, it was about a heroine who leads an unconventional life of brief romances, abortion, loveless marriage, and constant travel. The money from the book allowed her to return to New York City and live in a cottage on Staten Island while writing full time. During this time she drank, smoked, cursed, attempted suicide, and had a common-law marriage to biologist Forster Batterham, an anarchist. Day had believed she was barren but was pleasantly surprised when she became pregnant.

Day's religious upbringing had been virtually nonexistent as a child. However, in 1927, the same year she gave birth to her daughter, she underwent conversion to Roman Catholicism. Batterham was an atheist who thought religion was merely escapism, but Day had herself and her daughter baptized as Catholics when the baby was a few months old.

Catholicism intrigued Day because she saw it as aligned with the poor. Day believed, "The mystery of the poor is that they are Jesus, and what we do for them we do for him." In Day's view, the Bible supported anticapitalism and social activism. Day started working for the Fellowship of Reconciliation and began writing pieces for the liberal Catholic magazine *Commonweal.* During the Great Depression, in 1932 she began working with French intellectual Peter Maurin to develop communal farms to assist the urban poor. She spent much of her time on one of the farms on Staten Island.

Day had great success as the editor of the *Catholic Worker,* a monthly paper she cofounded with Peter Maurin in 1933. The paper began as an eight-page sheet with an initial printing of 2,500 copies that were distributed on May Day, an international labor day often marked with political demonstrations. Day raised the necessary $57 for the first printing from the donations of a priest and two nuns. Day called the paper the *Catholic Worker* because the majority of Catholics were poor working-class people. Circulation grew to 150,000 within three years. The readers of *Catholic Worker* formed communities that practiced voluntary poverty for spiritual discipline and solidarity with the poor. In 1934, the Catholic Workers founded St. Joseph's House of Hospitality in New York City to provide meals and housing to the homeless. By the end of the depression, the Catholic Workers had established 30 similar projects throughout the country. Day traveled by bus throughout the nation spreading the ideas of the *Catholic Worker* and visiting hospitality houses and cooperative farms.

In 1946, Day began calling her column "On Pilgrimage." The column chronicled the Catholic Worker movement as well as books she was reading. The *Catholic Worker* continues to sell for a penny a copy and in the 1990s still had a circulation of more than 100,000. The *Catholic Worker* also supported the establishment of cooperative farms in New England, New York State, Appalachia, the Midwest, and the Pacific Coast. The philosophy of the *Catholic Worker* emphasized the moral and political purpose of agricultural work, which not only provided food to those in need but also countered the alienation caused by industrialism. Day published a number of books, including *On Pilgrimage* in 1948, her autobiography, *The Long Loneliness* in 1952, *I Remember Peter Maurin* in 1958, and *Therese* in 1960. *Loaves and Fishes,* published in 1963, told the story of the Catholic Worker movement.

Throughout Day's writing and publishing career, her political views alienated some of her readers. Day's criticism of Spain's fascist dictator Francisco Franco during the Spanish Civil War of the 1930s cost her many Catholic readers who viewed Franco as a leader of the Catholic stand against the atheist communists. The *Catholic Worker* supported pacifism during World War II, which was an unpopular view at that time. During the 1950s, she was jailed for failure to participate in mandatory civil defense drills. During air raid drills, rather than going to shelters, Day and other protesters sat on park benches. Day was jailed three times during this period, once for an entire month. She demonstrated against the Vietnam War in the 1960s and for farmworkers in California. Day described herself as a Christian anarchist and was a neutral pacifist during all wars occurring in her lifetime.

Despite her sexual promiscuity in the 1920s, she opposed the relaxed sexual mores of the 1960s. In 1973, at age 76, Day was arrested while protesting with the United Farm Workers in California and was jailed one last time, for 10 days.

Despite her controversial pacifism and socialism, the University of Notre Dame, a Catholic institution, honored her as an outstanding Catholic in 1972. A movie about her life was made in 1996 called *Entertaining Angels: The Dorothy Day Story.* She lived in voluntary poverty until her death on November 29, 1980, in New York City at age 83. Toward the end of her life, when asked to contemplate its meaning, she stated: "I try to think back; I try to remember this life that the Lord gave me; the other day I wrote down the words 'a life remembered,' and I was going to try to make a summary for myself, and thought of our Lord, and His visit to us all those centuries ago, and I said to myself that my great luck was to have had Him on my mind for so long in my life!" When asked about the prospect of sainthood, Day responded, "Don't trivialize me by trying to make me a saint." Because she had no money, the archdiocese of New York paid for her funeral, which was held at Nativity Church in New York City, where the crowd of mourners overflowed onto the sidewalks.

The *Catholic Worker* continues to be published, and its central offices on East Third Street in New York City still serve as a soup kitchen.

On the 100th anniversary of Day's birth, John Cardinal O'Connor of New York suggested that Day be considered a candidate for sainthood, saying, "It has long been my contention that Dorothy Day is a saint." In 1983, three years after her death, Claretian missionaries in Chicago began collecting testimonies of miracles on her behalf. To be a saint in The Roman Catholic Church, a candidate must be credited with one documented miracle and Day already has one: The wife of sociologist Robert Coles prayed to Day and was healed. Day would become the fifth American saint in the Roman Catholic Church's history. As Tom McGrath, publisher of *U.S. Catholic,* has noted, "She's a saint for our times, someone that can help us make sense of the challenges of the time." In March 2000, the Vatican began to consider the process of canonization for Day.

Day began as a left-wing atheist but ended up serving others by blending her social activism with her acquired faith. Day's blend of Catholicism and communism preceded by more than 35 years liberation theology, a movement begun in Latin America that emphasized the application of religious faith to the problems of the poor. Day once said, "If I pray by making soup and serving soup, I feel I'm praying by doing. If I pray by saying words, I can sometimes feel frustrated."

Further Reading

Alleva, Richard. "Entertaining Angels." *Commonweal* 123, no. 18 (October 25, 1996): 18.

Coles, Robert. *Dorothy Day: A Radical Devotion.* Reading, Mass.: Addison Wesley, 1989.

Day, Dorothy. *The Long Loneliness: The Autobiography of Dorothy Day.* San Francisco: Harper San Francisco, 1997.

Dorothy Day Library on the Web. "Writings of Dorothy Day." Available online. URL: http://www.catholic-worker.org/dorothyday/index.cfm. Downloaded on December 27, 2000.

Dwyer, Maureen Keashon. "The Real Dorothy Day." *Momentum* 28, no. 4 (October 1997): 53.

Wren, Celia. "Dorothy Day." *Commonweal* 125, no. 16 (September 25, 1998): 18.

DEER, ADA ELIZABETH
(1935–) *Menominee Bureau of Indian Affairs Director*

Ada Deer led the Menominee Nation in its struggle to regain federal recognition and was later the first American Indian woman to serve as director of the Bureau of Indian Affairs (BIA). Ada Elizabeth Deer was born on the Menominee reservation in rural northern Keshena, Wisconsin, on August 7, 1935, in a one-room log cabin that lacked heat and running water. She was the oldest of nine children, of whom only five survived childhood. Her father, Joseph, was a Menominee who had been sent to Indian boarding schools for his education and worked in the tribe's lumber mill. Her mother, Constance Wood, was of Scottish-English ancestry and had grown up in a wealthy Philadelphia family. Against her family's wishes, she became a nurse and took a job with the Bureau of Indian Affairs on the Menominee reservation, where she met her husband.

Ada Deer survived the taunts of whites in local schools and graduated from high school in 1954, the same year Congress passed the Menominee Termination Act, which was to end the federally recognized status of her tribe. Ada Deer won a scholarship from the University of Wisconsin, Madison, and another from her tribe to attend college. She became the first Menominee student to graduate from the University of Wisconsin, receiving a B.A. degree in social work in 1957. Deer next received her M.S.W. degree from the School of Social Work at Columbia University in 1961. She was the first member of her tribe to receive a graduate degree. For a short time she studied law at the University of Wisconsin, Madison, and at the University of New Mexico. She was also a fellow at the Harvard Institute of Politics in 1977. Her first job after graduation was in Minneapolis as a social worker at the Edward F. Waite Neighborhood House. As part of the federal termination program, the government sought to relocate reservation Indians to cities. Many cities, such as Minneapolis, experienced a large increase in their population of urban Indians because of these poli-

cies. In 1964, Deer began a three-year job as the community services coordinator for the Bureau of Indian Affairs in Minneapolis.

In the 1970s, Deer led a successful campaign to regain federal recognition for her tribe. The 1953 termination of the tribe's federal status had devastated the tribe economically, socially, and culturally. Because the tribe members were unable to pay individual property taxes, most of the Menominees' former land holdings were sold, and the tribal hospital and school were closed. But in 1970 Deer led a grassroots movement to stop the land sale. She was the cofounder of the Determination of the Rights and Unity for Menominee Shareholders (DRUMS) and became the vice president of the National Committee to Save the Menomineee People and Forest, whose larger goal was to repeal the tribe's termination. In this position Deer led two years of intensive lobbying, which resulted in the Menominee Restoration Act, signed by President Nixon in December 1972. This act restored federal recognition to the tribe. The tribe elected Deer as its chair, and she served in this position for two years.

From 1977 until 1993, she taught social work at the University of Wisconsin. She was a founding director of Americans for Indian Opportunity and was also active in Planned Parenthood, the Urban League, and the National Women's Education Fund. In 1978 and 1982, she ran unsuccessfully for the Wisconsin secretary of state position. In 1984 Deer served as vice-chair of the presidential campaign of Vice President Walter Mondale and congressional Representative GERALDINE FERRARO. She served as a board member of the Native American Rights Fund from 1984 to 1990 and as its chair for the 1989–90 term. In 1991, Deer joined the Women's Studies Program at the university. The following year she ran as the Democratic candidate for the House seat from Wisconsin's Second Congressional District but lost to Scott Klug, the Republican incumbent.

In 1993, she became the first American-Indian woman appointed as the assistant Interior Secretary for Indian Affairs. The Bureau of Indian Affairs has had a long and sometimes troubled relationship with American Indian tribes. Deer knew that changing the bureau would be difficult but approached the task hoping to "make a dent every day." The BIA is the largest bureau within the Interior Department, with a staff of 14,000. In 1994 Deer insisted that an American Indian serve as chair of the National Indian Gaming Commission for the first time ever.

Her tenure at the BIA was not without controversy, however. By November 1994 the National Congress of American Indians discussed asking her to resign. In January 1995 the All Indian Pueblo Council gave her a vote of no confidence. Native corporations sued her in December 1995 over a dispute involving their North Slope (Alaska) oil resources and $2.4 billion in missing funds.

Accomplishments during her tenure included: extension of federal recognition to 12 tribes, approval of 145 tribal-state gaming compacts in 24 states, and recognition of government-to-government relationship with 223 Alaska Native villages.

After the 1996 election, President Bill Clinton announced his plans to replace Deer at the BIA. In 1997 Deer chaired the National Indian Gaming Commission for a year before becoming the director of the American Indian Studies Program at the University of Wisconsin at Madison, a position she continued to serve in as of 2001. An American Indian activist for more than 30 years, Deer remains committed to Indian issues, noting, "It takes a tribe to raise a child."

Further Reading

Adams, Rebecca. "An Activist Chief for Indian Affairs." *National Journal* 26, no. 39 (September 24, 1994): 2234.

"Ada Deer to Run Bureau of Indian Affairs." *Congressional Quarterly Weekly Report* 51, no. 20 (May 15, 1993): 1238.

Adare, Sierra. "Deer Uses Her Experiences." *News From Indian Country,* no. 20 (October 31, 2000): 14A.

Deer, Ada. *Speaking Out.* Chicago: Children's Press Open Door Books, 1970.

Graf, Karen. "Ada Deer: Creating Opportunities for Minority Students." *On Wisconsin* 9 (April 1998): 8.

Savilla, Elmer, "Ada Bids Adieu to Interior." *Indian Country Today* (November 17, 1997): A1.

 ## DIX, DOROTHEA LYNDE
(1802–1887)   *Mental Health Reformer*

Dorothea Dix was a reformer for improved treatment of the mentally ill and served as superintendent of nurses during the Civil War. Dorothea Lynde Dix was born on April 4, 1802, in Hampden, Maine, the first child of Mary Bigelow Dix and Joseph Dix. Dix's family was poor. Her mother's prolonged illnesses and her father's alcoholism left Dix largely responsible for the home. Her father made very little money from tenant farming, preaching, and selling his printed sermons. The family moved frequently—sometimes as often as three or four times a year. Her extended family had a more prosperous background than her nuclear family: Her paternal grandfather was a wealthy physician, chemical manufacturer, and land developer in Boston. From the time she was 12, Dix lived with her grandmother in Boston. In 1816, at age 14, Dix founded a successful school in Worcester, where she taught for three years. When she was 19, she opened a successful school for girls in Boston in 1821. At this time, she also met Anne Heath, a woman from a wealthy family who would become her lifelong friend and companion.

For the next 20 years Dix taught and wrote books. She published five books between 1824 and 1829, including a popular science textbook for elementary students called *Conversations on Common Things,* which had 60 reprintings. Dix left teaching in 1836. She struggled with lung problems and depression after being displaced from her family mansion following her grandmother's death.

In 1841, she started a Sunday school class in the East Cambridge, Massachusetts, jail. She was horrified by the conditions she found there. Mentally ill women were living in the jail, naked, filthy, and chained. There was no heat, since officials argued that "lunatics" could not feel the cold and would burn themselves and the building if they were given any source of heat. Dix spent a year touring every jail in Massachusetts. She found that the mentally ill were routinely locked away in jails or in their families' attics. She wrote letters of protest and outrage to local authorities that were published in local newspapers.

In 1843, she reported these conditions to the Massachusetts legislature. In the written report that accompanied her testimony, she documented the conditions of nearly 1,000 insane inmates. She said, "I proceed Gentlemen, briefly to call attention to the present state of Insane Persons confined within the Commonwealth, in cages, closets, stalls, pens! Chained, naked, beaten with rods, and lashed into obedience!" Her exposé resulted in the renovation of an asylum in Worcester. She put the findings of her survey in a petition to the general court as well. The state legislature voted to reprint her petition as a government publication and distributed 5,000 copies throughout the state. A few months before her 41st birthday, *Memorial to the Massachusetts Legislature* was published. Dix was a persistent and effective lobbyist, and the bill Dix drafted was passed by the Massachusetts legislature in 1843. She served as researcher, reporter, author of amendments, and architect of the asylum itself. She expanded her research and reports into other states including Rhode Island, Connecticut, Tennessee, New Jersey, New York, and even into Canada.

Dix claimed that her work was simple obedience to the voice of God. She spent the next 40 years of her life documenting abuse of mental patients throughout the United States. She successfully spurred legislative reforms in 15 states and personally oversaw the establishment of 32 mental hospitals. There were only 13 mental hospitals when Dix began her work in 1843, but by 1880 there were 123. In 1844, she cofounded Medical Superintendents of American Institutions for the Insane, a landmark organization in the field of psychiatry. Dix also proposed changes in prison conditions in her 1845 book, *Remarks on Prisons and Prison Discipline in the United States.*

At a time when the federal government was giving millions of acres of land to private railroads, Dix lobbied for legislation to use income from the sale of western lands to permanently fund mental health programs. In the 1840s and 1850s, the House and Senate debated her land bill. For Dix, medical welfare was not charity, but a right. The bill to use federal land grants to endow mental hospitals passed the Senate by a two-thirds majority in 1854 but was vetoed by President Franklin Pierce. Pierce based his veto on the idea that if the government took responsibility for the insane poor, then they would also have to take care of the poor in general. According to Pierce, the bill Dix lobbied for would have set a precedent for a welfare state.

Dix investigated mental institutions in her travels to Russia, France, Turkey, and Scotland and influenced the pope to investigate conditions in Italy. At a time when women's public activity was still discouraged, her campaign on behalf of others fit into the female ideal of selflessness.

During the Civil War, from 1861 until 1866, Dix served without pay as superintendent of nurses for the Union in the U.S. Sanitary Commission. Military officials were unaccustomed to female nurses, so Dix deliberately sought applicants who were plain-looking and older than 30. She authorized a modest dress of black or brown skirts without hoops. Jewelry was not allowed. More than 3,000 women served as Union army nurses under her command. When the war was over, she returned to her work on behalf of the mentally ill.

Dix was the only New England social reformer to organize successfully in the South. She was an old-line Whig, an early conservative political party. Dix did not support the women's rights or antislavery movements. She did not support the abolitionist movement and argued that it was hypocritical to urge "our Southern countrymen to break the bonds of the slave and bid him free—while here we hold men in dungeons—and chains—and in prisons then simply because their minds are darkened."

Dorothea Dix died on July 17, 1887, at age 79 in a Trenton, New Jersey, hospital that she had founded. According to her instructions, she was placed in a plain casket and had a simple granite headstone with nothing but her name inscribed. Dix is buried in Mount Auburn Cemetery, near Boston. She left $50,000 of her estate to be used for industrial training and education, $100 to the African church in Washington, D.C., and $100 to each of the nurses whom she had supervised in the Civil War.

The executor of her estate commissioned a Unitarian minister to write an account of her life. The result, *The Life of Dorothea Lynde Dix,* was published in 1891. The volume was more a collection of her letters and papers than an account of her life. Her papers are stored at the Houghton Library at Harvard University. Among the 10,000 items in the collection are journals, diaries, letters, needlework samples, and locks of her hair. The institutions she built are still standing.

Dix's concerns are still pertinent today: Government budget cuts of funds for mental hospitals in the 1980s led some patients to be discharged from institutions to live on the streets. A recent survey of U.S. jails revealed that one-third of the nation's jails still regularly hold people with serious mental problems.

Further Reading

Brown, Thomas. *Dorothea Dix: New England Reformer.* Cambridge, Mass.: Harvard University Press, 1998.

Dix, Dorothea Lynde. *Asylum Prison, and Poorhouse: The Writings and Reform Work of Dorothea Dix in Illinois.* Carbondale: Southern Illinois University Press, 1999.

———. *On Behalf of the Insane Poor: Selected Reports 1843–1852.* Manchester, N.H.: Ayer, 1971.

———. *Remarks on Prisons and Prison Discipline in the United States.* New York: Patterson Smith, 1984.

Gollaher, David. *Voice for the Mad: The Life of Dorothea Dix.* New York: Free Press, 1995.

Tiffany, Francis. *Life of Dorothea Lynde Dix.* 1891. Reprint, Salem, Mass.: Higginson Book Company, 1993.

 DOLE, MARY ELIZABETH
ALEXANDER HANFORD
(1936–) *Presidential Candidate,
Secretary of Transportation*

Elizabeth Dole sought the Republican presidential nomination in 2000 after a lifetime of public service. Mary Elizabeth Alexander Hanford was born on July 29, 1936, in Salisbury, North Carolina, to Mary and John Van Hanford. Her father was a successful florist and a strong cold war–era anticommunist who built a bomb shelter in the backyard. Her mother was a music instructor who gave up her career when she married. The family was Methodist. Around the age of one, Elizabeth gave herself the nickname of Liddy.

She entered Duke University in Durham, North Carolina, and she majored in political science and international affairs. Her mother would have preferred that she study home economics, which was, as her mother stated, a "natural prelude to marriage." During her freshman year she ran unsuccessfully for class representative. She attended debutante balls in nearby Raleigh but remembers, "As an international affairs major, I was more interested in writing a paper examining the decision-making process leading up to America's use of the first atomic bomb."

After graduation she worked as a secretary at the Harvard Law School Library. In the summer of 1959, she studied English history and government at Oxford University in England. The following fall she began a master's program in teaching, with a joint major in government. During the summer of 1960 she worked as a secretary in Washington, D.C., for Senator B. Everett Jordan, a Democrat from North Carolina. She considered herself a Democrat at this time and worked on behalf of Lyndon Baines Johnson's vice presidential campaign in 1960. Friends from Harvard remember her as a liberal who provided free legal representation to indigents. During the summers of 1961 and 1962 she worked at the United Nations. She began studies at Harvard Law School in 1962, one of only two dozen women in a class of 550. She passed her bar exam in 1966 and took a managerial-level job at the Department of Health, Education and Welfare (HEW).

She met her future husband, Republican senator Bob Dole of Kansas, in the early 1970s. He served as Republican National Committee chairman and was a strong supporter of President Nixon. In 1972, while Hanford was working as President Richard Nixon's deputy assistant for, and then director of, consumer affairs, she focused on consumer fraud, the quality of nursing home care, and the regulation

Elizabeth Dole, political appointee
(Courtesy of Elizabeth Dole)

of the auto industry. In 1973, President Nixon appointed her to the Federal Trade Commission. In 1975, she married Bob Dole. She was 39 and her husband 52 when they married. It was her first marriage and his second marriage. By 1976, when Bob Dole became the Republican vice presidential candidate, she had joined the Republican Party.

In 1981, President Ronald Reagan appointed Elizabeth Dole to head the White House Office of Public Liaison. In 1983, she was chosen to head the Department of Transportation, the first woman to hold this position, the only female cabinet member in the Reagan administration, and the seventh woman to serve in the cabinet. As transportation secretary, she led the fight to privatize the publicly owned Conrail railroad and campaigned to raise the drinking age to 21. She initially stalled safety initiatives, including requirements to make her car manufacturers install air bags and automatic seat belts. But later, her vigorous advocacy of seat belt use resulted in major accomplishments. State legislatures passed laws requiring seat belt usage, and the

number of people using them nationwide tripled during her tenure. She also supported passage of a 1983 bill that mandated a center-mounted third brake light on automobiles. However, she was criticized for ignoring air safety issues; many felt she was unable to respond to the growing needs of airports and air traffic control systems.

In 1988 the Gallup poll of the 10 most admired women in the world included Elizabeth Dole. She was mentioned as a possible vice-presidential candidate for Republican presidential contender George H. W. Bush in 1988, but Senator Dan Quayle was chosen instead. President Bush appointed her secretary of labor in 1989. She was the only woman in the cabinet and the highest-ranking woman in that administration. During her 22 months as secretary of labor, she opposed federal minimum wage legislation, the Family and Medical Leave Act, parental leave and child care legislation, and other legislation backed by moderate Republicans in Congress. Consequently, organized labor gave her low marks. Other political observers felt she had done the best she could to represent labor in a Republican administration and that her efforts were limited by a probusiness administration. She has said, however, that she felt left out of major policy and political decision making in the administration. In 1990 she became the first member of President Bush's cabinet to resign.

Dole left service in the federal government to become president of the American Red Cross in 1991, a position she held for eight years. She was the first woman to head the Red Cross since its founder, CLARA BARTON, in 1881. As president, she turned the organization's $30 million deficit into a surplus of $100 million. She supervised 30,000 employees and 1.3 million volunteers. She turned down her first year's salary of $200,000 to set an example for an organization based on the work of volunteers. She also pledged to donate a certain percentage of her speaking fees to the charity. From 1991 to 1994 she earned more than $875,000 in speaking fees and was paid as much as $20,000 for an individual appearance. Two weeks after a *Los Angeles Times* story appeared that examined a discrepancy between the donation she claimed to have made to the American Red Cross and the amount that appeared on her income tax return, she gave a check for $74,635 to the charity. Critics also charged Dole with rewriting a Red Cross AIDS prevention manual to satisfy the religious right. Media pundits noted that the timing of her directive occurred while her husband, presidential candidate Robert Dole, was trying to increase his appeal to conservatives. The issue surfaced when chapter executives complained to the press. An internal memo of the Red Cross advised employees to state that the decision involved their entire board, not just Dole. Elizabeth Dole never responded publicly to the charges.

Inspectors from the U.S. Food and Drug Administration found a dangerous lack of control over the blood bank operations of the Red Cross and screening of donations from persons with AIDS at the start of her tenure. A couple of years earlier, in 1988, the Red Cross publicly acknowledged that it had distributed 24 pints of blood tainted with HIV, the virus that causes AIDS. When Dole assumed leadership in 1991 she responded by spending $120 million to improve the Red Cross blood services, including reequipping local centers, centralizing the computer system, and consolidating 53 blood testing centers into 10 regional labs to offer more effective screening for HIV, the virus that causes AIDS.

Business Week analysts gave Dole an A-plus rating for public relations and a C for management skills and employee relations. Critics of her personal work style claim she is a poor manager who gets obsessed with unimportant details and is overly ambitious with self-promotion. Many in the general public admired her as an organized and effective female role model.

In 1996, her husband ran as the Republican presidential candidate but lost to incumbent President Clinton. Elizabeth Dole addressed the 1996 Republican National Convention, something no other presidential candidate's wife had ever done. She announced her intention to retain her position as head of the American Red Cross if her husband won the presidential election. This would have made her the first employed first lady in history. Dole declared her candidacy for the Republican nomination for president in 2000. She ran second in national polls to George W. Bush. More than 50 percent of her big donors were women, twice the number in other campaigns. Dole was only the second woman to bid for her party's presidential nomination; the first had been Maine senator MARGARET CHASE SMITH. At times Dole seemed to emphasize the historic role she played as a female candidate. She hired a plane to fly over the Women's World Cup soccer finals with a banner that read, "Go team USA! Make history—Elizabeth Dole." At other times she seemed somewhat ambivalent about the role of gender in her campaign, in *Newsweek* noting, "I am not running because I'm a woman; I don't want people voting for me because I'm a woman." When *U.S. News and World Report* asked Dole if she considered herself a feminist, she responded, "I think if it means that you had some sort of prepackaged answers that are handed down by the political correctness club, no. But if it means that you want equal opportunity for women, more freedom for women—absolutely." Dole left the race after several months, citing financial constraints.

Dole has written about being born again while working in the Reagan White House in 1982. She claims to read her Bible for 30 minutes each day and has long supported prayer in schools and opposed abortion. As she stated to the Christian Coalition, "It is wrong that our children are not allowed a silent moment of prayer in school, that a constitutional amendment is necessary to insure a child's right to pray. And it is right that we protect the sanctity of life, that we replace abortion with adoption, require a parental notification, and that we continue the ban on federal funding." She also supported a measure to deny public services, except for emergency medical care, to illegal immigrants. During her presidential campaign, however, she took a more centrist position on abortion than did candidate George W. Bush and promised not to personally pursue a ban on abortion. Dole said she opposed abortion, except in cases of rape or incest or to save the life of the mother. She also represented a more moderate stance on gun control than did other Republican candidates, supporting the banning of certain assault weapons and requiring safety locks on guns. In a 2000 Gallup poll of the most admired women, she came in third, behind HILLARY RODHAM CLINTON and television talk show host Oprah Winfrey. Dole was then mentioned as a possible vice-presidential nominee, outpacing other potential nominees in early Gallup polls. In March 2001 she reportedly declined to serve as U.S. ambassador to the United Nations in the administration of President George W. Bush because that position did not carry cabinet rank. Elizabeth Dole is a candidate, in 2002, for a Senate seat from North Carolina and remains one of the most prominent women in the Republican Party.

Further Reading

Baumgardener, Jennifer. "Why Not Elizabeth Dole." *Nation* 268, no. 13 (1999): 6–7.

Brunei, Frank. "With Eye on the Vice Presidency." *New York Times,* January 3, 2000, A14.

Dole, Bob, and Elizabeth Dole. *Unlimited Partners: Our American Story.* New York: Simon and Schuster, 1988.

Dole, Elizabeth. *A Few Good Women: Breaking the Barriers to Top Management.* Old Tappan, N.J.: Prentice Hall, 1998.

Nicholas, John. "Will Any Woman Do?" *Progressive* 63, no. 7 (July 1999): 31–32.

Reed, Julia. "Elizabeth Dole." *Newsweek* 134, no. 2 (1999): 28–30.

Zengerle, Jason. "Liddy Lite." *New Republic* (February 1999): 9–10.

 ## DORR, RHETA LOUISE CHILDE
(1866–1948) *Journalist*

Rheta Dorr covered stories for the *New York Tribune* and the *New York Post* with a special focus on women's problems. Rheta Louise Childe was born on November 2, 1866, in Omaha, Nebraska. She was the second in a family of four girls and two boys. Her father, Edward Parson Childe, was a druggist whose ancestors had been among the earliest settlers in the Massachusetts Bay Colony. Her

mother, Lucie Mitchell Childe, was a housewife. The family was Episcopalian.

Rheta Childe had feminist tendencies from a very young age and remembered being bothered by women's gravestones that listed them merely as wives. She said, "It was a family joke that from infancy it was easy to irritate me by a most casual allusion to the tradition of male superiority. Whenever a neighbor dropped in to announce that the Smiths had a new baby—I had an acute attack of nerves. I dropped my playthings, scrambled to my short legs, jumped up and down and shrieked: 'Lil girls just as good as lil boys!'" She recalled another incident that provoked her feminist sensibilities: "The crushing formula: 'Aw, you're nothing but a girl' failed to crush me. In fact the boy who uttered those hateful words in my hearing was liable to find himself with a fight on his hands, a fight waged without regard to rules of civilized warfare."

At age 12, against her father's wishes, she snuck out of her house to hear women's rights advocates ELIZABETH CADY STANTON and SUSAN B. ANTHONY speak, and promptly paid dues to become a member of the National Woman Suffrage Association (NWSA). On the following day, the *Nebraska State Journal* listed the names of those who had joined the NWSA, and her disobedience to her father was quickly apparent.

She viewed the inequality in the typical patriarchal family as based on economic disparity between the genders. As a teenager she washed windows to earn spending money for school clothing. While she was a student at Nebraska State University, a professor gave Dorr a copy of *A Doll's House,* the play by Henrik Ibsen, which resonated with her own observations. Ibsen offered a compelling critique of the limitations women faced in 19th-century society in this work.

After college, rather than teach, which was considered a respectable, if temporary, pursuit for a woman (providing only a stopgap until marriage), Dorr decided to work at the post office. Her father was a prominent Democrat, and when applying for the job, she gave the impression that her father was requesting the position for her as a political favor. Her family was upset about her being employed in such a public position but when her father insisted that she quit, she threatened to leave home. She worked at the post office for two years, then moved to New York City in 1890 with a friend. While living in New York, in 1892 she met and married John Pixley Dorr, who was 20 years her senior. They moved to Seattle, Washington, the following year. She gave birth to a son in 1896, and the marriage dissolved shortly after that. She separated from her husband in 1898, but kept his name and never formally divorced.

While married, she had been publishing newspaper stories. After her separation, she and her two-year-old son returned to New York. She hoped to make a living as a writer, but discovered that newspapers were unwilling to hire her. In her first attempt to find employment as a journalist, she was told that women writers could not receive a salary. For many years she peddled special-interest stories at $5 a column and recalled, "I was at this time, and for a long time after, in danger of becoming what I dreaded to be, a man-hater. As far as I could see I lived in a world entirely hostile to women; a world in which every right and every privilege were claimed by men. Men exacted everything, gave nothing, throwing contempt into the bargain. Every man's hand was held out to help young fellows beginning life. Almost any recent college graduate could get a trial week in a newspaper city-room. The brightest woman waited in the office-boy's coop."

She did eventually find employment with the *New York Tribune* and the *New York Post.* In the beginning Dorr was hired because the papers wanted to get more women readers for their department-store advertisers. Dorr was expected to report on women's club activities. She also covered stories on professional women. She started writing a regular column on women and their work. Her salary was significantly lower than those of the men on staff, since women reporters were just "an experiment."

At times, editors wanted her to cover women's conventions with an angle that ridiculed the pro-

ceedings, but she refused. Many of her stories investigated the working conditions and salary inequities women faced in employment, especially in factories. Dorr joined the Women's Trade Union League (WTUL), whose main goal was to gain equal pay for equal work for female workers. Dorr did not support special protective legislation for women workers because she feared that would label women as inferior. (Protective labor legislation set safety and work hour limits on female employees that restricted their employment opportunities.)

In 1905, by lobbying Congress for a bill to authorize investigations by the Bureau of Labor, Dorr was instrumental in securing the first official investigation into the conditions of working women.

She also reported on women's activism in the Russian Revolution. She had first traveled to Russia in 1906, and she returned in 1917, the same year she published a book, *Inside the Russian Revolution,* based on her observations. She also served as a war correspondent during World War I. She published war experiences in 1918 in *A Soldier's Mother in France.* During these years, Dorr also organized suffrage marches in the United States and went to England to assist the suffragists there. She smuggled $20,000 to them by carrying the money sewn into her corset.

In 1918, *Good Housekeeping* magazine commissioned Dorr to write a series of biographical articles on Emmeline Pankhurst, the leader of the British suffrage movement, and so Dorr traveled with Pankhurst extensively and became her adviser during an American tour. Dorr also founded and edited the *Suffragist,* a newspaper largely written by ALICE PAUL and Dorr, which advocated militant tactics, such as those used by British suffragists, in the struggle for suffrage in the United States. Militant tactics included imprisonment, hunger strikes, marches, street meetings, and heckling public officials.

She wrote a series of articles on women and work for *Hampton's Magazine* that were later published as a book titled *What Eight Million Women Want.* The collection examined the organization of women's clubs, suffrage associations, trade unions, and consumers' leagues. Dorr was also a member of a luncheon club called the Heterodoxy, which featured speakers on political topics.

Dorr briefly joined a New York branch of the Socialist Party around 1918, and was well acquainted with such leading radicals as EMMA GOLDMAN, ELIZABETH GURLEY FLYNN, John Reed, and Upton Sinclair, but she returned to what she felt was suffrage. She said, "Always after consorting with them I went back to the suffragists and the feminists who, it seemed to me, were working towards a definite goal, constructive, progressive, and sane."

Dorr died in 1948, a few years after the end of World War II. She had reported fairly on feminist activities in the United States and abroad. She once reflected on her life's work: "The vague thing which the anti-suffragists and even the old suffrage-leaders spoke of with bated breath, feminism, held an eternal attraction for me. I thought my next job ought to be waking women up to feminism."

Further Reading

Dorr, Rheta. *Inside the Russian Revolution.* 1917. Reprint, New York: Arno Press, 1970.
———. *A Woman of Fifty.* 1924. Reprint. San Francisco, Calif.: Signal, 1980.
———. *Women's Demand for Humane Treatment of Women Workers in Shop and Factory.* New York: The Consumers League of the City of New York, 1909.

 ## DUNIWAY, ABIGAIL JANE SCOTT
(1834–1915) *Suffragist*

Abigail Jane Scott Duniway was founder of the Oregon Equal Suffrage Association. Abigail Jane Scott was born on October 22, 1834, on a Groveland, Illinois, farm to Ann Roelofson Scott and John Tucker Scott. She was the second daughter in a family of nine children. In 1852, her father moved the family to the Northwest Territory, in what would become Oregon. Her mother and three-year-old brother died of cholera on the 2,400-mile journey. She taught school for a year in Eola, Oregon, and then married Benjamin Charles Duniway in 1853. She had six children, five sons and one daughter, during the next 15 years.

She had a hard life raising six children on the family farm in Lafayette, Oregon. She started a business making and selling thousands of pounds of butter annually to help make ends meet. Her husband lost the family farm when a friend defaulted on a loan that he had cosigned. Duniway had no knowledge of the deal. She resented laws that allowed men to make any decision they pleased in regard to family assets without the consent or even knowledge of their wives. When her husband became disabled from an accident, Duniway became the sole support of the family. She returned to teaching, ran a boardinghouse, and operated a millinery shop to provide for the family.

In 1871, Duniway began publishing a weekly newspaper in Portland called the *New Northwest,* which she headed for 16 years. Her sister and her children helped her publish the paper, which featured news supporting women's rights. Her only previous publishing experience had been as author of a novel, *Captain Gray's Company,* written in 1859 while she lived in Portland. In the novel her fictional character had proclaimed, "When woman's true history shall have been written, her part in the upbuilding of this nation will astound the world."

In 1871, she managed suffrage leader SUSAN B. ANTHONY's speaking tour in the Northwest. During this time Duniway herself began lecturing in the Northwest for suffrage. In 1873, she founded and served as president of the Oregon Equal Suffrage Association. She also served as honorary president of the Oregon Federation of Women's Clubs and as president of the Portland Woman's Club. She played a pivotal role in gaining suffrage in Washington Territory in 1883 and in Idaho in 1896, but the Oregon victory took several more years to achieve.

Suffrage was finally passed in Oregon in 1912, eight years before its federal passage. Oregon became the seventh state to approve women's suffrage. Governor Oswald West of Oregon remembered hearing Duniway speak when he was a boy and agreeing with her arguments. Thirty years later, he asked Duniway to author the official Woman Suffrage Proclamation for the state. She and the governor signed the suffrage bill she had authored for Oregon; this made Duniway the first female voter in the state. Duniway also served as vice president of the National American Woman Suffrage Association (NAWSA) from 1884 until Susan B. Anthony's death in 1906.

Duniway wrote her autobiography, *Path Breaking,* in 1914, two years after the Oregon suffrage victory and a year before her death. The title reflected her independent outlook as an activist who had opposed Prohibition, which many suffragists supported. Duniway believed in entrepreneurial opportunities for women, which could afford them economic independence. Her opposition to Prohibition was based on a concern for governmental and/or religious coercion in individual lives. She also feared that working for Prohibition would drain energy from the suffrage movement and delay the passage of suffrage acts by mobilizing additional opposition.

Abigail Scott Duniway died on October 11, 1915. A park in Portland, Oregon, and a public school in East Portland bear her name. In 1944, the Oregon Shipbuilding Company named a "liberty ship" in her honor. In 1981, members of the Oregon legislature unanimously nominated her to represent their state in the National Woman's Hall of Fame. After devoting her life to the suffrage struggle, Abigail Scott Duniway saw her efforts succeed in her home state of Oregon, but she died five years before national suffrage was attained.

Further Reading

Moynihan, Ruth Barnes. *Rebel for Rights: Abigail Scott Duniway.* New Haven, Conn.: Yale University Press, 1983.

Smith, Helen. *Presumptuous Dreamers: A Sociological History of the Life and Times of Abigail Scott Duniway, 1834–1871.* Portland, Ore.: Smith, Smith and Smith Publishing Company, 1974.

Ward, Jean. *Yours for Liberty: Selections from Abigail Scott Duniway's Suffrage Newspaper.* Corvallis: Oregon State University Press, 1999.

E

 EASTMAN, CATHERINE CRYSTAL
(1881–1928)   *Founder of the American*
Civil Liberties Union, Peace Advocate

Socialist, labor lawyer, journalist, and suffragist Crystal Eastman founded the American Civil Liberties Union (ACLU) and coauthored the Equal Rights Amendment (ERA). Catherine Crystal Eastman was born on June 25, 1881, in Marlborough, Massachusetts, to Anna Bertha Ford Eastman and Samuel Elijah Eastman. Her parents were Congregational ministers. She graduated from Vassar College in 1903 and completed a master's degree in sociology from Columbia University in 1904 and an LL.B. (bachelor of laws) degree from New York University Law School in 1907, where she was second in the class. She lived in Greenwich Village and worked evenings in a settlement house.

Her first job was investigating labor conditions for the Russell Sage Foundation's Pittsburgh Survey. (The study of more than 1,000 industrial accidents was conducted in New York.) Her report, *Work Accidents and the Law,* in 1910 led Governor Charles Evans Hughes to appoint her to the state's Commission on Employer's Liability and Causes of Industrial Accidents, Unemployment, and Lack of Farm Labor. She was the first woman appointed to such a position. She served on the commission from 1909 to 1911 and drafted the nation's first worker's compensation law for New York State. The law was later adopted by the federal government. In 1913, President Woodrow Wilson appointed her as an attorney for the U.S. Commission on Industrial Relations.

Eastman married insurance salesman Wallace Benedict in 1911 and lived for a short time in Milwaukee, where in 1912 she ran an unsuccessful campaign for women's suffrage in Wisconsin. In 1913, she returned to New York and cofounded, with militant suffragist ALICE PAUL, the Congressional Union for Woman Suffrage (CUWS), which later became the National Woman's Party (NWP).

In 1915, Eastman founded the Woman's Peace Party, heading the radical New York branch, which became the Women's International League for Peace and Freedom. (It remains the nation's oldest women's peace organization.) At the same time she served as director of the American Union Against Militarism (AUAM), which lobbied against U.S. entry into World War I. The AUAM was successful in its efforts to help the United States avoid war with Mexico in 1916. It also campaigned against U.S. imperialism in Latin America and the Caribbean. The organization worked against the draft and supported conscientious objectors. It also opposed arms profiteering by military industrial corporations.

In 1916, her marriage to Benedict having ended, Eastman married another antiwar activist, British poet Walter Fuller. The following year, she founded and served as lead attorney of the National Civil Liberties Bureau, which evolved into the current American Civil Liberties Union. She originally founded the organization to defend conscientious objectors during World War I and to protect the Bill of Rights. She explained she wanted the organization "To maintain something over here that will be worth coming back to when the weary war is over."

At the end of World War I, Eastman resumed her suffrage activism. She was blacklisted (denied work) during the 1919 to 1921 Red Scare. She was one of the four authors of the Equal Rights Amendment (ERA) in 1923. Commenting on the ERA, Eastman noted, "This is a fight worth fighting even if it takes ten years." Eastman was one of the few socialists to support the ERA, but she opposed protective labor legislation, feeling that it allowed employers to discriminate against women. Protective labor legislation regulated safety conditions and work hours for female workers. These restrictions prevented women from gaining employment opportunities in some fields. She was a strong supporter of birth control reform and wrote pieces for *The Birth Control Review.* Eastman wrote for several feminist publications, including *Equal Rights,* the journal started by Alice Paul, and a London feminist weekly, *Time and Tide.* With her brother, Max Eastman, she copublished the socialist journal *The Liberator.* (Her brother was also editor and publisher of the socialist journal *The Masses.*)

Eastman's husband died from a stroke in 1927, and Crystal Eastman died of nephritis on July 8, 1928, in Erie, Pennsylvania, at age 48. Eastman once wrote, "Life is a big battle for the complete feminist."

Further Reading

American Civil Liberties Union. "Crystal Eastman." Available online. URL: http://www.aclu.org/library/eastman.html. Downloaded on January 11, 2001.

Cook, Blanche Wiesen, editor. *Crystal Eastman on Women and Revolution.* New York: Oxford University Press, 1978.

 EDELMAN, MARIAN WRIGHT
(1939–) *Founder of the Children's Defense Fund*

Yale-trained attorney Marian Wright Edelman founded the Children's Defense Fund. Marian Wright was born on June 6, 1939, to Maggie Leola Bowen Wright and Arthur Jerome Wright, the youngest daughter in a family of five children. She was named after singer Marian Anderson.

Her father, a minister at Shiloh Baptist Church, was raised in segregated Bennettsville, South Carolina. Her family built the Wright Home for the Aged for the elderly poor in their community. Recalling her upbringing, Edelman said, "Working for the community was as much a part of our existence as eating and sleeping and church. I did it as a kid like other kids go to the movies. It is what I was raised to be."

When her father died in 1954, her mother continued to run the Wright Home for the Aged. Her brother Harry took over her father's ministerial role. Edelman's family was an important source of inspiration for her. She said, "I was taught that service is the rent each of us pays for living."

She attended Spelman College in Atlanta, Georgia, one of the oldest colleges for African-American women in the United States, and got involved in civil rights sit-ins and protests. During the same year, black and white students throughout the South started the sit-in movement to desegregate public facilities. Edelman participated in a sit-in at the cafeteria in the Atlanta city hall and was arrested with 14 other Spelman students. In 1960, she studied briefly in Paris, France; Geneva, Switzerland; and the Soviet Union. She graduated as valedictorian from Spelman in 1960. After volunteering at the local office of the National Association for the Advancement of Colored People (NAACP), she decided to become an attorney.

She entered Yale Law School in 1960 and in the summers went to Greenwood, Mississippi, to work with the Student Nonviolent Coordinating Committee. She worked for voter registration in Mississippi in 1963. After receiving her law degree in 1963, she returned to the South to head the NAACP Legal Defense Fund and became the first African-American woman admitted to the bar in Mississippi. She led Senator Robert Kennedy on a tour so he could see firsthand the poverty in the Mississippi Delta country and met her future husband, Robert Edelman, an assistant to the senator, during this assignment.

In 1968, she moved to Washington, D.C., and started the Washington Public Policy Research Center, a civil rights advocacy group that focused on issues impacting the poor. Also in 1968, she married Peter Edelman, in what was the first interracial marriage in Virginia since the 1967 decision by the U.S. Supreme Court that struck down state laws against such marriages. The Edelmans' three sons were raised in both their mother's Baptist tradition and their father's Jewish tradition.

After President Richard Nixon vetoed a child care bill, she came to believe that the group with the least political power were children. In 1973, she founded the Children's Defense Fund. She became such an effective lobbyist that she was called the "101st senator." In 1980, she became the chair of the board of trustees of Spelman College, the first African American and the second woman to hold the position. She was disheartened in the 1980s when the Reagan administration dismantled so much of the welfare system, comparing her position to that of "being caught in an avalanche." In 1983, the *Ladies' Home Journal* named her among the top 100 most influential women in America.

Her books include *Children Out of School in America* and *Portrait of Inequality: Black and White Children in America.* Harvard University Press issued her 1986 W. E. B. DuBois lectures at Harvard as a book, *Families in Peril: An Agenda for Social Change* (published 1987). Her 1992 book, *The Measure of Our Success: A Letter to My Children and Yours,* was part autobiography and part social commentary, written in the form of a letter to her sons. Marian Wright Edelman has devoted her considerable talents to improving the lives of our nation's children. She has influenced numerous legislators, including Senator HILLARY RODHAM CLINTON, and shaped national policy on such issues as infant mortality, day care, child abuse, and teenage pregnancy.

Further Reading

Boykin, Terri. "An Interview with Marian Wright Edelman." *Southern Exposure* (1995): 40.

Edelman, Marian Wright. *Guide My Feet: Prayers and Meditations on Loving and Working for Children.* New York: Harperperennial Library, 1996.

———. *Lanterns: A Memoir of Mentors.* Boston: Beacon Press, 1999.

———. *The Measure of Our Success: A Letter to My Children and Yours.* Boston: Beacon Press, 1992.

F

 ## FEINSTEIN, DIANNE
(1933–   ) *Senator, Mayor*

A respected senator since 1992 who is committed to a political agenda that benefits women and children, Dianne Feinstein was also the first female mayor of San Francisco. She was born on June 22, 1933, one of three daughters of a gifted San Francisco surgeon and professor, Leon Goldman. Her mother, Betty Goldman, a Russian immigrant with roots in the Russian Orthodox Church, was an abusive alcoholic who attempted suicide before being institutionalized when Feinstein was an adult. Tests revealed that her mother had suffered from a brain disorder.

Her father was a Republican, but her uncle Morris Goldman, who lived with the family, was an urban Populist who took Dianne to political meetings and influenced her political outlook. She went to a Jewish religious school to please her father, but her mother enrolled her as the first Jewish student to attend the exclusive Convent of the Sacred Heart High School, from which she graduated in 1951.

She attended Stanford University, originally thinking of becoming a doctor, but she earned a D in genetics and an A in political thought. Her interest in politics was apparent by 1954 during her junior year, when she conducted a poll to test the support among students for a female candidate for student government. The survey revealed that students would prefer an orangutan, giraffe, or donkey to a female candidate. Gauging her chances, she decided to run for vice president rather than president of the student body, and she won. The next year, she graduated with a B.A. degree in history.

A year after graduating she married a prosecuting attorney, Jack Berman, who was 11 years her senior, and they had a daughter. The couple divorced after three years. Feinstein commented, "He wanted to keep me barefoot and pregnant. I could not be that kind of wife." She served on the California Women's Board of Terms and Parole from 1960 to 1966. She also served on the San Francisco Mayor's Committee on crime during the same time. Her second husband, Bert Feinstein, was a surgeon 20 years her senior who supported her political interests. She became a widow when he died of cancer in 1978 and would marry again in 1980, when she married investment banker Richard Blum.

In 1970, Feinstein became the first woman to serve on the San Francisco Board of Supervisors, a position she held for eight years, from 1970 to

1978, and served as president of that board for four years. She made two unsuccessful bids for mayor prior to 1978. During her tenure as president of the Board of Supervisors, in 1978, terror struck just a few doors from her City Hall office. Supervisor Daniel White assasinated Council Member Harvey Milk and Mayor George Moscone. As a result, Feinstein became acting mayor. She was reelected to two additional terms as mayor, once with 81 percent of the vote. She served as mayor of San Francisco for a decade, from 1978 to 1988.

During her tenure as mayor, Feinstein improved garbage collection and public transportation, and she increased public housing. Commercial office space doubled, one measure of the economic growth she oversaw. Her term was not without controversy, however. She closed gay bathhouses in 1980, vetoed domestic-partners legislation in 1982, and vetoed comparable worth bills. Yet, in 1969 as a candidate for the Board of Supervisors she had introduced one of the first pieces of legislation in America that prohibited discrimination against gays, and some of her gay friends had commitment ceremonies in her home. Feinstein disliked discrimination of any kind and appeared to support gays on a private level; but public policy support was not always consistent. Feinstein voted to support a ban on discrimination against gay municipal employees on April 3, 1972. She also raised taxes to cope with increased homelessness in the city and with the AIDS epidemic. In 1984, Walter Mondale considered her as a vice presidential candidate but instead selected GERALDINE FERRARO.

Feinstein was narrowly defeated in her run against Peter Wilson for governor of California in 1990. During her campaign, she promised that half the jobs in her administration would go to women. Feinstein won a special election to the U.S. Senate in 1992 to fill the seat vacated by newly elected governor Pete Wilson and was reelected two years later. Her opponent, millionaire Republican representative Michael Huffington, spent $30 million in his unsuccessful campaign. She easily won reelection in her 2000 campaign against Representative Tom Campbell, a Republican, of San Jose.

In the 2000 election Feinstein placed fourth in a national poll that surveyed voter preference for Democratic vice-presidential candidates. Democratic presidential nominee Al Gore reportedly did not select Feinstein as his running mate because of questions concerning her husband's business affairs—the same reason given by 1984 presidential candidate Walter Mondale in his selection process. Currently, Feinstein supports abortion rights and also supports the death penalty. She is considered to be tough on crime. Feinstein coauthored campaign finance reform legislation with Republican senator John McCain.

Further Reading

"Dianne Feinstein." *CQ Weekly* 57, no. 42 (October 30, 1999): 54–55.

Johnson, John. "Feinstein Posts an Easy Victory." *Los Angeles Times*, November 8, 2000, A3.

Morris, Celia. *Storming the Statehouse.* New York: Scribner, 1992.

Nichols, John. "Feinstein Faces a Double-Team." *The Progressive* 64, no. 8 (August 2000): 26–29.

Roberts, Jerry. *Dianne Feinstein: Never Let Them See You Cry.* San Francisco: Harper, 1995.

Whitney, Catherine. *Nine and Counting: The Women of the Senate.* New York: Perennial, 2001.

 ## FELTON, REBECCA ANN LATIMER
(1835–1930)   *Senator*

Rebecca Felton was the first female to officially serve in the U.S. Senate. Rebecca Ann Latimer was born on June 10, 1835, in Decatur, Georgia, and raised in rural Georgia in a privileged family. Her father was a merchant and a farmer. She graduated first in her class from the Madison Female College in 1852. The following year she married Dr. William Felton, a physician who was a Methodist minister 12 years her senior. They had five children, only one of whom lived to adulthood, and lived on the family farm in Cartersville, Georgia. Hardship during the Civil War claimed the lives of two of their children. The Feltons identified with the Populist Party, which traditionally was more represented among small farmers than the aristocracy.

Dr. Felton was active in politics, serving as a congressman and in the Georgia legislature. Felton organized all her husband's campaigns and wrote his speeches, but she was a prominent Georgia leader in her own right. She advocated free public education, a rare point of view in the South. She also supported women's admission to state universities. She started a vocational training school for women, the Georgia Training School for Girls in Atlanta. She joined the Women's Christian Temperance Union and supported women's suffrage. She lobbied on behalf of prisoners, against chain gangs, and against housing women and juveniles with male prisoners. Felton experienced some legislative success in these areas. In 1908 the practice of convict leasing was outlawed in her state.

As Felton grew older, she became more conservative on labor and racial issues. She was critical of Catholics, Jews, African Americans, and child labor laws. Her views on race matched those of many other elite white southerners of the time. In 1910, she began writing a column for the *Atlanta Journal* that continued until her death 20 years later. In 1911, she wrote a book, *My Memoirs of Georgia Politics*. She was a delegate to the 1912 Progressive Party convention. She held isolationist views, which influenced her opposition to World War I. In 1919, she wrote her second book, *Country Life in Georgia in the Days of My Youth.*

In 1922, Georgia senator Thomas Watson died in office, and the governor appointed Felton to fill the senate position. At the age of 87 she became the first female senator in U.S. history. A man had been elected to the vacated seat, so officially she held the position for only one day, but she made a short speech in the Senate on that day. Her official seating in the Senate had a great deal of symbolic importance, because women had gained suffrage only a few years earlier. Women around the country had lobbied for her official swearing-in. In her brief address to her senatorial colleagues, Felton stated, "Mr. President, the women of this country are going

to come and sit here. There may not be very many the next few years, but in time they will come."

Rebecca Felton returned to Georgia and died eight years later, at age 94, on January 24, 1930, in Atlanta. She is buried in Cartersville. Her papers are stored at the University of Georgia Library. Her brief tenure in the U.S. Senate was precedent setting.

Further Reading

Felton, Rebecca Latimer. *Country Life in Georgia in the Days of My Youth.* 1919. Reprint, New York: Signal, 1980.
Georgia Women of Achievement. "Rebecca Ann Latimer Felton." Available online. URL: http://www.netsrq.com/ ~dbois/felton.html. Downloaded on December 30, 2000.

 FERRARO, GERALDINE
(1935–) *Congressional Representative, Vice-Presidential Candidate*

In 1984, Geraldine Ferraro became the first woman to be nominated as a candidate for vice president of the United States. Geraldine Ferraro was born August 26, 1935, in Newburgh, New York, to Antonetta Corrieri Ferraro and Dominick Ferraro, an Italian immigrant from Marcianese, Italy. Her father, who owned a restaurant and dime store, died when she was eight. Her mother supported the family by sewing in the garment district (an area on the West Side of Manhattan between approximately 35th Street and 41st Street where clothing manufacturers traditionally located). Ferraro graduated from high school in 1952 at age 16.

Ferraro earned a college degree through scholarships at Marymount Manhattan College, a Catholic women's college. She completed her B.A. degree in English in 1956. After graduating, Ferraro taught second grade while attending law school classes at night at Fordham University. She was one of two women in a class of 200 men. Several of her classmates resented her presence, and some male professors believed she was taking a man's rightful place in law school.

In 1960, she completed her J.D. degree at Fordham with honors, then married real-estate broker John Zaccaro. She retained her maiden name in honor of her mother and split the first fee that she collected as an attorney with her mother. Ferraro had three children and for a dozen years worked primarily in her home.

From 1974 to 1978, she was an assistant district attorney in Queens, New York. She worked in the Special Victims Bureau, handling many child abuse, domestic violence, and sexual assault cases. Her experiences during these few years turned her into a liberal.

Ferraro served in the U.S. House of Representatives from 1979 to 1985, representing Queens, a largely ethnic and blue-collar district. She was one of only 17 congresswomen in office at the time. Speaker of the House Thomas P. "Tip" O'Neill served as her mentor. By her third term, she was serving on the House budget committee. Her voting record was that of a mainstream liberal Democrat. She took a pro-choice stance on abortion despite her Roman Catholic background. John Cardinal O'Connor publicly chastised her for her views. However, Ferraro would not agree to impose the teachings of the Catholic Church on the issue of abortion on the general public, which is comprised of many faiths. The Catholic Church had never attacked Catholic male politicians such as Ted Kennedy, who held similar views on abortion. In 1982, she cosponsored the Economic Equity Act, which, had it been successful, would have achieved many of the goals of the defeated Equal Rights Amendment (ERA). She was reelected in 1980 and again in 1982 with 73 percent of the vote. However, she sometimes had difficulty using the House members' entrance because the House guards did not recognize her.

In 1984, she became the first female vice-presidential candidate nominated by a major political party. At the time, the gender gap, the difference between men's and women's voting preferences, was being widely discussed in the media. Democratic presidential candidate Walter Mondale had considered two other women as potential running mates: Kentucky governor Martha Layne Collins and San Francisco mayor DIANNE FEINSTEIN. In her accept-ance speech at the Democratic National Convention, Ferraro noted, "By choosing a woman to run for our nation's second highest office, you send a powerful signal to all Americans. There are no doors we cannot unlock." Within weeks after her nomination, the House Ethics Committee began investigating her husband's finances. Ferraro recalled, "I really didn't expect all the slurs and innuendos about being Italian." The Mondale-Ferraro ticket lost to incumbents Ronald Reagan and George H. W. Bush, but her candidacy had made history. As Senator Edward Kennedy of Massachusetts noted, "By his choice of Geraldine Ferraro, Walter Mondale has already done more for this country in one short day than Ronald Reagan has done in four long years." As Mondale himself acknowledged in his concession speech, "We didn't win, but we made history. And that fight has just begun."

In 1985, Ferraro received a $1 million advance for writing her campaign memoir, titled *Ferraro: My Story*. She sought the Democratic nomination for the U.S. Senate from the state of New York in 1992, but lost by one percentage point to Robert Abrams in a race that also included popular New York City politicians Elizabeth Holtzman and the Reverend Al Sharpton. In 1993, President Bill Clinton appointed Ferraro as the U.S. representative to the United Nations Human Rights Commission. In 1996 she became cohost of the CNN television show *Crossfire*. She lost another Senate bid in 1998 to Representative Charles Schumer.

In June 2001, Ferraro made public that she had been diagnosed with multiple myeloma, a blood cancer, in December 1998. She went public in part because she was being treated with thalidomide, known for causing serious birth defects in the 1950s in Europe where it was used to treat morning sickness. The United States had blocked the drug in 1960, but now doctors are experimenting with it for treatment of cancer and other illnesses.

As of 2001, she worked at Weber McGinn, a lobbying firm based in Arlington, Virginia, and as a commentator on Fox News. Geraldine Ferraro was the first female vice-presidential candidate on a major party ticket, one indicator of the growing influence of women in politics.

Further Reading

Dwyer, Jim. "Ferraro Is Battling Blood Cancer with a Potent Ally: Thalidomide." *New York Times,* June 19, 2001, B1, B4.

Ferraro, Geraldine. *Changing History: Women, Power, and Politics.* Wakefield, R.I.: Moyer Bell Ltd., 1998.

———. *Framing a Life: A Family Memoir.* New York: Scribner, 1998.

Peterson, Bill. "Candidate Ferraro." *Washington Post,* July 20, 1999, C13.

Rosin, Hanna. "Geraldine Ferraro." *New York* 31 (February 2, 1998): 22.

Russell, Jan. "Geraldine Ferraro." *Working Woman* 21 (November/December 1996): 28–31.

 ## FLYNN, ELIZABETH GURLEY
(1890–1964)   *Labor Activist*

Elizabeth Gurley Flynn, a radical political activist for more than five decades, was known as "the Rebel Girl" of the Industrial Workers of the World (IWW), a radical labor organization. Elizabeth Gurley Flynn was born on August 7, 1890, in Concord, New Hampshire. Her parents were Irish nationalists and socialists. She was raised in poor New England textile-mill towns and in the blue-collar Bronx borough of New York City. Her mother, Annie Gurley Flynn, was a member of the Knights of Labor and the Irish Feminist Club in New York City. Her father, Thomas Flynn, belonged to the Socialist Labor Party and joined the IWW.

Flynn joined the IWW when she was 16 years old, and that year at the Harlem Socialist Club she made her first public speech: "What Socialism Will Do for Women." She joined the striking miners in the iron range of Minnesota in 1907, then traveled to Spokane, Washington, where she was jailed twice for her radical speeches.

The next year she became active in the free speech fights of 1909. Free speech fights occurred in cities where ordinances were passed to forbid street meetings near employment agencies, where labor organizers and the unemployed often demonstrated. Challengers to the ordinances would stand on crates and read part of the Constitution of the United States or the Bill of Rights. Flynn took part in 26 such confrontations between 1909 and 1916. She once explained her attraction to the IWW by saying: "My father and mother were Socialists, members of the Socialist Party. So all of us of the younger generation were impatient with it. We felt it was rather stodgy. Its leaders were, if you will pardon me for saying so, professors, lawyer, doctors, ministers, and middle-aged and older people, and we felt a desire to have something more militant, more progressive and more youthful and so we flocked into the new organization, the IWW."

She married an IWW organizer from Minnesota, Jack Jones, in 1908 and had two children, though only one survived infancy. The marriage ended after two years.

Flynn gained a national reputation during the 1912 textile strike in Lawrence, Massachusetts, which was also known as the Bread and Roses Strike. When hours in the mills were reduced to 54 per week, wages were cut correspondingly, and a spontaneous strike of the largely female and child labor force occurred. Fourteen thousand workers went on strike, leaving the mills empty for three months. Flynn worked as an organizer in the strike. While working in Lawrence, she met anarchist Carlo Tresca, with whom she lived for 13 years.

From 1910 to 1917, she worked as an organizer for the IWW and was attracted to their philosophy that the problems of women could not be separated from those of the working class. She was arrested in 1917 during World War I, with 168 other IWW members, for alleged violation of the Espionage Act. Next, she helped organize defense committees during the first Red Scare of 1919, when hundreds of radicals were arrested and imprisoned. In 1920, she founded and chaired the International Labor Defense for Sacco and Vanzetti, two Italian anarchists accused of a Massachusetts robbery and murder. She headed their defense committee for seven years, until their execution in August 1927. Exhausted after her work on the Sacco and Vanzetti case, she spent a decade recovering her health in Portland, Oregon.

She was a founding member of the American Civil Liberties Union (ACLU) in 1920 and served on its board of directors until 1940. In 1937, she joined the Communist Party, and three years later the ACLU board, in a purge of communist members, expelled her.

She wrote a biweekly column for the *Daily Worker* and served as chair of the Communist Party's women's commission for 10 years. She ran unsuccessfully for a Bronx congressional seat in New York in 1942, and later ran unsuccessfully for a seat on the city council, using the slogan, "Clean Jim Crow out of New York." She believed that in spite of unsuccessful electoral campaigns, her presence helped move mainstream groups toward more progressive ideas.

In 1951, she and other Communist Party leaders were prosecuted under the Smith Act for their political views. The 1940 Smith Act banned the advocacy of the overthrow of the government and was used to suppress communists and other leftist groups in the United States. Smith and other communists were convicted of violating the Smith Act. Her supporters argued for her right of free speech to express her political views. She served two and one-half years in Alderson Prison in West Virginia. Her autobiography, *I Speak My Own Piece,* and a memoir of her time in prison, *Alderson Story,* were published during her incarceration. Flynn could have accepted deportation to the Soviet Union rather than prison, but her life goal was to work to improve her own country. In 1961, at age 71, she became the first female chairperson of the Communist Party in America, a position she held until her death three years later.

In 1962, the U.S. State Department revoked her passport. In response, Flynn and historian Herbert Aptheker a communist and acquaintance of Flynn, brought a successful lawsuit all the way to the U.S. Supreme Court, which ruled that her passport could not be withheld because of her political beliefs. After regaining her passport, Flynn took her first trip to the Soviet Union and other communist countries in Eastern Europe.

Elizabeth Gurley Flynn died of gastroenterocolitis while visiting Moscow in 1964. She received a state funeral in Red Square, and then, as she had requested, her remains were flown home for burial in Chicago's Waldheim Cemetery, near the graves of labor leader Big Bill Haywood and the Haymarket martyrs, labor leaders who were framed for throwing a bomb and hanged in 1887. In 1976, the ACLU rescinded her expulsion posthumously. She remained an unabashed radical throughout her life, steadfast in her commitment to justice.

Further Reading

Camp, Helen. *Iron in Her Soul: Elizabeth Gurley Flynn and the American Left.* Pullman: Washington State University Press, 1995.

Flynn, Elizabeth Gurley. *Words on Fire: The Life and Writing of Elizabeth Gurley Flynn.* Piscataway, N.J.: Rutgers University Press, 1987.

Voice of the Rebel Worker. Available online. URL: http://www.geocities.com/CapitolHill/5202/. Downloaded on January 3, 2001.

 ## FRIEDAN, ELIZABETH NAOMI GOLDSTEIN (Betty Friedan)
(1921–) *Founder of the National Organization for Women (NOW)*

Betty Friedan, a founder of the National Organization for Women (NOW), wrote *The Feminine Mystique* in 1963. Her book launched the modern women's movement. Elizabeth Naomi Goldstein was born in Peoria, Illinois, on February 4, 1921. Her mother, Miriam Horowitz, was raised in a wealthy family and had been editor of the women's page of a local newspaper before her marriage. Her father, Harry Goldstein, was a Jewish immigrant from Russia who owned Goldsteins' Jewelry Store. Betty's mother, Mirram, had wanted to attend Smith College, but at her parents' insistence she attended a local college in Illinois.

Betty skipped the second and fourth grades. She was such a bookworm that her father limited her reading to five books a week. While she was in high school, she founded a literary magazine and was valedictorian of her class. Despite these accomplishments, her high school experience also had negative aspects. She was ostracized because she was Jewish. During her junior year in high school she read a biography about Marie Curie and felt inspired, but a teacher squelched her enthusiasm by telling her there was no future in science for girls. She was advised to consider a career as a doctor's receptionist or a lab technician instead.

She attended Smith College, where once again she felt snubbed because of her Jewish background. As editor in chief of the college newspaper, she wrote an exposé on the snobbery of wealthy, eastern white Anglo-Saxon Protestant (WASP) students. However, the college president threatened to expel reporters if the story appeared in the paper, and the students decided to drop the story. Nevertheless Betty Goldstein made her point by including a blank page in the paper which she had stamped with the word *censored.*

A psychology major, she graduated summa cum laude in 1942 as class valedictorian. Her Russian Jewish father, fearing his daughter would be ashamed of him, did not attend the graduation ceremony.

She won a research fellowship to pursue graduate work in psychology with the noted psychoanalyst Erik Erikson at the University of California, Berkeley. One year later she returned to New York City, where she worked as a labor reporter for *The Federated Press.* She earned the same salary as workers on factory lines. Consequently, she wrote scathing articles about the unequal pay women received and the unfair opportunities for promotion that women experienced. She wrote a 40-page pamphlet during this time, explaining how lower wages for female workers undermined the wages of males. Many considered unions controversial, so her activist writings on behalf of workers appeared as the first entries in Federal Bureau of Investigation (FBI) files that were compiled on her.

In 1947, she married Carl Friedan, returning to work after the birth of their first child. She was fired when her employer discovered her second pregnancy. Friedan became a housewife in an 11-room home in suburban Rockland County, New York. She was not a conventional housewife, however, as she continued working as a freelance writer for women's magazines such as *Redbook* and *Ladies' Home Journal.* Her daughter was expelled from a carpool because Friedan sent a taxi to pick up the children when it was her turn to drive.

In 1957, Friedan sent questionnaires to her Smith College classmates regarding their upcoming 15th class reunion. She received 200 responses to her questionnaire. Eighty-nine percent of the alumni were housewives. The main regret they expressed to Friedan was not being able to apply their education to professional work. Friedan submitted an article based on this research to women's magazines, but her work was rejected. The male editors at *McCall's* would not even consider her efforts. *Redbook* editors told her only sick women would identify with her conclusions. But the publisher W.W. Norton gave her a $1,000 advance to write a book based on her study. She spent five years completing the book, which became the best-seller *The Feminine Mystique,* published in 1963. In her book, Friedan examined the ways in which women were restricted to subservient roles and labeled the discouraging frustration faced by white, middle-class housewives as "the problem that has no name." She called the concentration of women in suburbia a "comfortable concentration camp," a seemingly exaggerated description of the experience of white, middle-class women. Her book was seen as a landmark that brought about the rebirth of U.S. feminism. A sociologist described it as "one of those rare books, which launches a major social movement." The book sold more than 3 million copies and was translated into 13 languages. Excerpts were printed in *Ladies' Home Journal, Good Housekeeping, Mademoiselle,* and *McCall's.* Friedan faced public ridicule and threats of bodily harm because of her standpoint.

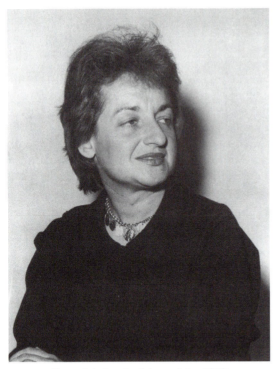

Betty Friedan, feminist activist, 1960
(Prints & Photographs Division,
Library of Congress, Washington, D.C.)

In 1966, she cofounded NOW and served as its president. The group had its genesis at a national gathering of the federal government's Equal Employment Opportunity Council (EEOC), which she had decided to report on. A small group, frustrated with the unwillingness of the EEOC to enforce sexual discrimination laws, met in her hotel room. The following day the 32 founding members drew up plans for NOW on a paper napkin during their lunch break. They called the group the National Organization for Women, not *of* women, because they did not wish to exclude men.

The organization started with $135 in its treasury. NOW's first success in 1967 brought an end to the practice of gender-specific help-wanted ads through an EEOC ruling, but it took a year of picketing the *New York Times* before that newspaper would comply.

Another early issue that NOW dealt with was the discrimination faced by airline stewardesses, who were forced to retire when they reached age 30 or got married.

Splits in NOW occurred over the group's support of abortion rights and lesbian visibility. Friedan was one of the leaders who initially refused to support lesbian visibility in the organization, believing such a stance would harm the movement.

Friedan's marriage was marred by domestic violence. She occasionally used makeup to cover her black eyes when she appeared at events. Friedan feared divorce because of the stereotype of feminists breaking up marriages and families. After 22 years, however, Friedan's marriage was dissolved in 1969. Much as she had feared, her ex-husband told the press, "She hates men. Let's face it, they all do—all those activists in the women's lib movement."

Friedan was also a cofounder of the National Abortion Rights Action League (NARAL) in 1969 as well as an organizer of the Women's Strike for Equality in 1970. At the 1970 annual NOW convention, Friedan revealed her plans for a nationwide demonstration in support of women's rights to take place on August 26—the 50th anniversary of women's suffrage. Women gathered in cities across the nation, 50,000 in New York City alone. The demands of the women's strike were free abortion on demand, free 24-hour child care centers, and equal opportunity in education and jobs. Friedan stepped down as head of NOW in 1970. By the time she left, NOW had grown to 3,000 members. In 1971, Friedan helped cofound the National Women's Political Caucus (NWPC).

After leaving NOW, Friedan worked as a visiting professor, teaching classes in sociology at both Temple University and Queens College. She was also a visiting lecturer at Yale University. Her 1976 book *It Changed My Life* was a collection of articles on the women's movement. In her 1981 book *The Second Stage,* Friedan critiqued "the feminist mystique" and asserted that the focus on the rights of lesbians and women of color had alienated mainstream women from the women's movement and groups such as NOW. In 1993, she authored a book called *The Fountain of Age* in which she addressed the mystique of aging. In 1997 she wrote *Beyond Gender: The New Politics of Work and Family.* In 1998 the Academy of the Arts in New York recognized her with a Lifetime Achievement Award for Literary Arts. She published an autobiography, *Life So Far,* in 2000, and was also the subject of a documentary, *Intimate Portrait: Betty Friedan.* NOW, which Friedan founded, remains the largest feminist organization in the United States.

Further Reading

Friedan, Betty. *Beyond Gender: The New Politics of Work and Family.* Washington, D.C.: Woodrow Wilson Center Press, 1997.

———. *The Feminine Mystique.* New York: W.W. Norton, 1963.

———. *It Changed My Life: Writings on the Women's Movement.* New York: Random House, 1976.

———. *Life So Far: A Memoir.* New York: Simon and Schuster, 2000.

———. *The Second Stage.* New York: Summit Books, 1981.

Hennessee, Judith Adler. *Betty Friedan: Her Life.* New York: Random House, 1999.

Horowitz, Daniel. *Betty Friedan And the Making of the Feminine Mystique.* Amherst: University of Massachusetts Press, 1998.

FULLER, SARAH MARGARET
(1810–1850) *Journalist*

Margaret Fuller was both the first professional literary critic and the first female foreign correspondent in the United States. Sarah Margaret Fuller was born on May 23, 1810, in Cambridge, Massachusetts. Her Harvard-educated lawyer-legislator father, Timothy Fuller, was disappointed that his first child was a girl. Colleges were not open to women at the time, so her father educated her at home. Unlike most women of her era, she was taught a classical curriculum usually considered to be exclusively for white males. She was reading classics in Latin before most other children even

learned the alphabet. Fuller attended a finishing school in Groton, Connecticut. By the time she was 20, she was already a part of the intellectual society in Cambridge and at Harvard.

She was hired by Bronson Alcott, the father of author Louisa May Alcott, to teach in his Temple School. She then taught for a couple of years in Providence, Rhode Island, at the Green Street School.

Fuller returned to Boston in 1839 and for the next several years earned a living by holding intellectual seminars in her home, the majority of which were for women only. Since social mores strongly discouraged women from speaking publicly, Fuller did not identify her talks, which trained middle-class women in philosophy and argument, as lectures.

She was also a member of the Transcendental Club, a new literary movement with political overtones. Transcendentalism denounced the limited roles of women. Other club members were Bronson Alcott, Ralph Waldo Emerson, and other New England intellectuals.

With Emerson, Fuller cofounded and edited the nation's first literary journal, the *Dial,* a quarterly publication of the transcendentalist movement.

Fuller published an essay in the *Dial* in 1843, and in 1844 she published her first book, *Summer on the Lakes.* After the publication of her book, publisher Horace Greeley offered her a job at the *New York Tribune* as literary critic, and she became the first U.S. woman to make a living as a journalist. She articulated her feminist theory in her next book, *Woman in the Nineteenth Century,* published in 1845. The book was based on her 1843 essay published in the *Dial* and titled "The Great Lawsuit: Man versus Men. Woman versus Women" in which she called for women's full equality: "Man cannot, by right, lay even well-meant restrictions on woman . . . what woman needs is to grow, as an intellect to discern, as a soul to live freely and unimpeded." Some historians believe her book spurred the formation of the Seneca Falls Women's Convention in 1849. As she explained: "I believe that at present women are the best helpers of one another. Let them think, let them act, till they know what they need. We only ask of men to remove arbitrary barriers."

For Fuller, transcendentalism offered a path to the liberation of women, with its emphasis on harmonious, androgynous individuals. Fuller asserted: "Male and female are perpetually passing into one another. . . . There is no wholly masculine man, no purely feminine women." In her book, she critiqued the institution of marriage and advocated free love. Her book even argued that prostitution was the consequence of antiquated courtship and marriage practices. Influenced by abolitionist thought, she wrote, "As the friend of the Negro assumes that one man cannot by right hold another in bondage, so should the friend of Woman assume that Man cannot by right lay even well-meant restrictions on Woman."

In 1846, Greeley promoted her to foreign correspondent for the *Tribune,* and in this capacity she traveled to England, France, and Italy. In 1847, she became involved in the revolutionary drive to unify Italy. She entered a relationship with revolutionary aristocrat Giovanni Angelo, Marchese d'Ossoli, and bore his child in 1848, when she was 38. They married a year later.

During the French siege of Rome, Fuller ran one of the hospitals in the city. Her experiences in Italy led her to accept and support socialism. The Roman republic was defeated in 1849, and the couple fled to Florence. While living in Florence, she worked on a history of the 1848 Italitian unification—a period of cultural nationalism.

On her return trip to the United States, the ship she was sailing on, the *Elizabeth,* sank near Fire Island, New York, on July 19, 1850, and all aboard drowned. Fuller died at sea at age 40. Friends searched for her body, but only the body of her two-year-old son was recovered. Friends published her memoirs and other writings posthumously, including in 1856 *At Home and Abroad,* a collection of her articles on Europe. Her intellectual gifts exhibited the potential all women might reach.

Further Reading

Fuller, Margaret. *The Letters of Margaret Fuller.* Ithaca, N.Y.: Cornell University Press, 1995.

———. *Margaret Fuller's New York Journalism: A Biographical Essay and Key Writings.* Nashville: University of Tennessee Press, 1995.

———. *The Portable Margaret Fuller.* New York: Penguin, 1994.

———. *The Woman and The Myth: Margaret Fuller's Life and Writings.* Boston, Mass.: Northeastern University Press, 1994.

———. *Woman in the Nineteenth Century.* Mineola, N.Y.: Dover, 1999.

Watson, David. *Margaret Fuller: An American Romantic.* New York: Berg, 1989.

G

 GILMAN, CHARLOTTE ANNA PERKINS STETSON
(1860–1935)   *Political Writer*

Charlotte Perkins Gilman was a best-selling feminist author of the late 19th and early 20th centuries. Charlotte Anna Perkins was born on July 3, 1860, in Hartford, Connecticut, the second child of Mary A. Fitch Westcott Perkins and Frederic Beecher Perkins, a librarian and magazine editor who came from the wealthy Beecher family. Both of her great aunts on her father's side, Harriet Beecher Stowe and Catharine Beecher, were well-known writers. Her father abandoned his daughter and wife shortly after Charlotte's birth, leaving them dependent on family charity. Poverty caused the family to move often. Charlotte's parents later divorced. Unlike most girls, young Charlotte was more interested in physical exercise and reading philosophy than in clothes and jewelry.

She attended the Rhode Island School of Design in 1878 and 1879. While still a teenager, she worked as a commercial artist and art teacher. She married artist Charles Walter Stetson when she was 24. The couple had a daughter nine months later, in 1885. After the birth of her daughter, Charlotte Stetson suffered from serious postpartum depression. Physicians at that time often treated women's illnesses by restricting them from physical activity, and her enforced seclusion resulted in a total breakdown. Her depression improved on a trip to California but then recurred a few months later when she returned to the Northeast. The couple separated in 1888 after four years of marriage and divorced in 1894. Charlotte Perkins refused to accept support from her ex-husband and tried to support herself, her daughter, and her mother by lecturing and writing.

One of her first published pieces was also one of her most famous, *The Yellow Wallpaper,* a fictional account of her mental breakdown presented with a feminist slant. First published in *New England Magazine,* it chronicled the nervous breakdown of a female artist tormented between her avocation as a writer and the demands of marriage and motherhood.

Charles Stetson, her ex-husband, married her close friend Grace Ellery Channing, and Perkins sent her and Charles's nine-year-old daughter to live with them in 1894.

In 1895, Perkins lived at Hull-House in Chicago for a few months and honed her interest in economic issues. But unlike Hull-House founder JANE ADDAMS, she was not at ease living among the poor. Perkins abandoned the idea of becoming a social worker and cited depression as her reason for leaving Hull-House after just three months. She referred to the environment at Hull-House as "Little Hell."

In 1898, she published *Women and Economics,* which was originally titled *Economic Relation of the Sexes as a Factor in Social Development.* This was her first and what many consider her best nonfiction work. She argued that the primary vehicle of women's oppression was their economic dependence on men. She noted that institutions such as religion, education, marriage, and the family reinforced this subordination. *Women and Economics* proposed that women's true liberation could only occur through economic independence. She believed that women's work in the home was central to their exploitation. That belief caused her to support ideas about communal living, model communities, and kitchenless apartments. She proposed using multifamily buildings with staffs hired to care for cooking, laundry, and children. She compared marriage to prostitution, insisting they both involve an exchange of money for sex. Some of her writing criticized the mixing of races or nations. Her later works on sexuality, birth control, and eugenics expressed some racism, ethnocentrism, anti-Semitism, and nativism.

Her second marriage was to a younger cousin, Houghton Gilman. The couple lived in New York. In 1909, she began publishing the magazine *Forerunner,* which lasted for seven years and 86 issues. The most famous features were her utopian pieces, especially *Herland,* a futuristic vision of an all-female feminist society that reproduced through parthenogenesis. A frequent theme in *Herland* was women ridding themselves of illness or male domination by joining the workforce, similar in some respects to the ideas BETTY FRIEDAN would express several decades later in her 1963 book *The Feminine Mystique.*

Gilman's other books included *Moving and Mountain* in 1911, *With Her in Ourland* (a sequel to *Herland*) in 1916, and *His Religion and Hers* in 1923.

The decline of the progressive era and of feminism, after the passage of suffrage, made Gilman's works less popular. She was a professed Fabian socialist who condemned capitalism. (Fabians were a British socialist group who believed that class conflict could be addressed by existing political institutions rather than by violent revolutions. They helped create the Labour Party and remain active as a research and policy advocacy group.) Gilman was horrified by the sexual freedoms of the Roaring Twenties and believed that the influence of Freud would increase the sexual exploitation of women. Her writings were out of print by the time of her death but were rediscovered in the 1970s with the rebirth of modern feminism. The Feminist Press reprinted *The Yellow Wallpaper* in 1973, allowing a new generation to examine her ideas.

After her husband died in 1934, she discovered she had breast cancer. Her autobiography, which she had written in 1925, was published posthumously in 1935 under the title *The Living of Charlotte Perkins Gilman.* When her cancer was deemed incurable, she took her own life on August 17, 1935, at age 75, in Pasadena, California. In a final note, she wrote, "When one is assured of unavoidable and imminent death, it is the simplest of human rights to choose a quick and easy death in place of a slow and horrible one." Her works continue to influence new generations of feminists.

Further Reading

Gilman, Charlotte Perkins. *The Abridged Diaries of Charlotte Perkins Gilman.* Richmond: University Press of Virginia, 1997.

———. *Charlotte Perkins Gilman: A Nonfiction Reader.* New York: Columbia University Press, 1991.

———. *Herland, the Yellow Wallpaper, and Selected Writings.* New York: Penguin, 1999.

———. *The Living of Charlotte Perkins Gilman: An Autobiography.* Madison: University of Wisconsin Press, 1991.

Golden, Catherine. *The Captive Imagination: A Casebook on the Yellow Wallpaper.* New York: Feminist Press, 1992.

Lane, Ann. *To Herland and Beyond: The Life and Work of Charlotte Perkins Gilman.* Richmond: University Press of Virginia, 1997.

GINSBURG, RUTH BADER
(Joan Ruth Bader)
(1933–) *Supreme Court Justice*

Ruth Bader Ginsburg headed the women's rights project for the American Civil Liberties Union (ACLU) and argued half a dozen gender equity cases before the U.S. Supreme Court, before becoming a justice of the Supreme Court herself in 1993. She is the second woman to serve in this position. She was born Joan Ruth Bader on March 15, 1933, in the Brooklyn, New York, neighborhood of Flatbush, the second child of Celia and Nathan Bader. Her grandparents were Jewish immigrants who had escaped pogroms (massacres of Jews) in Russia and eastern Europe. During Ruth's childhood, she experienced discrimination: Some stores carried signs that read "No Jews Allowed." Her mother had wanted to attend college but was prevented from doing so by her father, who maintained that higher education was a waste for women. He sent Celia to work in New York City's garment district after she finished high school at age 15. Celia's earnings paid for her brother's college tuition.

Nathan Bader ran a small business as a furrier and haberdasher in Brooklyn. Tragedy struck the family when Ruth's older sister died from meningitis at age eight. Because she had been deprived of higher education, Celia Bader saved $8,000 for Ruth's college education. During her first year of high school Ruth learned that her mother had cervical cancer. The night before her high school graduation, her mother died at age 47. Ruth Bader did not attend her graduation the next day but instead made arrangements for her mother's funeral.

She entered Cornell University in 1950 on a full scholarship. She lived in a separate dormitory for Jewish girls that had been created by the university. She completed her B.A. degree in government studies in 1954. She then married Martin Ginsburg, whom she had met on a blind date, and had two children. Her husband came from a wealthy Long Island family. Ginsburg had planned to attend law school, possibly Harvard, but her

husband was in the army and was stationed at Fort Sill, Oklahoma, where they lived for two years. Though she had a degree from one of the best colleges in the nation, the only job she could find was that of a clerk-typist at the local social security office. When her supervisor discovered Ginsburg was pregnant, she was refused a promotion.

Following her husband's two-year army assignment, Ginsburg started at Harvard Law School. She was one of nine women in a class of 500. A Harvard dean invited the nine women to dinner and questioned them as to why they were taking places that could have gone to men. In addition, she was refused entry to Harvard's Lamont Library, as it was off-limits to females.

When her husband got a job in New York, the family relocated and she completed her degree at Columbia Law School, tying for first in her class. She served on the staff of the *Harvard Law Review* and *Columbia Law Review,* positions limited to the schools' top students. She had made law review at two Ivy League schools but after graduation found that "Not a single law firm in the entire city of New York bid for my employment." She was also turned down for a clerkship with Supreme Court justice Felix Frankfurter, who told her he was not ready to hire a woman. Ginsburg was the sole support of her family at this time, because her husband was being treated for a rare and usually fatal testicular cancer that had spread to four lymph nodes. Eventually, she found a job clerking for a federal judge for two years. After that, she wrote two books on Swedish law.

In 1963, she joined the faculty at Rutgers School of Law, becoming its second female law professor and one of only 20 in the nation. She was promoted to full professor in 1969. In 1971, she was hired by Harvard University to teach a course on women and the law. In 1972, she accepted a position at Columbia University, where she remained until 1980, and became the first woman hired there to receive tenure.

Ginsburg founded and served as volunteer director of the ACLU women's rights project. She won five of the six precedent-setting cases she argued before the U.S. Supreme Court including *Frontiero v. Richardson* in 1973; *Weinberger v. Wiesenfeld* in 1975; *Edwards v. Healy* in 1975; *Califano v. Goldfarb* in 1975; *Craig v. Boren* in 1976; and *Duren v. Missouri* in 1978. The cases addressed double standards for men and women in a number of areas including spousal social security benefits, jury duty, military benefits, and estate administration. Ginsburg was compared to Thurgood Marshall, the great civil rights lawyer who won landmark cases on racial discrimination before serving on the U.S. Supreme Court. In explaining her approach to gender equity, Ginsburg once stated, "If I had an affirmative action program to design, it would be to give men every incentive to be concerned about rearing children." She put her words into action by allowing male

Ruth Bader Ginsburg, justice of the U.S.
Supreme Court
(U.S. Supreme Court)

and female court clerks to have flexible work schedules that would allow them to share child care responsibilities.

In 1980, President Jimmy Carter appointed Ginsburg to the U.S. Court of Appeals for the District Columbia, the second highest level of the judicial system in the nation. She served on this bench for 13 years, during which time her rulings were not always viewed as liberal. For example, in 1984 she upheld the navy's and the Central Intelligence Agency's dismissal of gay employees solely on the basis of their sexual orientation.

In 1993, Justice Byron White retired from the Supreme Court and President Bill Clinton nominated Ginsburg to fill the vacant seat. Clinton was the first Democratic president to appoint a U.S. Supreme Court justice in a quarter of a century. The American Bar Association (ABA) gave Ginsburg their highest rating. During her nomination process she wore her mother's circle pin, as she had for all six of her previous arguments before the United States Supreme Court. She acknowledged: "My greatest inspiration was my own mother. She never had the opportunity to go to college, but she taught me to pursue learning. She gave me confidence in myself that is invaluable." Ginsburg was the second woman nominated to the U.S. Supreme Court; the first was Sandra Day O'Connor, nominated by President Ronald Reagan in 1981.

Ginsburg has been viewed as a centrist; she votes as often with her Republican colleagues as with her Democratic ones. At age 66, Ginsburg had surgery for colon cancer. She continues to serve as a justice on the U.S. Supreme Court. In her Supreme Court acceptance speech she acknowledged her mother's influence: "I want to thank my mother, Celia Bader, the bravest and strongest person I have known, who was taken from me too soon. I pray that I may be all that she would have been had she lived in an age when women could aspire and achieve and daughters are cherished as much as sons."

Further Reading

Comiskey, Michael. "The Case of Ruth Bader Ginsburg." *PS, Political Science and Politics* 27, no. 2 (June 1994): 224.

Ginsburg, Ruth. *The Supreme Court: A Place for Women.* Saint Louis, Mo.: Washington University, 2001.

Halberstam, M. "Ruth Bader Ginsburg." *Cardozo Law Review* 19, no. 4 (1998): 1441.

United States Senate. *Nomination of Ruth Bader Ginsburg.* Washington, D.C.: United States Government Printing Office, 1993.

GOLDMAN, EMMA
(1869–1940)   *Anarchist Leader, Writer*

Emma Goldman was one of the best-known women radicals in American history. In her annual lecture tours she spoke against government and organized religion and in favor of civil liberties, sexual freedom, free speech, unions, the eight-hour workday, feminism, and birth control. Emma Goldman was born on June 27, 1869, in Kovno, Russia, to lower-middle-class Lithuanian Jews, Taube Bienowitch Goldman and Abraham Goldman. She fled from Russia and an arranged marriage when she was 15. She settled in Rochester, New York, and married Jacob Kershner, thus gaining citizenship. Goldman worked in garment factories for $2.50 a week for four years.

Goldman started attending socialist meetings in Rochester and was spurred to activism by the Haymarket trial of 1886, in which eight anarchists were accused of setting a dynamite explosion that killed eight police officers. Four of the eight defendants were hanged.

In 1889, Goldman divorced her husband, moved to New York City, and joined the anarchist movement. Anarchism was a response to the growing size and power of economic and political institutions that accompanied 19th-century industrialization. As an anarchist Goldman believed that all governments were oppressive. She opposed all forms of institutionalized authority, including marriage.

She believed passionately in free speech and was jailed several times for exercising that right. In the severe depression of 1893, she told the unemployed that they had a "sacred right" to steal bread to feed their families and was promptly jailed for a year for this comment. Anarchist Leon Czolgosz blamed her and other anarchists for inciting his 1901 assassination of President William McKinley, though she had denounced the use of violence in 1900.

Goldman viewed the suffrage movement as merely wanting a piece of the pie in a system that was inherently corrupt and should be overthrown. She believed that it was the economic oppression of women within the capitalist system that kept them subordinate. In 1908, her ex-husband was stripped of his citizenship in a move that was motivated by determination to rescind the citizenship of "Red Emma," as she was called. One of her most influential essays, *The Traffic in Women,* written in 1910, argued that capitalism created unemployment and underpaid the labor of women, thereby forcing many women into prostitution. According to Goldman, the difference between marriage and prostitution was "merely a question of degree whether a woman sells herself to one man, in or out of marriage, or to many men." Goldman published *Anarchism, and Other Essays* in 1910 and *The Social Significance of Modern Drama* in 1914.

In 1916, she instructed a New York City audience in the use of contraceptives and was arrested once again. Her support of birth control was based on her familiarity with overpopulated immigrant slums and the frequency of early maternal deaths.

Viewing World War I as imperialist, Goldman expressed strong pacifist views. With her partner, anarchist Alexander Berkman, Goldman organized the No-Conscription League to resist the draft. In 1917, she served two years in prison for urging men to refuse their draft notices. Due to wartime censorship, in 1917 the government shut down publication of the periodical she had founded in 1906, *Mother Earth,* which alluded to her idea of nurturing a better world.

She was deported to the Soviet Union with other radicals during the Red Scare of 1919 and subsequently became one of the first leftists to condemn the new Soviet system. She was disappointed with the Communist, or Bolshevik, Revolution in Russia and found no free speech there. In the end, she was as critical of Lenin's Communist state as she was of capitalism. She published *My Disillusionment in Russia* in 1923.

Goldman married a Welsh miner in 1925 in order to obtain British citizenship. She published two volumes of her autobiography, *Living My Life,* in 1931. She returned to the United States only once, for a brief visit in 1934. She spent her last few years raising funds in Canada to fight Francisco Franco's fascist regime in Spanish Civil War. She worked in London and Madrid on behalf of the Spanish Republican government.

Emma Goldman died in Toronto, Ontario, Canada, on May 14, 1940. The U.S. government allowed her to be buried next to the graves of the four men who had been hanged in the Haymarket trial. Emma Goldman had devoted her life to addressing injustice through radical politics.

Emma Goldman, socialist and radical
(Prints & Photographs Division,
Library of Congress, Washington, D.C.)

Further Reading

Chalberg, John. *Emma Goldman: American Individualist.* New York: HarperCollins, 1991.

Falk, Candace. *Love, Anarchy, and Emma Goldman.* New Brunswick, N.J.: Rutgers University Press, 1990.

Goldman, Emma. *Anarchism, and Other Essays.* 1910. Mineola, N.Y.: Dover, 1970.

Haaland, Bonnie. *Emma Goldman: Sexuality and the Impurity of the State.* New York: Black Rose, 1993.

Morton, Marian. *Emma Goldman and the American Left.* New York: Twayne, 1992.

University of California, Berkeley. "Emma Goldman Papers Project." Available online. URL: http://sunsite.berkeley.edu/Goldman/project.html. Posted on April 25, 1996.

GRASSO, ELLA ROSA GIOVANNI OLIVA TAMBUSSI
(1919–1981) *Governor*

Ella Grasso was the first woman elected governor of a state without first succeeding her husband into the office. Ella Rosa Giovanni Oliva Tambussi was born on May 10, 1919, in Windsor Locks, Connecticut, to Italian immigrant parents. She completed her primary schooling in private and parochial schools. In 1940, she completed her B.A. degree and in 1942, her M.A. degree from Mount Holyoke, a private women's college in South Hadley, Massachusetts. The summer following her graduation she married Thomas Grasso, a school principal. They had two children. Around this time, Grasso first became active in politics, working for the League of Women Voters in 1943. She also worked for the Democratic Party in many capacities, including speechwriter. During World War II she worked as the assistant director of research in communication for the Federal War Manpower Commission.

Grasso had to overcome religious prejudice against Catholics and sexism against women when seeking political office. She was elected to the Connecticut state legislature in 1952 and reelected in 1954. She became the first woman elected as floor leader in the state body in 1955. In 1958, she began serving the first of what would be three consecutive terms as secretary of state in Connecticut. She was a leader in the development of a new state constitution that went into effect in 1960. In 1970, Grasso was elected to the U.S. House of Representatives. She was reelected to a second term in 1972. She usually voted along liberal Democratic lines, supporting a minimum wage, the Equal Rights Amendment, welfare, and benefits for veterans and the elderly. She opposed reproductive rights and affirmative action. While in Congress she worked for the Emergency Employment Act of 1971 and the Higher Education Act of 1972. She also worked for passage of appropriations for sickle-cell anemia (a genetic blood disorder mainly affecting African Americans) and assisted in drafting the Comprehensive Employment and Training Act.

In 1974, Grasso was elected governor of Connecticut, the first woman to be elected on her own merit. In 1924, NELLIE ROSS had been elected governor of Wyoming in order to complete her husband's term after his death, but she failed to gain reelection. Miriam Amanda Ferguson had been elected governor of Texas in 1921 to finish her husband's term, but she was impeached.

Grasso was an extremely popular governor, winning reelection in 1978 with more than 75 percent of the votes. Grasso returned $7,000 of her salary to the state treasury as a gesture that the cuts she planned to make in state government would start with her own paycheck. Her austerity budget only allowed spending on programs mandated by law and for necessary facilities such as hospitals. Through these measures she was able to balance the state budget, create a surplus, and avoid implementing a state income tax. In the 1978 blizzard that hit the state, she directed emergency operations around the clock at the state armory. She was openly feminist and worked with Congressional representative BELLA ABZUG of New York on the International Women's Conference of 1975.

In 1980, at the middle of her second term, Grasso announced that she was resigning from office due to a diagnosis of ovarian cancer. She died in Hartford, Connecticut, on February 5, 1981. She

Governor Ella Grasso, 1978
(From the 1978 Connecticut State Register
and Manuals Secretary of State, Hartford, Conn.)

was buried in St. Mary's Cemetery, in Windsor Locks, Connecticut. She never lost an election.

Further Reading

Purmont, Jon. "Ella Grasso: As She Saw Herself." *Connecticut Review* 17 (spring 1995): 23–29.
Women in Congress. "Ella Tambussi Grasso." Available online: URL: http://clerkweb.house.gov/womenvio/ Bio/grasso.htm. Downloaded on January 3, 2001.

GRIFFITHS, MARTHA WRIGHT
(1912–)   *Congressional Representative*

Martha Griffiths, a congressional representative known as the "Mother of the ERA," became

Michigan's first female lieutenant governor. Martha Wright was born in Pier City, Missouri, in 1912 in a family with two children. Her father, Eldridge Wright, was a letter carrier; her paternal grandmother had been an active suffragist. Martha's mother, Nellie Sullinger Wright, worked as a substitute postal carrier and took in boarders to finance her daughter's education.

Martha Wright attended the University of Missouri. While in college she worked for the campus radio station and also captained the debate team, as she had in high school. In her sophomore year at the university she met Hicks George Griffiths. They married in 1933. Her husband had been admitted to Harvard but chose to attend the University of Michigan Law School instead, because it admitted women. The couple both attended the law school, and in 1940 they were the first married couple to graduate from that school. They worked for the American Automobile Insurance Company after graduation, but Griffiths was paid $10 less per week than her husband. The couple eventually opened a private law practice.

Griffiths was unsuccessful in her first run for public office in 1946 when she ran as a candidate for the Michigan House of Representatives. She was elected two years later and served two terms as a member of the Michigan legislature from 1949 to 1952. She was one of only two women out of 100 state representatives in the legislature. Her male colleagues praised her, saying that she "reasoned like a man." In 1952, she served for two years as a judge in Detroit—the first female to do so. She was elected to Congress in 1954 and reelected for the next 20 years.

Griffiths was an ardent supporter of women's issues and a sponsor of the Equal Rights Amendment (ERA). One of her greatest successes was the passage of the landmark 1964 Civil Rights Act, which included legislation against sex discrimination. This victory for women's rights occurred because a conservative southern representative, Howard Smith, believed erroneously that the best way to prevent civil rights legislation banning racial discrimination from passing was to add legislation regarding sex discrimination. Although Smith introduced the sex-discrimination provision, Griffiths is considered its author. Griffiths explained, "I used Smith." When he offered the amended piece of legislation as a joke the House floor accordingly erupted with laughter. After the votes were cast, however, the amendment had passed with sex discrimination included in its provisions. Once the legislation was enacted, however, there were still difficulties, because the Equal Employment Opportunity Commission (EEOC) refused to enforce the law regarding sex discrimination. Griffith also led hearings on the Equal Pay Act of 1963.

In 1966, Griffiths was asked to serve as honorary president of the National Organization for Women (NOW), but she declined, instead serving on its advisory board. She ran hearings on discrimination that airline stewardesses faced in being fired if they married or turned 30. She asked an airline executive during the hearing, "What are you running, Mr. Mason, an airline or a whorehouse?" A former congressional colleague recalls her advocacy of women's rights and stated, "I remember her fight for the stewardesses. . . . And whenever I see an older stewardess, I think of Martha."

It was Griffith's 1973 petition that got the ERA out of the Judiciary Committee, where it had been ignored for decades. As she stated, "I seek justice— not in some distant tomorrow, not by some study commission, but now while I live." Democratic support for the amendment outnumbered Republican support by three to one. Griffiths went to House Minority Leader Gerald Ford and "told him I felt sure I would get enough signers, and it would look very bad if there were not more Republicans." Ford lined up 17 Republicans to support the petition, and it passed. The House passed the ERA by a vote of 315 to 15; 64 members refrained from voting. A strong anti-ERA lobby immediately formed that included Eagle Forum leader PHYLLIS SCHLAFLY. They argued that women would now be drafted and unisex bathrooms would replace separate facilities for men and women. Griffiths termed this strategy the "potty argument." The

ERA was ultimately defeated—too few states ratifred it to make it part of the Constitution.

Griffiths sponsored legislation to outlaw the discrimination women faced in obtaining credit, insurance, education, and social security payments. She holds 29 honorary Ph.D.s. She retired from public life for a few years, then, at 71, returned in 1983 to serve two terms as lieutenant governor of Michigan. Martha Griffiths advanced the cause of the ERA and women's rights as one of the most effective early feminist legislators.

Further Reading

George, Emily. *Martha W. Griffiths.* Washington, D.C.: University Press of America, 1982.

National Women's Hall of Fame. "Martha Wright Griffiths." Available online. URL: http://www.greatwomen.org/griffiths.htm. Downloaded on January 6, 2001.

Veteran Feminists of America. "Martha Griffiths." Available online. URL: http://www.bizwomen.com/VFOA/vios/g002.html. Downloaded on January 6, 2001.

 ## GRIMKÉ, ANGELINA EMILY
(1805–1879) *Abolitionist, Writer*

Daughter of a prominent South Carolina slaveholding family, Angelina Grimké moved north in the 1820s and became one of the first women to speak publicly on behalf of abolition and women's rights. Angelina Grimké was born on November 26, 1805, in Charleston, South Carolina, the daughter of a well-known South Carolina judge. She lived her entire life with her sister Sarah, who was 13 years older than she. Sarah was her godmother and acted as a surrogate mother to her. Their father, Judge John Faucheraud Grimké, fought in the Revolutionary War, served in the South Carolina legislature, and operated a large cotton plantation. Their mother, Mary Smith Grimké, came from an upper-class family in Charleston. They were raised as Episcopalians. Slaves served as nursemaids to all 14 of the Grimké children. The girls were not allowed a secondary education. They read Bible stories to slave children but were not allowed to teach the slaves to read the stories because that was against the law.

Sarah traveled to Philadelphia for a visit and became a Quaker, a member of the Society of Friends religious organization, many of whom were opposed to slavery. Sarah found she could no longer live in the South because of the slavery there, and when she returned to Philadelphia in 1829, Angelina went with her, and she also became a Quaker and opposed slavery. Her religious beliefs influenced her commitment to antislavery activism. Grimké became active in the abolitionist movement in 1833, telling William Lloyd Garrison, "This is a cause worth dying for." In addition to supporting an end to slavery, she also criticized racism in the North. She became a brilliant speaker for the American Anti-Slavery Society, one of the first women to speak publicly. Women who spoke in public to audiences of men and women were still controversial figures, and Grimké faced open opposition by the clergy as well. The Massachusetts clergy published a pastoral letter in 1837 that was read from pulpits in churches across the state. It claimed, in part, that when a woman "assumed the place and tone of man as public reformer . . . her character becomes unnatural." She wrote, "The Bible then is the book I want you to read in the spirit of inquiry, and the spirit of prayer. Even the enemies of Abolitionists, acknowledge that their doctrines are drawn from it."

In 1836, Grimké published a book, *Appeal to the Christian Women of the South,* that outlined her objections to slavery. The book was expanded from a letter she had originally published in 1835 in William Lloyd Garrison's abolitionist newspaper, *The Liberator.* She declared, "But perhaps you will be ready to query, why appeal to women on this subject? We do not make the laws, which perpetuate slavery. No legislative power is vested in us; we can do nothing to overthrow the system, even if we wished to do so. To this I reply, I know you do not make the laws, but I also know that you are the wives and mothers, the sisters and daughters of those who do; and if you really suppose you can do nothing to overthrow slavery, you are greatly mistaken."

Grimké's book was the first antislavery work to be authored by a southerner for southerners. The fact that Grimké had grown up in the South and came from a respectable family underlined the huge impact of her work. Grimké was convinced that the women of the South could overthrow the system of slavery and urged those she addressed to teach their servants to read, pay them wages, and allow them to decide if they wished to leave. She also encouraged southern women to petition clerical and state governing bodies. Grimké proposed that slavery was "opposed to Christian principles and to everything Jesus had taught." When copies of the book reached Charleston, the postmaster burned them, and local police warned the Grimké family that their daughter should not return to the South. She and her sister Sarah became permanent residents in the North.

Critics branded Grimké as sinful and loose, a "Devil-ina." Other women also criticized her for her public speaking. Catharine Beecher, an otherwise liberal advocate of education for women, criticized Grimké for addressing mixed audiences in an 1837 essay, arguing that it was not a "woman's place" to speak in public. Grimké responded by writing *Letters to Catherine Beecher,* published in 1838. Grimké argued in favor of women working for abolition on the grounds that the Bible cited examples of women taking public stands. Grimké and her sister became notorious merely because they lectured openly. The press described them as old maids, as embittered spinsters, and as cranks who spoke in public to attract men. Despite the hostile criticism, the sisters addressed at least 40,000 to 50,000 people during the first 23 weeks they lived in New England, appearing at 88 meetings in 67 towns. In pamphlets and speeches Grimké argued that it was women's right—even their duty—to petition and organize politically. Both *Appeal to Christian Women of the South* and *Letters to Catherine Beecher* defended women's rights to organize and hold leadership positions in the abolitionist movement. As she would remind male abolitionists, "Can you not see that woman could do and would do a hundred times more for the slave, if she were not fettered?" Grimké became the first American woman to speak before a legislative body when she presented an antislavery petition to the Massachusetts state legislature in February 1838.

Grimké married abolitionist Theodore Weld in 1838. In their marriage vows, she did not make the traditional promise to obey him. Weld also renounced his legal rights as a husband to own and manage his wife's property. Both black and white friends attended the ceremony. Grimké was expelled from the Philadelphia Society of Friends for marrying a non-Quaker. The couple had three children.

During the Civil War she wrote articles with her sister Sarah in support of the Union, including an 1863 piece titled *An Appeal to the Women of the Republic.* However, Grimké's activism declined after marriage and motherhood as ill health, poverty, and domestic work curtailed her political participation. In 1839, Grimké, her sister Sarah, and her husband Theodore coauthored a comprehensive biblical analysis of the institution of slavery, *American Slavery As It is: Testimony of a Thousand Witnesses.* Their analysis was important since many southerners based their defense of slavery upon Scripture. The Grimkés refuted these arguments in their text. After the Civil War they opened a coeducational school in Bellville, New Jersey, and later a progressive school at the Raritan Bay Community in New York. In 1870, both women cast ballots in a local election as a protest gesture for women's suffrage.

Sarah Grimké died six years before her sister. After Sarah's death, Grimké suffered a series of strokes that left her paralyzed during the last six years of her life. Grimké died in Boston on October 26, 1879. Grimké made the transition from Charleston belle to exiled abolitionist.

Further Reading

Browne, Stephen Howard. *Angelina Grimké: Rhetoric, Identity, and the Radical Imagination.* Detroit: Michigan State University Press, 2000.

Japp, Phyllis M. Esther and Isaiah: "The Abolitionist-Feminist Rhetoric of Angelina Grimké." *Quarterly Journal of Speech* 71(3) (1985): 335–348.

Lerner, Gerda. *The Grimké Sisters from South Carolina: Pioneers for Women's Rights and Abolition.* New York: Oxford University Press, 1998.

Spartacus Educational. "Angelina Grimké." Available online. URL: http://www.spartacus.schoolnet.co.uk/ USASgrimke.htm. Downloaded on December 26, 2000.

Todras, Ellen. *Angelina Grimké: Voice of Abolition.* New York: Linnet Books, 1999.

Vielhaber, Mary E. "An Abandoned Speaking Career: Angelina Grimké." *Michigan Academician* 17(1) (1984): 59–66.

H

HALE, CLARA (Mother Hale)
(1905–1992) *Founder of Hale House*

Known as Mother Hale, Clara Hale founded New York City's nonprofit Hale House in 1975 to offer care to hundreds of abandoned and orphaned children. Clara McBride was born in Elizabeth, North Carolina, on April 11, 1905. She herself was orphaned at 16. She married after high school and then moved to Brooklyn. After her husband, Thomas Hale, died of cancer in 1932, she worked as a domestic in Brooklyn to support her three children. Dissatisfied with the quality of day care she found, she quit her job to care for her children and opened a day care center in her house for other children. She became a foster parent in 1940. She cared for dozens of children of all cultural backgrounds, often seven or eight at a time.

After Clara Hale retired in 1969 at age 65, Hale's daughter Lorraine brought home a drug-addicted mother and her child in need of assistance. Lorraine asked if her mother would care for the infant if she covered the expenses. Six years later, in 1975, Hale's home was officially licensed as a child care facility called the Center for the Promotion of Human Potential, but it became known as Hale House. The operation evolved into a full-fledged hospital to care for babies born addicted to drugs. Hale had no prior knowledge of how to care for these infants. At one time she had in her home 22 babies born of heroin-addicted women. She cared for the infants in her five-room Harlem apartment until they were six months old. The older children referred to her as Mommy Hale.

In the 1980s, some of the children she sheltered were afflicted with AIDS. Hale House was the only volunteer-run child-care agency for African-American children in the country. Hale cared for more than 500 unwanted children.

Hale earned her high school equivalency diploma shortly before her death. President Ronald Reagan recognized her as an American hero in 1985, and she received 17 honorary doctorates. A 1985 interview of Clara and Lorraine Hale covers the philosophy of Hale House, its origins, and details on the treatment available to adults and on caring for newborns going though withdrawal. A 1992 video, *Hale House: Alive With Love,* tells the story of how Dr. Lorraine Hale found a heroin addict and her infant daughter on a New York sidewalk nearly thirty years earlier, and sent them to her mother for help. This act of kindness from a stranger began the work of Hale House.

In 1996 a life-size bronze statue was unveiled in her honor in New York City. Clara Hale died on December 18, 1992, following a stroke.

Lorraine Hale, who had worked with her mother for more than 25 years, continues her mother's work. Lorraine Hale resigned as head of Hale House on May 14, 2001, following charges of misspent money, operating without a board of directors, and spending more on soliciting funds than on children's services. Only $54,000 of the $8 million raised in 2000 was spent on providing for the children. She allegedly borrowed $15,800 from Hale House to renovate her private residence and more funds to produce her husband's off-Broadway play. Her salary had been $200,000 a year; her husband, who served as director of public relations at Hale House, had a salary of $110,000 a year.

Several videos have been made that examine the work of Dr. Hale and her mother. As Clara Hale stated, "If you can't hold children in your arms, please hold them in your heart."

Further Reading

Bernstein, Nina. "At Hale House, Broken Bonds." *New York Times,* May 13, 2001, 1.

Coulter, Nancy. "Clara Hale: One of the Vocal Minorities." Available online. URL: http:///www.suite101.com/article.cfm/womens_issues/5338. Posted on February 17, 1998.

Foundation for National Progress. "Hale's Children," Available online. URL: http://bsd.mojones.com/mother.jones/JA95/greider2.html. Downloaded on December 29, 2000.

Hale, Clara, Dr. Lorraine Hale, James Briggs Murray. *An Interview with Mother Hale and Dr. Lorraine Hale.* VHS. L & S Enterprises, 1985.

Hale, Lorraine. *Hale House: Alive With Love.* VHS. L & S Video Enterprises, Inc., 1992.

Kershaw, Sarah. "Hale House, a Source of Local Pride, Is Now a Source of Concern in Harlem." *New York Times,* April 23, 2000, B9.

Pristin, Terry. "Hale House's Fund-Raising Is Prompting More Questions." *New York Times,* April 18, 2001, B1, B11.

Renee Johnson. "Another Moment in History: Mother Hale." Available online. URL: http://sma.ncsu.edu/Nubian/Archives/Fall1998/091798/Health/clara_hale.html. Downloaded on December 29, 2000.

 HAMER, FANNIE LOU TOWNSEND
(1917–1977)   *Civil Rights Leader*

Fannie Lou Hamer was a field worker for the Student Nonviolent Coordinating Committee (SNCC) and founder of the Mississippi Freedom Democratic Party (MFDP). Fannie Lou Townsend was born in Ruleville, in Montgomery County, Mississippi, on October 6, 1917. She grew up in a tar paper shack, sleeping on a cotton sack stuffed with dry grass under a roof patched with tin. When she was two, she moved with her family to Sunflower County, where she would live for the rest of her life.

Her mother, Lou Ella, and father, Jim Townsend, had 20 children; Fannie Lou was the youngest. The family worked as sharecroppers. As Fannie Lou recalled, "Life was worse than hard. It was horrible! We never did have enough to eat and I don't remember how old I was when I got my first pair of shoes, but I was a big girl. Mamma tried to keep our feet warm by wrapping them in rags and tying them with string." And when the family prospered enough to buy two mules and a cow, a white farmer poisoned the animals with Paris green, an insecticide.

The children of sharecroppers attended school only four months a year, December through March, when they were not needed in the fields. Fannie Lou Townsend started picking cotton when she was six years old. She quit school when she was 12, after completing the sixth grade and had to work full time to help support her family. She married Perry Hamer in 1944. He was a tractor driver and sharecropper on a nearby plantation, and the couple adopted two children.

Hamer had been a plantation timekeeper for 18 years when she attended her first civil rights meetings, which were mass meetings of SNCC. The meetings were held in her hometown of Ruleville and facilitated by James Foreman of SNCC and James Bevel of the Southern Christian Leadership Conference (SCLC). Hamer was so inspired by her first meeting that she led 17 people to the courthouse to register to vote. The information the applicants wrote on their forms regarding their residency was used by white citizen's councils to harass them. Their literacy tests included reciting and interpreting sections of the Mississippi state constitution. The test took all day to complete. On the ride home, their bus driver was stopped and fined $100 for driving a bus of "the wrong color."

Hamer did not pass the exam on her first attempt but returned every month until she did pass a few months later. Her boss insisted that she withdraw her voter application but Hamer refused. She remembered telling her boss, "'Mr., I didn't register for you; I was trying to register for myself.' He said, 'We're not ready for that in Mississippi.' He wasn't ready, but I been ready a long time. I had to leave that same night."

The landowner had fired her entire family. Her husband and daughter were arrested, and police searched her home without a warrant. The family lost their car, furniture, and house. Officials thought of numerous ways to harass Hamer. They even presented her with a $9,000 water bill for a house that did not have running water. She was shot at and threatened. Nobody would hire her.

In 1963, she became a registered voter and began working as a field secretary for SNCC in Mississippi. Hamer was one of the first African Americans, out of a population of 20,000, to register to vote in Sunflower County. To finally pass the exam, she had memorized sections of the Mississippi state constitution. On election day, however, she still was unable to vote because she did not have money to pay the poll tax. The poll tax was used by elite white southerners to disenfranchise poor African Americans and whites.

Her weekly salary as a SNCC organizer was $10. Most SNCC volunteers were younger than Hamer, had better educations, and had no families to support. She was arrested and severely beaten in Winona, Mississippi, for running a citizenship school. The beating left her with kidney damage and a blood clot in her left eye that permanently limited her sight. Another beating occurred when she tried to integrate a bus station in South Carolina. She lost the nerves in her arm from this beating.

In 1964, she was elected vice president of the Mississippi Freedom Democratic Party (MFDP) and led the delegation of dissenters to the Democratic National Convention in Atlantic City. The group challenged the seating of the Mississippi Democratic delegation, which was all white, although the state was 90 percent African American. The delegation opposed civil rights and rejected the national party platform. The MFDP was endorsed by several states, including California, Michigan, Massachusetts, and Colorado. They also received support from 25 congressional representatives.

Hamer's address to the convention was televised. She recounted the abuses she and many other African Americans received in the South and asked, "Is this America? The land of the free and the home of the brave? Where people are being murdered, lynched, and killed because we want to register and vote!" President Lyndon Johnson attempted to stop her address by scheduling a press conference to interrupt her presentation. However, later that evening Hamer's testimony appeared on the evening news.

Vice-presidential candidate Hubert Humphrey and Minnesota senator Walter Mondale extended a compromise to MFDP by offering to seat two of their delegates, but Hamer refused, stating, "Two at-large seats were token rights, on the back row, the same as we got in Mississippi. We didn't come all this way for that mess again." When pressured by Humphrey, Hamer responded, "Well Mr. Humphrey, do you mean to tell me that your position is more important to you than 400,000 black lives?" To get her delegation onto the convention floor, Hamer borrowed passes from supportive delegates, and she led her group in singing freedom songs on the convention floor.

She visited Africa in the fall of 1964, was active on the National Council of Negro Women, and was a cofounder of the National Women's Political Caucus.

Changes did occur as a result of the MFDP's activism. The Democratic Party pledged not to seat an all-white delegation at the next convention in 1968. They kept that promise by seating an integrated group rather than the all-white group, which appeared again at the convention. As Hamer noted, "I was determined to see that things were changed." When she went to the 1968 Democratic National Convention in Chicago, she received a standing ovation and was elected to the Democratic National Committee.

In 1969, she founded the 680-acre Freedom Farm Cooperative, a nonprofit agency, to help needy families grow food. In 1970, the National Council of Negro Women started the Fannie Lou Hamer Day Care Center in her honor. She ran unsuccessfully for the Mississippi state senate in 1971. Fannie Lou Hamer died of cancer on March 15, 1977, in Bayou, Mississippi, a few months short of her 60th birthday. Her most famous motto was engraved on her tombstone in Ruleville, Mississippi: "I'm sick and tired of being sick and tired."

Further Reading

DeMuth, Jerry. "Tired of Being Sick and Tired." *Nation* 198 (June 1964): 549.

Hamer, Fannie Lou. "It's In Your Hands." In *Black Women in White America: A Documentary History,* edited by Gerda Lerner. New York: Vintage, 1972.

Hamlet, Janice. "Fannie Lou Hamer: The Unquenchable Spirit of the Civil Rights Movement." *Journal of Black Studies* 26 (May 1996): 560–76.

Lee, Chana Kai. *For Freedom's Sake: The Life of Fannie Lou Hamer.* Champaign: University of Illinois Press, 1999.

Mills, Kay. *This Little Light of Mine: The Life of Fannie Lou Hamer.* New York: Plume, 1994.

Norton, Eleanor Holmes. "The Woman Who Changed the South: A Memory of Fannie Lou Hamer." *Ms.* 6 (July 1977): 98.

 ## HAMILTON, ALICE
(1869–1970) *Industrial Health Advocate*

Alice Hamilton pioneered the field of industrial toxicology. She was born on February 27, 1869, in New York City, but the family moved to Indiana when she was six weeks old. She grew up in Fort Wayne, Indiana, where she was tutored at home, followed by two years at Miss Porter's School, a finishing school in Farmington, Connecticut. Her father was from Ireland, her mother, Gertrude Pond, was from Germany and France. Her father was Presbyterian, her mother Episcopalian. As a child Hamilton thought of becoming a medical missionary.

Her older sister, the classical scholar Edith Hamilton, was a student at Bryn Mawr College in Pennsylvania, but Hamilton was interested in a medical education, something neither Bryn Mawr nor any other women's college in the Northeast offered. She received her M.D. degree in 1893 from the University of Michigan medical school. She noted, "The school was co-educational and had been so for some twenty years, so we women were taken for granted and there was none of the sex antagonism which I saw later in Eastern schools."

Few internships were open to women, but Hamilton completed two months at the Hospital for Women and Children in Minneapolis and then nine months in the New England Hospital for Women and Children, outside Boston.

Hamilton studied bacteriology in Munich from 1895 to 1896 accompanied by her sister, Edith Hamilton, who also studied in German universities. Since women were not officially admitted to German universities at the time, she had to find a liberal professor who would give her permission to attend his classes. The school she attended had three female students, all strangers to Germany. However, receiving any kind of degree was out of the question for Hamilton. The German authorities maintained that the only reason women wanted to attend a university was to become political subversives.

She followed her study abroad with more research at Johns Hopkins University, in Baltimore, Maryland. Hamilton said, "In spite of my year in Germany, nobody seemed to want my service."

Hamilton was hired as a professor to teach pathology at the Woman's Medical School of Northwestern University in Chicago in 1897. She lived at JANE ADDAMS's Hull-House, where she saw firsthand that many health problems of the immigrant poor were caused by their exposure to unsafe chemicals in their factory work. Hamilton believed she would not have taken up the causes of the working class and poor had she not lived at Hull-House, her primary home for more than 20 years. She investigated toxic substances that workers, mostly female, in the munitions industry were exposed to. Insights gained from her work led her to become a socialist. As Hamilton recalled, "It was while I was living in Hull House and working in bacteriological research that the opportunity came to me to investigate the dangerous trades of Illinois."

When Hamilton began her work, only lead poisoning was being investigated or an occupational cause of disease. Few researchers had made connections between toxicity and health. The American Medical Association (AMA) had never held a meeting on the subject. When employees became fatally ill, many employers would argue that it was a result of their alcoholism. In 1925, Hamilton researched and published *A Survey of Occupation Diseases,* and one year later the state of Illinois passed the workers' compensation law. She presented her findings in Illinois, New York, and Massachusetts, before legislative committees where she argued against the manufacturers and their representatives.

In 1910, Hamilton became director of the Illinois Occupational Disease Commission, the first such organization in the world. Her investigations resulted in passage of several state workers' compensation laws. The U.S. Commissioner of Labor asked her to continue her work on the national level, and she held an unpaid position in the Department of Labor from 1911 to 1921.

Hamilton was a pacifist during World War I and became involved in the founding of the Women's International League for Peace and Freedom. In 1915, she and Addams coauthored *Women at The Hague.* She became the first woman on the staff of Harvard Medical School in 1919. Since women were not admitted to the school as students until after World War II, all her students were male. In 1925, she published the classic *Industrial Poisons in the United States,* followed by *Industrial Toxicology* in 1934. She retired from Harvard in 1935.

Although she had been a pacifist during World War I, she did not oppose World War II. At the end of that war she served as president of the National Consumers League. She expanded her writing beyond academia in order to reach a mass audience, including publishing articles in *Ladies' Home Journal.* In 1943, she published her autobiography, *Exploring the Dangerous Trades.* Alice Hamilton died six months after her 100th birthday on September 22, 1970, in Hadlyme, Connecticut. Her work allowed succeeding generations of workers to enjoy safer working conditions.

Further Reading

Hamilton, Alice. *Exploring the Dangerous Trades: The Autobiography of Alice Hamilton.* Boston: Little, Brown and Company, 1943.

Harbison, Raymond. *Hamilton and Hardy's Industrial Toxicology.* Saint Louis, Mo.: Mosby Year Book, 1998.

Sicherman, Barbara. *Alice Hamilton: A Life in Letters.* Cambridge, Mass.: Harvard University Press, 1984.

 HARPER, FRANCES ELLEN WATKINS
(1825–1911)   *Abolitionist*

Frances Harper was an author, a member of the Underground Railroad, and one of the first African-American women to be hired as an abolitionist lecturer. Frances Watkins was born on September 24, 1825, in Baltimore, Maryland, a slave city, to free parents. There was much debate over her race during her lifetime because of her skin tone. Many referred to her as "red mulatto," a reference to her mixed American Indian and African-American ancestry. Many free African Americans, before the end of the Civil War, had such backgrounds through intermarriage with American Indians.

By the time she was three she was an orphan. Her uncle William Watkins, a shoemaker and minister, was very active in antislavery activities, and she attended the William Watkins Academy for Negro Youth, which he had founded. At the academy she received an education that was superior to that received by most other women of that time. Nonetheless, she could find employment only as a seamstress and a baby sitter.

When she was 20, in 1845, she published her first volume of prose, *Forest Leaves.* She published the first of 10 books of poetry in 1846 and became the most widely recognized black poet since Phillis Wheatley. Her writings were critical of what she saw as the patriarchal paternalism of African-American men and the overt racism of white women.

She was also an antislavery lecturer, delivering her first speech, "Education and the Elevation of the Coloured Race" in New Bedford, Massachusetts. Her lecture tours ranged throughout the United States and Canada.

Her uncle closed his school in 1850 because of the increasingly repressive climate for African Americans in Baltimore and moved his family to Canada. Watkins moved to Ohio and became the first female faculty member at Union Seminary, later renamed Wilberforce University. She faced resistance to her appointment because she was female. After teaching at Union Seminary for a couple of years, she lived in Little York, Pennsylvania, and by 1853 had moved to Philadelphia to work exclusively for the abolitionist cause. She lived with the family of William Still, whose home was the main Philadelphia depot of the Underground Railroad, which smuggled escaped slaves to freedom. She continued to publish essays and poems; some appeared in abolitionist William Lloyd Garrison's paper the *Liberator.* One of her essays, called "We Are All Bound Up Together," argued that the burdens of one group were "The Burdens of All." In 1853, a Maryland law was passed that allowed free African-Americans who entered the state to be sold back into slavery. Frances Watkins subsequently moved to Ohio.

In 1860, she married Fenton Harper, a widowed farmer who had three children. They settled in Columbus, Ohio. She gave birth to a daughter who died before reaching adulthood. When her husband died four years later, in 1864, she returned to lecturing full time.

Harper worked with the American Equal Rights Association but when leaders ELIZABETH CADY STANTON and SUSAN B. ANTHONY lobbied against passage of the Fifteenth Amendment, which would allow African-American men—but not women—to vote, Harper left the group. As she reasoned, there was no reason for "Black women to put a single straw in the way to prevent the progress of Black men."

Harper became a founder, with LUCY STONE, of the American Woman Suffrage Association, which endorsed the Fourteenth and Fifteenth Amendments. She lectured for the new organization. After the Civil War she lectured in the South on temperance and against white racial violence.

After Reconstruction she wrote on a wide range of topics, including lynching, in her *Sketches of Southern Life.* Her book *The Martyr of Alabama and Other Poems,* published in 1894, tells the story of slavery and Reconstruction through a series of poems. Her most popular work was the novel *Iola Leroy or Shadows Uplifted.* Published in 1883, it traced the story of a quadroon (a person of three-quarters white and one-quarter African-American ancestry) through the Civil War. The novel critiqued ideas concerning racial identity and the socioeconomic status of African-American women. It revealed slaves' perspectives of and participation in the Civil War and the ideas espoused by black intellectuals during and after Reconstruction. The protagonist, Iola Leroy, confronted the issues around which black women and their organizations rallied, including discrimination in the employment and education, settings, suffrage, temperance, and lynching. In 1896, she was a founder and vice president of the National Association of Colored Women (NACW). The NACW focused on job training, wage equity and child care. It raised funds for kindergartens and college scholarships. Harper lectured, raised funds, and served as an administrator of the NACW.

Frances Harper died on February 22, 1911, in Philadelphia at age 85. In the 1950s, her publisher discarded a number of her manuscripts and correspondence as rubbish when the business was sold, but the bulk of her writings have been preserved by the Library of Congress and Howard University and have been reprinted by Beacon Press, the Feminist Press, and Oxford University Press. Her work affected the lives of thousands who read her books and articles, heard her lectures, or were assisted on the Underground Railroad.

Further Reading

University of Michigan Press, Ann Arbor. "Atlanta Offering: Poems by Frances Ellen Watkins Harper." Available online. URL: http://www.hti.umich.edu/bin/amv-idx.pl?type=header&id=Harper. Downloaded on December 7, 2000.

Foster, Frances. *A Brighter Coming Day: A Frances Ellen Watkins Harper Reader.* New York: Feminist Press, 1990.

Harper, Frances E. W. *Complete Poems of Frances E. W. Harper.* Oxford, England: Oxford University Press, 1988.

———. *Iola Leroy or Shadows Uplifted.* Boston: Beacon Press, 1999.

———. *Minnie's Sacrifice, Sowing and Reaping, Trial and Triumph: Three Rediscovered Novels.* Boston: Beacon Press, 2000.

 ### HARRIS, PATRICIA ROBERTS
(1924–1985)   *Secretary of Health, Education and Welfare*

Patricia Roberts Harris was the first African-American woman to head a United States embassy and the first African-American woman to serve in a president's cabinet. Patricia Roberts was born on May 31, 1924, in Mattoon, Illinois, the only daughter of Chiquita and Bert Roberts. She grew up in Chicago, where her father worked as a dining-car porter. In 1942, she began attending Howard University on a scholarship. While at Howard, she participated in one of the first student sit-ins, to integrate the Little Palace cafeteria.

Harris graduated summa cum laude from Howard in 1945 and then pursued graduate work at the University of Chicago and American University in 1949. She served as the program director at the Chicago Young Women's Christian Association (YWCA from 1946 to 1949.). Three years later she began work as the assistant director of the American Council on Human Rights, a Washington, D.C., civil rights organization.

In 1944, she married attorney William Beasley Harris, a law professor she had met at Howard. She worked full time as the national director of the Delta Sigma Theta sorority from 1953 to 1959, while also attending George Washington University Law School. She graduated first in her class in 1960, then worked as a trial attorney at the U.S. Department of Justice. Harris then went to work as associate dean of students and also as a lecturer in law at Howard University.

In 1963, Harris was promoted to full professor and served as cochair of President John F. Kennedy's National Women's Committee for Civil Rights. In 1965, President Lyndon Johnson appointed her ambassador to Luxembourg, making her the first African-American female to serve as ambassador to a European nation. She was also the first African-American female to serve in the United Nations as an alternate delegate.

She returned to Howard University as a professor of law and in 1969 served briefly as dean of the law school, the first female to serve as dean of a law school. She gave the seconding address for President Lyndon Johnson's nomination at the National Democratic Convention in 1964, thus becoming the first African-American female to make a presidential nomination. In 1972, she was the first African-American woman to chair the Democratic National Committee.

Harris became the first African-American female cabinet member as the U.S. secretary of the Department of Housing and Urban Development (HUD) in President Jimmy Carter's cabinet in 1976, a position in which she served until 1979. She was then appointed to a position as secretary of the Department of Health, Education and Welfare (HEW), which she held until the Reagan administration took office in 1981.

In 1982, Harris ran unsuccessfully against Marion Barry for mayor of the District of Columbia. The following year, she joined the faculty at George Washington University's National Law Center, where she taught for only two years before dying of cancer on March 23, 1985. The 23rd stamp in the U.S. Postal Service's Black Heritage series was issued in her honor. Patricia Harris served as a visible and gifted role model in public service.

Further Reading

Afro-American Almanac. "Patricia Roberts Harris." Available online. URL: http://www.toptags.com/aama/bio/women/pharris.htm. Downloaded on December 8, 2000.

Chealham, Cheryl Smith. *African American Women in the Legal Academy.* Cleveland, Ohio: Case Western Reserve University Law Library, 1994.

Columbus State University. "Patricia Roberts Harris." Available online. URL: http://students.colstate.edu/dst/SororHarris.htm. Downloaded on December 8, 2000.

 HAVILAND, LAURA SMITH
(1808–1898) *Abolitionist*

Laura Haviland organized one of the first Underground Railroad stations in Michigan, aiding 40,000 to 100,000 slaves during her lifetime. Laura Smith was born in 1808 in Kitley Township, Ontario, the first child of Daniel Smith, a Quaker minister, and the former Sene Blancher of Vermont. When Laura was seven, her family moved to Cambria, New York. Her mother and a neighbor supervised her education.

She married Charles Haviland, a Quaker farmer from Royalton, New York, when she was 16. Many Quakers, including the Havilands, opposed slavery and worked on the Underground Railroad, a secret system that helped escaped slaves reach freedom. The couple decided to homestead in Michigan, where they set up the first Underground Railroad station in that state.

In 1837, she and her husband cofounded the Raisin Institute, one of the first schools in the country to admit black students. The school started with fifty students, many of whom were fugitives from slavery.

Haviland led many escaped slaves to Canada. Her work was so successful that southern slave owners offered a $3,000 reward for her capture.

During the Civil War, she served as a hospital inspector. Following the Civil War, she served as an officer in the Freedmen's Aid Society, helping former slaves relocate to Kansas. She earned $40 a month, the first salary she received for her labors.

Haviland was a founder of the Women's Christian Temperance Union in Michigan. She believed that suffering the abuses of an alcoholic husband was similar to slavery. She also founded the State Public School for Dependent Children at Coldwater, Michigan, and the Industrial Home for Girls at Adrian, Michigan. She suggested that the term "reform school" be dropped and "industrial school" be used instead.

In 1882, she published her memoirs, *A Woman's Life Work.* The first edition in 1881 had 2,500 copies printed. The volume went through five editions. The book revealed her activism in the Underground Railroad and the Civil War. To make absolutely certain that skeptics would not discount her story, in later editions she included letters and testimonials from public officials who knew her.

Laura Haviland died on April 20, 1898, in Grand Rapids, Michigan. Four services were held in her honor. The first service was held at a Methodist church with two African-American ministers and two white ministers. Two choirs also participated, one African American and one white. A second service was held at the Girls Industrial School in Adrian; a third service in the town of Adrian; and a final service at the Friends' Meeting House. A historical marker stands at the Raisin Valley Friends Church, where she is buried. A statue in her honor was erected in front of Adrian City Hall in 1909 by the Adrian Woman's Christian Temperance Union. The statue shows her seated, holding a copy of *A Woman's Life Work* in her lap. The descendants of those assisted on the Underground Railroad number in the thousands and serve as a living legacy of Haviland's work.

Further Reading

Danforth, Mildred. *A Quaker Pioneer: Laura Haviland: Superintendent of the Underground.* New York: Exposition Press, 1961.

Haviland, Laura, *A Woman's Life Work.* 1881. Reprint, New York: Arno Press, 1969.

Michigan Historical Center. "The Civil War Gallery." Available online. URL: http://www.sos.state.mi.us/history/museum/explore/museums/hismus/prehist/civilwar/undergrou.html. Downloaded on December 9, 2000.

 HEIGHT, DOROTHY IRENE
(1912–) *President of the National Council of Negro Women*

Dorothy Height has served as president of the National Council of Negro Women (NCNW) since 1957. Dorothy Irene Height was born on March 24, 1912, in Richmond, Virginia, to Fannie Borroughs Height and James Edward Height. When Dorothy was four, her family moved from Richmond to Rankin, Pennsylvania, a small mining town outside Pittsburgh. Her mother worked as a nurse for cancer patients. Her father was a building contractor as well as the choirmaster and Sunday school superintendent at the local segregated Baptist church. Height was a straight-A student at Rankin High School, and played center on the basketball team. She graduated from Rankin High in 1926, at age 14, younger than her classmates, since school officials had advanced her two grade levels.

After graduating from high school, Height applied to Barnard College in New York City but was refused admission since Barnard had racial quotas and already had two black students attending. Instead, she attended New York University on a scholarship. She completed her undergraduate degree in three years and her master's degree in educational psychology in her fourth year, graduating in 1933. Height taught briefly at the Brownsville Community Center in Brooklyn.

In 1935, she found employment as a caseworker for the New York City Welfare Department and began course work at the New York School of Social Work. The Harlem rioters of 1935 had demanded black representation in the Welfare Department. Height did not participate in the riots but received her position in response to those demands. She accepted a position with the Young Women's Christian Association (YWCA) in 1938, eventually serving on its national board.

Height testified before the New York City Council on the plight of domestic workers who worked in what she termed a "slave market," for substandard wages. In 1937, Height met MARY MCLEOD BETHUNE, the education leader and president and founder of the National Council of Negro Women (NCNW). In 1939, Height moved to Washington, D.C., to serve as executive secretary of the YWCA Phillis Wheatley Home. Height developed programs to assist the influx of women seeking federal employment during World War II. In 1944, she returned to New York City and began serving full time on the national board of the YWCA. In 1946, due to her efforts in interracial education, the YWCA adopted an interracial charter.

In 1957, Height became president of the NCNW. In 1960, she served as consultant to the U.S. secretary of state following her study of women's organizations in five African countries. During this era of civil rights activism, the NCNW held voter education drives in the North and voter registration drives in the South. The NCNW raised funds to assist students who opted to postpone college in order to work in the civil rights movement. Height played a pivotal role in bringing the YWCA into social issues. In 1963, as secretary of the YWCA's Department of Racial Justice, she led the process to desegregate all facilities of the YWCA. Height was known as a moderate leader in the civil rights movement. She did not publicly support the early calls for black power.

Height contributed to the empowerment of women by serving under ELEANOR ROOSEVELT on President John F. Kennedy's Commission on the Status of Women and later serving as chairperson of the commission. Height directed the use of a Ford Foundation grant to the NCNW. The grant totaled $300,000 and was donated to initiate a program called Operation Woman Power that would help women open their own businesses.

Height was an organizer for the 1975 International Women's Year conference in Nairobi, Kenya. She also led a struggle to erect the monument to Mary McLeod Bethune in Washington's Lincoln Park, the first to an African American in the nation's capital. Height oversees an organization of 90 workers at NCNW, which encompasses 240 local groups and 31 national organizations. Additionally, Height holds a number of honorary degrees, including one from Harvard University. Her papers are stored in the office of the National Council of Negro Women in Washington, D.C. Dorothy Height is one of the most effective and longest-serving leaders in the African-American community.

Further Reading

DeRamus, Betty. "Living Legends." *Essence* 29, no. 10 (February 1999): 92.

Gateway. "Dorothy Height." Available online. URL: http://www.gatewayva.com/pages/bhistory/1999/heights.html. Downloaded on December 1, 2000.

National Council of Negro Women. *Dorothy I Height: Legend, Linkage, Legacy.* Washington D.C.: National Council of Negro Women, 1992.

 ## HERMAN, ALEXIS
(1947–   )   *Secretary of Labor*

As U.S. secretary of labor, Alexis Herman was the highest-ranking African-American woman in the Clinton administration. Alexis Herman was born on July 16, 1947, in Mobile, Alabama. She was born out of wedlock to Gloria Broadus Caponis, and Alex Herman. Her mother, who was 25 years younger than Herman's father, returned to school after Herman's birth to become a schoolteacher. Alex Herman was a businessman who sued to integrate the Democratic Party in Alabama and later became the state's first African-American ward leader.

When Herman was five, her father's car was forced off the road by a car full of Klansmen, members of a white supremacist group opposed to civil rights. Alex Herman had his daughter hide on

the floorboard and gave her a gun before he left the car. He told her that if anyone except him opened the car door, she was to pull the trigger of the gun. The Klansmen beat her father for his political and civil rights activities.

Herman graduated from the Heart of Mary High School in Mobile in 1965. She completed a B.S. degree from Xavier University in New Orleans, Louisiana, in 1969 and did her graduate work at the University of South Alabama in Mobile.

She worked for Catholic Charities as a social worker after graduation. In 1972, Herman developed the Minority Women Employment Program (MWEP) in Atlanta, Georgia, and two years later, when the program expanded nationally, she served as its director. She chaired the National Commission on Working Women and sat on the board of the National Council of Negro Women. In 1979, she was recognized by *Ebony* magazine as one of "50 Future Leaders." In 1980, she was named an "Outstanding Young Woman of the Future," by *Ladies' Home Journal.*

Herman became director of the Women's Bureau of the U.S. Department of Labor from 1977 to 1980 during the administration of President Jimmy Carter. In 1977 she was 29—the youngest person to hold the position. She was also the senior African-American woman at the U.S. Department of Labor. In 1988, she served as chief of staff for the Democratic National Committee (DNC). In 1991, she became deputy chair of the DNC and also served as chief executive officer of the 1992 Democratic National Convention Committee.

In 1993, Herman served as the White House director of public liaison. President Clinton then nominated her as secretary of labor. Her nomination was controversial because of her strong probusiness views. Organized labor eventually accepted her nomination. After the third-longest confirmation process on record, 113 days, she was confirmed by an 85-3 vote in the Senate and succeeded Robert Reich. She was the first African American to serve in that position, and the fourth woman. In 1997, three months into her term she successfully negotiated an end to the 10-day United Parcel Service strike. One of her more innovative programs was Youth Opportunity, an outreach effort on youth unemployment and training. She married physician Charles Franklin on February 12, 2000. Herman would have served as a White House chief of staff in an Al Gore presidency, but when Democrats lost the 2000 election Herman retired to private life. Her leadership highlighted the immense talents that African-American women bring to public service.

Further Reading

"Alexis Herman." *Washington Post.* Available online. URL: http://washingtonpost.com/wp-srv/politics/govt/admin/herman.htm. Downloaded on December 28, 2000.

Duffy, Michael. "Confirmation Hearings of Alexis Herman." *Time* 149, no. 5 (February 3, 1997): 26.

Edwards, Tamala. "Labor of Love." *Essence* 28, no. 11 (March 1, 1998): 86.

Gerhart, Ann. "A Cabinet Member's Farewell." *Washington Post,* January 18, 2001, C1.

Henneberger, Melinda. "Married to the Job." *New York Times Magazine,* March 5, 2000, 21.

Herman, Alexis. "Employment Opportunities for Black Women in the 1980's." *Black Collegian* 10 (April/May 1980): 96–99.

Randolph, Laura. "Secretary of Labor Alexis Herman." *Ebony* 53, no. 1 (November 1, 1997): 124.

Whigham-Desir, Marjorie. "The Magnolia Mediator." *Black Enterprise* 30, no. 10 (May 2000): 143–48.

 ## HERNANDEZ, ANTONIA
(1948–   )   *Civil Rights Lawyer*

Antonia Hernandez served as president of the Mexican American Legal Defense Fund (MALDEF), a Latino civil rights organization. Antonia Hernandez was born on May 30, 1948, in Torreón, in the province of Coahuila, Mexico. She was the oldest of six children. Her father was a gardener; her mother, a homemaker. Her family immigrated to East Los Angeles when Hernandez was eight. Her family life was a happy but economically poor one. She grew up with a strong

sense of ethnic pride, which she attributed partly to her upbringing in Mexico. She said, "When I came to the United States, I was very proud of who I was. I was a Mexican. I had an identity. I had been taught a history, a culture of centuries of rich civilization so I had none of the psychoses of people who don't know who they are."

She earned a B.A. degree and teaching certificate from the University of California in Los Angeles (UCLA) in 1973. While working in a counseling program she decided to pursue a law degree, saying she "realized that we couldn't help the kids as teachers unless we did something about the laws that were holding them back." Professors urged her to attend Harvard or Stanford, but she choose UCLA in order to remain near her family.

After completing her J.D. degree in 1974, she became an attorney for the East Los Angeles Center for Law and Justice, handling police brutality cases. In 1977, she married attorney Michael Stern and had three children. In 1978, she left her work in poverty law to join the staff of the U.S. Senate Judiciary Committee. She took a brief leave of absence to coordinate Senator Ted Kennedy's southwestern campaign for the Democratic presidential nomination.

In 1980, MALDEF asked Hernandez to join its Washington, D.C., staff. She worked her way to the top position by 1985. She had encountered difficulty in school as a Spanish-speaking child, and this led her to support bilingual education as an adult. Hernandez remembered the problems she faced by having no transitional support to the English language. She was involved in lawsuits to pressure employers to compensate bilingual workers whose second-language skills were a part of their job. Hernandez served as an advocate on issues of immigrant rights, employment discrimination, educational inequities, U.S. Census data, redistricting, voting, and language rights. One of her successes was defeating the Simpson-Mazzoli immigration bill, which would have required Latinos to carry identification cards. One aspect of the Simpson-Mazzoli bill was later incorporated into the 1988

Immigration Reform and Control Act (IRCA). The IRCA was meant to deter illegal immigration by requiring employers to verify the immigration status of employees. Many employers were willing to risk mandated fines in order to pay low wages to undocumented immigrants.

In 1987, her leadership of MALDEF was challenged by an executive committee of MALDEF but the courts as well as the full board of the organization reinstated her. Her detractors had questioned her administrative abilities. The man who would have replaced her, former New Mexico governor Tony Anaya, would have been paid $40,000 a year more than Hernandez earned though it is difficult to prove that the difference in salary was based solely on gender.

Hernandez has retained the ability to identify with recent immigrants to the United States and with those who do not "make it" in the American system. Hernandez tells new immigrants, "I made it. But just because I made it cannot be used as an example that it works. I say 'Don't look at me, look at all those who didn't make it.' Because you're not judged by whether you made it, whether the minority made it. You're judged by whether the majority makes it."

Further Reading

"Antonia Hernandez." *Hispanic* (December 1990): 17–18.
"Antonia Hernandez." *Hispanic Business* (February 1992): 10.
"Hispanic Heritage Awards Salutes Excellence." *Hispanic Outlook in Higher Education* 10, no. 3 (October 22, 1999): 6.
Salas, Abel. "In the Trenches with MALDEF." *Hispanic* (October 31, 1997): 32. Films for the Humanities, VHS, 1996.

 HERNANDEZ, MARIA LATIGO
(1893–1986) *Civil Rights Activist*

Maria Latigo Hernandez worked with preeminent organizations in the Mexican-American civil rights movement, including the Orden Caballeros de America, La Liga por Defensa Escolar, and La Raza Unida Party. Maria Latigo was born in 1893 in Mexico. After the Great Revolution of 1910, her family fled to Texas, settling in Hebbronville. She married Pedro Hernandez in 1915, and in 1918 they moved to San Antonio, where they ran a grocery store.

The Mexican-American community had several civic groups, which assisted with burial services and health care. In 1924, Hernandez joined one of the groups, La Orden Hijos de America. Hernandez was trained as a midwife and offered her services to low-income people who were unable to afford medical care. Hernandez was not interested in joining the organization that hoped to become an umbrella of all the Mexican-American groups, the League of United Latin American Citizens (LULAC), because LULAC organized women in a separate auxiliary, and she did not approve of that policy.

Many Mexican-American leaders at that time were assimilationists who advocated using only English to speed their acceptance in mainstream society. However, Hernandez continued to speak and write Spanish in her speeches and articles. She became a pioneer advocate of bilingualism in education.

In 1929, Hernandez and her husband founded a civil rights organization called Orden Caballeros de America. She also formed the group La Liga Por Defensa Escolar en San Antonio in 1934. The group used direct action, such as marches and rallies, to challenge inequities in education: Mexican American schools sometimes had teacher-to-student ratios of 1 to 130 and lacked heat in classrooms, while schools in Anglo communities were better equipped and better staffed. In addition to public protests, the group lobbied the state board of education for improvements. As Hernandez stated to the board, "The students are not at fault for being born with black eyes and brown hair and not with blue eyes. We are all supported by the stripes and stars of the flag. I want you to take this gesture of this community as a protest and disgust over the terrible conditions." She also campaigned for Democratic presidential candidate Franklin Delano Roosevelt in the Mexican-American community.

In the 1930s, she began the first Spanish-language radio program in San Antonio, *La voz de las Américas,* on KABC radio. It began as a half-hour segment but was soon expanded to an hour-long show. In 1945, she wrote a book addressing the importance of political work, *México y los cuatro poderes que dirigen al pueblo* (Mexico and the four powers that guide the people). In the 1960s, she started a weekly television show, *La hora de la mujer* ("The Hour of the Woman") on KWEX. When in 1970 La Raza Unida Party (RUP) started to organize unregistered Mexican-American voters and elect candidates, Hernandez became involved. She died in 1986, survived by five children, 19 grandchildren, 23 great-grandchildren, and eight great-great-grandchildren. Hernandez was an early and effective civil rights leader.

Further Reading

Groller, Ingrid. "Law in the Family." *Parents* 60 (March 1985): 96–100+.

Hernandez, Maria L. Interview by Angie del Cueto Quiros, April 19, 1975, Benson Latin American Collection, University of Texas at San Antonio.

 HEUMANN, JUDY
(1947–   )   *Disability Rights Activist*

In 1993, the Clinton administration appointed disability rights activist Judy Heumann assistant secretary of education. Judy Heumann was born on December 18, 1947, in Brooklyn, New York, to Ilse and Werner Heumann. Her family was Jewish. Her father had emigrated from Germany at the age of 14 and operated a butcher shop with his brother. Heumann contracted polio when she was 18 months old, which left her physically disabled. Her parents struggled to gain equal access to education for their daughter. The local school principal refused to enroll her, and so Heumann's early schooling consisted of home instruction, with a teacher visiting her family's apartment two or three times a week. After her mother's prolonged battle with the school board, Heumann was finally allowed to attend school by the middle of her fourth-grade year. However, she was assigned to a class for children with disabilities, whose teachers appeared not to expect very much from their students. Heumann also had to be bused to a school an hour and a half from Brooklyn, since that was the only school that would take disabled students. Heumann attended summer camps with other disabled children, but no disabled adults worked there to serve as role models for the children.

After eighth grade, Heumann was again forced to return home for instruction, as no local high school would accept students in wheelchairs. Heumann's mother sought support from the March of Dimes (a nonprofit organization supporting birth defect and disability research and education) to help convince the school board to allow her daughter into a high school, but the March of Dimes explained that the group did not get involved in political issues. Heumann's mother then organized a group of parents of disabled children who pressured the school board to admit their children into the high schools. Heumann was finally allowed to attend high school, but she was placed in a separate homeroom with other disabled students.

At her graduation ceremony, Heumann's father lifted her to the stage to receive a scholastic achievement award, but the principal tried to block them. When her father insisted that she appear on the stage with the other students, the event had its effect, as Heumann later recalled. "It was one more example of the discrimination disabled people face all the time. You never know when something like that is going to happen. It can hit you when you least expect it, and ruin some occasion you've planned for months. You never feel totally safe."

Heumann entered Long Island University, majoring in speech and theater. She had wanted to major in education but her vocational counselor said the state would not pay for teaching courses since they would not lead to a career. Heumann took the education classes on the side, and she studied hard. She rarely dated and remembered one day when a boy asked her if she knew someone who might like to go on a double date with his friend. Clearly, he never considered Heumann as a potential date.

Heumann completed coursework to become a teacher in 1970. She failed the New York City Board of Education's medical exam because of her disability. Heumann called the American Civil Liberties Union (ACLU), but they refused to take her case because they did not feel it was a matter of discrimination. Heumann then contacted a friend of hers who was a student reporter for the *New York Times*. After the paper ran the story, titled "You Can Be President, Not Teacher, with Polio," three attorneys offered to represent Heumann in a lawsuit against the school board. The board of education settled out of court, and Heumann started teaching in the same "disabled class" she had attended as a fourth-grader. She taught for the next three years both in classes of disabled students and in nondisabled second grade classes.

During the same time she was attempting to gain employment as a teacher Heumann was engaged as an activist. In 1970, at age 22, Heumann founded Disabled in Action (DIA), a political group whose aim was to gain civil rights for the disabled. In 1972, when President Nixon vetoed a bill to fund disability programs, DIA members joined disabled veterans to protest at Nixon's New York City campaign headquarters, and later that year at the Lincoln Memorial in Washington, D.C. The group also demonstrated against the Jerry Lewis telethon, an annual fund-raising broadcast, for what they believed was its belittling portrayal of the disabled as pitiful, helpless dependents.

In 1973, Heumann moved to Berkeley, California, to study at the University of California. During this time she spent 18 months as a legislative assistant to Senator Harrison Williams, the chair of the Senate Labor and Public Welfare Committee. In this position she worked to draft two significant pieces of legislation, the Education of All Handicapped Children Act, intended to correct inequities in public school systems, and Section 504 of the Rehabilitation Act, which would guarantee basic civil rights to the disabled. Heumann also helped draft the Americans with Disabilities Act. She earned a master's degree in public health administration in 1975. From 1975 to 1982, Heumann served as deputy director of the Center for Independent Living (CIL).

In April 1977, Heumann led one of the most important disability rights demonstrations in U.S. history. Congress had passed the new Rehabilitation Act in 1973. Section 504 of the act made it illegal for any agency or institution that received federal funding to discriminate against a person because of a disability. But four years later, the act still had not been drawn up, signed, and enforced by Joseph Califano, then secretary of the Department of Health, Education and Welfare (HEW). Disability activists across the country staged a series of demonstrations, but their 26-day takeover of HEW offices in San Francisco, which Heumann led, was the longest. Hundreds of people with disabilities occupied the building as Heumann, their spokesperson, told reporters, "We will not accept more segregation! There will be more sit-ins until the government understands this." On April 28, 1977, Califano signed Section 504 regulations into law, and the demonstrators ended their occupation.

Ms. magazine cited her as one of 80 women to watch in the 1980s, and the California state legislature named her its Woman of the Year in 1980. In 1993, President Bill Clinton appointed Heumann as assistant secretary of education. She is in charge of the Office of Special Education and Rehabilitation Services (OSERS), overseeing a staff of 370. She married accountant Jorge Pineda in 1994, and they now live in Washington, D.C. After the administration of President George W. Bush took office in January 2001. Heumann began a consulting firm, Heumann and Associates. Her accomplishments highlight the potential contributions people with disabilities can make despite the enormous social barriers they face.

Further Reading

Heumann, Judy. Letter to author, May 21, 2001.

Kent, Deborah. *Extraordinary People With Disabilities*. New York: Children's Press, 1996.

McMahon, Brian. *Enabling Lives*. Boca Raton, Fla: CRC Press, 2000.

 HOBBY, OVETA CULP
(1905–1995)   *Secretary of Health, Education and Welfare*

Oveta Culp Hobby was the first commanding officer of the Women's Army Corps, known as the WACs, and the first secretary of the U.S. Department of Health, Education and Welfare (HEW). She became the second woman in U.S. history to serve in the president's cabinet. Oveta Culp was born on January 19, 1905, in Killeen, Texas, to Emma Hoover Culp, a suffragist, and Isaac William Culp, an attorney and politician. The second of seven children, Culp was intellectually advanced for her age. She completed her education at the Mary Hardin Baylor College for Women in Belton, Texas, and in 1925, she earned a law degree at the University of Texas Law School. At age 20 she had already become the assistant city attorney in Houston. In 1925 she ran unsuccessfully against a Ku Klux Klan candidate for the Texas House of Representatives. She lost the race by 4,000 votes. A woman was not elected to the Texas House from Harris County until 42 years later. Culp never sought elective office again, but she served as parliamentarian of the Texas legislature from 1926 to 1931. In 1931, she married the publisher of the *Houston Post,* former governor William Hobby, whom she had met while working in the circulation department of the *Post.* He was 30 years her senior. They had two children. In 1937 she published a book on parliamentary law entitled *Mr. Chairman.* In 1939 and 1941 she again served briefly as parliamentarian in the Texas House. She worked at the *Houston Post,* advancing from research editor to executive vice president by 1938.

Six months before the Japanese attack on Pearl Harbor, in June 1941, she became head of the Women's Interest Division of the Army's Public Relations Bureau. In this position she developed the Women's Army Corps, a women's noncombatant auxiliary of the army. The work of Hobby was supported by a bill to establish the corps authored by congressional representative Edith Nourse. Hobby was chosen to head the Women's Army Corps (WAC) when it was created in 1942 and served in this capacity until 1945. Before 1943 it was known as the Women's Auxiliary Army Corps (WAAC). In three years, she recruited and trained 100,000 women to fill military posts all over the world. She began the appointment as director of the WACs at the rank of major and was promoted to colonel in 1943. When she began the corps, Congress had agreed that women could perform 54 army jobs. By the end of her tenure, women were working in 230 different army jobs. At the end of her service, Colonel Hobby received the Distinguished Service Medal, the first women to receive this award. There was discussion in Congress of making her a general, but this did not occur.

After the war and her retirement from the WACs, Hobby returned to her work in the media in Texas. In 1945, she served as the station director for KPRC-TV and seven years later was named coeditor and publisher of the *Houston Post.* In 1953, she headed the Federal Security Agency under President Dwight Eisenhower. Later that year, her position was made part of the president's cabinet and renamed the Department of Health, Education and Welfare. She also improved the administration of food and drug laws, expanded funds for mental health, and established a hospital insurance program. She served as HEW's first secretary until 1955, when she returned to Houston to take care of her husband, who had become ill. Treasury Secretary George Humphrey responded to news of her resignation by stating, "What? The best man in the Cabinet?"

Oveta Culp Hobby (right), 1943, political appointee
(Prints & Photographs Division, Library of Congress, Washington, D.C.)

She was the first woman to be appointed to the presidential cabinet since FRANCES PERKINS served as secretary of labor in 1933. After Hobby's husband's death in 1964, she became the publisher of the *Houston Post.* She served as director of the Corporation for Public Broadcasting in 1968. In 1983, she was listed as one of the 20 most powerful Texans. She sold the *Houston Post* that same year for $100 million. She died on August 16, 1995, in Houston, Texas. Her innovative and visible leadership exemplified at the contributions women could make in public service.

Further Reading

Barned, Bart. "Oveta Culp Hobby Dies at 90." *Washington Post,* August 17, 1995, B4.

Barron, James. "Oveta Culp Hobby, founder of the WACs and first Secretary of Health, Dies at 90." *New York Times,* August 17, 1995, B13.

Chapman, T. "Influential Oveta Culp Hobby Left Lasting Legacy for Women." *Houston Business Journal* 31, no. 45 (March 23, 2001): A30.

"Obituary." *Time* 146 (August 17, 1995): 27.

"Oveta Culp Hobby." *Current Biography* 56, no. 10 (October 1995): 59.

"Oveta Culp Hobby." *U.S. News & World Report* 119 (August 28, 1995): 28.

Sutphen, Debra Lynn. "Conservative Warrior: Oveta Culp Hobby and the Administration of America's Health, Education, and Welfare, 1953–1955." Dissertation Abstracts: DAI 1999 59(9): 3619-3620-A. DA9907122.

 ## HUERTA, DOLORES FERNANDEZ
(1930–   )   *Vice President of the United Farm Workers*

Dolores Huerta was cofounder and vice president of the United Farm Workers and the Fund for the Feminist Majority. Dolores Fernandez was born on April 10, 1930, in the small mining town of Dawson, New Mexico, the second child of Alicia Chavez and Juan Fernandez.

After her parents divorced she moved to Stockton, California, with her mother and two brothers. Her mother worked in canneries at night and waitressed during the day to provide for her family. Her mother also started a restaurant and hotel that served poor farmworkers' families. Her mother was an important role model for Huerta in many ways, and she recalled, "I never had to cook for my brothers or do their clothes like [in] many traditional Mexican families."

Her father was a more remote role model but also a source of pride because of his work as secretary-treasurer in the Congress of Industrial Organizations (CIO). He was elected to the New Mexico state legislature in 1938.

She faced racism in school, including a specific incident with a teacher she recalled: "When I was in high school I got straight As in all my compositions. But the teacher told me at the end of the year that she could not give me an A because he knew that somebody was writing my papers for me." She graduated from Stockton High School, and a classmate recalled, "When we were in school, she was very popular and outspoken. She was already an organizer, but I didn't think she'd get so serious and work for such a cause."

After high school, she married Ralph Heal and had two daughters, but the marriage ended in the early 1950s. She married a second time, to Ventura Huerta, with whom she had five children. They later divorced but she kept the name Huerta. She reasoned that the relationship failed because, "I cared more about helping other people than cleaning our house and doing my hair." Her final relationship was with Richard Chávez, brother of well-known activist César Chávez. Huerta was the mother of 11 children. She earned a teaching certificate at Stockton College and worked as a teacher for a year in 1955. She said she left teaching when, "I realized one day as a teacher I couldn't do anything for the kids who came to school barefoot and hungry."

She began her activism in the late 1950s, working for the Community Service Organization (CSO), a grassroots advocacy group and Mexican-American self-help association that tried to register Chicano voters and held citizenship classes. Founded in Los Angeles, CSO had branches throughout California and the Southwest. When Huerta began working with the CSO, she was still politically conservative, "a registered Republican," as she has said. César Chávez was also working for CSO as executive director. Huerta became a successful lobbyist for the CSO, winning the extension of old-age pensions to noncitizens, the right to register voters door to door, and the right to take driver's license examinations in Spanish. She and Chavez left the more urban-oriented CSO, however, to work with rural farmworkers.

In 1962 she and Chávez formed the National Farm Workers Association, which later became the United Farm Workers (UFW) of America. Huerta joined Chávez in Delano, California, for a grape picker's strike, one of their first actions. It was accompanied by a nationwide boycott, which proved successful in winning the very first contracts for farmworkers. Huerta negotiated the contract and became the first female Chicana negotiator in U.S. labor history. One landowner described her effectiveness this way: "Dolores Huerta is crazy. She's a violent woman, where

Dolores Huerta speaking at a United Farm Workers rally in Los Angeles, California, in 1998
(Joycelyn Sherman)

women, especially Mexican women, are usually peaceful and pleasant." She later organized the lettuce, Gallo wine, and international grape boycotts. Like other organizers, Huerta earned $5 a week. Her children seldom had a permanent residence.

Huerta dates her feminist consciousness to 1968, when she met and spoke with GLORIA STEINEM. She said, "Women in the fields get treated very badly—with additional humiliation and indignities." Huerta was also a cofounder of the Coalition of Labor Union Women (CLUW) in 1974. Her efforts on behalf of guest workers and those who lived, worked, and paid taxes in the United States without the benefits of citizenship

helped bring about the Immigration Act of 1985. She was severely beaten in 1988 by police in San Francisco at a protest against Vice President George H. W. Bush and needed emergency surgery for a ruptured spleen and six broken ribs. She later settled out of court, with San Francisco agreeing to pay her $825,000 in damages.

Huerta won the Martin Luther King Jr. Award from the National Association for the Advancement of Colored People, the Woman of Courage award from the National Organization for Women, and the American Civil Liberties Union Bill of Rights Award. In 1993 she was inducted into the National Women's Hall of Fame, and she won three prestigious awards, one of which was the American Civil Liberties Union (ACLU) Roger Baldwin Medal of Liberty Award. She continues to lead on active life of travel and work on behalf of the farmworkers' cause and women's rights. In thinking about her life's work, Huerta commented, "I think we brought to the world, the United States anyway, the whole idea of boycotting as a nonviolent tactic. I think we showed the world that nonviolence can work to make social change. . . . I think we have laid a pattern of how farm workers are eventually going to get out of their bondage." She currently serves as the secretary-treasurer of the United Farm Workers, vice president of the Coalition for Labor Union Women, vice president of the California AFL-CIO, and board member for the Fund for the Feminist Majority.

Further Reading

Drake, Susan Samuels. "Dolores Huerta." *Progressive* 64, no. 9 (September 2000): 34–38.

Felner, Julie. "Dolores Huerta." *Ms.* 8, no. 4 (January/February 1998): 46–49.

Genasci, Lisa. "UFW Co-Founder Comes Out of Shadow." *Los Angeles Times,* May 11, 1995, B1.

Lopez, Lalo. "Si Se Puede." *Hispanic* 9, no. 8 (August 1996): 41–44.

"March For Strawberry Workers' Rights." *La Prensa* 7, no. 42 (April 20, 1997): 1A.

Rose, Margaret. "From the Fields to the Picket Line: Huelga Women and the Boycott: 1965–1975." *Labor History* 31 (1990): 271–93.

"Corrido de Dolores Huerta." *Sing Out* 35, no. 1 (1990): 60–61.

 ## HUGHAN, JESSIE WALLACE
(1875–1955)   *Peace Advocate*

Jessie Hughan was a tireless organizer of leading pacifist organizations at the turn of the last century, including the Fellowship of Reconciliation and the War Resisters League. Jessie Wallace Hughan was born on December 25, 1875, in Brooklyn, New York, to Margaret and Samuel Hughan, the third of four children. Her father, a Scot, emigrated from

England to the United States. Her mother's family was of English, Scottish, and French heritage and had been in North America since the 17th century.

Hughan attended public school on Staten Island, then attended Northfield Seminary in Massachusetts. In 1894, she enrolled in Barnard College, earning her A.B. degree in 1898. While at Barnard, she founded the nationwide sorority Alpha Omicron Pi, with three other students in 1897. She continued her studies of economics at Columbia University. She became a socialist in 1907 and chose to write her doctoral thesis on socialism. In 1910, she completed her dissertation, *The Present Status of Socialism in America,* and received her Ph.D. She taught in public high schools in Naugatuck, Connecticut; White Plains, New York; and throughout New York State.

Hughan made several unsuccessful bids for office, beginning in 1915 when she was a candidate for alderman in New York City on the socialist ticket. In 1918, she ran for secretary of state. In 1920, she ran for lieutenant governor and then for U.S. senator in 1924. She never won an election but believed that a socialist presence on the ballot would pressure other parties to debate and adopt more liberal reforms.

At the beginning of World War I, she was a cofounder, along with three other women, of the Anti-Enlistment League. She was active in the 1915 founding of the Fellowship of Reconciliation (FOR), a Christian pacifist organization that later became active on civil rights issues. Her antiwar activities put her teaching career at risk, and she was constantly monitored by supervisors. This did not deter her, however, as she started another pacifist group in 1922 called the Committee for Enrollment Against War.

Hughan was instrumental in bringing together members of FOR, the Women's Peace Union, and the Women's Peace Society in 1923 to form the War Resisters League. She served as secretary of this organization until 1945. She organized "No More War" parades and coordinated peace education and conscientious objector efforts for the United Pacifist Committee. In 1940, she formed the Pacifist Teachers League. She took a strong stance against civilian public service camps, where conscientious objectors were forced to work without pay.

Hughan retired from teaching in 1945 and died at her Manhattan home on April 10, 1955. Her papers from 1905 through 1955, including an unfinished biography of Hughan by Annie Ridley Crane Finch, are stored at the Swarthmore College Peace Collection. The Jessie Wallace Hughan Memorial Fund was established in her honor to recognize published works that promote peace. Her legacy thus continues in the work of other peace activists.

Further Reading

Leland, Wilma Smith. *Jessie Wallace Hughan: Woman of Courage.* New York, New York: W. S. Leland, 1989.

Phenomenal Women of the Web. "Jessie Wallace Hughan." Available online. URL: http://members.aol.com/taylorteri/hughan.html. Downloaded on December 11, 2000.

HUTCHINSON, ANNE MARBURY
(1591–1643) *Religious Leader*

Anne Hutchinson was a leader of the opposition to orthodox Puritan dogma in 17th-century Massachusetts. Anne Marbury was born in 1591, in England during the reign of Queen Elizabeth I. She was the eldest daughter of Anglican clergyman Francis Marbury and his second wife, Bridget Drydent. Her father was a dissident minister who had been imprisoned because of his religious views. Francis Marbury had been censured (or silenced by the church) during Anne's early years, so he took charge of her education, which included in-depth doctrinal study. He also provided a role model as someone who was willing to question authority.

She learned nursing and midwifery from her mother, skills that made women leaders in the community. The Marbury family lived in the village of Alford in Lincolnshire, except for a few in Anne's teens, when they lived in London.

Anne Hutchinson, religious leader
(Prints & Photographs Division, Library of Congress, Washington, D.C.)

Back in Alford, she married merchant William Hutchinson in 1612. She gave birth to 15 children in 17 years, but lost three as infants. The Hutchinsons became followers of Anglican minister John Cotton, vicar of the nearby Lincolnshire parish of Boston. Cotton had fled Anglican authorities and joined the Puritan religious dissidents who were then immigrating to North America. Hutchinson was 43 years old when her family followed Cotton, in 1634, to the Massachusetts Bay Colony.

Hutchinson held twice-weekly meetings in her home that were considered a challenge to Puritan orthodoxy in the colonies. She stressed the importance of inner faith over outward piety. The meetings attracted up to 80 men and women. Church elders approved of a few women meeting to pray together but not of a woman who drew crowds. Hutchinson was viewed as unfit as much for her "unwomanly" manner as for her theological lectures. As Governor John Winthrop put it, "you have mainted [sic] a meeting . . . that hath been condemned . . . as a thing not tolerable nor comely in the sight of God nor fitting for your sex." She, in turn, denounced all Boston Puritan clergy, except Cotton and her brother-in-law, John Wheelwright.

In 1637, she stood trial, charged with having "troubled the peace of the commonwealth" through actions "not fitting for her sex." The formal charge was "Traducing the ministers and their ministry." Her former mentor, Reverend Cotton, joined her accusers and charged her with "that filthy sin of the community of women, and all promiscuous and filthy coming together of men and women. Though I have not heard you have been unfaithful to your husband in his marriage covenant, yet that will follow. . . ." Cotton also ordered the other women of the colony to disassociate themselves from Hutchinson. Her influence was substantial; some of her male supporters had refused to join the militia in battles against the native Pequot tribe, who warred with the colonists.

The Puritans, who had left England in search of religious freedom, could not extend that freedom to others. Hutchinson was found guilty, excommunicated, and banished from Massachusetts.

The Hutchinsons moved to Rhode Island in 1636, where other dissidents who had been exiled from Massachusetts two years earlier had settled. After her 51-year-old husband died in 1642, Anne Hutchinson moved with her six youngest children to New Netherland, a Dutch colony that later became New York and New Jersey. The colony was attracting other New Englanders who were uncomfortable with religious orthodoxy.

Hutchinson farmed on Long Island Sound, between the modern cities of the Bronx and New Rochelle. A river and highway in the area bear her name today. In 1643, she and all but her youngest child were killed in a war between the Dutch colonists and Algonquians. She lived in the British colonies in America for only nine years before her death but remained an icon of American intellectual life and the ideal of free speech.

Further Reading

Buckingham, Rachel. "Anne Hutchinson: American Jezebel or Woman of Courage." Available online. URL: http://cpcug.org/user/billb/hutch.html. Downloaded on December 15, 2000.

Burnham, Michelle. "Anne Hutchinson and the Economics of Antinomian Selfhood in Colonial New England." *Criticism* 39, no. 3 (1997): 337 (22).

Gale Group. "Anne Hutchinson." Available online. URL: http://www.gale.com/freresrc/womenhst/hutchin.html. Downloaded on December 15, 2000.

Lang, Amy Schrager. *Prophetic Women: Anne Hutchinson and the Problem of Dissent in the Literature of New England.* Berkeley: University of California Press, 1987.

Rimmer, Robert. *The Resurrection of Anne Hutchinson.* Amherst, N.Y.: Prometheus Books, 1987.

Tobin, Lad. "A Radically Different Voice: Gender and Language in the Trials of Anne Hutchinson." *Early American Literature* 25, no. 3 (1990): 253–70.

HUTCHISON, KAY BAILEY
(1943–) *Senator*

Kay Bailey Hutchison, a Republican from Texas, is the first woman to have represented her state in the U.S. Senate. Kay Bailey was born on July 22, 1943, in Galveston, Texas. The senator's heritage in Texas is historic. Her great-great-grandfather, Charles S. Taylor, one of Texas's earliest white settlers, signed the Texas Declaration of Independence. Her father, Allan Bailey, was a developer, and her mother, Kathryn, was a homemaker. The family is Episcopalian. Bailey grew up in the small Texas town of La Marque, just outside of Galveston. She was a high school prom queen. After graduating from the University of Texas at Austin, where she had been a cheerleader, she was one of just a dozen women in a class of 500 at the University of Texas School of Law. Regarding her decision to attend law school, Hutchison remarked, "I decided to go to law school because I hadn't found a husband." (After law school she was married to a medical student for less than a year.) She graduated from law school in 1967. After graduation she could not find a job in a law firm. She remembers hearing such responses as, "We like you, but if we hire a woman and she gets married and moves away, the huge investment we've made in training you is gone." After driving by a television station, she decided to stop in and ask about becoming an on-air reporter. Before entering politics, she worked for four years as a correspondent for KPRC-TV in Houston, from 1967 to 1971. In 1971 Bailey became Houston's first female television reporter. She switched from a career in journalism to politics under the mentorship of former U.S. ambassador to Great Britain and Nixon adviser Anne Armstrong (also a Texan).

In 1972, Hutchison became the first Republican woman elected to the Texas House of Representatives. She was twice reelected to that body. In the legislature she met Ray Hutchison, a Republican legislator. She would marry Hutchison in 1978. President Gerald Ford appointed her vice-chair of the National Transportation Safety Board in 1976. She worked with SARAH WEDDINGTON (the attorney who won the 1973 *Roe v. Wade* case) to prevent rape victims' names from being published in the media. She supported some abortion rights, but not federal funding for abortions. She ran for Congress in 1982 but lost to future Dallas mayor Steve Bartlett. Hutchison found few nonincumbent political campaigns that interested her for several years. She spent the next eight years working in a decorating showroom.

In 1990 she was elected Texas state treasurer. This marked the first time a Republican woman had been elected to a statewide office in Texas. As treasurer, she not only trimmed her agency's budget more than any other state official but also spearheaded the successful fight against a state income tax, a popular stance in a state traditionally critical of the idea of taxation. She served as

cochair of the 1992 Republican National Convention, delivering the welcoming speech.

Hutchison was elected to the U.S. Senate in 1993 with more than 67 percent of the vote—the largest margin of victory ever for a Republican in Texas—in a special election to replace Senator Lloyd Bentsen, whom President Bill Clinton had appointed as treasury secretary. Hutchison said she would serve only two terms. She was the first Texas Republican since 1875 to hold the senate seat.

One of Hutchison's first actions as senator came in 1993, when Hutchison and Republican senator NANCY KASSEBAUM of Kansas joined with Democratic women in opposing abortion restrictions. Hutchison supports federal funding for abortion only in cases of rape, incest and life-endangerment.

In 1994 Hutchison was indicted on four felony courts and one misdemeanor that could have resulted in a sentence of 20 years in prison. She was charged with using state funds, employees, and computers for personal and campaign purposes when she was state treasurer from 1991 to 1993, and then tampering with computer records to destroy evidence of her misdeeds. Former state workers also claimed that she was an obsessive boss who lashed out at employees, including striking a worker on at least one occasion. Heraide Sharon Amman, the daughter of former Texas governor John Connally, was reportedly hit by Hutchison with a notebook when she couldn't find a phone number quickly enough. Eventually, Hutchison was acquitted on all charges.

Senator Hutchison was a deputy majority whip in the Senate. In 1996 she sponsored and passed the federal antistalking bill, which made stalking across state lines a crime. She also sponsored homemaker individual retirement account (IRA) legislation that significantly expanded retirement opportunities for stay-at-home spouses. Democratic Senator BARBARA MIKULSKI cosponsored the IRA bill. Hutchison devised the federal welfare funding formulas that were implemented in cuts to the federal welfare budget in 1996. At the 1996

Texas Republican convention, religious conservatives tried to oust Hutchison from the proceedings because of her support of abortion rights. After a loud floor fight the supporters of presidential candidate Robert Dole were finally able to retain Hutchison's position as a delegate to the national convention.

She entered her Senate reelection campaign with funding of more than $6 million, the most money any senator raised for a 2000 race. Her campaigns received more than $1.2 million in contributions from the oil industry. Some questioned her efforts in spearheading a vote to pass a rider in 1999 to stop the U.S. Department of the Interior from collecting full royalties from oil companies that drill on public land. Large oil companies saved millions through this discounted royalty payment to the public. In 2000 Hutchison headed a Republican marriage tax penalty task force, which drafted a successful marriage tax relief plan. In 2000 Hutchison was elected vice-chair of the Republican conference. She was reelected in the 2000 election by a large margin.

Hutchison is considered to have a very bright future in national politics. She has expressed no interest in a cabinet position or other presidential appointment in a Republican White House, but during the 2000 election year, she was frequently mentioned as a possible candidate for governor of Texas in 2002. In March 2001 Hutchison ended speculation that she might seek the Republican nomination by declining to run. She remains one of the most visible women in the Republican Party.

Further Reading

ABC News Biography. "Kay Bailey Hutchison." Available online. URL: http://www.abcnews.go.com/reference/congress/TXS1.html. Downloaded on December 12, 2000.

Carnia, Catalina. "Hutchison won't rule out future run for governor." *Dallas Morning News,* January 5, 2000. Available online. URL: http://dallasnews.com/texas southwest/14346KAY05.html. Downloaded on December 15, 2000.

Current Biography Yearbook. "Kay Bailey Hutchison." New York: H.W. Wilson, v. 58, 1997.

"No Bid for Governor." *New York Times,* March 15, 2001, A22.

Pianin, Eric. "Trying to Put the Icing on a Tax Break." *Washington Post,* May 24, 2000, A35.

Senator Kay Bailey Hutchison. "Official home page of Senator Kay Bailey Hutchison." Available online. URL: http://www.senate.gov/~hutchison/. Updated July 28, 2000.

U.S. Senate Biography. "Kay Bailey Hutchison." Available online. URL: http://www.senate.gov/hutchison/bio.htm. Downloaded on December 15, 2000.

Whitney, Catherine. *Nine and Counting: The Women of the Senate.* New York: Perennial, 2001.

J

 JACKSON, HELEN MARIA FISKE HUNT
(1830–1885)   *Critic of Federal Indian Policy, Author*

Helen Hunt Jackson was a 19th-century writer and social reformer involved in American Indian rights. Helen Maria Fiske was born in Amherst, Massachusetts, on October 14, 1830, to Deborah Waterman Vinal Fiske and Nathan Welby Fiske. Her father was a stern Congregational minister and professor; her mother, a writer. Jackson benefited from an elite education at Abbott Institute, a select boarding school. Her classmate, neighbor, and lifelong friend was Emily Dickinson. Helen Fiske was orphaned as a teenager. In 1852, she married Edward Bissell Hunt, a U.S. Army captain and West Point engineer. They traveled extensively as her husband's career dictated.

In 1865, after the deaths of her husband and two children, she began a writing career, eventually producing more than 30 books. She sometimes used male pseudonyms in seeking publication. After 12 years of widowhood, in 1873 Hunt visited Colorado, where she met and married businessman William Jackson. Some

scholars believe that her new home in the West brought her into closer contact with the plight of American Indians.

Jackson's interest in issues of the American Indian surfaced publicly in 1879 when she heard Chief Standing Bear, a leader of the Ponca tribe, speak in Boston. Though she had not been sympathetic to other social movements for women's rights or abolition, Jackson devoted the remaining six years of her life to the rights of American Indians, and she remains best known for this work. In 1884, she published *A Century of Dishonor,* which exposed the history of U.S. government interactions with Indians and charged the Bureau of Indian Affairs (BIA) with a record of broken treaties and gross corruption. She had diligently researched her muckraking report in New York's Astor Library. At her own expense, Jackson sent each member of Congress a copy of her book inscribed with a quote from Benjamin Franklin: "Look upon your hands! They are stained with the blood of your relations." The book led to the formation of the Indian Rights Association.

Jackson was commissioned by U.S. Department of the Interior to report on the conditions of

Indians in California. She served as an official agent to the Indians and then used her literary talents to publicize their situation. That project formed the basis of a second book, *California and the Missions,* published in 1883.

Her most popular book was a romantic novel, *Ramona,* published in 1884, which told the story of a young woman who married an Indian man against the wishes of her family. Jackson had intended that *Ramona* serve as a catalyst for social change the way that Harriet Beecher Stowe's novel *Uncle Tom's Cabin* had led some to reevaluate the system of slavery. While most Indian reformers of the time were anti-Catholic Protestant Christians, Jackson had presented a sympathetic picture of the Catholic Church in her novel. The novel was retold in three films and one stage play. While her main focus was exposing the mistreatment of Indians, like other white reformers of the time, Jackson endorsed an assimilationist view, believing that Indians could be "saved" by Christianity, mainstream education, and "civilization."

Jackson broke a leg shortly after the publication of *Ramona* and never recovered, dying less than one year later at age 54. Her most significant works were published just a few years before her death. She had done more than any other white person to raise consciousness regarding the status of American Indians. She might have pushed public awareness further had she lived longer. Her books and articles were extremely influential among such white reformist groups as the Women's National Indian Association (WNIA), the Indian Rights Association (IRA), and the Lake Mohawk Conference.

After her death these organizations continued her work on behalf of the California Mission Indians. The 1892 passage of the Act for the Relief of the Mission Indians in the State of California was based on Jackson's recommendations made as agent to the Mission Indians. Her connection to the rights of American Indians was so strong that she had stated to a friend, "I shall be found with 'Indians' engraved on my brain when I am dead.—A fire has been kindled within me, which will never go out."

Further Reading

Jackson, Helen Hunt. *California and the Missions.* 1883. Reprint, Boston: Little, Brown, 1916.

———. *A Century of Dishonor: A Sketch of the United States Government's Dealings With Some of the Indian Tribes.* 1884. Reprint, Stillwater: University of Oklahoma Press, 1995.

———. *The Indian Reform Letters of Helen Hunt Jackson, 1879–1885.* Stillwater: University of Oklahoma Press, 1998.

———. *Ramona: A Story.* 1884. Reprint, New York: New American Library, 1988.

Mathes, Valerie Sherer. *Helen Hunt Jackson and Her Indian Reform Legacy,* Stillwater, University of Oklahoma Press, 1997.

Narkiewicz, Beverly S. "Poets and Friends, Emily Dickinson and Helen Hunt Jackson." *American History* 30, no. 5 (December 1, 1995): 42.

 ## JONES, MARY HARRIS (Mother Jones)
(1830–1930)   *Labor Leader*

Mary Harris Jones, popularly known as "Mother" Jones, worked as a labor organizer for the United Mine Workers (UMW) and was a founding member of the Industrial Workers of the World (IWW), a radical branch of the labor movement. Mary Harris was born on May 1, 1830, in Cork, Ireland. She was the first child of tenant farmers Mary and Richard Harris. Her father was forced to leave Ireland for defying the English. He immigrated to the United States, worked on canals in upstate New York, and became a U.S. citizen. He sent for his family in 1838. Mary learned dressmaking from her mother.

She did well in school and was the first in her family to graduate from high school. She attended a teacher's college, when many poor immigrant girls worked as maids. She completed college in 1847 at age 17 and taught in Toronto and Maine. She moved to Chicago in 1859 and opened a dressmaker shop.

In 1861, she went to teach in Memphis, Tennessee, earning a third of the salary that male teachers were paid. Also that year she met George

Jones, an iron molder, and they married. She gave birth to four children in six years. He became an organizer for the Iron Molders International Union. A yellow fever epidemic claimed the lives of Jones's husband and their four children, leaving her a widow at age 37. She wore black for the rest of her life.

Jones returned to Chicago in 1867, but the shop she then opened was destroyed in the Great Chicago Fire of 1871. While homeless due to the Great Fire, she started attending Knights of Labor meetings. This group, founded in 1869, was the first to try to organize all workers, regardless of their trades. At a time when 12- to 14-hour days were the norm, the Knights called for eight-hour workdays. As the nation moved from an agrarian to an industrial economy, many workers were impoverished and had no pension or health care. The Knights welcomed all workers, skilled or unskilled, black or white, male or female. Jones began working for the Knights of Labor at a time when few women had joined the group, and very few women worked as organizers. In her 60s she became an organizer for the UMW. Her advanced age, gray hair, and shawl caused workers to refer to her affectionately as "Mother."

Jones was a union organizer in the days before unions were solidly established. In the 1870s, there were only 30 national unions. A lawyer once called her "the most dangerous woman in the country today." When a college professor praised her as a great humanitarian, she responded, "Get it right. I'm not a humanitarian, I'm a hell raiser." From 1900 to 1920 she organized miners in Colorado, Arizona, Michigan, Minnesota, West Virginia, and Pennsylvania. She was involved in garment workers' strikes in New York and steelworkers' strikes in Pennsylvania. Jones excelled in using the power of the media to bring attention to her causes through her own arrests or by leading marches of miners' wives or working children.

She worked undercover in mills in Alabama, Georgia, and South Carolina to expose abuses. Jones was particularly concerned with the issue of child labor; in some areas of the country, children accounted for one-third of all workers. In 1903, she led the "March of the Mill Children," drawing the nation's attention to the issue of child labor by organizing a cross-country march from Pennsylvania to Long Island. She led 100 mill child workers to the residence of President Theodore Roosevelt. A federal child labor law was finally passed 35 years later in 1938, eight years after her death.

Jones thought socialism would improve workers' lives. In 1905, she joined other socialists to form the IWW. One of the most violent strikes she participated in was the 1913 Colorado Coal Strike. As she later recalled of the strikers, "They had only the constitution. The other side had bayonets. In the end bayonets always win." The Ludlow Massacre in Colorado occurred when a tent colony of miners and their families was attacked with machine guns in April 1914. Jones testified on the assault before the U.S. Congress. A truce was called and grievance committees for the mines were established.

Jones was a versatile strategist who once advised jailed women in Pennsylvania in 1910 to sing all night long so that the jailers and townspeople could not sleep. The women were released five days later. Jones enlisted miners' wives to frighten strikebreakers (known as scabs). Women armed with brooms, mops, and pans chased scabs away and patrolled the striking area. Under the orders of the local coal company, one town did not allow Jones to pass out leaflets to announce a meeting so Jones sent two men into town to wander the streets. One man acted as though he was hard of hearing, and the other man yelled the news to his companion about Jones's meeting.

She organized working-class women into auxiliaries of the unions and criticized men in general for not being as strong as women, but Jones opposed women's suffrage. Part of her opposition was due to her distrust of politics. She stated, "I have never had a vote and I have raised hell all over this country!" Her opposition to suffrage may have also been due to the class-based nature of her politics and her belief that poor women needed food and shelter more than they needed the right to

President Coolidge and Mary Harris "Mother" Jones, 1924
(Prints & Photographs Division, Library of Congress, Washington, D.C.)

vote. She said, "God almighty made women, and the Rockefeller gang of thieves made the ladies." After women's suffrage was attained in 1920, she wrote in 1925, "The plutocrats have organized their women. They keep them busy with suffrage and prohibition and charity."

The Charles Kerr Company of Chicago published her autobiography in 1925. On her 100th birthday, a Movietone News cameraman tried to tell her how to speak on camera but she responded, "What the hell do you know about it? I was making speeches before you were born!" Mother Jones died a few months after that incident, on November 30, 1930. Workers from eight different trades served as her pallbearers. She asked to be buried at Mount Olive Hill, the miner's cemetery in Mount Olive, Illinois, because she wanted to "sleep under the clay with those brave boys." A friend had observed at her funeral that, "If Mother Jones had stayed in Ireland, she probably would have been hanged . . . or else, she would have been President of the Irish Republic."

A few years after her death, miners erected a huge granite monument at the cemetery in her honor. A progressive magazine still in circulation was named after her. In 1992, she was inducted into the U.S. Department of Labor's Hall of Fame in Washington, D.C.

She is featured in a display in the lobby, where a videotape about Mother Jones is available, and visitors can hear a recording of her Irish brogue. She says in the video, made from a film on her 100th birthday, that she wished she could "live another hundred years in order to fight to the end that there would be no more machine guns and no more sobbing of little children."

Further Reading

Foner, Phillip. *Mother Jones Speaks: Speeches and Writings of a Working-Class Fighter.* New York: Pathfinder Press, 1995.

Jones, Mary Harris. *The Autobiography of Mother Jones.* Chicago: Charles Kerr, 1925.

Tonn, Mari Boor. "Militant Motherhood: Labor's Mary Harris "Mother" Jones." *Quarterly Journal of Speech* 82 (February 1996): 1–21.

 JORDAN, BARBARA CHARLINE
(1936–1996)   *Congressional Representative*

Barbara Jordan was the first African-American woman elected to Congress from the South. Barbara Charline Jordan was born on February 21, 1936, to Arlyne and Benjamin Jordan. She was youngest of three girls. Her mother was a domestic worker, and her father was a warehouse clerk and Baptist minister. She grew up in Houston, Texas. Because of the disparities in resources under segregation, she attended schools that used textbooks that were outdated by at least 10 years. Students from her school were not allowed to use public libraries. After hearing African-American attorney Edith Sampson speak at her high school, Jordan decided she wanted to become a lawyer. She was a member of the honor society and graduated in 1952 in the top 5 percent of her class.

She attended Texas Southern University, where she studied political science and history and led the debate team. She graduated magna cum laude in 1956. Jordan was the first African-American student admitted to Boston University Law School. She completed her J.D. degree in 1959 and was one of only two women to graduate from the school that year.

Jordan worked for the Democratic Party to organize the African-American vote for John F. Kennedy in 1960. She returned to Houston in 1960 and practiced law for three years, using her parents' dining room as an office before saving enough money to open a more traditional office. She became the friend of other Texas politicians such as former Speaker of the House Sam Rayburn, future President Lyndon Johnson, and future governor ANN RICHARDS. She ran unsuccessfully for a seat in the Texas House of Representatives in 1962 and again in 1964. In 1966, she won election to the Texas State Senate, becoming the first woman elected and the first African American elected since 1883. She authored the state's first minimum-wage bill and supported civil rights legislation. During her first year in the Texas Senate, she was named outstanding freshman senator. In her 1968 reelection bid, she ran unopposed. President Lyndon Johnson said of Jordan, "She proved that black is beautiful before we knew what it meant."

In 1971, Jordan ran for the U.S. Congress in the newly created 18th Congressional District in Texas. She received 80 percent of the vote in a field that included four Democratic candidates. She served three terms in Congress. During this time she sponsored legislation to extend social security coverage to U.S. women who worked in the home. She authored an expanded Workman's Compensation Act and sponsored legislation to expand the Voting Rights Act of 1965. She gained national prominence during the Watergate hearings in 1974 when she served on the House Judiciary Committee. Jordan was one of 38 representatives responsible for making the decisions regarding articles of impeachment for President Richard Nixon. In 1975, *Time* magazine recognized her as one of its 10 most admired women of the year. A 1979 *Redbook* poll found that Jordan was selected as one of the top women who could potentially be president. In 1976, she was the first woman and the first African-American keynote speaker at a national party convention.

President Jimmy Carter offered Jordan a post in his cabinet as Secretary of the Department of

Health, Education and Welfare (HEW), but she declined. Some political analysts believed she wanted the attorney general position instead. In 1979, she left politics to work in education and served as distinguished professor at the University of Texas, Austin, Lyndon Baines Johnson School of Public Affairs. Her autobiography, *Barbara Jordan: A Self-Portrait,* was published in 1979. For 10 years she also hosted a public affairs program, *Crisis to Crisis with Barbara Jordan,* on public television. In 1982 she was awarded the university's Lyndon B. Johnson Chair of National Policy.

She gave another keynote address at the 1992 Democratic convention, this time from a wheelchair because of her multiple sclerosis, which had been diagnosed several years earlier in 1973. A school at the University of Texas is named in her honor. She donated her papers to her alma mater, Texas Southern University. President Clinton awarded her the Presidential Medal of Freedom in 1994. Princeton, Harvard, and 13 other universities awarded her honorary doctorates.

Barbara Jordan died in 1996. She was born in a poor, all-black segregated neighborhood in Houston, Texas, only four years after African Americans were allowed to vote in Texas. However, she rose to national prominence as an attorney and politician.

Further Reading

Groer, Annie. "Barbara Jordan." *Biography* 3, no. 1 (January 1999): 108–10.

Ivins, Molly. "She Sounded Like God." *New York Times Magazine,* December 29, 1996, 17.

Johnson, Linda Carlson. *Barbara Jordan: Congresswoman.* Woodbridge, Conn.: Blackbirch Press, 1990.

Rogers, Mary Beth. *Barbara Jordan: American Hero.* New York: Bantam Doubleday Dell, 1998.

"Ethics Watchdog Barbara Jordan Keeps Tabs on Texas." *Time* 137, no. 22 (June 3, 1991): 9–12.

K

KASSEBAUM, NANCY JOSEPHINE LANDON

(1932–) *Senator*

Nancy Landon Kassebaum was the fourth woman in history to be elected to the U.S. Senate and the first to be elected on her own terms, not as the widow of a senator. Nancy Josephine Landon was born July 29, 1932, to Alfred Landon and his second wife, Theo. Her father, a wealthy attorney, banker, and oil operator, was the governor of Kansas from 1932 to 1937 and a Republican presidential candidate in 1936. Nancy Landon met her husband, John Philip Kassebaum, when she was a sophomore at the University of Kansas. She completed a B.A. degree in political science in 1954. In 1955, she got married, and while her husband attended law school at the University of Michigan, she completed an M.A. degree in diplomatic history there. The couple had four children. She remained active in civic affairs as a member of the Maize School Board, the Kansas Governmental Ethics Commission, and the Kansas Committee for the Humanities. She raised her children in a suburb of Wichita and served as vice president of a family-owned firm that operated two radio stations.

After her divorce in 1975, she worked as a legislative aide in Washington, D.C., to Senator James Pearson of Kansas. When Pearson announced his retirement in 1978, Kassebaum became one of nine Republicans who sought the Republican nomination for his office. Her mother encouraged her but her father was reluctant to support her at first because he knew firsthand of the public and private demands entailed by a political career. She won the primary and general election, becoming the only woman senator. She was reelected in 1984 and 1990. She supported the Equal Rights Amendment, but refused to support an extension of the ratification deadline. She worked to impose economic sanctions against South Africa for its apartheid policies, and served on the Foreign Relations Committee. She supported abortion rights and was viewed as a moderate on social issues. She also authored the Federal Health Insurance Portability and Accountability Act, better known as the Kassebaum-Kennedy Act, after its sponsors, Senator

Edward Kennedy, D-Mass. and Senator Nancy Kassebaum, R-Kan. The legislation was drafted to prevent insurance companies from denying coverage to those clients with preexisting conditions or dropping coverage for people who changed jobs. She advocated ending all federal funding for welfare and food stamps.

She served three terms before retiring for "purely personal" reasons. In 1996, Kassebaum was the first holder of the Mary Louise Smith Endowed Chair in the Carrie Chapman Catt Center for Women and Politics at Iowa State University. (Mary Louise Smith was the only woman to chair the National Committee of the Republican Party, a position she held from 1974 through 1977.)

Kassebaum married former Tennessee senator and Republican majority leader Howard Baker in 1996. It was the first marriage between a senator and former senator.

In 1997 President Bill Clinton appointed former senator Kassebaum to lead a public education project on campaign finance reform. In April 2001, President George W. Bush appointed Kassebaum to chair the Presidential Appointee Initiative advisory board, which made recommendations on how to streamline the recruitment and nomination process for presidential appointees.

Nancy Kassebaum's service and achievements as one of the first female senators offered an important role model to those who followed.

Further Reading

Chen, Edwin. "Political Elders Tapped." *Los Angeles Times,* March 18, 1997, A15.

Clines, Francis. "Weary of Political Noise, a Senator Sees a Peaceful Farm in Her Future." *New York Times Biographical Service* 26 (December 1995): 1792–93.

Greenfield, Meg. "Let Nancy Do It." *Newsweek* 125 (March 27, 1995): 74.

Kassebaum, Nancy. "The Intersection of Hope and Doubt—The Agenda for the Future." *Vital Speeches of the Day* 63, no. 2 (1996): 36(4).

"Profile: Senator Nancy Kassebaum." *U.S. News and World Report* 118, no. 4 (January 23, 1995): 4.

Raines, Franklin. "Commentary: Uncle Sam Wants a Few Good Appointees." *Los Angeles Times,* April 5, 2001, B11.

Werber, Serafini. "Grand Finale: After 18 Years in the Senate." *National Journal* 28, no. 10 (1996): 527 (5).

 ## KELLER, HELEN ADAMS
(1880–1968)   *Disability Advocate*

Helen Keller was an internationally known disability rights activist at the turn of the 20th century. Helen Adams Keller was born June 27, 1880, in the small southern town of Tuscumbia, Alabama. She was the first child of Kate and Arthur Keller. Her father was a wealthy landowner and newspaper publisher who had been a captain in the Confederate army. Kate was the captain's second wife and was 20 years his junior.

When Keller was 19 months old she contracted scarlet fever, which caused her to lose her sight and hearing within a few weeks. At the time, many assumed that blind and deaf people were also simpleminded. Some family members felt that Keller should be committed to a mental institution, but her mother refused to give up hope. Helen had invented 60 hand signs of her own, which her family could understand. Her mother read the book *American Notes* by Charles Dickens, in which he described his meeting with Laura Bridgman, a Boston girl who had lost her sight and hearing. Bridgman was taught how to read at the Perkins Institution for the Blind in Boston by using a manual alphabet. Spanish monks who had taken a vow of silence had invented the manual language, and a sign language was also used as the trade language among many American Indian tribes.

Her mother wrote to the Perkins Institution requesting a teacher for her daughter. The school sent 21-year-old Anne Mansfield Sullivan. Sullivan came from an impoverished background and had been valedictorian of the Perkins class of 1886. At this time northerners were still viewed with suspicion in the South. Keller would remember the arrival of Anne Sullivan in March 1887: "My birthday can never mean as much to me as the arrival of Anne Sullivan on March 3, 1887. That was my soul's birthday."

A month after Sullivan's arrival she had her first breakthrough when she held Keller's hand under water and spelled the word manually into her hand. Keller would remember, "It was as if I had come back to life after being dead." By the end of the day Keller had learned 30 words. Her hands would sometimes talk in her sleep. When she first went to the ocean and tasted it she signed angrily, "Who put salt in the water?"

By age 12, Keller had become familiar to the American public through newspaper stories. She used her fame to raise funds for an impoverished deaf and blind five-year-old named Tommy Stringer. Stringer would have been sent to the poorhouse in Pennsylvania, but through Keller's intervention, he was sent to Perkins.

Keller wanted to attend Boston's Horace Mann School for the Deaf in order to learn to speak, but her vocal cords were weak and untrained. She never learned to speak clearly but did learn lipreading as well as Braille. She learned to lip read by placing one hand on her teacher's lips while the teacher said the name of an object and placing her other hand on the object itself. (Frenchman Louis Braille invented a raised alphabet for the blind in 1826, and the first machine for writing Braille was developed in 1892).

Keller attended Perkins, the only blind student who was also deaf. When Keller arrived at Perkins she recalled, "What a joy to talk to other children in my own language . . . in the school where Laura Bridgman was taught. I was in my own country." The school library had the largest collection of books for the blind in the United States. Keller's fluency with her fingers was clocked at 80 words per minute.

At a time when women were not encouraged to pursue higher education, Keller wanted a college degree. When her father had a reversal of fortune, Mark Twain assumed financial responsibility for Keller's schooling, commenting; "It won't do for Americans to allow this marvelous child to retire from her studies because of poverty. If she can go on with them, she will make a name that will endure in history for centuries."

In 1896, Keller entered the Cambridge School for Young Ladies in Boston to prepare for Radcliffe College's entrance examinations. The tips of her fingers bled from studying. Keller received scholarship offers from Cornell and the University of Chicago but declined them, saying, "If I went to any other college it would be thought that I did not pass my examinations for Radcliffe." She entered Radcliffe in 1900 and studied languages and philosophy. In 1902, while she was still at Radcliffe, *Ladies' Home Journal* offered her $3,000, which was then an average American's yearly salary, to write the story of her life. In 1903, this story was expanded into a very successful book, *The Story of My Life,* which was translated into 50 languages. In 1904, Keller graduated cum laude from Radcliffe.

In 1908, she followed the literary success of her first book by writing *The World I Live In,* which explained how she compensated for her lack of vision and hearing by using other senses.

Her teacher, Anne Sullivan, was politically conservative, against suffrage for women and socialism. Keller, in contrast, was a pacifist and a staunch suffragist who marched in Votes for Women parades. She also supported birth control, condemned child labor and capital punishment, and became a socialist. Traditional biographers have often ignored her radical politics. Keller had a red flag of Russia over the desk in her study and also supported the Industrial Workers of the World (IWW), a radical union. Keller thought that blindness was more common in the working class and poor due to industrial accidents and inadequate medical care. She also spoke of the blindness prostitutes suffered, a result of the venereal disease syphilis, not

Helen Keller touching a statue, 1912
(Prints & Photographs Division,
Library of Congress, Washington, D.C.)

considered a fitting topic for ladies of her class background.

Keller also contributed money to the National Association for the Advancement of Colored People (NAACP), and her letters of support were published in its magazine, *The Crisis.* These were radical acts for a white person from Alabama in the 1920s.

She supported the Russian Revolution and was lucky to escape the red purges in America in the 1920s, but she was criticized for her socialist views. Her articles on the women's movement and political economy were rejected by publishers. Her 1913 collection of essays, *Out of the Dark,* which dealt with political topics, received a lukewarm reception.

In 1914, a Scottish woman, Polly Thomson, was hired as Keller's secretary-housekeeper and remained her companion for the next 46 years. In 1924, Keller joined the three-year-old American Foundation for the Blind as a fund-raiser, touring 123 cities and raising more than $1 million, a huge sum in the 1920s. Keller also worked to standardize the Braille system, which until 1932 comprised five different reading systems. Keller was finally successful in getting the Louis Braille system accepted as the standard. She also organized a global meeting for the American Foundation for the Blind that had representatives from 32 nations.

Her teacher and companion for 50 years, Anne Sullivan, died in 1936. The last book Keller wrote, in 1955, was about Anne Sullivan and simply titled *Teacher.* At age 47 Keller wrote *My Religion,* about the new church she joined, which had been founded by Emmanuel Swedenborg, a Swedish mystic. About her religious views, Keller said, "The spiritual world offers no difficulty to one who is deaf and blind. Nearly everything in the natural world is as vague, as remote from my sense, as spiritual things seem to the minds of most people." Keller read the Bible so much that the Braille dots were worn off some pages.

A movie about her life, *The Unconquered,* won an Academy Award, and in 1959 William Gibson wrote *The Miracle Worker,* a Pulitzer Prize–winning play about her life that was also made into a film in 1962. President Lyndon Johnson awarded Keller the Presidential Medal of Freedom in 1964.

Polly Thompson died in 1960, and Keller had a stroke the following year. She retired from public life at age 81 due to her stroke, and the during next seven years she endured a series of strokes. Helen Keller died June 1, 1968, in Westport, Connecticut, a few weeks before her 88th birthday. She had once said, "Life is either a daring adventure or nothing."

Further Reading

Einhorn, Lois. *Helen Keller, Public Speaker: Sightless but Seen, Deaf but Heard.* Westport, Conn.: Greenwood, 1996.

Herrmann, Dorothy. *Helen Keller: A Life.* New York: Knopf, 1998.

Hurwitz, Johanna. *Helen Keller: Courage in the Dark.* New York: Random House, 1997.

Keller, Helen. *Helen Keller's Journal.* 1938. Reprint, Murrieta, Calif.: University of Temecula, 1991.

———. *Story of My Life.* 1902. Reprint, New York: Doubleday, 1991.

———. *Teacher.* 1955. Reprint, Westport, Conn.: Greenwood, 1985.

 ## KELLEY, FLORENCE MOLTHROP
(1859–1932)   *Labor Advocate*

Florence Kelley led efforts to enact protective labor legislation. She was born in Philadelphia, the youngest daughter of Caroline Bonsall Kelley and William Kelley. Her parents had been active abolitionists. William Kelley was a Republican member of the House of Representatives, known for his radical views on race and the support of protectionist trade. Florence Kelley earned a bachelor's degree from Cornell University in 1882. She then studied at the University of Zurich, one of the few European universities that accepted women students. Kelley became a socialist and also translated socialist theorist Friedrich Engels's work from German into English. She married a young Russian medical student in 1890, and they had three children.

In 1891, Kelley became a resident of Chicago's Hull-House settlement. She met the women of Hull-House when she went to Illinois to take advantage of the more liberal divorce laws in that state. In 1897 she divorced her husband for physical and mental abuse and resumed using her maiden name. Kelley gained custody of her children in the divorce, but they often stayed with her mother in Philadelphia while Kelley engaged in campaigns.

She earned a law degree from Northwestern University in 1894 and served as the chief factory inspector for the state of Illinois from 1893 to 1897. She was the first female inspector for the state, and she focused on sweatshops in the Chicago area. Under Governor John Peter Altgeld her efforts resulted in Illinois passing an act that limited women's work hours and banned child labor. The next governor of Illinois was not as supportive of reform measurers as Altgeld, so Kelley returned to the East Coast. She was branded as too radical for labor inspection posts in other states.

In 1899, she moved to New York and resided at Lillian Wald's Henry Street Settlement. Kelley became the executive secretary of the National Consumers' League, a position she held from 1899 until her death. She organized more than 60 chapters of the league, which used consumer pressure to ensure that products were manufactured and marketed under safe conditions, thus monitoring the products of sweatshops. She helped organize the New York Child Labor Committee in 1902. Kelley worked closely with the consumers' league in Oregon to help defeat a challenge to the 10-hour-day for women in 1908. In that case, *Muller v. Oregon,* the Supreme Court ruled that restricted work hours for women were constitutional. In the 1920s, the U.S. Supreme Court would reverse this position and find protective legislation for women unconstitutional, arguing that the right of suffrage that women had gained canceled their need for special workplace protections. Kelley would continue to argue, "Why are seals, bears, reindeer, fish, wild game in the national parks, buffalo, migratory birds, all found suitable for federal protection; but not the children of our race and their mothers?"

Kelley lobbied for national legislation modeled on what she had achieved in Illinois. Her ideas on industrial reform were published in 1905 in *Some Ethical Gains Through Legislation.* She played a pivotal role in introducing minimum wage legislation by publishing articles and speaking on the subject, beginning in 1909. Three years later, Kelley assisted in the founding of the Federal Children's Bureau in 1912. She also joined the Eugene Debs Socialist Party of America in 1912 and would remain a member until her death. By 1913, nine states had passed minimum wage laws.

She was a founder of the National Association for the Advancement of Colored People (NAACP) and the Women's International League for Peace and Freedom. She also opposed World War I. Her last legislative victory was in 1921 with the passage of the Sheppard-Towner Maternity and Infancy Protection Act, which afforded infants and mothers accessible prenatal and maternal care. As the federal and state governments became more conservative, her influence waned. She was also an active suffragist and served as vice president of the National Woman Suffrage Association and campaigned in states from California to Georgia. She opposed other suffragists who supported the Equal Rights Amendment (ERA), because she was concerned that the protective legislation for women, for which she had lobbied for so many years, would be nullified by that amendment.

Florence Kelley died on February 17, 1932, in Philadelphia, Pennsylvania. She had worked to remove many of the abuses workers suffered under rapid industrialization. Many of the laws enacted under President Franklin Roosevelt's New Deal had originated with Florence Kelley and other reformers during the Progressive era. Her legacy included establishing a minimum wage, setting maximum working hours, working for laws to protect women and children from unsafe working conditions, and authoring most of the child labor laws. She dedicated her life to end the abuses of unregulated industrial capitalism.

Further Reading

Goldmark, Josephine Clara. *Impatient Crusader.* Westport, Conn.: Greenwood, 1981.

Kelley, Florence. *Modern Industry in Relation to the Family, Health, Education, Morality.* 1913. Reprint, Los Angeles: Hyperion Press, 1975.

Sklar, Kathryn Kish. *Florence Kelley and the Nation's Work: The Rise of Women's Political Culture, 1830–1900.* New Haven, Conn.: Yale University Press, 1995.

Sklar, Kathryn ed. *Notes of Sixty Years: The Autobiography of Florence Kelley.* Chicago: Charles H. Kerr, 1986.

Florence Kelley, labor reformer
(Still Picture Branch, National Archives, College Park, MD)

 KENNEDY, FLORENCE RAE
(Flo Kennedy)
(1916–) *Feminist Activist*

Florence Kennedy was a preeminent attorney, writer, public speaker, and advocate of black feminism in both white feminist organizations and organizations created by women of color in the 1970s. Florence Rae "Flo" Kennedy was born on February 11, 1916, in Kansas City, Missouri, the second of five daughters of Zella and Wiley Kennedy. Her childhood years were spent in Missouri and California. She recalls her father staring down Ku Klux Klan members at their home and said, "My parents gave us a fantastic sense of security and worth. By the time the bigots got around to telling us we were nobody, we already knew we were somebody."

Even before starting high school, Kennedy had decided on a career as an attorney. After completing high school, she worked in a hat shop and performed with her sisters on a radio show in Kansas City. Her activism began when she helped organize a boycott against Coca-Cola through the Negro Chamber of Commerce and the local branch of the National Association for the Advancement of Colored People (NAACP). The boycott was waged to force the Coca-Cola Company to hire African Americans.

In 1942, Kennedy moved to New York City and entered Columbia University. As early as 1946 she exhibited a sharp social perception regarding issues of race and class in an essay she wrote for a sociology class, "A Comparative Study: Accentuating the Similarities of Societal Position of Women and Negroes." Her essay was critical of capitalism and the ways in which industry marginalizes and subordinates women and African Americans. She completed her B.A. degree and applied to the Columbia Law School but was denied admission because the quota for women students had already been filled. After she threatened to file a discrimination lawsuit, Columbia admitted her. She completed her law degree in 1951.

In 1954, she established a successful law practice, representing such performers as Billie Holiday and Charlie Parker and later defending activist H. Rap Brown. She was one of the founders of the National Organization for Women (NOW) but became disenchanted with what she felt was the conservative nature of its politics, so she joined radical feminist groups. She protested with other radical feminists at the Miss America pageant in 1968. In 1969, she formed a legal team that filed a class-action lawsuit regarding the constitutionality of New York State abortion laws.

In 1972, she filed a complaint against the Catholic Church for its financial support of anti-abortion groups. In the 1970s, she also organized a "pee-in" at Harvard when the previously all-male institution was hesitating in the installation of women's bathrooms. By the mid 1970s, Kennedy had moved from practicing law to becoming a full-time activist.

She coauthored one of the first books on the issue of abortion, *Abortion Rap*. The idea for the book came from a consciousness-raising rap session (discussion) with a radical feminist group, the Redstockings, organized for women to talk publicly about the taboo topic of abortion. Her book was a collection of stories about women's decisions and experiences with abortion when it was still illegal and underground. Many black nationalists at the time were against not only abortion, but also the use of birth control, arguing that African-American women could contribute to a black revolution by having babies. Kennedy wrote an essay in *Abortion Rap* that critiqued this position.

In 1971, Kennedy founded the Feminist Party, which supported the presidential candidacy of SHIRLEY CHISHOLM. Her support of Chisholm was crucial, because Chisholm received little support from other feminist and black leaders. In 1973, Kennedy cofounded the National Black Feminist Organization (NBFO). The group was short-lived due to financial difficulties, but made its mark as the first black feminist organization. By 1974, the Feminist Party had 175 chapters.

At the turn of the 21st century, Kennedy remained active in Democratic politics and hosted *The Flo Kennedy Show* on a New York City public-access television channel. As her activism continues into her 80s she says, "I never stop to wonder why I'm not like other people. The mystery to me is why more people aren't like me."

Further Reading

Kennedy, Florence, with Diane Schulder. *Abortion Rap.* New York: McGraw-Hill, 1971.

———. *Color Me Flo: My Hard Life and Good Times.* Englewood Cliffs, N.J.: Prentice-Hall, 1976.

———. "A Comparative Study: Accentuating the Similarities of the Societal Position of Women and Negroes." In *Words of Fire: An Anthology of African-American Feminist Thought,* edited by Beverly Guy-Shefall. New York: New Press, 1995.

KIRKPATRICK, JEANNE JORDAN
(1926–   )   *United Nations Ambassador*

Jeanne Kirkpatrick served as the U.S. ambassador to the United Nations from 1981 to 1985. She was the first woman to hold the post and the first woman to sit on the National Security Council. Jeanne Jordan was born in Duncan, Oklahoma, on November 19, 1926. Her father was an oilman—a drilling contractor. Both her parents were active Democrats.

Jordan attended Stephens College in Missouri for two years, then transferred to Barnard College in New York. She graduated from Barnard College in 1948 and received her master's degree in 1950 and doctorate in 1968, both in political science from Columbia University. While at Columbia, she was deeply influenced by several professors who were political refugees from war-torn Europe and had strong views regarding the totalitarianism of Nazi Germany and Stalinist Russia.

From 1955 to 1972 she worked for the Department of Defense, in an intelligence and research bureau headed by Evron Kirkpatrick, a former political science professor 15 years her senior. She married him one year later in 1955. They honeymooned at a political science conference at Northwestern University. She worked as a research analyst at the U.S. State Department and served on several Democratic Party committees. In 1956 she joined the Communism in Government project at the Department of Defense. She worked in this position until 1962. The next decade she worked in the home raising three children.

Kirkpatrick began teaching at Georgetown University in 1967, focusing on political theory, European government, French politics, and politics and

Jeanne Kirkpatrick, political appointee
(Prints & Photographs Division,
Library of Congress, Washington, D.C.)

personality. In the 1970s she wrote several books, including *Leader and Vanguard in Mass Society* (1971), *Political Women* (1974), which examined the role of women in state legislatures, and *The New Presidential Elite* (1976). As a Democrat she was active in the political campaigns of Hubert Humphrey and served on the Credentials Committee at the 1976 Democratic National Convention. She later became disenchanted with the Democratic Party and publicly criticized the foreign policy of President Jimmy Carter. She became a full professor at Georgetown University in 1978.

An article she wrote in 1979 changed the course of her career when Ronald Reagan noticed it. At first she thought the article was not worth publishing, but "Dictatorships and Double Standards" appeared in the November 1979 issue of *Commentary*. In it she argued that U.S. policy makers should distinguish between authoritarian regimes that it could assist and become allies with, and totalitarian regimes. According to her viewpoint, the authoritarian regime of General Anastasio Somoza in Nicaragua had been replaced with the totalitarian regime of Daniel Ortega, and the authoritarian regime of the Shah of Iran had been replaced with the totalitarian rule of the Ayatollah Khomeini. Her views correlated closely with those of the Reagan administration. She became a foreign policy adviser for President Ronald Reagan in 1980. Reagan appointed Kirkpatrick as the U.S. ambassador to the United Nations. She served four years and became one of the longest-serving ambassadors in that post. She was given cabinet rank and served on Reagan's national security team. Kirkpatrick advocated a hard line toward the Soviet Union. Kirkpatrick was criticized for her tolerance of authoritarian regimes. Critics accused her of accepting bribes and falsifying documents that accused the USSR of shooting down a Korean passenger jet. She denied all charges. In 1985 she returned to teaching at Georgetown, officially joined the Republican Party, and worked as a political commentator.

Kirkpatrick was mentioned as a potential presidential candidate in the 1988 election. In 1990, she wrote *The Withering Away of the Totalitarian State*. She delivered a keynote speech at the 1996 Republican Convention in San Diego, California.

Kirkpatrick is a professor at Georgetown University, a senior fellow at the American Enterprise Institute (AEI), and a founding codirector of Empower America, a conservative public policy organization. She remains active in Republican Party politics.

Further Reading

Gerson, Allan. *The Kirkpatrick Mission: Diplomacy without Apology: America at the United Nations, 1981–1985.* New York: Free Press, 1991.

Kirkpatrick, Jeanne. "Dictatorships and Double Standards." *Commentary* (November 1979): 34–45.

———. *The Kennedy-Khrushchev Pact and the Sandinistas.* Washington: Cuban American National Foundation, 1985.

———. *Leader and Vanguard.* Cambridge: Massachusetts Institute of Technology, 1971.

———. *The New Presidential Elite: Men and Women in National Politics.* New York: Russell Sage, 1976.

———. *Political Women.* New York: Basic Books, 1974.

KUHN, MARGARET ELIZA (Maggie Kuhn)
(1905–1995)   *Founder of the Gray Panthers*

When Maggie Kuhn was forced to retire at age 65, she launched the Gray Panthers, a public advocacy group to address ageism. The name was modeled on that of the Black Panthers, an African-American organization. Margaret Eliza Kuhn was born on August 3, 1905, in Buffalo, New York. At the time of her birth her parents had been living in Memphis, Tennessee, but her mother traveled home to Buffalo for labor and delivery so that her daughter would not be born in the segregated South. Her family was Presbyterian.

Kuhn completed a B.A. degree from Flora Stone Mather College of Case Western Reserve University in 1926. Kuhn was engaged twice but never married, she said, due to "sheer luck. If I had married them my life would have been over."

Her first job after graduation was with the Young Women's Christian Association (YWCA) in Cleveland, Ohio, and then in Philadelphia, Pennsylvania, when her family relocated there. She worked at the YWCA in Philadelphia from 1930 to 1941, then continued her work in New York City during World War II. Following the war she worked in Boston, Massachusetts, for the General Alliance for Unitarian and Other Christian Women.

She returned to Philadelphia in 1948 to be near her aging parents. She accepted a position as associate secretary of the Presbyterian Church's Social Education and Action Department, focusing on issues of urban poverty and health care. Kuhn served as editor of the organization journal *Social Progress*, which became *Church and Society* in the 1960s. At the time she was forced to retire, she was the coordinator of programs in the Division of Church and Race.

After a 25-year career as an employee of the United Presbyterian Church, she was forced into retirement in 1970. The church presented her with a retirement gift of a sewing machine, but Kuhn recalled, "I never opened it. I was too busy." She started a group in 1970 with five other female friends who had also been forced into retirement. The group was originally named Consultation of Older and Younger Adults with its headquarters in Philadelphia, and branches in eastern cities such as New York City and Washington, D.C. Kuhn additionally helped to develop the National Caucus on the Black Aged.

The Gray Panthers grew to a peak membership of 60,000 and lobbied to rewrite mandatory retirement laws. The group was intergenerational from its beginning, however. At its peak in the early 1980s, almost 40 percent of its membership was younger than 50. The Gray Panthers were successful in raising the mandatory retirement age to 70. They were also active in addressing nursing home abuses, patients' rights, and health care delivery. The group lobbied for mandatory geriatric-medicine courses in medical schools and more realistic portrayals of older adults in the media.

Kuhn authored several books, including *You Can't Be Human Alone, Let's Get Out There and Do Something About Injustice, Maggie Kuhn on Aging,* and her autobiography, *No Stone Unturned: The Life and Times of Maggie Kuhn,* published in 1991.

Maggie Kuhn died at home on April 22, 1995, in Philadelphia, just months before her 90th birthday and less than a month before the Gray Panthers celebrated their 25th anniversary.

The Gray Panthers remain active, with nearly 40,000 members. The 220-feet of records of Kuhn and the Gray Panthers are stored at the Urban Archives of Temple University, in Philadelphia. Her advocacy caused many to reexamine societal attitude regarding elders.

Further Reading

Altus, Deborah. "Maggie Kuhn on Intergenerational Home Sharing." *Communities* no. 82 (spring 1994): 45.

Hessel, Dieter T. *Age in a New Age: Study, Action Guide for Maggie Kuhn on Aging.* New York: United Presbyterian Program Agency, 1979.

———. *Maggie Kuhn on Aging: A Dialogue.* Philadelphia: Westminster Press, 1977.

Kuhn, Maggie. *No Stone Unturned: The Life and Times of Maggie Kuhn.* New York: Ballantine, 1991.

"Obituary." *Time* 145 (May 1, 1995): 33.

Shapiro, Bruce. "Obituary." *Nation* 260 (May 29, 1995): 744–45.

L

 LaDUKE, WINONA

(1959–) *Anishinabe Environmental Activist, Vice-Presidential Candidate*

Harvard-educated Winona LaDuke returned to her Anishinabe White Earth Reservation in northern Minnesota to found a land recovery project and address environmental racism. (*Environmental racism* refers to the disproportionate share of environmental devastation carried out in communities of color.) She also ran as the vice-presidential candidate of the Green Party in 1996 and 2000.

Winona LaDuke was born on August 18, 1959. Her family lived in an American Indian neighborhood in east Los Angeles. Her father, Vincent LaDuke, was a Mississippi band member of the Anishinabe (Chippewa/Ojibway) from the White Earth Reservation. During the 1950s, the Eisenhower years, he traveled to Washington, D.C., to take part in protests regarding the status of American Indians. While on one of these trips he met Betty Bernstein, a Russian Jewish painter from New York who had worked with American Indians in Santa Fe, New Mexico. In 1958, LaDuke's parents married on the White Earth Reservation, 220 miles northwest of Minneapolis, Minnesota. The couple moved to California, where Vincent LaDuke worked as an extra in Hollywood movies. Her parents divorced in 1964 when LaDuke was five, so LaDuke went to live with her mother in Ashland, Oregon. Her father became known as Sun Bear, a leader in the New Age movement, and her mother became an art professor.

Her high school guidance counselor told her not to apply to college but to attend a vocational technical school. However, after completing high school in 1976, LaDuke attended Harvard University in Cambridge, Massachusetts. A speech she heard by Cherokee activist Jimmy Durham had a great impact on her. She began working for Durham, researching the health implications of uranium mining. She spent the summer in Arizona working with Navajo who were organizing protests against uranium mining on their reservation. She began working with the International Indian Treaty Council (IITC), a nongovernmental organization of the United Nations. She was just 18 when she testified before the United Nations for the IITC on the issues of mining and multinational corporations on reservations.

LaDuke completed a degree in native economic development at Harvard in 1982, then

Winona LaDuke, American Indian leader
(Keri Picket)

attended the Massachusetts Institute of Technology (MIT). She completed a master's degree in rural development at Antioch College in Yellow Springs, Ohio, in 1989.

LaDuke returned to live on the White Earth Reservation in rural Minnesota, working as a high school principal. While serving as principal she began an Anishinabe language immersion program for preschoolers during the day and for adults in night classes. The program, called Wadison, or "nest," trained a small group of children and their families to become fully literate in Anishinabe. She also initiated the use of Anishinabe words on reservation road signs.

In 1988, she married Randy Kapashesit, a leader of the Cree tribe from Moose Factory, Ontario. The couple had two children but separated in 1992

since, as LaDuke has acknowledged, "I couldn't give up who I am and what I believe for my husband."

In 1989, she was a recipient of one of Reebok's first International Human Rights Awards. With the $20,000 in award money, LaDuke founded the White Earth Land Recovery Project (WELRP), to repurchase tribal lands that were under white ownership. American Indians owned only 8 percent of reservation lands. An 1867 treaty formally acknowledged an 837,000-acre reservation for White Earth, one of seven Anishinabe tribes in northern Minnesota. Questionable sales and foreclosures due to unpaid land taxes reduced the reservation to less than one-tenth its original size. The majority of the reservation fell into the white control during the 1880s when the General Allotment Act led to a further loss of tribal lands. By 1934, only 7,890 acres remained under Anishinabe ownership. Loss of land forced many Anishinabes into even deeper poverty, and by the 1930s more than half the tribal members had fled to urban areas.

By 2001, only 5,000 of 20,000 tribal members reside on the reservation, and WELRP had repurchased 1,200 acres. WELRP's priority is to recover burial grounds and lands containing endangered species and/or medicinal plants. LaDuke hopes to meet the goal of purchasing 750 acres a year from private owners at market value. The federal government annexed and still owns over 25,000 acres of the reservation. WELRP operates as a nonprofit organization outside the traditionally male-dominated tribal council.

LaDuke became an activist on environmental racism, which targets Indian lands for uranium mining, strip mining, mercury contamination, toxic waste dumping, and nuclear bomb testing. In 1994, *Time* magazine named LaDuke as one of the 50 Leaders for the Future. Since 1995 she has served as program director for "Honor the Earth" tours, at which music groups such as the Indigo Girls perform to raise money and political support for American Indian concerns. The first tour raised $250,000 in funds for American Indian groups. LaDuke was named "Woman of the Year" by *Ms.* magazine in 1997. She serves as cochair of the Indigenous Women's Network (IWN).

LaDuke serves on the board of directors of the environmental group Greenpeace. She remains committed to encouraging a better society for all Americans, including the first inhabitants. LaDuke insists that Americans give up their mythology of the history of America and their denial of the holocaust of American Indians. LaDuke maintains, "That's the foundation of America, this whole idea of Manifest Destiny, the great emptiness that is out there. You cannot discover something if somebody lives there. You create a mythology that it's this vast, untamed wilderness and that nobody was there. The mythology of America says that there were 'a few' Indians, and those Indians died mysteriously. We

had some mistakes, like Sand Creek* in Colorado or Wounded Knee*."

Lack of jobs on the White Earth Reservation is a continuing crisis. The median annual income for tribal members who reside there is just $3,500 a year. As LaDuke acknowledges, "Indian people are poor because of structural poverty. Structural poverty means you don't actually control your land, your economy." WELRP also helps develop projects on the reservation such as a wild rice cooperative and a 200-acre maple syrup project.

LaDuke has said that "A lot of non-Indians find me acceptable because I am educated, lighter-skinned, and a woman." Yet she remains committed to using her educational privileges to benefit her nation. According to LaDuke, "To not struggle is to lose your will."

Further Reading

LaDuke, Winona. *All Our Relations.* Boston, Mass.: South End Press, 1999.

———. "The Dilemma of Indian Forestry." *Earth Island Journal* 9, no. 3 (summer 1994) 36.

———. *Last Standing Woman.* Stillwater, Minn.: Voyageur Press, 1997.

———. "Like Tributaries to a River: The Growing Strength of Native Environmentalism." *Sierra* 81, 6 (1996) 38.

"Native Struggles for Life and Land." *Multinational Monitor* 20, no. 12 (December 1999): 19.

Paul, Sonya. "Winona LaDuke." *Progressive* 59, no. 100 (1995): 36.

Steiner, Andy. "Winona LaDuke." *Utne Reader* no. 86 (March/April 1998): 98–99.

 LaFLESCHE PICOTTE, SUSAN
(1865–1915)   *Omaha Tribal Physician*

Susan LaFlesche was the first American Indian woman trained in medical schools as a doctor. She returned to her tribe, the Omaha, to work as a

---

* These were places where the U.S. military massacred American Indians.

physician and spent her life working on behalf of her nation.

Susan LaFlesche was born on the Omaha Reservation near Macy, Nebraska, on June 17, 1865. She was the youngest of four daughters. Her father, Joseph LaFlesche (Insta Maza, or Iron Eye), was the son of a French fur trader. Her mother, Mary Gale (Hinnuagnun, or the One Word), was the daughter of a U.S. Army physician. Joseph LaFlesche was half white and half Ponca, while Mary LaFlesche was half white and half Omaha. Her father was the last recognized chief of the Omahas, from 1853 until 1866, and supported a policy of assimilation for his tribe. He encouraged conversion to Christianity, lived in a frame house instead of the traditional Omaha earth lodge, and farmed. He sent all his children to white schools.

After completing school on the reservation with Presbyterian and Quaker missionaries, LaFlesche attended the Elizabeth Institute for Young Ladies in New Jersey. In 1882, she returned home to teach. She left again in 1884 to study at the Hampton Normal Agricultural Institute in Virginia, a school for African Americans and American Indians. The institute had been founded in 1868 to educate former slaves; the first Indian students were accepted 10 years later. LaFlesche graduated from the institute with honors in the spring of 1886. She was awarded a gold medal for achieving the highest examination score in her class.

The following fall LaFlesche entered the Woman's Medical College in Philadelphia, Pennsylvania. The Women's National Indian Association (WNIA), founded by white liberals in 1879, funded all her education expenses. While at college, LaFlesche resided in the Young Women's Christian Association (YWCA) housing. She was chosen as corresponding secretary of the YWCA and began wearing her hair in the same style as her white classmates. Her studies were demanding. She had weekly examinations in chemistry, anatomy, and physiology. She also took classes in which she learned to dissect cadavers. LaFlesche graduated at the head of her medical class of 36 students in the spring of 1889, becoming the first American Indian woman to receive training as a doctor of medicine from white society. (For centuries, American Indian women in many tribes had been part of a long tradition that recognized them as trained medical practitioners—medicine women.)

LaFlesche was selected by a competitive examination to serve as a resident physician at the Woman's Hospital in Philadelphia. After a four-month internship in Philadelphia, LaFlesche returned to the Omaha Reservation. She had written the Commissioner of Indian Affairs in the spring of 1889 requesting an appointment as physician for the Omaha. She served as a physician for the Omaha Agency from 1889 to 1891, providing medical care as the only doctor for the 1,300 Omaha tribal members. During her first winter, two epidemics of influenza among the Omaha claimed many lives. She also nursed the Omahas through a serious measles epidemic.

In addition to providing medical services, LaFlesche also served as interpreter, adviser, and teacher to the tribe. She implemented public health campaigns against the use of public drinking cups and against the distribution of alcohol among the Omaha.

LaFlesche married Henry Picotte, of Yankton Lakota and French ancestry, in 1894. Of the four LaFlesche sisters, Susan LaFlesche was the only one to marry another American Indian; the others married white men. The couple resided in Bancroft, Nebraska, where she treated both white and Indian patients. The couple had two sons.

After her husband died in 1905 from alcohol poisoning, she was the sole support for her mother and two sons. LaFlesche was appointed as a missionary to the Omahas by the Presbyterian Board of Home Missions. In 1906, her work resulted in a congressional stipulation that every property deed on the Omaha reservation would prohibit the sale of alcohol. In 1910, she headed a tribal delegation to Washington, D.C., to discuss issues of Indian citizenship with the U.S. secretary of the interior.

LaFlesche published articles on Omaha tribal history and wrote stories for publications such as the WNIA's magazine, *The Indian's Friend*. LaFlesche worked to establish a hospital in Walthill, which was opened in 1913 and named in her honor. By 1914, her chronic ear infection was diagnosed as cancer. She had a series of operations, but her health declined drastically.

She died at age 50 on September 18, 1915. The hospital named in her honor served as a care center for the elderly before being restored in 1989 and renamed the Susan LaFlesche Picotte Center. The center displays photos and artifacts from her life. Her medical skills and determination to serve the Omaha nation left a legacy that continued to benefit future generations.

Further Reading

Mathes, Valerie Sherer. "Susan LaFlesche Picotte, M.D.: Nineteenth-Century Physician and Reformer." *Great Plains Quarterly* 13, no. 3 (summer 1993) 172–86.

Tong, Benson. *Susan LaFlesche Picotte, M.D.: Omaha Indian Leader and Reformer.* Norman: University of Oklahoma Press, 1999.

 ## LATHROP, JULIA CLIFFORD
(1858–1932) *Settlement House Leader*

Julia Lathrop was the first woman to head a federal bureau, the Children's Bureau in the U.S. Department of Labor. Her activism began at Hull-House, in Chicago, where she implemented a number of programs that benefited women and children, including the first juvenile court in the world.

Julia Lathrop was born in Rockford, Illinois, the eldest of five children born to William Lathrop and Sarah Potter Lathrop. Her father was a leader in the Republican Party who served in the state assembly and later in Congress. Her mother was a suffragist. Lathrop studied at Rockford College, where she met JANE ADDAMS, the founder of Hull-House. Lathrop completed her bachelor's degree in 1880 from Vassar College. She worked in her father's law office for a decade. In 1890, she moved to Chicago's Hull-House, the third settlement house in America, founded to serve the needs of people in poor neighborhoods. Lathrop lived at Hull-House for 20 years.

In 1893, she began serving on the Illinois State Board of Charities, working to improve the standard of care for the disabled. While working there, in 1899 she established in Chicago the first juvenile court in the world. She resigned from the Board of Charities in 1901 in protest against the low quality of care the mentally ill received in the more than 100 institutions she inspected. Lathrop traveled to Europe to study the treatment of the insane there. In 1903, she was involved in founding the first graduate school in social work at the University of Chicago and served as its director for a year. In 1905, she returned to the Illinois State Board of Charities and worked for the disabled again until 1909.

In 1912, President William Howard Taft appointed Lathrop as the first director of the U.S. Children's Bureau in the Department of Labor, making her the first woman to head a federal bureau. After Taft was defeated in his reelection bid, President Woodrow Wilson retained her as director of the bureau. The bureau conducted studies on maternal and infant mortality, nutrition, juvenile delinquency, juvenile courts, child labor, and mothers' pensions. Lathrop developed a plan for uniform birth registration across the nation. The bureau was also responsible for enforcement of the first federal child labor law, passed by Congress in 1916.

Lathrop was elected as the first president of the National Conference of Social Work in 1918. She wrote numerous articles in the area of social work that were published in both scholarly journals and popular magazines. Lathrop worked to assure passage of the Sheppard-Towner Act of 1921, which provided federal funds to states to obtain assistance for single mothers and children. When Lathrop resigned in 1921 she was replaced by Grace Abbott, another reformer from Hull House.

After retiring from her federal post, Lathrop returned to Rockford, Illinois, to live with her sister. She served as president of the Illinois League of Women Voters from 1922 to 1924 and as the U.S. commissioner to the Child Welfare

Committee of the League of Nations from 1925 to 1931. She also served on a presidential commission that studied conditions at New York's center for immigration on Ellis Island. In 1925, she served on the Child Welfare Committee of the League of Nations.

Lathrop died in Rockford, Illinois, in 1932 at age 73. She remains best known for her advocacy on behalf of children, a group often unable to lobby on its own accord.

Further Reading

Addams, Jane. *My Friend Julia Lathrop.* 1932. Reprint. Manchester, N.H.: Ayer, 1974.

Lathrop, Julia. *The United States Children's Bureau.* 1912, Reprint. Manchester, N.H.: Ayer, 1972.

⧖ LOW, JULIETTE MAGILL KINZIE GORDON (Daisy Low)
(1860–1927)   *Founder of the Girl Scouts*

Juliette Low founded the Girl Scouts of America in 1912 as a vibrant program that continues to encourage the aspirations of girls worldwide.

Juliette Magill Kinzie Gordon was born on October 31, 1860, in Chicago, Illinois. She was named after her grandmother. Her mother's family was influential in the founding of Chicago. Her father's family was prominent in Savannah, Georgia, where her grandfather was mayor. Her father, Captain William Gordon, had been a captain in the Confederate army; her mother, Eleanor Kinzie Gordon, was a northerner. Juliette was the second of six children. Her childhood nickname was Daisy. A childhood ear infection left her deaf in one ear, and rice thrown at her wedding caused an ear infection that created deafness in her other ear. She was deaf for the rest of her life.

Juliette began attending finishing schools at age 18, first at Stuart Hall and Edge Hall in Virginia, and in 1877 at Madame Charbonnier's school in New York City. She enjoyed history and art. She married William Mackey Low, a wealthy English-

man, in 1886. When Mackey died in 1904 after 18 years of marriage, he left his estate to his lover. Low was unable to have children.

After her husband's death, Low planned to study sculpture in Paris, but in 1911, she met Sir Robert Baden Powell, an English officer who had founded the Boy Scouts in 1908. The Boy Scouts had already spread to several counties by the time Low heard of the organization. Powell's sister Agnes had formed the Girl Guides in England in 1910. Low became interested in the idea and formed a troop near her family estate in Scotland.

Upon returning to America at age 52, Low formed the first American Girl Guide troop in Savannah, Georgia. The first meeting was on March 12, 1912, with 17 12-year-olds attending. Low opened a national headquarters for the organization in Washington, D.C., in 1913; it later moved to New York. (Low sold her pearls to finance the move to the larger New York office.) Within a year there were Girl Guide troops from Georgia to New England and as far west as Chicago, thanks to Low's organizing skills. A similar organization, the Camp Fire Girls, was already in operation, and though merger talks between the two organizations occurred, they remained separate groups. Low adopted the name that had been proposed for the possible joint group and in 1915 changed her Girl Guides into the Girl Scouts of America, a name that matched that of the Boy Scouts of America. Low's management ability helped the membership of the Girl Scouts exceed that of the older Camp Fire Girls group within just a few years.

The first American Girl Scout handbook was written by naturalist Walter John Hoxie and contained many stereotypes of the time period regarding female pursuits. Early merit badges were awarded in categories such as maid, dairymaid, laundress, and cook. However, the emphasis on ecology and physical fitness would increase over the years. In 1916, Low edited a new version of the Girl Scout Handbook that included new badges in areas such as aviation. The group began selling its famous cookies in the early 1920s, just before Low's death.

She stepped down from presidency of the Girl Scouts in 1920.

Low was diagnosed with cancer in her early 60s but continued working to expand the Girl Scouts. She died on January 18, 1927, in Savannah. She was buried in her Girl Scout uniform, according to her wishes. Her birthday on October 31 is still celebrated by millions of Girl Scouts as Founder's Day. Her Savannah home is now a museum, the Juliette Low National Center. In 1948, the U.S. Post Office issued a stamp in her honor. Her adventurous spirit and exceptional organizational skills created an enduring institution that mentors young girls worldwide.

Further Reading

Brown, Fern. *Daisy and the Girl Scouts: The Story of Juliette Gordon.* New York: Whitman, 1996.

Juliette Low World Friendship Fund. Available online. URL: http://jfg.girlscouts.org/GS/wagggs/jlwff.htm Downloaded November 20, 2000.

Minn-Ia-Kota Girl Scout Council. "History of the Girl Scouts Organization." Available online. URL: http//www.minn-ia-kota.org/html/history.html. Downloaded November 20, 2000.

Pace, Mildred Mastin. *Juliette Low.* Ashland, Ky.: Jesse Stuart Foundation, 1997.

⊠ LUCE, ANN CLARE BOOTHE
(1903–1987)   *Diplomat, Writer, Congressperson*

Clare Boothe Luce became the first female ambassador to a major nation when President Dwight David Eisenhower appointed her as the U.S. ambassador to Italy. She served as a congressional representative from the state of Connecticut from 1942 to 1946 and was also a successful playwright.

Ann Clare Boothe was born on April 10, 1903, in New York City, to Ann Clare Snyder Boothe and William F. Boothe. She was the child of a traveling salesman who marketed pianos and patent medicines and sometimes worked as a violinist. Her mother, Ann Boothe, was a chorus girl. Her father abandoned the family when she was nine and thereafter she grew up in poverty. She did not have a religious upbringing. Her mother pretended to be a widow to her children and the world, and worked as a waitress. Documents uncovered after Luce's death revealed that her parents had never actually married, but her mother had used her father's name. When she was a teen her mother married a physician, Albert Austin, who served as a congressional representative from Connecticut.

Ann Clare Boothe worked as a child actress. She completed her schooling at Miss Mason's School in Tarrytown, New York, in 1919. When she was 16, she wrote in her diary that she wanted to become fluent in four languages, marry a publisher, have three children, and write something that would be remembered. At 16 Clare ran away from home and worked in a factory making paper flowers. She was paid $18 a week. She used her wages to study typing and shorthand.

She was on the honor roll in school, served as editor of the school newspaper, and was a good enough swimmer to try out for the U.S. Olympic Team at age 17. After graduation, she enrolled in business school, then worked as a social secretary for Alva Vanderbilt Belmont, a benefactor of the suffrage movement. In 1920 on a transatlantic voyage she met another wealthy suffragist, Mrs. Oliver Belmont, and at only 18 went to work for Mrs. Belmont and the National Woman's Party. Boothe married millionaire George Tuttle Brokaw in 1923 and had a daughter the following year. In four years she had four early miscarriages. She divorced her abusive, alcoholic husband in 1929 when she was 26 years old. Her divorce settlement left her with $26,000 a year for life.

After her divorce she resumed using her maiden name of Boothe. She worked in editorial positions for two Condé Nast publications: *Vogue* (1930–31), and *Vanity Fair* (1931–34). Her first book, *Stuffed Shirts,* was published in 1931.

In 1935, she married Time-Life publishing tycoon Henry Luce and devoted herself to a playwriting career. Her first play, *Abide with Me,* was produced on Broadway the year she married. The play was the story of a young woman who was

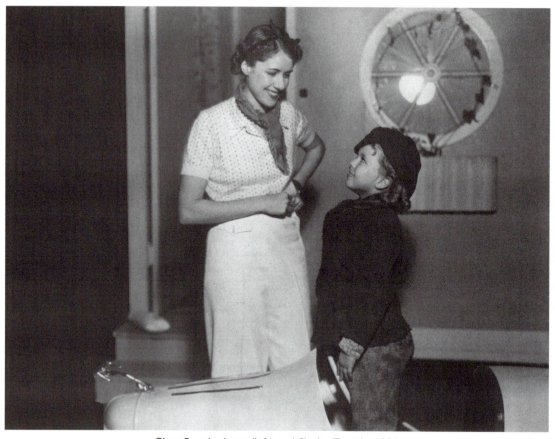

Clare Boothe Luce (left) and Shirley Temple, 1936
(Prints & Photographs Division, Library of Congress, Washington, D.C.)

married to a rich, older, alcoholic husband. Her second play, *The Women,* had a feminist perspective and an all-woman cast. Produced in 1936, *The Women* was a Broadway hit that offered a critical view of wealthy women who lead self-centered lives. Her husband got a more favorable review of the play in *Time* magazine than the theater critic had originally written. The play would be made into a 1939 movie directed by George Cukor and starring Joan Crawford and Norma Shearer. It remained her best-known play. She had another hit with *Kiss the Boys Goodbye* in 1938. Critics praised all her plays for their wit, and all were later turned into films, except for her last play, *Child of the Morning,* written in 1951.

Luce worked as a war correspondent at the start of World War II, publishing articles for *Life* magazine and a nonfiction book, *Europe in the Spring,* in 1940. The book, which argued against isolationism, was reprinted eight times. *Margin for Error,* another play, was produced in 1940. It had an anti-Nazi theme.

Luce was elected to Congress from the suburban fourth district of Connecticut in 1942 and reelected in 1944. She was the first woman elected to Congress from the state of Connecticut. She was the only female member of the House Military Affairs committee. Her stepfather had previously represented the same district. In 1944, she made the keynote address at the Republican

Party's national convention. After the 1944 death of her daughter in a car accident, Luce did not seek reelection in 1946. She also converted to Catholicism shortly after her daughter's death, and the story of her conversion was printed in *McCall's* magazine. She received an Oscar nomination in 1949 for her original story for the comedic film *Come to the Stable,* about two nuns.

Her husband started the picture magazine she had envisioned, *Life,* and years later she championed the start of another magazine, *People.*

In 1953 she failed to win a U.S. Senate nomination. A 1953 Gallup poll showed she was fourth on the list of the most admired women in the world, after ELEANOR ROOSEVELT, Queen Elizabeth II, and Mamie Eisenhower. She wanted the vice presidential position in President Eisenhower's 1956 campaign but the spot went to Richard Nixon instead. Luce became the first female ambassador to a major nation when President Eisenhower appointed her as the U.S. ambassador to Italy in 1953. Eisenhower had first asked her to serve as secretary of labor. Her increasingly conservative views were in conflict with the views of some large unions. A 1956 Gallup poll ranked her as the second most admired woman in the world. She served as ambassador until 1957. She resigned after suffering arsenic poisoning from paint dust in her bedroom. That year, the University of Notre Dame awarded her the Laetare medal, given to outstanding American Catholic laypersons.

When the press suggested that President Eisenhower consider a female vice presidential candidate, Luce was mentioned as a possibility, as was Maine senator MARGARET CHASE SMITH. Luce wanted to be appointed ambassador to the Soviet Union. However, in 1959, Eisenhower appointed her as ambassador to Brazil. She resigned after one month, following a fight for confirmation in the Senate, where she faced opposition because of her increasingly conservative views. After converting to Catholicism in 1946, her views had become more staunchly anticommunist and right wing. Luce seconded the nomination of conservative candidate Barry Goldwater at the Republican convention in 1964 and cochaired his campaign committee. She remained a maverick of sorts, however, admitting that she and her husband used LSD twice in 1966. Her husband, Henry Luce, died in 1967. She served on the Foreign Intelligence Advisory Board, intended to access foreign intelligence overseas, under Presidents Richard Nixon, Gerald Ford, and Ronald Reagan. In 1974 she supported President Richard Nixon during the Watergate scandal and threat of impeachment and wrote a letter attacking *Time* for its harsh treatment of Nixon. In her support of Nixon, Luce contacted Katherine Graham, publisher of the *Washington Post,* and told her that the spirit of Henry Luce had told her to denounce the *Post* for its Watergate coverage. Katherine Graham replied that the spirit of her late husband had told her to tell Luce to "shove it."

In 1983 she was awarded the Presidential Medal of Freedom. In 1985 she stated, "If I had it to do over again I would never have left the theater. I wouldn't have scattered my talents." When asked late in life about her regrets she replied, "I wish I'd kept a diary." Luce died in Washington, D.C., on October 9, 1987, at age 84 from cancer. She left more than 300 feet of papers in 800 boxes to the Library of Congress. Her will allowed for her handwritten diaries recorded while she was on LSD be made public 10 years after her death. She left the bulk of her $70 million estate to advance the careers of women in science and engineering. The feminist content and sharp wit in her plays continues to entertain and inform contemporary audiences.

Further Reading

Conroy, Sarah Booth. "Corralling Clare Boothe Luce." *Washington Post,* June 2, 1997, D2–3.

Fearnow, Mark. *Clare Boothe Luce.* Seattle, Wash.: Greenwood, 1995.

Luce, Clare Boothe, ed. *Saints for Now.* San Francisco: Ignatius Press, 1993.

Luce, Clare Boothe. *The Women.* New York: Dramatists Play Service, 1998.

Martin, Ralph. *Henry and Clare: An Intimate Portrait of the Luces.* New York: Putnam, 1991.

Morris, Sylvia Jukes. *Rage for Fame: The Ascent of Clare Boothe Luce.* New York: Random House, 1997.

M

MacKINNON, CATHARINE ALICE
(1946–   )   *Feminist Attorney, Writer*

Feminist attorney Catharine MacKinnon used her abilities and educational privilege to challenge violence against women, whether in the form of sexual harassment, pornography, or the sexual assault of women in the Bosnian war.

Catharine Alice MacKinnon was born on October 7, 1946, in Minneapolis, Minnesota, to Elizabeth Valentine Davis and George E. MacKinnon. Her father was a congressional representative who ran unsuccessfully for governor of Minnesota before becoming a federal judge for the U.S. Court of Appeals for the District of Columbia.

MacKinnon was her class valedictorian in high school. She attended Smith College, as her mother and grandmother had, and graduated in 1969 in the top 2 percent of her class. MacKinnon graduated from Yale Law School in 1977 and taught Yale's first women's studies course. Ten years later, she would complete her Ph.D. in political science from Yale University.

In 1977, having just completed law school, MacKinnon and a few former Yale classmates filed a sexual harassment lawsuit, *Barnes v. Costle.* At this time sexual harassment was not considered a form of discrimination, but the women won their case in a unanimous decision. The United States Court of Appeals ruled that if a female employee experienced retaliation for rejecting sexual advances from her supervisor, it was a violation of sex discrimination covered under Title VII. MacKinnon published *Sexual Harassment of Working Women* in 1979. In 1986, she was the cocounsel for the first sexual harassment case brought before the U.S. Supreme Court in *Meritor Savings Bank, FSB v. Vinson.* The court ruled in favor of the complainant, finding that sexual harassment was a violation of Title VII of the 1964 Civil Rights Act. It ruled that a "hostile environment" can be considered a form of sexual harassment actionable under Title VII. This provided a clearer definition of what constituted sexual harassment on the job and under what circumstances the employer could be held liable for the actions of subordinates.

With feminist writer Andrea Dworkin, MacKinnon drafted antipornography ordinances that were passed in Indianapolis, Indiana, and Minneapolis, Minnesota. The ordinances were designed to allow a woman to sue the producers and distributors of pornography for civil rights violation. In 1983, MacKinnon had a one-year appointment at the University of Minnesota Law School, teaching (with Dworkin) a course on pornography. She was asked by the Minneapolis Zoning Commission to testify on a proposed ordinance to restrict the location of sex industry businesses. For MacKinnon and Dworkin, pornography represented hate literature that encouraged violence against women. But in 1985 the U.S. Court of Appeals for the Seventh Circuit ruled Dworkin and MacKinnon's ordinance unconstitutional. The Supreme Court affirmed this ruling in 1986 in the *Hudnut v. American Booksellers Association* case, and the ordinance was then invalidated.

MacKinnon wrote *Feminism Unmodified: Discourses on Life and Law* in 1986. She and Dworkin published *Pornography and Civil Rights: A New Day for Women's Equality* in 1988 to highlight their arguments regarding pornography. Their basic premise stated that pornography creates a hostile environment for women, functioning much like harassment. In 1989, MacKinnon published *Toward a Feminist Theory of the State.* MacKinnon became a professor of law at the University of Michigan Law School in 1990 and remains in that position.

In 1992, the Supreme Court of Canada accepted the approach she created regarding the regulation of pornography. MacKinnon continued her crusade for women's rights in 1994 when she filed a lawsuit pro bono on behalf of Croatian and Muslim women who were raped during warfare in Bosnia-Herzegovina. The lawsuit sought remedies for those women under international law. Catherine MacKinnon continues to employ legal strategies in her efforts to decrease violence against women.

Further Reading

MacKinnon, Catharine. *Sexual Harassment of Working Women: A Case of Sex Discrimination.* New Haven, Conn.: Yale University Press, 1979.

———. *Feminism Unmodified: Discourses on Life and Law.* Cambridge, Mass.: Harvard University Press, 1987.

———. *Toward a Feminist Theory of the State.* Cambridge, Mass.: Harvard University Press, 1989.

———. *Only Words.* Cambridge, Mass.: Harvard University Press, 1993.

MacKinnon, Catharine, and Andrea Dworkin. *In Harm's Way: The Pornography Civil Rights Hearings.* Cambridge, Mass.: Harvard University Press, 1997.

———. *Pornography and Civil Rights: A New Day for Women's Equality.* Minneapolis, Minn.: Organizing Against Pornography, 1988.

Minson, J. P. "Social Theory and Legal Argument: Catherine MacKinnon on Sexual Harassment." *International Journal of the Sociology of Law* 19, no. 3 (August 1991) 355–78.

 MANKILLER, WILMA PEARL (A-ji-luhsgi Asgaya-dihi, "Flower and Protector of the Village")
(1945–) *Cherokee Chief*

Wilma Mankiller was the first female chief of a major American Indian nation, serving as chief of the Western Cherokee from 1985 to 1995. Mankiller was born on November 18, 1945, in the Indian Hospital in Tahlequah, Oklahoma, the capital of the Cherokee Nation of Oklahoma. She was the sixth in a family of eleven children. Her father, Charley Mankiller, was Cherokee, and her mother, Clara Irene Sitton, was Dutch/Irish. Her father's family was directly descended from tribal members who were forced to march from Cherokee homeland in the southeastern United States in 1838 to what was supposed to be permanent Indian Territory but later became the state of Oklahoma. During the march, known as the Trail of Tears, one in four Cherokee died.

Mankiller grew up in extreme poverty in Oklahoma in a home without electricity or running water. Her family picked crops in seasonal work, and wild game supplemented the family diet. Mankiller's first awareness of feeling different from others came when she attended school in floursack clothing.

Her family relocated to San Francisco when she was 11 as part of the Bureau of Indian Affairs

Relocation Program, which aimed to move large numbers of Indians from reservations to urban areas. The program was part of an official federal termination policy, which sought to end the legal recognition of all Indian tribes. The move to California was difficult for Mankiller, one she has remembered as being her own personal Trail of Tears. The family went from rural poverty to urban poverty. Her family's new neighborhood was so crime-ridden that no ambulance would respond to calls made in that area after dark.

Mankiller entered the fifth grade in San Francisco, where she experienced difficulty in school. Other children made fun of her accent and last name, which refers to warriors who protected Cherokee villages and signifies Cherokee military ranking. She has no fond memories of her urban school experience, but recalls that the Mankiller family participated in events at the San Francisco Indian Center. Indian centers were an outgrowth of the mass migration of Indians from reservations to cities and they offered displaced tribal members from many different Indian nations a gathering place and outlet for cultural continuity.

Mankiller graduated from high school in San Francisco in the summer of 1963, but as no one in her family had ever gone to college, she did not consider this option. Mankiller took a dead-end clerical position after high school. She soon met and married Hugo Olaya of Ecuador in Reno, Nevada, in November 1963. Their first child, Felicia, was born in August 1964, and another daughter, Gina, was born two years later. During this time Mankiller suffered from kidney infections, an early sign of the polycystic kidney disease with which she was later diagnosed and which claimed her father's life in 1969. Although her husband wanted to restrict her activities to the home, Mankiller started attending Skyline Junior College and then San Francisco State College, where she studied sociology.

Mankiller continued her involvement in San Francisco Indian Center community projects, and

at age 24, worked to raise funds and supplies for the 1969 American Indian occupation of Alcatraz Island. Several of her siblings participated in this occupation, which drew national and international attention to the plight of American Indians. The protest was located on Alcatraz Island because it was abandoned federal property, near a large urban Indian and student population, and located in the liberal environment of the San Francisco Bay Area. Protestors believed that the Fort Laramie Treaty of 1868 had guaranteed tribes the right to abandoned federal property. Protestors pursued a claim to the island through the legal system and the court of public opinion but were ultimately unsuccessful in gaining title to the land.

The takeover of the island was led by young, urban American Indian college students and supported by members of the Indian community, like Mankiller, on the mainland. A new militancy among Indian youth was another outgrowth of the federal government policy of relocating Indians from reservations to urban areas—the exact opposite of what the policy was intended to achieve. The occupation of Alcatraz contributed to the end of the federal termination policy. The occupation began in November 1969, and by the time it ended, in June 1971, the termination policy had been formally rescinded. This involvement at Alcatraz began Mankiller's life of activism and service. As she has recalled, "The name of the island was Alcatraz . . . it changed my life forever." When the Alcatraz occupation ended in 1971, Mankiller became a fundraiser and legal advocate for the Pit River tribe in California. She also served as director of the Native American Youth Center in East Oakland.

The new insurgency among American Indians led to changes in U.S. government policy regarding tribal self-determination. In 1907, the federal government had disbanded the government of the Western Cherokee Nation and divided its lands. In 1971, the nation was legally reinstated on 7,000 square miles in northeastern Oklahoma. Shortly afterward, in 1977, Mankiller and her daughters moved back to Oklahoma after her divorce, and she began to work for the Cherokee Nation as its economic stimulus coordinator. One primary goal in this position was to encourage Cherokee to train in environmental health and science fields.

Mankiller earned a bachelor's degree in social work in 1979 from Flaming Rainbow University in Stillwell, Oklahoma. While commuting to the University of Arkansas at Fayetteville for a master's program in community planning, she had a near-fatal car accident in November 1979. She had crashed head-on into another car that was trying to pass into the oncoming lane. The driver of the oncoming car, her best friend, Sherry Morris, was killed in the accident. Doctors predicted that Mankiller would spend the rest of her life in a wheelchair, but after 17 operations she regained her mobility. A year after the car accident, in 1980, she noticed an increasing muscle weakness that made it difficult to perform daily activities such as brushing her hair. While watching Jerry Lewis's Labor Day fund-raising telethon for muscular dystrophy, she realized that she was experiencing the symptoms they were describing in the program. But Mankiller was diagnosed instead with myasthenia gravis, a paralyzing nerve disease, and she underwent thymus surgery and steroid therapy in January 1981. (Almost a decade later, in 1990, she underwent a kidney transplant, with her brother Don serving as donor.) Mankiller faced her life-threatening illnesses with courage and believes that the outcome strengthened her spiritually.

After surviving these ordeals, she returned to work in January 1981 as director of community development for the Cherokee Nation. She achieved great success with the nationally praised Bell Community Revitalization Project, which constructed homes and brought running water and utilities to impoverished communities. She wrote a successful grant that provided funding to help build a 26-mile waterline for the rural Cherokee community. While working on this project she met Charlie Soap, a Cherokee whom she married in October 1986.

Cherokee chief Ross Swimmer selected Mankiller as his running mate for deputy chief in 1983. Mankiller's first response was to refuse Chief Swimmer's suggestion, but she reconsidered because she felt she could be an even more effective advocate for poor Cherokee in such a position. Mankiller had expected some conservative backlash to her liberal views and activist past but was surprised when campaign attacks focused on her gender. Opponents argued that her candidacy was against tradition: It would lower Cherokee status and respect among other Indian nations if a woman led them. She received death threats and had her tires slashed during her campaign. While her candidacy represented a "step forward," as Mankiller said, it was also a "step backward" to precolonial times when the Cherokee were matrifocal and matrilineal, and the women's council played an important political role. She made an effective point for many when she argued that her candidacy could be viewed as a return to Cherokee tradition. While Alcatraz was the pivotal point in her political awakening, she also acknowledged being influenced by the women's movement and aware of women's liberation groups in San Francisco.

Mankiller's successful election as deputy chief in August 1983 received national attention. She acknowledged, "Prior to my election, a young Cherokee girl would never have thought that [she] might grow up and become chief." Mankiller supervised the daily operation of an Indian nation that covered 14 counties. She supervised health clinics, child care, water projects, housing construction, and Head Start programs. Two years into their term, in September 1985, Chief Swimmer accepted President Ronald Reagan's offer to become director of the Bureau of Indian Affairs in Washington D.C., and Mankiller was sworn in as the first female Cherokee chief, in December 1985, at age 40. She met a great deal of resistance at the start of her term. Some tribal members thought that they just needed to wait two years and then remove her from office in the next election, but she changed attitudes toward

Wilma Mankiller, American Indian leader, 2001
(Wilma P. Mankiller)

a female head of state during her tenure. In 1987, she successfully ran for the position of chief and won another four-year term. During her tenure, three health centers and nine children's programs were added to the facilities on Cherokee land. She pursued many projects, including a new education plan, Cherokee language and literacy institutes, a comprehensive health care system, child and youth projects, college scholarships, and environmental and economic development. In 1990, Chief Mankiller signed a landmark agreement with the federal government that gave the Cherokee Nation, rather than the Bureau of Indian Affairs, the right to directly control federal allocations. In 1991, she

won reelection with a landslide 83 percent of the vote. Her tenure as chief also opened the door to leadership for other women, as the 15-member Cherokee tribal council changed its composition and eventually included six women. She decided not to run again in 1995 due to poor health. (In 1995 she was diagnosed with lymphoma.)

Mankiller holds honorary doctorates from Yale University and Dartmouth College. In 1986, she was inducted into the Oklahoma Hall of Fame and elected to the National Women's Hall of Fame, and in 1987 she was named Woman of the Year by *Ms.* magazine. In 1996, she taught and lectured at Dartmouth College as a Montgomery Fellow. She also battled lymphoma with chemotherapy and became a grandmother during this time. In 1998, President Clinton awarded her the Presidential Medal of Freedom, and she had a second kidney transplant. In 1999, she was diagnosed with breast cancer. Despite all her health problems, she continues to lecture on issues of importance to her.

Mankiller overcame a childhood of poverty and life-threatening illnesses to become a highly respected leader.

Further Reading

Griffin, Connie. "Relearning to Trust Ourselves: An Interview with Chief Wilma Mankiller, Tahlequah, Oklahoma." *Woman of Power* 7 (summer 1987): 38–40.

Gale Group. "Wilma Pearl Mankiller." Available online. URL: http://www.gale.com/gale/chw/mankill.html, Downloaded November 22, 2000.

Kallen, Stuart. *Native American Chiefs and Warriors.* San Diego: Lucent Books, 1999.

Mankiller, Wilma. *Mankiller: A Chief and Her People.* New York: St. Martin's Press, 1993.

Nelson, Andrew. "Wilma Mankiller." *Salon.com.* Available online. URL: http://www.salon.com/people/bc/2001/11/20/mankiller/index.html?x./ Downloaded January 23, 2002.

Sonneborn, Liz. *A to Z of Native American Women.* New York: Facts On File, 1998.

Wallace, Michele. "Wilma Mankiller." *Ms.* (January 1988): 68–69.

Whittemore, Hank. "She Leads a Nation." *Parade Magazine* (August 18, 1991): 4–5.

  MASON, BRIDGET
(Biddy Mason, Bridget Smith)
(1818–1891) *Entrepreneur, Philanthropist*

Bridget Mason went to court to win her freedom from slavery, worked as a nurse and midwife, and became a founding entrepreneur and philanthropist of Los Angeles, California.

Bridget "Biddy" Smith was born on August 15, 1818, in Hancock County, Georgia. She was of mixed African-American and three American Indian heritages; Choctaw, Seminole, and Geegi.

She was enslaved on a Mississippi plantation owned by Rebecca Crosby Smith and Robert Marion Smith. As was the custom, slaves took their master's surnames and religious backgrounds.

Bridget had three daughters. Their father was thought to be her master. In 1847, her master converted to the Mormon faith and moved his family and slaves to the Utah Territory. Bridget and her family had been promised their freedom if they accompanied the family to Utah. They lived in Utah for three years, until Brigham Young, a leader of the Mormon church, recruited volunteers to establish a new Mormon settlement in San Bernardino, in southern California. California had been admitted to the Union in 1850 as a free state and slavery was outlawed there. Five years later, Robert Smith decided to move the household to Texas, a slave state.

At the start of the journey to Texas, Bridget made a daring escape. She went to court hoping to win the right to remain in California for herself, her sister, and their children. She successfully sued her master in the court in 1856, because the owners lived in the free state of California, the enslaved status of Bridget was null and void. Winning freedom for herself and her daughters, even though women were not allowed to give testimony in court at that time. Her court decision came a year before the U.S. Supreme Court's Dred Scott decision, which mandated that escaped slaves in free states be returned to their owners. She had won her freedom in court and so no longer had the legal status of a slave.

She chose a new surname, Mason, taken from the name of a Mormon apostle, Amasa Mason Lyman, who had led the Mormons to San Bernardino. Mason moved to Los Angeles, where she worked as a nurse and midwife.

Mason had a shrewd business sensibility and was able, 10 years after gaining her right to remain in California, to purchase several lots of land. She was one of the first African-American women to own land in Los Angeles. The land she bought became the center of the commercial district of Los Angeles. In 1884, Mason sold part of her land, and on the remaining land she built commercial buildings with spaces for rent. As was one of Los Angeles's first real estate investors and developers, Mason accumulated a fortune of $300,000, making her one of the richest women and one of the richest African Americans in Los Angeles.

Mason was a generous philanthropist. She purchased the freedom of numerous African-American children and supported their schooling. She established homes to care for the aged and ill. She personally delivered medical care to prisoners. After a flood in the 1880s, Mason set up open-ended accounts with a local grocer for those who had been displaced. She assisted people of all races through various charities, and lines of needy people formed outside her home on a daily basis. In 1872, she founded and financed the first African-American church in Los Angeles, the First African-Methodist Episcopal Church. Mason donated the land on which the church was built and paid the taxes as well as the minister's salary.

Bridget Mason died on January 15, 1891. She was buried in an unmarked grave at Evergreen Cemetery in Los Angeles. Nearly a century later, in 1988, a tombstone marking her grave was erected by the city of Los Angeles. November 16, 1989, was declared Biddy Mason Day, and a memorial listing her achievements was unveiled at a park near the site of her original property holdings. The church she built and supported continues to thrive with a membership of more than 3,000. Mason began life in slavery and ended it by generously assisting disadvantaged people of every race.

Further Reading

Distinguished Women of Past and Present. "Bridget 'Biddy' Mason." Available online. URL: http://www. distinguishedwomen.com/biographies/mason-b.html. Downloaded November 23, 2000.

McCLOUD, JANET RENEECKER
(1934–) *Tulalip Activist*

Janet McCloud was one of the key leaders in the fish-in movement, which began in Washington State in the early 1960s and took a stand regarding the fishing treaty rights of Indian tribes.

Janet Reneecker was born on March 30, 1934, on the Tulalip Reservation in Washington State. Her childhood was turbulent, marked by alcohol, abuse, and foster homes. McCloud claims that her first political action occurred at age six, when she gathered younger children behind her and kept a child molester at a distance.

She had an early first marriage and divorce, then married Don McCloud, a Puyallup-Nisqually truck driver. The couple had eight children. They lived in Yelm, a few miles south of the Nisqually River near Olympia, Washington. McCloud's activism began with the issue of American Indian fishing rights in 1961. One event that spurred McCloud's activism occurred that year when state game wardens broke into her home, searching for deer meat. McCloud recalled her response to the intrusion, "I just got mad. I asked them, 'Do you have a search warrant?' They did. It said 'John Doe'." According to McCloud, another motivating factor spurring her activism was the need to keep busy in order to deal with the overwhelming grief that she felt after her sister died in 1961.

Washington State officials routinely arrested American Indians for fishing, in direct violation of their treaty rights. The 1854 Medicine Creek Treaty guaranteed Northwest Indian tribes unrestricted use of natural resources. But pressure had grown to manage rivers exclusively for sport fishing. Fish-in protests began as a response to Washington State policy, which tried to use state laws to restrict Indian fishing rights. With high poverty rates, the permission to fish was a significant contribution to a family's diet. As McCloud recalled, "Feeding the family was tough, and we were so glad if we could get a fish or a deer." When her brother-in-law and other men were arrested, McCloud and other women began fishing in their stead.

When McCloud turned to the large Yakama tribe for support, she was ridiculed because she was a woman and of mixed blood. As McCloud summarized, "Now you hear them talk and they act macho, they act belligerent, they act rough, but when it comes right down to the bottom line, they couldn't fight their way out of a paper bag. The only people I've ever seen them fight is Indian women and children. And yet they're controlling everything now."

In 1964, she founded a civil rights organization, Survival of American Indians Association (SAIA), to raise bail funds. She served as editor of the group's newspaper, *Survival News,* which gave an Indian view of the fishing rights controversty. Celebrities such as Marlon Brando and Dick Gregory joined the ranks of those who were arrested. In 1973 the American Indian Movement (AIM) held a two-month standoff with the FBI and corrupt tribal government at the Pine Ridge Reservation in South Dakota. At an AIM conference following the occupation of Wounded Knee, McCloud proposed that one of the main issues AIM should address was the need for Indian men to lead the fight against domestic violence in their communities. McCloud was one of the visible women in the Red Power movement who challenged the men on their sexism.

After a decade of protest, the 1974 *United States v. Washington State* case, more popularly known as the Boldt decision after Judge Hugh Boldt, recognized the treaty rights of tribes regarding fishing.

McCloud established the Northwest Indian Women's Circle in the 1980s, which focused on issues such as sterilization abuse and problems with the foster care placement and adoption of Indian children. McCloud was a founding member of Women of All Red Nations (WARN), an offshoot of AIM.

In 1985, McCloud was a delegate to the United Nations Conference on Women held in Nairobi, Kenya. She has been a member of the Indigenous Women's Network, a coalition of native women's groups from Chile to Canada who recognize McCloud as their founding mother. McCloud has earned respect through her activism and her role as a mother of eight children, grandmother of 25 and 10 additional adopted grandchildren, and 10 great-grandchildren. McCloud is an elder whom American Indian communities continue to lean on for encouragement, wisdom, and guidance.

Further Reading

Bomberry, Dan. "Sage Advice from a Longtime Activist." *Native Self-Sufficiency* 6 (1981): 4–5, 20.

Emery, Marg. "Indian Women's Groups." *Indian Truth* (May–June, 1981): 20–21.

Payne, Diane. "Each of My Generations Is Getting Stronger: An Interview with Janet McCloud." *Indian Truth: Special Issue on Native Women* 239 (May/June, 1988): 5–7.

Trahant, Mark. "The Center of Everything." *Seattle Times,* July 4, 1999. Available online. URL: http://www.alphacdc.com/sapadawn/center.html. Downloaded on November 23, 2000.

 ## MIKULSKI, BARBARA ANN
(1936–) *Senator*

Maryland native Barbara Mikulski was elected to the U.S. House of Representatives in 1976. In 1986, she was elected to the U.S. Senate, becoming the 16th woman to serve in the Senate. She was the first Democratic woman to gain a Senate seat in her own right, without inheriting the position from her husband, and is also the first Democratic woman to have served in both houses of Congress.

Barbara Ann Mikulski was born in Baltimore, Maryland, on July 20, 1936. She is the great-granddaughter of Polish immigrants who owned a local bakery. Her great-grandmother came to the United States at age 16 with no money or job. Barbara was the oldest of three daughters. Her parents, Christine and William Mikulski, owned a neighborhood grocery store in east Baltimore where Mikulski worked during high school. Mikulski was educated at local parochial schools. She completed a B.A. degree at Mount St. Agnes College in Baltimore in 1958, and then an M.S.W. degree at the University of Maryland School of Social Work in 1965.

Mikulski was employed as a social worker for the local Catholic Charities organization and then for the Baltimore city welfare department, for which she handled cases of child abuse and neglect. Her first political involvement was in the late 1960s when the city of Baltimore made plans to build a 16-lane highway through the historical African-American Fells Point neighborhood. She was an organizer of the community resistance to the proposed project. In 1971, Mikulski first sought public office and was elected to the Baltimore city council, where she served for five years.

She was elected representative for the third district United States congressional seat in 1976. She became the first woman ever appointed to the energy and commerce committee. Among her legislative victories was legislation to fund battered women's shelters. She cosponsored a congressional resolution to establish National Women's History week in 1981. Mikulski served in the House of Representatives for 10 years before deciding to run for a Senate seat.

Mikuski was elected to the U.S. Senate in 1986, becoming the 16th woman elected to the Senate. She was the first Democratic woman to hold a Senate seat not inherited from a husband and the first woman to win a statewide election in Maryland. She was reelected to a second and third term in the Senate with 71 percent of the vote both times. Her opponent in the second reelection campaign was conservative Republican LINDA CHAVEZ. Mikulski serves as chair of the appropriations subcommittee for the U.S. Department of Housing and Urban Development (HUD). She also serves on the labor and human resources committee and the small business committee. In 1994, she was unanimously elected as secretary of the Democratic conference, the first woman elected to a Democratic leadership position in the Senate. After the 2000 election Mikulski was selected to serve as secretary of the Democratic caucus. Throughout her political career, she has returned each night to her home in the ethnically rich city of Baltimore. Mikulski, born in a family and neighborhood of working people, remains connected to her Baltimore roots.

Following the 2000 election, Senator Mikulski cosponsored legislation to help low-income families obtain medical treatment for children with disabilities, led the fight against discrimination against those with genetic disorders, and introduced legislation to stop cuts in Medicare home health reimbursements. She continues to serve on the Appriations Committee, Senate Select Committee on Intelligence, and Health, Education and Pensions Committee (HELP).

Further Reading

Edmunds, Lavinia. "Barbara Mikulski." *Ms.* 15 (January 1987): 63+.

Whitney, Catherine. *Nine and Counting: The Women of the Senate.* New York: Perennial, 2001.

 ### MILLETT, KATHERINE MURRAY
(Kate Millett)
(1934–)   *Feminist Activist, Writer*

Kate Millett's best-selling 1970 book, *Sexual Politics,* was the first major volume of feminist literary criticism. It led to a reexamination of misogyny in literary works.

Katherine Murray Millett was born into an Irish Catholic family on September 14, 1934, in St. Paul, Minnesota. Her father was an engineer who deserted his family when Millett was 11 years old. Her mother, Helen Millett, had a college degree but experienced difficulty finding a job and finally tried selling insurance. Millett was sexually molested as a young girl.

Millett attended the University of Minnesota and graduated magna cum laude at 17. Millet's paternal aunt, Dorothy Millett Hill, whom Millett called AD, offered to fund Millett's graduate education at Oxford University. Millett earned first-class honors in English literature in 1958 with a specialization in the Victorians.

She briefly taught kindergarten in the Harlem area of New York City, and then at the University of North Carolina. During this time she felt drawn to sculpting and moved to Tokyo in 1961 to pursue this interest. While in Japan, she taught English at Waseda University. She returned to the United States and married sculptor Fumio Yoshimura in 1965 to make him a citizen and prevent his deportation. (They divorced in 1985.) She entered a doctoral program in English and comparative literature at Columbia University in 1966 and taught English at Barnard College. Barnard fired her for participating in a student strike at Columbia in 1968.

Millett's reading of Simone de Beauvoir's *The Second Sex* while at Oxford had sparked her initial interest in feminism. Millett served as the first chair of the education committee for the National Organization for Women (NOW) from 1965 to 1968. She also joined the civil rights group Congress of Racial Equality (CORE) in 1966.

Millett's 1970 best-seller, *Sexual Politics,* published when she was 36 years old, examined the misogyny in the works of a number of male writers, including Henry Miller, Norman Mailer, and D. H. Lawrence. She was given $4,000 advance from Doubleday publishers and received support from feminist scholars ROBIN MORGAN and Shulamith Firestone in editing the volume. The book was based on her dissertation, which had been awarded with distinction. *Sexual Politics* became an instant best-seller, with 80,000 copies sold in its first six months of publication. The book was reissued in 1990. *Time* magazine once dubbed her "the Mao Tse-Tung of Women's Liberation." She completed her doctorate, also awarded with distinction, from Columbia University.

Her publicly acknowledged bisexuality garnered national headlines in 1970. In 1973, she was diagnosed as manic-depressive, institutionalized, and prescribed lithium. She experienced side effects from the medication, including hand tremors, diarrhea, and kidney damage.

Millett abandoned the academic structure of *Sexual Politics* when she published the autobiography *Flying* in 1974. *Sita,* published in 1977, recounted a three-year love affair with a female university administrator and mother. Sita, the subject of the book, committed suicide in 1978. Mil-

lett went to Iran in 1979 to work for women's rights but was rapidly expelled. *AD,* published in 1995, recounted her relationship with her aunt. A 1990 memoir, *The Loony Bin Trip,* spoke frankly about her struggles with mental illness and her periods of institutionalization.

In 2000, the University of Illinois Press reissued a 30th anniversary edition of *Sexual Politics* and three other works: *Flying, The Loony-Bin Trip,* and *Sita.* Millett struggles to earn a living by running a small Christmas tree farm, but she made a major literary contribution to feminist theory.

Further Reading

Millett, Kate. *A.D., A Memoir.* New York: W. W. Norton, 1995.

———. *Flying.* 1974. Reprint. Champaign: University of Illinois, 2000.

———. *The Loony-Bin Trip.* 1990. Reprint. Champaign: University of Illinois, 2000.

———. *The Politics of Cruelty: An Essay on the Literature of Political Imprisonment.* New York: W. W. Norton, 1995.

———. *Sexual Politics.* 1970. Reprint. Champaign: University of Illinois Press, 2000.

———. *Sita.* 1976. Reprint. Champaign: University of Illinois Press, 2000.

 ## MINK, PATSY TAKEMOTO
(1927–)   *Congressional Representative*

In 1965, Patsy Mink became the first Asian-American woman and the first woman of color elected to the United States Congress from Hawaii. She has served a total of six terms in the House—she took a brief hiatus following her first term then was again elected to the same position in 1990, serving five more consecutive terms.

Patsy Takemoto was born on December 6, 1927, in Paia, Maui, Hawaii to Mitama Tateyama Takemoto and Suematsu Takemoto. Her family was Protestant. Her father worked as a civil engineer, and Patsy Takemoto enjoyed an upper-middle-class upbringing. She was so bright that she started school at age four. When she was 14 her father was briefly arrested after the bombing of

Pearl Harbor. She was the first female student body president at her high school. She graduated as valedictorian of her class at Maui High School, then enrolled at the University of Hawaii in Honolulu, planning to become a doctor. She was elected president of the premedical students' club and was a member of the varsity debate team.

She transferred to the University of Nebraska in 1947. She moved into the international house, which was reserved for students of color. When she discovered this, she wrote a letter of protest to the local paper. Other protests followed and the university changed its policies. Mink became very ill in 1948 and had to return to Hawaii to complete her bachelor's degree, majoring in zoology and chemistry. She was not accepted at any of the medical schools to which she applied following her college graduation, however. She would later recall, "I wish someone had told me then that medical schools in the United States [usually] didn't admit women students, except for one all-female school."

She worked briefly at the Honolulu Academy of Arts, where the female director suggested that she apply to law school. She was accepted into the University of Chicago and there she met her future husband, John Francis Mink, a graduate student in geophysics. She married and graduated in 1951. Still, no law firm was willing to hire Mink, even as a law clerk. She remembered, "My reaction was disbelief that just being a woman was a disqualification for a job." She worked at the University of Chicago Law School library until the eighth month of her pregnancy. Seven months later the family moved to Hawaii. Mink became the first Japanese-American female attorney in Hawaii but again found herself unemployable, so opened her own firm. Mink also taught business classes at the University of Hawaii.

Mink became involved with the Hawaii Young Democrats and worked in the 1954 elections. She served as vice president of the group from 1957 to 1959. She decided to seek election and easily won a seat in the Territory of Hawaii House of Representatives in 1956. In 1959 she was elected to the Territory of Hawaii Senate. While in the Senate, Mink authored equal pay legislation that mandated that women receive the same pay as men for the same job.

Hawaii became a state in 1959, and Mink ran for the U.S. Congress but was defeated by Daniel Inouye. She gave the speech for the civil rights plank at the Democratic National Convention in 1960. In 1962, she was reelected to the Hawaii State Senate. In 1964, she ran for the U.S. Congress again and won. Mink sponsored the Women's Education Equity Act and was an early critic of the Vietnam War. She was the first Asian-American to run for the presidency in the 1972 primary campaign. Mink was reelected to Congress six times, serving for 12 years. She then ran unsuccessfully for the U.S. Senate. She worked for three years as assistant secretary for oceans and environmental affairs in the Carter administration then returned to Hawaii.

She was elected to the Honolulu City Council where she served from 1983 to 1987 and acted as chair from 1983 to 1985. She ran unsuccessfully for governor of Hawaii in 1986, and for mayor of Honolulu in 1988. Mink ran for Congress again in 1990 and won.

She has been reelected to Congress five more times and serves on the education committee and the workforce and government reform committee. Mink has been a member of the congressional caucus for women's issues since 1990. Patsy Mink pursues an active legislative agenda in order to improve social conditions for women and families.

Further Reading

Almanac of American Politics 2000. "Patsy Mink." Available online. URL: http://www.freedomchannel.com/img/2000/people/hi/rep_hi02.cfm. Downloaded November 25, 2000.

Davidson, Sue. *A Heart in Politics: Jeanette Rankin and Patsy Mink.* Seattle: Seal Press, 1994.

Jade Magazine. "Congresswoman Patsy Mink: A Profile in Strength and Perseverance." Available online. URL: http://www.jademagazine.com/2mink.html. Downloaded November 25, 2000.

Matsuda, Mari. *Called From Within: Early Women Lawyers of Hawaii.* Honolulu: University of Hawaii Press, 1992.

MOLINA, GLORIA
(1948–   )   *Los Angeles County Supervisor*

Gloria Molina is the first Latina to be elected to the California State Assembly, the first Latina elected to the Los Angeles City Council, only the third Latina elected to the council in this century, and the first woman ever elected to the Los Angeles County Board of Supervisors.

Molina was born on May 31, 1948, in Los Angeles, California, the oldest daughter of 10 children born to Concepción and Leonardo Molina, who had emigrated from Mexico a year before her birth. She graduated from Pico Rivera High School, then enrolled in Rio Hondo College to study design. When she was 19, Molina took a job as a legal assistant to help support her family after her father had an accident. While working full time, she continued her education by attending night classes at East Los Angeles College, where she completed her coursework in 1968.

Molina attended California State University, Los Angeles, for two years and then began working as a job counselor for the East Los Angeles Community Union, (TELACU), an organization focused on economic development. She married Ron Martinez, a businessman, and the couple had one daughter.

In 1973, she was the founding president of a Latina organization, Comision Femenil de Los Angeles. She served as national president of the organization from 1974 to 1976. She was also a founding member of Hispanic American Democrats (HAD) and the National Association of Latino Elected and Appointed Officials (NALEO).

In 1974, Molina became the administrative assistant to California State Assemblyman Art Torres. Three years later she was appointed by President Jimmy Carter as Director of Intergovernmental and Congressional Affairs in the U.S. Department of Health and Human Services. In 1980, Molina returned to California and served as chief deputy to Willie Brown, the speaker of the California Assembly.

In 1982, Molina ran for the state assembly against an opponent who was better financed, but she won and became the first Latina ever elected to the California State Assembly. She recalled, however, "When I went to the Assembly, one man said to me, 'Oh, I'm so glad we have you, we need someone like you to work on bilingual education and child care.'" She served in the state assembly from 1982 to 1987.

Molina's work as a legislator has been recognized with numerous awards, including Woman of the Year in 1983 from the Mexican American Opportunity Foundation, and in 1984 an award from *Ms.* magazine. *Working Woman* magazine cited her as "one of the ten women of power to watch in the 90s," and she was listed by *Time* magazine as a member of a "Galaxy of Rising Stars." She was also recognized by *Hispanic Business Magazine* as one of the most influential Latinas in the nation. She shaped a number of legislative bills, including one to prevent discrimination against immigrants in auto insurance charges. She also shaped a neighborhood notification policy for agricultural spraying and legislation to protect tuition-free community colleges. Additionally, she lobbied against placing a prison in East Los Angeles. In 1987, she won a seat on the Los Angeles City Council, and in 1991 became the first woman ever elected to the Los Angeles County Board of Supervisors, one of the most influential positions in California State. Los Angeles County is the largest county in the United States, with a population of 10 million. A 1991 survey of Latinos conducted by Univision, a Spanish-language television network, found that Molina was the most admired Latina leader in the nation. In 1992, Democratic presidential candidate Bill Clinton appointed Molina as cochair of his national campaign, the first Latina appointed to cochair the campaign committee of a Democratic presidential nominee. Gloria Molina's clear-thinking political leadership offers a positive role model to all young people.

Further Reading

Democratic National Committee. "Gloria Molina: DNC Vice Chair." Available online. URL: http://www. democrats.org/hq/leadership/bios/molina.html. Downloaded November 26, 2000.

Hewett, Joan. *Getting Elected: The Diary of a Campaign.* New York: Lodestar Books, 1989.

Los Angeles Democratic National Convention. "Gloria Molina." Available online. URL: http://www.lc2000.org/ gmolina.htm. Downloaded November 26, 2000.

Thompson, Mark. "The Political Heirs of Gloria Molina." *California Republic* 1, no. 2 (March 26, 1991): 26–28.

 MORGAN, ROBIN
(1941–) *Journalist*

Robin Morgan is a well-known feminist writer of the second wave of feminism in the 20th century and a former editor of *Ms.* magazine. After suffrage was attained by "first wave" feminists in 1920, feminist activism was less visible until the 1960s when a "second wave" of feminist activism began.

Robin Morgan was born on January 29, 1941, in Lake Worth, Florida, to Faith Berkeley Morgan. From ages two through 16 she was a child actress in theater, radio and television. She starred in the popular television series *Mama.* She graduated from the Wetter School in Mount Vernon, New York. Morgan completed a B.A. degree from Columbia University in 1960 and became an associate literary agent with Curtis Brown. She left this position two years later in 1962 to become a freelance writer. In 1962, Morgan married Kenneth Pitchford, a poet and publicly acknowledged bisexual male. Their son was born in 1969. The couple divorced in 1983.

Morgan was part of a group of women writers who took over the left-wing journal *Rat* for a 1970 issue and renamed it *Women's Rat.* Her piece in that special issue, "Goodbye to All That," gained national prominence. In her article, Morgan critiqued the sexism in the 1960s civil rights and peace movements, two movements in which she had been active. In 1965, she joined the first Women's Liberation Caucus of both the Congress on Racial Equality (CORE) and the Student Nonviolent Coordinating Committee (SNCC).

Morgan became a founding member of preeminent second-wave feminist groups such as Women Against Pornography, New York Radical Women, and a radical offshoot of New York Radical Women called the Women's International Terrorist Conspiracy from Hell (WITCH) that staged symbolic protests like the hexing of Wall Street in addition to more ordinary actions, and as picketing bridal fairs. Morgan was involved in prominent events such as the 1968 picketing of the Miss America pageant in Atlantic City where the protestors threw curlers, girdles, dishcloths, stenography pads, and other objects they saw as manifestations of women's oppression into a trash can. In 1970, Morgan organized the first feminist antipornography demonstration in New York City. Morgan coined the phrase "Pornography is the theory, and rape the practice." Morgan has published more than 14 books. One of the best-known nonfiction works that she edited was *Sisterhood Is Powerful: An Anthology of Writing from the Women's Liberation Movement* (1970), one of the first collections of articles and essays from the second wave. Morgan published two early volumes of poetry, *Monster: Poems* in 1972 and *Lady of the Beasts: Poems* in 1976.

Morgan was a contributing editor to *Ms.* magazine from 1977 until its one-year hiatus from publication in 1989, due to financial reasons. Her autobiography, *Going Too Far: The Personal Chronicle of a Feminist,* was published in 1978. In 1982, Morgan published another volume of poetry, *Depth Perception: New Poems and a Masque.*

Morgan also served as editor of one of the first anthologies on the status of women and feminism globally, *Sisterhood Is Global: The International Women's Movement Anthology* (1984). Morgan went on to found the Sisterhood Is Global Institute, the first global feminist policy group.

In addition to nonfiction, Morgan published a novel, *Dry Your Smile,* in 1987.

When *Ms.* magazine resumed publication in 1990 as a bimonthly periodical, Morgan served as its editor until 1993. While working as editor, she received an honorary doctorate in humane letters from the University of Connecticut. She remains active in the Sisterhood Is Global Institute. Robin Morgan has used her considerable writing and editorial skills to further the cause of feminism both nationally and internationally.

Further Reading

Morgan, Robin. *The Anatomy of Freedom: Feminism in Four Dimensions.* Magnolia, Mass.: Peter Smith Publishing, 1994.

———. "Good News and Bad, Robin Morgan." *Women's Studies Quarterly* 24, no. 1–2 (spring 1996): 46.

———. *Sisterhood Is Global: The International Women's Movement Anthology* 1970. Reprint, New York: Feminist Press at City University of New York, 1996.

———. *Word of a Woman: Feminist Dispatches.* New York: W. W. Norton and Company, 1994.

 ## MOSELEY-BRAUN, CAROL
(1947–) *Senator*

Carol Moseley-Braun was the first African-American female senator and only the second African American elected to the Senate since Reconstruction.

Carol Moseley was born on August 16, 1947, in Chicago, Illinois. Her father was a Chicago police officer. She attended the University of Illinois at Chicago as an undergraduate and completed a law degree from the University of Chicago. Moseley worked for three years as a prosecutor in the U.S. attorney's office. She was so successful in this position that her work was recognized with the Attorney General's special achievement award.

In 1978, she was elected to the Illinois House of Representatives and made education a priority in the legislation she drafted. A 1980 bill she introduced provided higher salaries for professors. Among the bills she sponsored was one in 1984 that allowed people on welfare to attend college without losing benefits. She also was the chief sponsor of the 1985 Urban School Improvement Act, which increased the influence of parents' councils at every school in Chicago. In addition to sponsoring bills to reform education she also worked to ban discrimination in housing and private clubs. Moseley-Braun also introduced a bill to bar the state of Illinois from investing funds in South Africa because of their system of apartheid, a strict system of segregation maintained by the rule of a white minority.

After serving two terms in the Illinois House she became the first woman and the first African-American to serve as assistant majority leader. She also served as the legislative floor leader for Chicago mayor Harold Washington. She served a total of 10 years in the legislature, and every year the Independent Voters of Illinois recognized her with the Best Legislator Award.

In 1987, Moseley Braun left the House and was elected to the office of Cook County Recorder of Deeds. In this position she was once again the first female and the first African American to hold an executive office in Cook County government.

In 1992, when she ran for the Democratic nomination for the U.S. Senate from Illinois, Moseley-Braun could afford only one television commercial. She ran against a two-term incumbent in the general election and was outspent by 20 to 1. She was nevertheless elected senator in 1992 with 53 percent of the vote. She became the second African American elected to the Senate since Reconstruction; the first was Edward Brooke of Massachusetts in 1966.

One of her most memorable stands in the Senate occurred in 1993 when she challenged efforts by Republican senators Jesse Helms of North Carolina and Strom Thurmond of South Carolina to renew the Confederate battle flag on an emblem of the United Daughters of the Confederacy, a renewal that had been routinely granted every 14 years since 1893. The Senate had earlier approved the patent but reversed itself and voted

75-25 to reject the application. After the vote, Helms taunted Moseley-Braun by singing "Dixie" when she entered an elevator. Helms boasted to Senator Orrin Hatch, also on the elevator, "I'm going to make her cry." Moseley-Braun retorted, "Senator Helms, your singing would make me cry if you sung 'Rock of Ages'." As Moseley-Braun viewed it, "On this issue, there can be no consensus. It is an insult. It is absolutely unacceptable to me and to millions of Americans, black or white, that we would put the imprimatur of the United States Senate on a symbol of this kind." She later blocked Helms again in his attempt to cut funds to promote the Martin Luther King Jr. holiday.

In the Senate she served on the Judiciary Committee, the Banking, Housing and Urban Affairs Committee, and the Small Business Committee. She also served on the Juvenile Justice and the Courts and Administrative Practice Subcommittee of the Judiciary Committee.

Moseley-Braun faced charges of alleged mishandling of her campaign finances related to her former fiancé and campaign manager. An Internal Revenue Service (IRS) investigation of these charges became public during her reelection campaign in 1998, and she lost the election. The Federal Election Commission investigation found an unreconciled amount of $311.28 for personal expenses, far short of the original accusation of $200,000. The Internal Revenue Service claims against her were based on media accounts, which some thought had been falsely planted by opponents. The racial motives of some parties were questionable. An IRS agent in Chicago who made allegations against her wrote in his report, "After all, if 'they' are 'smart nough' to get elected, they are 'smart nough' to go to jail." Charges against her were dropped.

She was subsequently nominated by President Bill Clinton as ambassador to New Zealand. Senator Jesse Helms fought against her confirmation and warned her to "look for another line of work." Helms told the committee that he would consider her nomination only if she apologized

for, "the display that she provoked over the little symbol for a wonderful group of little old ladies."

The Moseley-Braun nomination was approved by a 98-2 vote in the Senate. Republican senators Jesse Helms and Peter Fitzgerald of Illinois, who had defeated her in the 1998 election, voted against her. She became one of seven African-American women to serve as an ambassador in President Bill Clinton's administration. After the administration of President George W. Bush took office, Moseley-Braun retired to private life. Carol Moseley-Braun exuded confidence and ambition, which propelled her into leadership positions.

Further Reading

Alvarez, Lizette. "Moseley-Braun Deflects Criticism." *New York Times,* November 6, 1999, A10.

Browning, Graeme. "Eighteen Months After She Was Sworn In." *National Journal* 26, no. 26 (June 25, 1994): 1504.

Kaufman, Susan. "Not Out of Nowhere—Carol Moseley-Braun." *New Directions for Women* 21, no. 5 (September 1992): 5.

Muwakkil, Salim. "Lessons From a Fall. What Happened to Carol Moseley-Braun?" *In These Times* 23, no. 1 (December 13, 1998): 19.

Shalit, Ruth. "A Star Is Born." *New Republic* 209, no. 20 (November 15, 1993): 18.

 ## MOTT, LUCRETIA COFFIN
(1793–1880)   *Abolitionist, Feminist*

Mott was one of the earliest abolitionists in the United States, and she organized one of the first women's rights convention in Seneca Falls, New York, in 1848.

Lucretia Coffin was born January 3, 1793, on Nantucket Island, Massachusetts, to Anna Folger Coffin and Thomas Coffin, a sea captain. Her family were Quakers, members of the Society of Friends, a faith that encouraged the equality of women. She was educated in public schools in Boston, Massachusetts, and at Nine Partners, a Quaker boarding school near Poughkeepsie,

New York. At age 15 she became an assistant teacher at the Nine Partners Quaker school. In 1811, after teaching for one year, she married Quaker abolitionist James Mott, who had been a teacher at her school. The couple had six children. The Quakers split into two factions in 1817, and the couple joined the more liberal faction led by Elias Hicks. In 1821, Mott was appointed as an official minister of the Society of Friends.

African-American leader Robert Purvis and others have found that the abolitionist work of Mott had preceded that of many people, including famous abolitionist William Lloyd Garrison. Mott was speaking in African-American churches as early as 1829. In 1833, the Motts helped organize the American Anti-Slavery Society. When the American Anti-Slavery Society decided to exclude women from membership, Mott helped form the Philadelphia Female Anti-Slavery Society. Once the policy of female exclusion was dropped from the American Anti-Slavery Society, Mott served on the executive board of its Pennsylvania branch. In 1837, Mott was one of the organizers of the Anti-Slavery Convention of American Women. In 1840, the Motts served as delegates to an international antislavery convention in London. At the convention, women were excluded from the proceedings. While at the convention, Mott and ELIZABETH CADY STANTON, outraged by their exclusion, planned a women's rights convention, which they held in 1848 in Seneca Falls, New York. Mott delivered the opening and closing addresses at the conference. She credited her interest in women's rights to her reading of feminist author Mary Wollstonecraft's *A Vindication of the Rights of Woman* published in 1792. Mott asserted in 1849 that woman "asks nothing as a favor, but as a right." Mott was elected as the first president of the American Equal Rights Association when the group was formed in 1866 to secure civil rights for ex-slaves and women.

After the Fugitive Slave Law was passed in 1850, Mott made her home a station on the

Lucretia Mott, suffragist
(Still Picture Branch, National Archives, College Park, MD)

Underground Railroad, which helped African-American slaves escape to freedom. She published a book in 1850, *Discourse on Woman,* which addressed the effects of poor education, limited employment opportunities, and low wages on women. She helped establish the Female Medical College of Pennsylvania. Mott also raised money to support the education of newly freed African Americans and for Swarthmore College, a coeducational institution founded by Quakers in 1864.

Lucretia Mott died on November 11, 1880, at Roadside, her country home north of Philadelphia, Pennsylvania, at age 87. Her efforts to ensure justice for women and African Americans set precedents and were ahead of her time.

Further Reading

Carlson, A. Cheree. "Defining Womanhood: Lucretia Coffin Mott and the Transformation of Femininity."

Western Journal of Communication 58, no. 2 (spring 1994): 85.

Hope Bacon, Margaret. "Lucretia Mott: Pioneer for Peace." *Quaker History* 82, no. 2 (Fall 1993): 63.

———. *Valiant Friend: The Life of Lucretia Mott.* Philadelphia, Pa.: Friends General Conference, 1999.

Sillars, Malcolm. "From Romantic Idealism to Enlightenment Rationalism: Lucretia Coffin Mott." *Rhetoric Society Quarterly* 25 (1995): 47–67.

   MURRAY, ANNA PAULINE (Pauli Murray)
(1910–1985)   *Feminist Attorney*

Pauline Murray battled exclusion based on her race and gender and broke barriers for women by entering the professions of law and the ministry.

Anna Pauline Murray was born on November 20, 1910, in Baltimore, Maryland. Her multiracial background included African-American, white, and American Indian ancestors. Murray lost both her parents at an early age and was raised by her maternal aunt Pauline and her grandparents in Durham, North Carolina. In 1927, Murray graduated as valedictorian of Hillside High School. She left the South in 1928 for New York in order to attend Hunter College, then an all-female institution. She was married for a few months before having the marriage annulled.

Murray paid for college by working several jobs. However, while in college she lived on such a restricted budget and diet that she had to seek medical care for malnutrition. Murray graduated from Hunter in 1933, one of only four African-Americans in a group 247 women.

After graduating from Hunter, Murray took classes at the Brookwood Labor College and worked for the Works Progress Administration (WPA), a New Deal program in which the federal government employed many citizens by having them work on a variety of to help relieve unemployment during the Great Depression jobs serving the public interest.

In 1938, Murray decided to attend graduate school and applied to the all-white University of North Carolina at Chapel Hill. When her applica-

tion was turned down because of her race, Murray campaigned against the school's policy of segregation. Her white relatives had donated significant sums to the same university. The result of her campaign against the University of North Carolina was that the state legislature set up separate graduate education programs for African Americans. A number of separate professional schools, including a law school, were established. African-American students were finally admitted to the University of North Carolina in 1951.

Murray continued to challenge racial prejudice. In 1940, she was arrested and jailed when she refused to go to the back of a segregated bus in Virginia.

Also in 1940, at age 30, Murray enrolled in Howard University to study law. She was the only female student in her class. While at Howard she became aware of sexism, or "Jane Crow" as she termed it. (The term *Jane Crow* was the gender equivalent of the term *Jim Crow,* which referred to statutes that legalized segregation between African Americans and whites in southern states.) On her first day of law school, a professor commented to the class—all men, except for Murray—that he did not know why women went to law school. Her response to such overt sexism was, "The professor didn't know it, but he had just guaranteed that I would be the top student in his class." She was elected as chief justice of the Howard Court of Peers, the highest student position on campus. Murray graduated from Howard in 1944 with honors. During the 1940s, she also participated in a sit-in to desegregate Washington, D.C., restaurants and other public facilities.

Murray next applied to earn a master's degree in law from Harvard University. They initially accepted her and awarded her a prestigious fellowship but reversed their decision when they discovered her gender. Their letter to her stated, "Your picture and the salutation of your college transcript indicate that you are not of the sex entitled to be admitted to Harvard Law School." Radcliffe women were allowed into Harvard classrooms in 1943 during World War II. Women were not allowed into the Harvard School of Medicine or Law School until

1945. Murray had been excluded from educational opportunities because of both her race and gender. However, she again refused to accept her exclusion without protest and wrote a letter to First Lady ELEANOR ROOSEVELT in her campaign to bring this injustice to light. Eleanor Roosevelt convinced President Franklin Roosevelt to write a letter to the president of Harvard on Murray's behalf, but to no avail. Consequently, Murray attended Bolt Law School at the University of California, Berkeley. She completed her L.L.M. degree in 1945. Her master's thesis, *The Right to Equal Opportunity in Employment,* was the first published on this topic.

She had moved to Brooklyn and, in 1949, Murray ran for the New York City Council from Brooklyn but lost to the Democratic incumbent. Two years later, Murray published her first book, *States Laws on Race and Color,* which U.S. Supreme Court justice Thurgood Marshall later acknowledged as his "bible" in the historic *Brown v. the Board of Education* case of 1954 (the case that outlawed segregation in public education). Her second book, on the history of her family, *Proud Shoes: The Story of an American Family,* was published in 1956. After teaching briefly at the Ghana School of Law she coauthored a book, *The Constitution and Government of Ghana,* published 1961. Murray had left Ghana after accusing Ghana's president, Kwame Nkrumah, of human rights violations. Nkrumah had established a one-party dictatorship. He eliminated his opposition through arrests and imprisonment without trial.

Murray returned to school and earned her doctor of jurisprudence degree from Yale University in 1965. While at Yale, she was appointed to the President's Commission on the Status of Women.

In 1966, Murray was a cofounder of the National Organization for Women (NOW). She generated the idea that women needed an organization similar to the National Association for the Advancement of Colored People (NAACP). NOW started with just 31 members and became the largest women's group in the nation within a few years.

In 1968, Murray became a tenured professor at Brandeis University. Murray rejected the tactics of

the black power movement, which took a militant stance regarding racial inequality, and remained fully supportive of integration. Murray also critiqued black power leaders for their sexism. Around this time, she also published a massive reference work on state race laws and published a prizewinning volume of poetry, *Dark Testament and Other Poems* (1970).

Murray challenged the exclusion of women from the Episcopalian priesthood by entering a seminary at age 62. In 1973, she enrolled at the New York General Theological Seminary and became an ordained Episcopalian minister in 1977, the first African-American woman in the United States to do so. Murray spent the next eight years serving as the minister of Holy Nativity Church in Baltimore, Maryland. She retired and moved to Pittsburgh in 1984.

Pauli Murray died of cancer on July 1, 1985, at age 75. Her autobiography, *Song in a Weary Throat: An American Pilgrimage,* was published in 1987, two years after her death. Pauli Murray used the law and ministry on behalf of social change.

Further Reading

Giddings, Paula. "Fighting Jane Crow." *Nation* (May 23, 1987): 689–90.

Murray, Pauli. *The Autobiography of a Black Activist, Feminist, Lawyer, Priest, and Poet.* Knoxville: University of Tennessee Press, 1989. Originally published as *Song in a Weary Throat.* New York: Harper and Row, 1987.

———. *Dark Testament, and Other Poems.* Norwalk, Conn.: Silvermine, 1970.

———. *Proud Shoes: The Story of an American Family.* New York: Harper and Row, 1987. Reprint, Boston: Beacon Press, 1999.

———. *States Laws on Race and Color.* 1951. Reprint, Athens: University of Georgia Press, 1997.

 MURRAY, PATTY JOHNS
(1950–) *Senator*

In 1992, Patty Murray became the first woman from Washington State elected to the U.S. Senate.

Patty Johns was born on October 11, 1950, in Bothell, Washington, one of seven siblings. Her parents were disabled veteran David L. Johns, who owned a five- and ten cent store, and Beverly McLoughlin Johns, an accountant. Patty graduated from Washington State University in 1972. She married Rob Murray in 1972 and had two children. She worked as a parent volunteer preschool teacher from 1977 to 1984 at the Shoreline Community Cooperation School. Murray worked as an instructor of parent education courses at Shoreline Community College from 1984 to 1987 and as a lobbyist for environmental and educational issues from 1983 to 1988. Murray served on the board of directors of the Shoreline School District from 1985 to 1989. She was both president of the board and its legislative representative.

She was elected to the Washington State Senate and served from 1988 to 1992. While in the state senate she served as Democratic whip from 1990 to 1992. Murray was recognized as Washington State Legislator of the Year in 1990.

A state official in Olympia, Washington, disregarded Murray, the former preschool teacher and school board president, and dismissed her efforts to preserve a parent-child preschool program with the remark that she was "just a mom in tennis shoes." But Murray adapted the remark as her slogan and a source of pride. As a candidate she emphasized her background, saying, "I have had a different life—I am not a millionaire; I had two working parents."

In 1991 she decided to challenge incumbent Democratic senator Brook Adams, who had been accused of sexual harassment by employees. He decided not to run and Murray beat incumbent Republican Representation Rod Chandler for the Senate seat. Murray became the first woman to serve in the U.S. Senate from Washington State when she was elected in 1992. In reviewing her Senate voting record, the *National Journal* rated her as having the most liberal record. As the daughter of a disabled veteran she was especially interested in serving on the Veterans Affairs Committee, to which she was appointed in 1996. Murray supported legislation to strengthen regulations against sexual harassment in the military. Murray voted against welfare reform budget cuts in 1996. She led the fight to allow military women to have abortions on overseas bases and earned a perfect score on her voting record from the National Abortion and Reproductive Rights Action League. The *National Journal* rated her the Senate's most liberal member.

Murray was reelected in 1998 over second-term Republican congresswoman Linda Smith. Murray serves on the Appropriations Committee, the Banking, Housing, and Urban Affairs Committee, and the Budget Committee. In January 2001 she sponsored negotiations on the *Seattle Times* newspaper strike. Summarizing her experience in the Senate thus far Murray stated, "My biggest surprise is the amount of time that people talk about issues that are irrelevant to "everyday, average people." Murray remains committed to working on behalf of "everyday, average people."

Further Reading

Biographical Directory of the United States Congress. "Patty Murray." Available online. URL: http://bioguide.congress.gov/scripts/viodisplay.pl?index=M001111. Downloaded November 27, 2000.

Broder, David. "Washington Senate Matchup." *Washington Post,* October 21, 1998, A14.

Doyle, Erica. "Leaving Her Mark." *Ms.* 10, no. 5 (August/September 2000): 20–21.

Lopez, Steve. "An Unconventional Fight." *Time* 152, no. 18 (November 2, 1998): 55–56.

Murphy, Kim. "For voters in Washington State." *Los Angeles Times,* October 28, 1998, 4.

Reaves, Jessica. "A Real Liberal Rocks the Senate." *Ms.* 8, no. 4 (January/February 1998): 31.

Victor, Kirk. "Fightin' Women." *National Journal* (August 2, 1997): 1544–47.

Whitney, Catherine. *Nine and Counting: The Women of the Senate.* New York: Perennial, 2001.

Women in Congress Biographies. "Patty Murray." Available online. URL: http://www.inform.umd.edu/EdRes/Topic/WomensStudies/GovernmentPolitics/WomeninCongress/Biographies/Senate/murray-patty. Downloaded November 27, 2000.

N

 NATION, CARRY AMELIA
MOORE GLOYD
(1846–1911)   *Temperance Advocate*

Carry Nation launched a one-woman crusade against liquor by smashing bars with a hatchet and thus garnerning headlines on behalf of her cause, to protect women and children from alcoholics. Because married women lacked property rights, they and their children were all too often abused by alcoholic husbands and fathers in previous centuries.

Carry Moore was born on November 25, 1846. She had a difficult childhood; the family was uprooted often and moved from state to state frequently. At age 13, Moore was sent to a boarding school in Independence, Missouri. Her family had been wealthy enough to own slaves, but during the Civil War, when Carry was 15, the Moores were impoverished. Her mother suffered from mental illness. She believed she was Queen Victoria and drove around in a coach, wearing royal purple gowns and a crown. Eventually her mother was committed to a mental institution.

The family took in boarders and eventually Carry Moore married one of them on November 21, 1867, when she was 20 years old. Her husband, Dr. Charles Gloyd, claimed to be a physician, but he was a teacher and a pronounced alcoholic. Her daughter Charline was born in September 1868. Her husband died six months after the birth of their daughter.

With a child to support and few job opportunities, the young widow worked as a teacher for four years. In 1877, she married David Nation, a businessman and preacher who was 19 years her senior. The family moved frequently from state to state for a few years, eventually settling in Medicine Lodge, Kansas.

In 1897, Nation formed a local chapter of the Woman's Christian Temperance Union (WCTU), which advocated abstinence from alcohol and worked to prohibit or limit its sale. The organization was already 20 years old when Nation became involved. She was involved with the organization in a quiet, reserved way for a decade, but she eventually came to the conclusion that more militant tactics were needed.

In 1899, she had begun closing saloons by praying and singing in front of them with groups of women and children. Since Kansas was a dry state (one in which alcohol sales were prohibited) the

Carry Nation aboard ship, 1904
(Prints & Photographs Division, Library of Congress,
Washington, D.C.)

saloon owners were in violation of the law, and Nation's protests drew attention to this. Nation soon employed the same tactic successfully in other towns.

In 1900, she began physically attacking saloon buildings, starting in Kiowa, Kansas. Armed with rocks and bricks she entered saloons and broke all the liquor bottles. She threw heavy cash registers and ripped doors off their hinges. Nation then used a hatchet to break up the furniture, and it was this symbol that made her famous. As Nation later recalled, "I felt invincible. My strength was that of a giant. God was certainly standing by me. I smashed five saloons with rocks before I ever took a hatchet."

Patrons were shocked at the sight of a woman acting violently. Nation was in her 50s when she embarked on her direct-action hatchet campaigns. Members of the state temperance union began carrying miniature hatchets as their symbol. A temperance publication called *The Hatchet* was begun in Guthrie, Oklahoma. Nation inspired rural housewives to board a train and head for Wichita, a city with numerous saloons.

In 1901, a few months after the start of her hatchet campaign, Nation's husband filed for divorce on grounds of desertion. The national WCTU was critical of Nation's destruction of property. The organization was led nationally by FRANCES WILLARD, who viewed Nation as eccentric. Nation did more than wield a hatchet, however. While in Kansas City, Nation helped to establish a shelter for the wives and children of alcoholics, an early model for today's battered women's shelters.

In 1904, Nation published her autobiography, *The Use and Need of Carry Nation.* The autobiography provided a source of income, which enabled Nation to care for her alcoholic daughter who, like her grandmother, was eventually committed to an insane asylum. Nation cared for her daughter for the remainder of her life. Sales of souvenir hatchets inscribed with "Carry Nation, Joint Smasher" also sold well.

Nation continued to mobilize women, sometimes running newspaper ads asking women to bring their hatchets with them to a specified place and time. Nation conducted her first saloon demonstration in 1899 and would hold her last in 1910.

Carry Nation died on June 2, 1911. She was buried with her mother in Belton, Missouri. A granite shaft marking her grave was erected in 1924 and simply reads "She hath done what she could." A memorial fountain was erected on the spot where she was first arrested in Wichita. Archives in the Kansas State Historical Society contain several of her hatchets. In 1950, her house in Medicine Lodge, Kansas, was dedicated as a memorial to Nation. Liquor laws were enforced in Kansas as a result of her activism, and it became a penal offense there to be found where liquor was dispensed. The story of Nation's direct confrontation with the liquor industry remained in the public imagination of succeeding generations.

Further Reading

Day, Robert. "Carry from Kansas Became a Nation All Unto Herself." *Smithsonian* 20 (April 1989): 147–48.

Grace, Fran. *Carry Nation: Retelling the Life.* Bloomington: Indiana University Press, 2000.

Schwarz, Frederic. "Carry Nation Took an Ax." *American Heritage* 51 no. 3 (May/June 2000): 107–08.

 ## NORTON, ELEANOR HOLMES
(1937–) *Congressional Representative*

Eleanor Holmes Norton was the first female chair of the Equal Employment Opportunity Commission (EEOC). In 1990, she was elected to Congress as the Democratic representative for the District of Columbia.

Eleanor Holmes was born on June 13, 1937, in Washington, D.C., part of a fourth-generation Washington family. Congress had abolished slavery in the District of Columbia in 1862, and her great-grandfather had walked off the southern plantation on which he was enslaved and migrated there. Many free African-Americans migrated to Washington, D.C., because of its lax enforcement of the Fugitive Slave Act. Holmes's father was one of the first officers in an entirely African-American fire department in 1902. She attended segregated public schools in Washington, D.C., and graduated from Dunbar High School in 1955, the only college preparatory school in Washington open to African Americans. She completed a B.A. degree from Antioch College in 1960 and then earned a master's degree in American history in 1963. In 1963 she was a member of the national staff of the March on Washington, which was then the largest U.S. civil rights march ever and perhaps best known for Martin Luther King Jr.'s "I Have a Dream" speech. Eleanor Holmes was a member of the primary civil rights organizations of the 1960s including the Student Nonviolent Coordinating Committee (SNCC) and the

Mississippi Freedom Democratic Party (MFDP), which challenged the all-white delegation from Mississippi at the 1964 Democratic Party National Convention.

She clerked for a federal judge from 1964 to 1965. She earned her J.D. degree in 1965 and married Edward Norton. The couple had two children. In 1963 Yale Law School awarded her the citation of merit as outstanding alumna of Yale Law School.

From 1965 to 1970, Norton served as the assistant legal director of the American Civil Liberties Union (ACLU) in New York City. She specialized in First Amendment cases involving free speech and represented a broad array of clients including Vietnam War protestors, feminists, segregationist governor George Wallace, and the Ku Klux Klan (KKK). She defended groups such as the Klan since she believed that "If the principle [of free speech] is going to live at all, it's got to live for anybody who wants to exercise it." Norton also defended Julian Bond when the Georgia House of Representatives attempted to deny him his seat because of his opposition to the Vietnam War. In 1970, she was appointed as head of the New York City commission on human rights by Mayor John Lindsay, the first woman to hold the position. She coauthored *Sex Discrimination and the Law: Causes and Remedies* in 1975.

In 1977, President Jimmy Carter appointed her as director of the EEOC. When she took over the EEOC, there was a backlog of 13,000 cases. Norton cut the backlog in half and increased the EEOC's productivity by 65 percent. Her tenure at the EEOC ended in 1981 when President Ronald Reagan appointed Clarence Thomas to the position. Norton became a professor of law at Georgetown University in 1982. She still serves in this position.

In 1990, Norton was elected as the Democratic congressional representative for the District of Columbia. She won reelection in 1996 with 90 percent of the vote and has been reelected four times. Norton authored 42 bills in Congress, and seven of her bills have become law, records of achievement that place her in the top 4 percent among her fellow legislators. Norton has cosponsored 458 bills, a record that places her in the top 3 percent among her peers. Norton serves as cochair of the Women's Caucus and is the first African American to reach the upper levels of the Women's Caucus leadership. She has received 70 honorary degrees. Norton originally proposed the Commission on Race in America that President Bill Clinton established. The commission held a series of hearings throughout the country in order to facilitate public attention and discussions regarding race relations. As an activist and politician, Eleanor Holmes Norton has remained on the cutting edge of national debates regarding race relations.

Further Reading

Cheatham, Cheryl Smith. *African American Women in the Legal Academy.* Cleveland, Ohio: Case Western Reserve University Law Library, 1994.

Norton, Eleanor Holmes. "Anita Hill and the Woman of the Year." In *Race, Gender and Power in America,* edited by Anita Faye Hill and Emma Coleman Jordan. New York: Oxford University Press, 1995.

"Norton Elected to Women's Caucus Vice-Chair." *Washington Afro-American* 103, no. 22 (January, 21, 1995): A1.

Kaufman, Leslie. "Eleanor Holmes Norton: A New Friend on the Hill." *Government Executive* 25, no. 4 (April 1993): 26–28.

Wright, James. "Congresswoman Norton Boasts of Proud Family History." *Washington Afro-American* 104, no. 2 (August, 26, 1995): B7.

NOVELLO, ANTONIA COELLO
(1944–)   *U.S. Surgeon General*

Antonia Novello is the first female and the first Latina to be appointed surgeon general of the United States. As the 14th surgeon general in the nation's history, she lobbied tobacco companies to stop targeting ads to children under age 18.

Antonia Coello was born on August 23, 1944, in Fajardo, Puerto Rico, to Ana Delia Flores Coello and Antonio Coello. Her father died when she was eight. Her mother, a schoolteacher and later a high school principal, raised Antonia and

her brothers. She graduated from high school at age 15. She suffered from a condition known as congenital megacolon in childhood, and every summer she had to undergo treatment for this disease. When she was 18, she had surgery to correct her condition. She suffered complications from the surgery for the next two years, until she traveled to the Mayo Clinic in the United States for a final operation that corrected her condition.

She earned her bachelor's degree at the University of Puerto Rico in 1965 and, from the same university, her medical degree in 1970. She graduated in the top 5 percent of her medical school class. Also in 1970, she married Joseph Novello, a U.S. Navy flight surgeon. The couple moved to Ann Arbor, Michigan, and continued their medical training at the University of Michigan Medical Center. There, Antonia Novello did her residency as a pediatrician and was chosen as the 1970 Intern of the Year. Novello had a hysterectomy in the 1970s and so the couple had no children.

Novello was a professor of pediatrics at Georgetown University in Washington D.C. She earned a master's degree in 1982 from Johns Hopkins University in Baltimore, Maryland. In 1986, she was named director of the National Institute of Child Health and Human Development.

In 1989, President George H. W. Bush nominated Antonia Novello as Surgeon General of the United States. Novello had served on several task forces on AIDS prior to her nomination. Her antiabortion views fit those of the Bush administration. Of her historic appointment, she stated, "The American dream is well and alive . . . today the West Side Story comes to the West Wing." She claimed that being a woman was an advantage in her work: "Being a woman, I learned diplomacy. We women have always learned how to wait until there comes your moment to speak." She also felt that her experience with congenital megacolon as a child allowed her to develop a sensitivity for the patient.

As surgeon general, Novello lobbied the liquor industry to end its targeting of advertising to minors. One of her concerns about alcohol was its involvement in sexual assaults and other violent crimes. She publicly addressed issues such as children with AIDS, teenage smoking and drinking, and women's health issues, such as rising lung cancer rates. She described the rise in smoking among women as "a case of the Virginia Slims woman catching up with the Marlboro Man."

She was also the first surgeon general to bring the issue of domestic violence under a national spotlight. In 1991, she announced that one-third of women murdered every year in the United States are killed by husbands, boyfriends, or ex-partners, and that for American women the home is more dangerous than city streets. In her efforts to educate the public about battered women, she pointed out that every five years, more lives are lost to domestic violence than the 58,000 American lives lost in the Vietnam War. Novello spoke of the contradiction between physician awareness of child abuse and spousal battering: "If they see an abused child, they know who to call to have the child taken from the home to safety. And they know that the law will protect someone who reports child abuse. But if they see an abused wife, they feel that reporting it may open a Pandora's box."

Her term as U.S. Surgeon General ended in 1993. Novello then worked on behalf of the United Nations Children's Fund (UNICEF) on issues related to health and nutrition. In 1991, she was appointed as commissioner of health for the state of New York, home to the largest population of Puerto Ricans outside Puerto Rico. Novello's daring advocacy on health issues that particularly affect women and children raised the quality of life.

Further Reading

Esterbook, Gregg. "Antonia Novello: U.S. Surgeon General Monitors Nation's Public Health." *Los Angeles Times,* January 12, 1992, 3.

Hawxhurst, Joan. *Antonia Novello, U.S. Surgeon General.* Brookfield, Conn.: Millbrook Press, 1993.

Krucoff, Carol. "Antonia Novello: A Dream Come True." *Saturday Evening Post* 263, no. 4 (May 1991): 38–41.

Puerto Rico Herald. "Antonia Novello." Available online. URL: http://www.puertoricoherald.org/issues/vol4n12/ProfileANovello-en.shtml. Downloaded November 28, 2000.

Virtual Office of the Surgeon General. "Antonia C. Novello." Available online. URL: http://www.surgeongeneral.gov/library/history/bionovello.htm. Downloaded November 28, 2000.

 O'HARE, CARRIE KATHLEEN RICHARDS CUNNINGHAM (Kate O'Hare)
(1877–1948)   *Socialist Leader*

Carrie Kathleen Richards O'Hare (known as Kate) joined the Socialist Party of America in 1901 and became one of its best-known organizers and journalists. O'Hare became the first female candidate for the U.S. Senate when the Socialist Party nominated her in 1916 in Missouri. She was jailed during World War I under the Espionage Act for her antiwar speeches.

Carrie Kathleen Richards was born near Ada, Kansas, on March 26, 1877, to Lucy Sullivan and Andrew Richards, a farming family in central Kansas. She was the fourth child and the eldest daughter. Both her parents' families had descended from colonial Americans. When the bank foreclosed on their farm, the family moved to a slum area in Kansas City, Missouri. Kansas City was the largest urban area between St. Louis and San Francisco at the time. She studied Latin and Greek at Central High School, graduating in 1892.

Richards earned a teaching certificate at Pawnee City Academy in southeast Nebraska. One-quarter of 19th-century women worked as teachers, generally earning half the salary of male teachers. She briefly taught at a rural school in Nebraska, then returned to her family in Kansas City, Missouri, in 1895 and worked as a machinist in her father's shop, eventually joining the International Order of Machinists union.

Her family was involved in Populist politics and Richards took courses to prepare for work as a missionary. Her spare time was devoted to temperance work and the local Florence Crittenton mission, which was attempting to rescue prostitutes by teaching them morals, job skills, and religion.

After hearing a speech by MARY HARRIS JONES (known as "Mother Jones"), Richards became interested in socialism. As she remembered, "Dear old Mother! That is one of the mile-posts in my life that I can easily locate . . . and that the only place for a sincere union man was in the Socialist party."

Although inspired by Jones, Richards was uncertain what socialism was, so she borrowed books and immediately began to study the topic. She founded the Socialist Labor Party with her father in 1899 and when the party split two years later, she joined the more moderate branch of the Socialist Party of America.

In 1901, she attended the International School of Social Economy for socialist organizers in Girard, Kansas, where she met Francis O'Hare. Francis O'Hare was a highly effective lecturer who traveled throughout the United States, England, Canada, and Mexico. She married him four days later. She gave birth to four children and began a career as a columnist for socialist periodicals such as *Appeal to Reason.*

In 1912, the O'Hares became coeditors and publishers of the weekly socialist paper the *National Rip-Saw,* published in St. Louis, Missouri. Francis O'Hare served as the business manager for the publication.

In 1910, Kate O'Hare ran for the seat representing the Second Congressional District in Kansas on the Socialist Party ticket. She lost, but won 5 percent of the vote. That year, she was elected to the national executive committee of the Socialist Party, the first woman to serve in this position. She became the first woman to campaign for a seat in the U.S. Senate when her party nominated her in 1916 to represent Missouri.

O'Hare supported suffrage for women and served as grand marshal of a 1913 suffrage parade in Washington, D.C. She also supported birth control, abortion, and divorce. One of her most famous articles on the status of working-class women, *Wimmin Ain't Got No Kick,* was published around this time as a pamphlet by the Socialist Party. It argued that working-class women were vulnerable to exploitation in industry, in the home where they reproduced workers, and in prostitution.

She was not on the vanguard of the left in her views on race, however. She believed that African Americans were inferior to whites and that African Americans should be given a separate section of the country in which to live. O'Hare had lived in Oklahoma briefly and had sympathy for the plight of American Indians but believed that their evolutionary stage was primitive compared to whites.

In 1917, O'Hare was indicted under the new federal Espionage Act, which made it illegal to give antiwar speeches, for speaking against U.S. entry into World War I. O'Hare was charged with advising draft resistance. Her speeches condemned war as imperialist and economically motivated. Federal surveillance agents had targeted her as the most dangerous woman in America and had been following her on the lecture circuit for a long time before they were able to charge her with a crime. At the trial, the prosecutor told the jury that O'Hare was dangerous because she was "shrewd and brainy." She was sentenced to five years in prison for her antiwar speech.

O'Hare served a 14-month sentence in the Missouri State Penitentiary, which she entered in 1919. Radical activist EMMA GOLDMAN was also an inmate at the facility. While in prison, O'Hare wrote *Kate O'Hare's Prison Letters,* which was published in 1919, and *In Prison,* published in 1920. In May 1920, she received a full pardon from President Calvin Coolidge. After being released from prison she devoted her energies to prison reform.

In 1922, she helped found Commonwealth, a socialist college in Mena, Arkansas. She taught at the college for two years and served as trustee and director for 17 years. The college was dissolved in 1940.

In 1928, she divorced Francis O'Hare and married Charles Cunningham, an engineer and businessman from San Jose, California. In 1934, she was involved in Upton Sinclair's "End Poverty In California" Democratic Party campaign for the governorship. Upton Sinclair was a Pulitzer Prize–winning novelist and social reformer. His best-known novel, *The Jungle,* was published in 1906. It exposed abuses in the meat-packing industry and led to reform of federal food inspection laws. From 1939 to 1940, she served as assistant director of the California Department of Penology. By this time she no longer identified herself as a socialist. By the 1940s and the beginning of World War II, U.S. society had become more conservative. Some U.S. leftists became more moderate in their political views. O'Hare's second marriage, to a businessman, and the accompanying personal prosperity may have shaped her public stances as well. O'Hare opposed communism and lived to see the declining influence of socialism in U.S. public debates.

Kate Richards O'Hare died on January 12, 1948, in Benicia, California, at age 71 from a heart attack. Services were held at the local Congregational church. O'Hare was cremated. Obituaries appeared in all major newspapers from coast to coast, including the *New York Times*. Some of her papers are stored in the Socialist Party of America collection, which is housed at Duke University in North Carolina. The life of Kate Richards O'Hare remains a testimony of a time in U.S. history more progressive than is often recognized in traditional accounts.

Further Reading

Miller, Sally. *From Prairie to Prison: The Life of Social Activist Kate Richards O'Hare.* Columbia: University of Missouri Press, 1993.
———. "Kate Richards O'Hare: Progression Toward Feminism." *Kansas History* 7 (winter 1984/85) 263–79.
University of North Dakota. "Kate Richard O'Hare Papers." Available online. URL: http://www.und.edu/dept/library/Collections/og220.html. Downloaded November 28, 2000.

P

PARKS, ROSA LOUISE McCAULEY
(1913–   )   *Civil Rights Activist*

Rosa Louise McCauley Parks's refusal to give up her seat on a segregated bus to a white man and move to the back of the bus is cited as the spark that launched the modern civil rights movement. The resulting Montgomery Bus Boycott lasted 381 days, ending in 1956 when the U.S. Supreme Court ruled that segregation in transportation was unconstitutional. Martin Luther King Jr. became the nationally known leader of the boycott, but it was the arrest of Rosa Parks that began the struggle.

Rosa McCauley was born on February 4, 1913, in Tuskegee, Alabama, the first child in her family. Her carpenter father was absent from her childhood, but her maternal grandfather was a strong influence. He had been born into slavery, the son of his master, but was so fair-skinned that other African Americans often thought he was white and sometimes tried to keep him out of their community meetings.

Her mother, Leona Edwards McCauley, worked as a poorly paid teacher. During the war her mother worked in Detroit, Michigan, and Rosa saw that African Americans in the North had more freedom than did African Americans in the South.

Rosa McCauley Parks attended the private Lab School at the all-black Alabama State Teachers College for a year and a half—through 11th grade. Parks married barber Raymond Parks in 1932, and they were both active in the local chapter of the National Association for the Advancement of Colored People (NAACP). Rosa Parks finished her high school diploma in 1934, an accomplishment she had delayed in order to care for her mother a few years earlier. In 1943, she was elected secretary of the Montgomery branch of the NAACP and also served as its youth adviser. She registered to vote in 1945, a dangerous action for African Americans in the South at this time. She had been refused in two previous attempts.

At the time of her arrest in 1955, Parks worked as a seamstress at the Fair Department Store and took buses to and from work. Buses throughout the South were racially segregated, and African Americans were expected to sit only in the back. As white passengers boarded the bus and filled the white front section of the bus, African Americans were supposed to stand and give up their seats in the

African-American back section. Her refusal to move to the back of the bus resulted in her arrest and a $14 fine. When the police officer arrived to arrest Parks, he asked, "Why don't you stand up?" and Parks replied, "I don't think I should have to." These few words would shake the world. While Parks has said that she was simply too tired to move that day, she had been an activist and leader in the civil rights community for a long time. Parks attended training for civil rights workers at the Highlander Folk School near Nashville, Tennessee, where such civil rights leaders as ELLA BAKER and SEPTIMA CLARK taught political strategy. As Parks would later recall concerning the day of her arrest, "I had enough. I wanted to be treated like a human being." Parks's arrest at age 42 caused her to lose her job.

The original plan for the bus boycott, developed by JOANN ROBINSON, the president of the

Rosa Parks, civil rights activist
(National Archives)

Women's Political Council, was to have a one-day boycott to protest Parks's arrest. The boycott lasted for 381 days. African Americans made up more than 70 percent of the ridership on the buses, so when they walked to work instead of riding, the boycott brought the local economy to a standstill. This boycott was one of the first successful mass challenges to southern segregation. The original demands called for more courteous treatment from the white drivers, the hiring of African-American drivers, and the right of African Americans to remain seated. Their segregation to the back of the bus was not originally challenged.

In 1957, she moved to Detroit with her husband and mother. Congressman John Conyers hired Parks as a staff assistant in 1965, and she worked for Conyers for the next 25 years. Parks remained active in the NAACP and the Southern Christian Leadership Conference (SCLC), another civil rights organization.

Detroit renamed its Twelfth Street in her honor in 1969. Her husband died in 1977. In 1980, readers of *Ebony* magazine voted her as the woman who had done the most to advance the civil rights of African Americans.

She still serves as deaconess of St. Matthew's African-Methodist Episcopal Church in Detroit. In 1987, she started the Rosa and Raymond Parks Institute of Self Development in Detroit to offer career training to African-American youth. She retired in 1988. In her honor, the Rosa Parks Freedom Award is bestowed annually by the SCLC. She was awarded the Presidential Medal of Freedom by President Bill Clinton in 1996 and the Congressional Medal of Honor in 1999. In January 2002, the *New York Times* reported that Parks's former home had been placed on the National Register of Historic Places. Rosa Parks has been called the mother of the civil rights movement. Her legacy will remain in the annals of history.

Further Reading

Brinkley, Douglas. *Rosa Parks.* New York: Viking, 2000.
Dove, Rita. "Rosa Parks." *Time* 153, no. 23 (June 14, 1999): 166+.

Parks, Rosa. *Dear Mrs. Parks: A Dialogue with Today's Youth.* New York: Lee and Low Books, 1996.

———. *Quiet Strength: The Faith, the Hope, and the Heart of a Woman Who Changed a Nation.* Grand Rapids, Mich.: Zondervan Publishing Company, 2000.

———. *Rosa Parks: My Story.* New York: Penguin, 1999.

"Rosa Parks." *Biography* 3, no. 12 (December 1999): 110.

PARSONS, LUCY GONZALEZ
(1852–1942)   *Labor Leader*

In the 1920s and 1930s, the Federal Bureau of Investigation (FBI) described Lucy Parsons as "more dangerous than a thousand rioters." Active in many leftist organizations at the turn of the 20th century, she was also noted for her writings published in leftist periodicals.

Lucy Parsons was born in Johnson County, Texas, in 1852. Parsons claimed to be Mexican and Creek Indian, and she occasionally used the name Gonzalez. However, current research suggest that she most likely had been an African-American slave in Texas.

In 1872, she married Albert Parsons, a radical Republican and former Confederate soldier. Because of miscegenation laws regarding their mixed marriage, they fled the South in 1872 under threats from the Ku Klux Klan (KKK). When the Reconstruction government came to an end in Texas, they moved to Chicago.

Parsons's dark skin may have made it hard for her to get a factory job. She opened a dress shop in Chicago. Parsons also began writing articles for socialist publications about the homeless, the unemployed, and the working women. She gave birth to the first of two children in 1879. Her son's birth certificate registered him as "Negro" and her daughter's birth certificate listed her as "nigger."

In 1879, she was involved with the Chicago Working Women's Union, which called for a suffrage plank in the Socialist Labor Party platform. The union wanted equal pay for women and an eight-hour work day.

In 1883, she cofounded the International Working People's Association (IWPA), an anarchist-influenced labor organization that insisted not only on the equality of people of color but also of women. One of her most famous articles in the IPWA weekly paper, *The Alarm,* appeared in an 1884. Entitled "To Tramps," it encouraged workers and the unemployed to direct violence against the rich. Her 1885 article entitled "Dynamite! The Only Voice the Oppressor of the People Can Understand," published in the *Denver Labor Enquirer,* urged its readers to "Learn the use of explosives!" Parsons argued that dynamite was the only weapon of defense against tyranny since dynamite could defy armies. Labor organizer MARY HARRIS JONES thought anarchists in general, specifically Lucy Parsons, were too violent. For anarchist Parsons, getting rid of the politician "is worth a good-sized revolution any time."

While she was primarily a labor activist in leftist organizations, Parsons also advocated the rights of African Americans. One of her most important pieces on this subject appeared in an 1886 issue of *The Alarm* and was titled "The Negro: Let Him Leave Politics to the Politician and Prayer to the Preacher." The article responded to a lynching of 13 African Americans and claimed that the cause of racism was capitalism: African Americans were victimized because they were poor. In Parsons view, "Are there any so stupid as to believe these outrages have been, are being, and will be heaped upon the Negro because he is black? Not at all. It is because he is poor. It is because he is dependent. Because he is poorer as a class than his white wage-slave brother of the North."

In May 1886, Parsons was involved in a general strike in Chicago for an eight-hour workday. Five days after the strike began, a rally was held at Haymarket Square to support the strike. During the rally, a bomb was thrown at police officers who had attacked demonstrators. Seven police officers died (some from police bullets) and seven workers also died. Parsons and many others thought the Haymarket event was the beginning of a social revolution that would sweep the United States as it had Russia. Her husband, Albert Parsons, was not even present at the rally, yet he was charged with the crime. (Later evidence suggested that the police captain might have been involved in the bomb throwing.) Police rounded up anarchist organizers, including Albert Parsons. Lucy Parsons traveled across the nation to raise defense funds for their appeal after a trial found them guilty.

A few months after the bombing, her husband and three other Haymarket defendants were hanged. Some 250,000 people lined the street for the "Haymarket martyrs," as they became known. Fifteen thousand were present at the cemetery. In 1889, her daughter died of lymphodenoma. Parsons buried her daughter in an unmarked grave near her husband's in Waldheim cemetery.

In 1892, Parsons published a journal entitled *Freedom, A Revolutionary Anarchist-Communist Monthly,* which launched attacks on both lynching and the system of involuntary servitude forced on African Americans in the South through state laws following the end of the Civil War. In an 1892 issue of *Freedom,* she wrote three articles on women and marriage, including one on rape and one on divorce. Parsons advocated divorce rights and birth control and wrote against sexual violence. She viewed women's oppression as deriving primarily from capitalism.

In 1893, a monument to the Haymarket martyrs was erected in Waldheim cemetery. At the ceremony Parsons and others wore small golden gallows, the symbol of the movement that had attempted to free the Haymarket martyrs. In her 1895 article "Cause of Sex Slavery," she stated, "The economic is the first issue to be settled . . . it is woman's economical dependence which makes her enslavement to man possible." She also wrote a weekly column for the *Liberator,* a left-wing periodical edited by Max Eastman.

In 1899, she committed her son to the Illinois Northern Hospital for the Insane after he had joined the army and had begun attending church. He died there 20 years later in 1919. Many find her action difficult to explain. In 1905 she participated in organizing the Industrial Workers of the World (an anarcho-syndicalist trade union), which published *The Liberator.* In 1927 she became a member of the of National Committee of the International Labor Defense—a communist-led organization that defended labor activists and unjustly accused African Americans such as the Scottsboro Nine and Angelo Herndon. She joined the Communist Party in 1939. Parsons had been part of the Socialist Party, the IWW, the Syndicalism League, and then the communist movement. Radical activist EMMA GOLDMAN viewed Parsons as an opportunist who, "goes with every gang proclaiming itself revolutionary, the IWW, now the communists."

Lucy Parsons died in her Chicago home in March 1942 when her wood stove caught fire. After her death the police seized and destroyed her letters, writings, and library. Three hundred people attended her funeral at Waldheim cemetery. Lucy Parsons remained determined in her efforts to improve the working conditions of the underpaid, unemployed, and disadvantaged.

Further Reading

Ashbaugh, Carolyn. *Lucy Parsons, American Revolutionary.* Chicago: Charles H. Kerr, 1976.

Parsons, Lucy. *Lucy Parsons Speaks.* Chicago: Charles H. Kerr, 2000.

 ## PAUL, ALICE STOKES
(1885–1977) *Suffragist*

Alice Paul incorporated the militant direct actions tactics of the British suffrage movement into the suffrage movement in the United States. She founded a radical suffrage organization, the National Woman's Party (NWP) and coauthored the Equal Rights Admendment (ERA).

Alice Stokes Paul was born on January 11, 1885, in Moorestown, New Jersey, a small community nine miles east of Philadelphia, Pennsylvania. (Moorestown is now a suburb of Mount

Laurel.) She was the oldest child of Tacie Perry Paul and William Paul. The family tree on her mother's side included state founder William Penn; on her father's side she was descended from the Winthrops of Massachusetts, a powerful colonial family. The Pauls were Quakers, members of the Society of Friends, who believed in equality between the sexes. Her father died of pneumonia when Paul was 16 years old.

She was raised in an upper-middle-class family and never had to work as a matter of economic necessity. Paul completed a B.A. degree in social work in 1906 at Swarthmore, the Quaker college that her grandfather William Perry had cofounded with famed abolitionist LUCRETIA MOTT. Paul then enrolled at the University of Pennsylvania, where she completed an M.A. degree in 1908. Paul then spent two years in England studying at another Quaker institution, the Woodbrooke Institute of Social Work at the University of Birmingham. She also studied at the London School of Economics.

Paul became disillusioned with social work because, "I could see that social workers were not doing much good in the world. . . . You knew you couldn't change the situation by social work." She became involved in the militant British suffrage campaign through the Women's Social and Political Union (WSPU) in Great Britain. Suffragist Christabel Pankhurst, cofounder (with her mother) of the WSPU, spoke at the University of Birmingham in the fall of 1908, and Paul found a cause to engage her. She worked with the Pankhurst family. Paul was arrested and imprisoned for taking part in demonstrations three times while in Great Britain. British women employed marching, demonstrations, hunger strikes, and property damage and endured arrests and forced feedings in the quest for suffrage.

Paul returned from England to the United States in 1910. She discovered that the National American Woman Suffrage Association (NAWSA) was too moderate for her tastes. Paul completed a Ph.D. from the University of Pennsylvania in 1912. Her dissertation examined the legal status of women in

Pennsylvania. She founded the Congressional Union for Woman Suffrage (CUWS) in 1913. Its newspaper, the *Suffragist,* also founded 1913, became more popular than the NAWSA's paper, the *Woman's Journal.* RHETA CHILDE DORR was the first editor of the *Suffragist.* CUWS members were primarily professional white, middle-class women. Paul was elitist and prejudiced, particularly against African Americans and Jews. She was known to state that she wanted a home where "some American people were left." Paul lived with a companion, Elsie Hill, the daughter of a Connecticut congressman, who had come to work for Paul in 1913.

Paul introduced the militant methods she had learned in England to the U.S. suffrage movement, beginning with picketing the White House. In 1913, she organized a march in Washington, D.C., for Woodrow Wilson's inauguration that drew 8,000 women. Males on the sidelines attacked the marchers. Troops were needed to restore order, and 40 people were hospitalized, while 200 were treated for injuries. When the marchers were attacked, the police stood by and watched. One police officer remarked, "If my wife were here I'd break her head." Paul was imprisoned three times during the U.S. campaign for suffrage and force-fed at one point in a hunger strike.

Paul served as the chair of the CUWS until 1917, when it merged with the Woman's Party to form the National Woman's Party (NWP). Paul served as the first chair until 1921. Paul was focused on a single issue. She felt that all efforts should be devoted toward suffrage rather than distracting issues such as birth control and divorce. A new generation of suffragists agreed with Paul and were interested in pursuing more radical tactics. Paul decided to target the party in power, the Democrats, and hold them accountable for the lack of suffrage. This stance made her a radical outsider. The radical NWP actively campaigned against Democratic incumbents and claimed credit for at least five Democratic losses.

In 1917, Paul was briefly imprisoned in a psychiatric ward for her activism. When Paul was arrested and sentenced to 60 days in the workhouse

Alice Paul, suffragist
(Prints & Photographs Division, Library of Congress,
Washington, D.C.)

recognized that "the real fight for equality can never be won in legislatures. . . . Women have an economic fight to win." Paul was successful in her lobbying attempts to include an equal rights statement in the 1943 United Nations charter. The ERA finally made it through Congress in 1970 when Paul was 87 years old.

Alice Paul died on July 9, 1977 in Moorestown, New Jersey, at age 92. The ERA she had worked so hard for was defeated in 1983, when it came just three states short of ratification. Opponents such as PHYLLIS SCHLAFLY of the Eagle Forum had argued that it would lead to unisex bathrooms and the breakdown of the American family. The Alice Paul Foundation in Moorestown, New Jersey, was founded in 1984 and worked to save Paul's birthplace and home in the suburb of Mount Laurel, New Jersey. Paulsdale, as her birthplace is called, was named a National Historical landmark in 1991 and is slated to become a national conference center for women and girls. Her legacy of the Equal Rights Amendment, however, has yet to be realized.

Further Reading

Ford, Linda. *Iron-Jawed Angels: The Suffrage Militancy of the National Women's Party.* Lanham, Md.: University Press of America, 1991.

Fry, Amelia. "Alice Paul and the ERA." *Social Education* 59, no. 5 (1995): 285–90.

Irwin, Inez Haynes. *Alice Paul and the Story of the National Woman's Party.* Fairfax, Va.: Denlinger's, 1921.

Lunardini, Christine. *From Equal Suffrage to Equal Rights: Alice Paul and the National Woman's Party, 1910–1928.* New York: New York University Press, 1986.

Rosen, Andrew. *Rise Up, Women! The Militant Campaign of the Women's Social and Political Union, 1903–1914.* Boston: Routledge and Kegan, 1991.

for picketing the White House, President Woodrow Wilson pardoned her. Yet Paul responded, "We're very much obliged to the president for pardoning the pickets but we'll be picketing again next Monday." While the media viewed all dissent as harmful, the arrests and trials of middle-class women were more likely to garner sympathy than those of other groups.

After suffrage was attained with passage of the Nineteenth Amendment, Paul earned law degrees from Washington College of Law (L.L.B., L.L.M.), and American University (D.C.L.).

In 1923 Paul coauthored the Equal Rights Amendment (ERA). The amendment she drafted read simply, "Men and women shall have equal rights throughout the United States and every place subject to its jurisdiction." Even Paul, however,

 PERKINS, FRANCES CORALIE
(Fannie Perkins)
(1880–1965) *Secretary of Labor*

As the secretary of labor during the New Deal era, Frances Perkins became the first female cabinet member in U.S. history. She served in that position for 12 years. As the first woman in such a high-profile position, she experienced criticism and constant scrutiny by both the press and the public.

Fannie Coralie Perkins was born on April 10, 1880, in Boston, Massachusetts, the first-born child of Susan Bean Perkins and Frederick Perkins. Her parents were Republicans, Congregationalists, and descendants of James Otis and Mercy Otis Warren, the famous Revolutionary War playwright. When Perkins was two, the family moved to Worcester, Massachusetts, where her father opened a stationery business. Her father became a supporter of suffrage after he heard suffrage leader ANNA HOWARD SHAW speak. Perkins graduated from Worcester Classical High School in 1898 at age 16, where she was a star debater and one of the few female students in attendance.

Perkins attended Mount Holyoke College in South Hadley, Massachusetts, where she majored in chemistry with a minor in physics and biology. Perkins was elected senior class president. An economics history course she took studied factory conditions in the local area, a project that raised Perkins's consciousness regarding workers. During her senior year, Perkins also heard FLORENCE KELLEY speak on campus. Kelley was the general secretary of the National Consumers' League, and had fought for child labor laws. Perkins later recalled that hearing Kelley speak "first opened my mind to the necessity for and the possibility of work which became my vocation."

Perkins switched her party affiliation from that of her parents' to the Democratic Party because she felt that that political group was more interested in the poor. Perkins had considered working as an analytical chemist after her graduation with an A.B. degree in 1902, but her parents opposed the idea of having her work in a traditionally male job. In the fall of 1904, Perkins taught physics and biology at the Ferry Hall School in Lake Forest, Illinois. During this time she started working at Hull House, the famous settlement house in Chicago founded by JANE ADDAMS.

In 1907, Perkins worked for two years as general secretary of the Philadelphia Research and Protective Association. While in Philadelphia, she joined the Socialist Party and enrolled in graduate courses in economics and sociology at the University of Pennsylvania. Perkins earned a degree in economics and sociology at Columbia University in 1910.

She became secretary of the New York Consumers' League from 1910 to 1912. The Consumers' League that Kelley had founded conducted inspections and issued reports on factories, evaluating safety, wages, hours, and working conditions. Perkins also marched in suffrage parades and worked for passage of a 54-hour-workweek bill in the New York legislature in 1912. Perkins favored improving the conditions of workers through legislation rather than unions, however.

Perkins married Paul Caldwell Wilson, an economist for the Bureau of Municipal Research in New York, on September 26, 1913. She kept her own name because, as she recalled, "My generation was perhaps the first that openly and actively asserted, at least some of us did, the separateness of women and their personal independence in the family relationship." Her daughter Susanna Winslow Wilson was born in 1916.

New York State governor Alfred Smith appointed Perkins to the New York State Industrial Commission in 1918, making her the first woman to occupy this position. Her salary of $8,000 a year made her highest-paid state employee in the United States. Franklin Roosevelt, New York State governor from 1929 to 1933, appointed Perkins to head the New York State Department of Labor, the largest such department in the nation. Perkins supervised 1,800 employees and branch offices in seven cities. The policies she implemented in this position affected one in eight factory workers in the country.

Paul Wilson's gambling on the gold market left the family destitute, and he suffered a nervous breakdown. From 1930 until his death in 1952, Perkins's husband spent half of his life institutionalized, suffering from serious depression.

In 1931, Roosevelt sent Perkins to England to study that country's system of unemployment insurance, and it was Perkins who first introduced the idea of unemployment insurance in the United States in 1931. The 54-hour workweek Perkins had lobbied for was further reduced to a 48-hour workweek under her guidance. New York State became the model for other states.

When Franklin Roosevelt was elected president of the United States, he appointed Perkins as Secretary of Labor in 1933. Congress had created the Department of Labor just 20 years earlier. The *Baltimore Sun*'s response to her appointment was representative of the view of some: "A woman smarter than a man is something to get on guard about. But a woman smarter than a man and also not afraid of a man, well, goodnight." As Perkins

Frances Perkins (right) with Mrs. Percy Pennypacker (center), Eleanor Rooosevelt (left)
in New York City, 1931
(Still Picture Branch, National Archives, College Park, MD)

viewed the opportunity, "I had been taught long ago by my grandmother that if anybody opens a door, one should always go through."

One of her first acts was to abolish the department's segregated lunchrooms, which were the norm in Washington, D.C., and many other areas of the country. Perkins did not criticize Roosevelt publicly but she thought that Executive Order 9066, which resulted in the internment of Japanese Americans during World War II, was "very wrong." Perkins helped draft pivotal New Deal legislation, such as the Social Security Act of 1935, the Civilian Conservation Corps Act, the National Industrial Recovery Act, Federal Emergency Relief Act, National Labor Relations Act, and the Fair Labor Standards Act of 1938, which ensured a 40-hour workweek and a minimum wage. It was Perkins who coined the term "Rosie the Riveter" to refer to women working in war industries.

Perkins faced criticism throughout her career from the press and conservative politicians. In 1939, a resolution was offered to the House Judiciary Committee calling for her impeachment because she had refused to deport Harry Bridges, a San Francisco Bay area union leader accused of being a communist. Perkins had publicly stated during the depression that married women should quit jobs so unemployed men might find work. Most jobs that women held, however, were segregated by gender, and so few men would have had the skills or interest in "women's" work. The *New York Times* once asked her if gender had limited her performance, and she responded that it had, "in climbing trees." During her years in Washington, D.C., she lived with Mary Rumsey, daughter of a railroad executive.

After the death of Franklin Roosevelt, Perkins briefly served under President Harry Truman. In 1946, she penned *The Roosevelt I Knew,* a tribute to her former boss and friend. Perkins had served 12 years in his cabinet as secretary of labor, the second-longest term of any cabinet member in history.

Her husband died in 1952. In 1957, at age 77, she began teaching at Cornell University's School of Industrial and Labor Relations, a position she retained until her death.

Frances Perkins died on May 14, 1965, in a New York City hospital after a series of strokes. Hundreds attended her funeral services in New York City and at Cornell University. She was buried between the graves of her parents and husband in a cemetery in Newcastle, Maine. She had shaped legislation regarding wages, hours, and social security, which improved the lives of all workers of her time and future generations.

Her papers are stored at the Schlesinger Library at Radcliffe College, and the Franklin Roosevelt Library in Hyde Park, New York. A 5,000-page oral history of Perkins is held at Columbia University. Perkins had secured more benefits for American workers than anyone before or since. As Secretary of Labor Willard Wirtz eulogized, "Every man and woman in America who works at a living wage, under safe conditions, and for reasonable hours, or who is protected by unemployment insurance or social security, is Frances Perkins' debtor."

Further Reading

Colman, Penny. *A Woman Unafraid: the Achievements of Frances Perkins.* New York: Macmillan, 1993.

Martin, George. *Madam Secretary: Frances Perkins.* Boston: Houghton Mifflin, 1976.

Mohr, Lillian Holmen. *Frances Perkins: The Woman in FDR's Cabinet.* Croton-on-Hudson, N.Y.: North River Press, 1979.

Pasachoff, Naomi. *Frances Perkins: Champion of the New Deal.* New York: Oxford University Press, 1999.

Severn, Bill. *Frances Perkins: A Member of the Cabinet.* New York: Hawthorn, 1976.

R

 RANKIN, JEANNETTE PICKERING
(1880–1973)   *Congressional Representative*

Jeannette Rankin was the first woman to be elected to the U.S. House of Representatives in 1917. She served another term in Congress in 1941. A lifelong peace advocate, she was the only member of Congress to oppose the entry of the United States into both World War I and World War II.

Jeannette Rankin was born on June 11, 1880, in Missoula, Montana, the oldest of seven children. Her mother, Olive Pickering, was of English ancestry and had left New Hampshire in 1878 to work as a teacher in Missoula, where she met John Rankin, a successful rancher and lumber merchant. Her father's family had emigrated from Scotland to Canada around 1800. Her family attended the Presbyterian church. Her father did not like the soldiers in their area who harassed local Indians, so antimilitary attitudes may have been adopted by his children as well.

Rankin, a biology major, graduated from the University of Montana in 1902 and taught for a short time afterward. Her father died in 1904. In the fall of 1908, she enrolled in the New York School of Philanthropy and Social Work, where the faculty included social reformers FLORENCE KELLEY and Booker T. Washington, anthropologist Franz Boas, and U.S. Supreme Court justice Louis Brandeis.

Rankin entered the University of Washington in 1909 as a graduate student and became involved in the suffrage campaign in Washington State. In 1913, Rankin became a field secretary for the National American Woman Suffrage Association (NAWSA). She spent the next two years campaigning for suffrage in 15 states.

Montana enfranchised women in 1914, six years before federal suffrage was granted through the Nineteenth Amendment. In 1916, Rankin ran for Congress. (The West had often offered women more opportunities to step outside their traditional roles than the East.) Rankin campaigned for Congress on a progressive Republican ticket, which supported federal suffrage for women, child labor laws, and Prohibition. She was elected in 1917 and was a member of Congress before most American women could vote. As Rankin stated, "The primal motive for my seeking a seat in the national congress is to further the suffrage work and to aid in every possible way the movement for a nationwide suffrage."

Just four days into her term in Congress she cast a vote against U.S. entry into World War I. The president of NAWSA, CARRIE CHAPMAN CATT, among others, had urged Rankin to vote in support of the war and President Woodrow Wilson because of the political damage a pacifist vote might do to her career and the cause of suffrage. But as Rankin stated in Congress, "I want to stand by my country, but I cannot vote for war." The House voted 373-50 to declare war on Germany. The first woman's vote in Congress had been cast against war. Nearly 50 men in Congress also voted against the war. While in Congress, Rankin fought for federal women's suffrage and proposed a maternity and infant health bill that passed as the Sheppard-Towner bill in 1921.

Rankin did not run for reelection to Congress but instead sought the Republican nomination for the Senate in 1918. She lost that bid and instead ran as a candidate of the National Party, an organization of progressives. Her 1916 antiwar vote may have cost her the Senate nomination.

In 1919, Rankin accompanied 25 delegates, including Hull House founder JANE ADDAMS and social reformer Florence Kelley, to the Second International Congress of Women, which evolved into the Women's International League for Peace and Freedom (WILPF). Rankin was one of five members on the national committee and also served as vice-chair of the American Civil Liberties Union (ACLU). She worked as a field secretary for WILPF and then, starting in 1929, as a lobbyist for the Women's Peace Union (WPU), an organization whose goal was to outlaw war by passing a constitutional amendment. By 1929, Rankin was also serving as a lobbyist and field organizer for another peace group, with which she would work with for 10 years, the

Jeannette Rankin, congressional representative
(Library of Congress)

National Council for the Prevention of War (NCPW).

In 1940, Rankin was elected to Congress, again representing Montana. Rankin cast the single vote against U.S. entry into World War II. During this term she also opposed the military draft and opposed increased government spending on armaments. Rankin did not run for reelection in 1942.

Rankin visited India seven times between 1946 and 1971 to observe the work of Indian independence activist and nonviolence advocate Mohandas Gandhi. At age 87, in 1967, she led 5,000 women in a group named the Jeanette Rankin Brigade in a march to protest the Vietnam War. At age 88, Rankin wanted to run for Congress again, but her health was not stable. In 1972, she was the first woman elected to the

National Women's Hall of Fame, established by the National Organization for Women (NOW). She remained an activist on peace issues for the remainder of her life.

Jeannette Rankin died on May 18, 1973, in Carmel, California, of a heart attack at age 93. Her ashes were scattered near Carmel on the Pacific Ocean. Her papers are stored at the Schlesinger Library at Radcliffe College.

When asked about the possibility of a female president during her first term in Congress, in 1917–19, Rankin had replied, "Why certainly. It is inevitable, and more important, very desirable. That time is not very distant—probably fifty years, possibly sooner." Her prediction had not come to pass in 2001.

Further Reading

Alonso, Harriet Hyman. "Woman in National Politics: Jeannette Rankin." *The Journal of American History* 82, no. 1 (1995): 382–84.

Davidson, Sue. *A Heart in Politics: Jeannette Rankin.* Seattle, Wash.: Seal Press, 1994.

Harris, Ted Carlton. *Jeannette Rankin; Suffragist, First Woman Elected to Congress, and Pacifist.* New York: Arno Press, 1982.

Jeansonne, Glen. "The Single Dissenting Vote." *American History* 34, no. 1 (April 1, 1999): 46–49.

 RAY, DIXY LEE (Margaret Ray)
(1914–1994) *Governor*

Dixy Lee Ray was governor of Washington State from 1976 to 1980. She served in a time of few female governors. She was only the second woman elected as a governor without following a husband in the office. Environmentalists criticized her support of the nuclear energy industry. She was an accomplished professor and the first woman to serve on the U.S. Atomic Energy Commission.

Margaret Lee Ray was born on September 3, 1914, in Tacoma, Washington. She was the second of five daughters born to Francis Adams Ray and Alvis Marion Ray, a commercial printer. Her nickname, Dixy, was short for "Little Dickens." After graduating from high school in 1933, she attended Mills College on a four-year scholarship. She also worked at janitorial and cafeteria jobs to support herself while in school. She completed a B.A. degree from Mills in 1937 and then earned an M.A. degree and teaching certificate from the same institution in 1938. Ray taught science in Oakland schools for four years. In 1942, a John Switzer Fellowship allowed her to enter a Ph.D. program in biology at Stanford University in Palo Alto, California.

In 1945, Ray was hired as an instructor in zoology at the University of Washington in Seattle. She was promoted to assistant professor in 1947, then to associate professor in 1957. Ray taught at the University of Washington for 31 years. She also served as director of the Pacific Science Center. In the 1960s and 1970s she hosted a science-oriented television program in Seattle.

President Nixon appointed Ray to a task force on oceanography in 1969 and also appointed her to the Atomic Energy Commission (AEC) in 1972. The next year, she chaired the commission. As chair of the AEC, she was one of the highest-ranking woman in government. She credited the feminist movement with her appointment, saying, "If it hadn't been for the women's liberation movement, I doubt the president would have appointed me." As an advocate of nuclear power she often debated environmentalists. She moved to Washington, D.C., in 1972, where some commented on her unconventional lifestyle; she lived in a house trailer with two dogs.

The AEC divided into two agencies in 1974. Ray moved to the State Department, where she served as assistant secretary in charge of the Bureau of Oceans, International Environmental and Scientific Affairs. Ray resigned from her commissions in 1975 in order to campaign for governor of Washington State.

Ray ran on the Democratic ticket at age 62 at a time when there were few female candidates. Before seeking political office, she had been an apolitical college professor, but she won her election by a large margin and served one four-year term. She supported nuclear power and worked to let super-tankers carry oil from Alaska through Puget Sound and also minimized the dangers of nuclear waste and oil spills in Puget Sound. During her tenure, there had been an improvement in the state's economic condition, and she balanced the budget. She also did well in her crisis management when Mount St. Helens erupted in 1980.

She lost the next Democratic primary, in 1980, and returned to lecturing and writing on science and public policy, including a book published in 1990 entitled *Trashing the Planet: How Science Can Help us Deal with Acid Rain.* Ray characterized environmentalists as being "anti-development, anti-progress, anti-technology, anti-business, anti-established institutions, and above all anti-capitalism." Ray was involved in founding the Wise Use movement, which argued that nature created more pollution than industry and that common environmentalist concerns, such as ozone depletion, were mere "scare tactics."

Ray was concerned with the obstacles she believed the environmental movement created to industrial and technological progress. She believed environmentalism was not based on science and tried to maintain itself by creating unnecessary alarm regarding global warning, acid rain, asbestos, PCBs, nuclear waste, radiation and pesticides. She claimed pesticides reduced the cost of food, thus allowing the poor to receive more nutritious fruits and vegetables. Numerous scientists and environmentalists critiqued many of her assertions, including that trees and volcanoes cause smog.

In retirement, she worked as an engineering consultant and continued to write and lecture on environmental policy. Dixy Lee Ray died on January 2, 1994. She maintained her support of nuclear energy throughout her life, although environmentalist groups viewed her position as both wrong and hardheaded. Dixy Lee Ray was one of the highest-ranking female political leaders of her time and provided an important role model of leadership to subsequent generations.

Further Reading

Bankoff, Barbara. "Is Environmentalism a Religion?" *Wall Street Journal,* December 3, 1990, A12.

Morris, Geoffrey. "Trashing the Planet." *National Review* (December 3, 1990) 52.

Ray, Dixy Lee. *Environmental Overkill: Whatever Happened to Common Sense?* Washington, D.C.: Regnery, 1993.

Ray, Dixy. *Trashing the Planet: How Science Can Help Us Deal With Acid Rain, Depletion of the Ozone, and Nuclear Waste (Among Other Things).* New York: Harper, 1992.

Turner, Wallace. "Dixy Lee Ray Key Issue." *New York Times,* August 24, 1980, 18(N), 27(LC).

RENO, JANET
(1938–)   *Attorney General*

Janet Reno was the first female attorney general of the United States. She was the last member to join the Clinton cabinet. In her acceptance speech she noted, "I will set an example that will enable people to understand, if a woman can be attorney general of the United States, she can do anything."

Janet Reno was born on July 21, 1938, in Miami, Florida, to Jane Wood Reno and Henry Reno. She was the oldest of four children. When she was eight, the family moved to property in the Everglades. Reno grew up in a log cabin her family built on a 21-acre plot of land. Her parents encouraged independent thinking. As Reno recalled, "My mother wouldn't let us have a television. She said it contributed to mind rot." Reno's father was a police reporter for the *Miami Herald,* and her mother worked from home as a freelance journalist.

Reno attended Coral Gables High School. Its student body came mainly from the upper and middle classes. She was active in the girls' athletic association, the French club, National Honor Society, National Forensic League, and debating club, and she lettered in softball and basketball.

Reno majored in chemistry at Cornell University, since her mother wanted her to become a medical doctor. In her senior year, Reno was elected president of the women's student government

Janet Reno, former attorney general
(U.S. Department of Justice)

association. She graduated from Cornell in 1960. She then attended Harvard Law School, which had first admitted women in 1950. There was only one women's restroom on the entire campus. Reno received her J.D. degree from Harvard in 1963. She was one of only 15 women in a class of 500 students.

Reno had difficulty finding a job after law school and was told by a friend in a law firm that, on at least one occasion, she was not hired because of her gender. In 1971, she served as director of the Florida House Judiciary Committee. Reno authored Florida's no-fault divorce laws and implemented a constitutional amendment to reform Florida's courts.

Reno lost a 1972 race for the Florida legislature. In 1973, she served as assistant to the state's attor-

ney. In 1978, at age 39, she was appointed Florida State Attorney, with a staff of 900 employees handling more than 100,000 cases a year. Reno took lessons to learn Spanish, an important skill in serving the large Latino population in Florida. She was reelected five times, holding this position for a total of 15 years. Reno ran unopposed in 1980.

Her tenure in office was not without controversy, however. In 1980, three days of riots broke out in Miami after five police officers, who had beaten an African-American insurance salesman to death, were acquitted by an all-white jury. Her 1988 reelection campaign took place at a time when the religious right was becoming stronger. In one debate she was asked about her sexual preference, but she refused to answer. She won reelection in 1988 with 68 percent of the votes.

Reno opposes capital punishment, but as state attorney, her office sought the death penalty in 103 cases. She stated her views on capital punishment: "I think that the only justification for the death penalty is vengeance—But I don't think that civilized society can engage in vengeance." Reno felt that, despite her personal beliefs, her job was to uphold the laws of the state of Florida. In the mid-1980s, she assumed custody of two 15-year-old twins after a friend's death. Reno said that mothering was "as important to me as anything I've done."

Reno created innovative projects, such as a drug court to give first-time offenders a second chance. She cracked down on domestic violence, even when the victim did not want to her office to press charges. Reno served on the board of the local shelter for battered women. She was a tough enforcer of child-support laws. These programs were so successful that they were copied statewide and nationwide. She ran unopposed again in 1992.

In February 1993, President Bill Clinton appointed Reno as U.S. attorney general. She had turned the job offer down the year before because her mother was dying of lung cancer. Reno, who is pro-choice on the abortion issue, promised to protect the safety of abortion providers who were being firebombed and harassed.

In her acceptance speech for attorney general, Reno stated her goals: "I hope to end racial, ethnic, and gender discrimination and disharmony in America by enforcing the laws to ensure equal opportunity for all Americans, and by restoring civil rights enforcement as one of the top priorities of the department."

Early in her term a standoff near Waco, Texas, between the Branch Davidian religious cult and the Federal Bureau of Investigation (FBI) ended tragically with the death by fire of 81 cult members. It was Reno who had ordered this final raid at Waco. She accepted full responsibility for Waco.

In 2000, seven-year-old Elián González was found floating at sea after his mother had died in the attempted escape from Cuba. The Cuban-American community became passionately involved in trying to keep Elián in the United States rather than have him returned to his father in Cuba. Reno tried to personally negotiate an end to the standoff but finally ordered federal agents to forcibly remove Elián and end the standoff.

Reno was the first attorney general to hold weekly press conferences. She became the longest-serving attorney general in 172 years. After Democrats lost the 2000 election, Reno's retirement plans included a road trip to Alaska in a new pickup truck, a 120-mile kayak trip in the Florida Everglades, and writing a memoir and a book on reducing violence.

In September 2001 she announced her candidacy for governor of Florida, running against Governor Jeb Bush. Reno was one of the most highly respected members of Clinton's cabinet.

Further Reading

Anderson, Paul. *Janet Reno: Doing the Right Thing.* New York: John Wiley and Sons, 1994.

Borreilli, Mary Anne. "Gender, Politics, and Change in the United States Cabinet: The Madeleine Korbel Albright and Janet Reno Appointments." In *Gender and American Politics: Women, Men, and the Political Process,* edited by S.T. Rinehart and J. Josephson. Armonk, N.Y.: M.E. Sharpe, 2000.

Goldberg, Jeffrey. "What Is Janet Reno Thinking?" *New York Times Magazine,* July 6, 1997, 16+.

Johnston, David. "Reno Ponders the Future." *New York Times,* January 20, 2001, A10.

Mayer, Jane. "Janet Reno, Alone." *New Yorker* 73 (December 1997): 40–45.

Rosen, Jeffrey. "The Trials of Janet Reno." *Vanity Fair* 57, no. 4 (April 1994): 148–55.

U.S. Congress. House. Committee on Government Reform and Oversight. *Janet Reno's Stewardship of the Justice Department.* H. Rpt. 106–1027. 106th Congress.

U.S. Congress. Senate. Committee on the Judiciary. *Nomination of Janet Reno to be Attorney General of the United States.* Washington D.C.: United States Government Printing Office, 1994.

Vise, David. "For Reno, Connections Made Outside Beltway." *Washington Post,* January 22, 2001, A17.

 RICHARDS, DOROTHY ANN WILLIS
(1933–) *Governor*

Ann Richards in 1990 became the second female governor of Texas. A longtime activist in Texas Democratic politics, she is noted for her sharp wit.

Dorothy Ann Willis was born on September 1, 1933, in the rural Texas town of Lakeview, near Waco, to Iona Warren Willis and Cecil Willis. The couple decided not to have other children because of the financial hardships they experienced in the Great Depression and their desire to offer their one child more opportunities than they had been able to enjoy.

Her father was a truck driver and her mother worked in a dry goods store. During World War II, she and her mother joined her father, who was stationed in San Diego, California. Her time in California, where racial segregation was not practiced as it was in Texas, allowed her to see how a world without overt segregation worked.

Dorothy Ann Willis graduated from Waco High School. In high school she participated in the "girls state" program, which allowed female students to role-play state government operations. She also participated in "girls nation" in Washington, D.C., where she shook hands with President Harry Truman. She married David Richards when they were both 19. In 1957, she gave birth to the first of her four children. She earned a bachelor of arts degree at Baylor in 1954 and completed additional course work at the University of Texas at Austin, where she earned her teaching certificate.

Richards's commitment to civil rights is long-standing. She helped form the Dallas Committee for Peaceful Integration in the 1950s. She worked on the 1958 campaign of Henry Gonzalez for governor of Texas. In the 1970s, when an east Texas judge visibly shuddered when shaking hands with an African-American man named Charlie Miles, Richards smiled and introduced herself to the judge as Mrs. Miles.

In 1971, she ran the successful campaign for *Roe v. Wade* attorney SARAH WEDDINGTON for the Texas House of Representatives. In 1975, Richards entered politics herself and was elected Travis County Commissioner.

Richards dates the beginning of her feminist consciousness to the 1977 International Women's Year convention, held in Houston, Texas. She served on President Carter's Commission on Women. In the 1970s, she was an active member of the Texas Women's Political Caucus.

In 1982, she was elected Texas state treasurer, the first woman in more than 50 years to be elected to a state-level position. During that campaign, her opponent charged that Richards was a recovering alcoholic, and Richards responded with a frank acknowledgment that voters seemed to appreciate. Her marriage came to an end on February 1, 1984, when her husband divorced her and married a younger woman. Richards's 1988 keynote address at the Democratic National Convention turned her into a celebrity with her quip about George H. W. Bush being born with a "silver foot in his mouth."

Richards was elected governor of Texas in 1990, the first woman elected to the position in her own right. (The only previous female governor, Miriam "Ma" Ferguson, had acted as a surrogate for her husband, Jim "Pa" Ferguson, who left office in 1917 to avoid being impeached. "Ma" served as governor from 1926 to 1934.) Richards was also the first liberal Democrat elected governor in Texas since 1936. Richards published her autobiography, *Straight From the Heart,* in 1989. She currently works in Washington, D.C., as a lobbyist. Many admired her robust approach to politics and found her quick wit refreshing.

Further Reading

Collins, Gail. "The Unsinkable Meets the Unthinkable." *Working Woman* 20 (March 1995): 52+.

Marvel, Mark. "Ann Richards." *Interview* 25 (February 1995): 28+.

Richards, Ann. *Straight From the Heart: My Life in Politics and Other Places.* New York: Simon and Schuster, 1989.

Siegel, Dorothy, *Dorothy Ann Richards: Politician, Feminist, Survivor.* Berkeley Heights, Calif.: Enslow Publishing, 1996.

Smith, Evan. "Two Fisted Texan." *Mother Jones* 21 (March/April 1996): 60+.

Tolleson-Rinehart, Sue. *Claytie and the Lady: Ann Richards, Gender, and Politics in Texas.* Austin: University of Texas Press, 1994.

RICHARDS, ELLEN HENRIETTA SWALLOW
(1842–1911)   *Founder of Home Economics*

Ellen Richards was a pioneer in the fields of home economics and chemistry. Richards was the first woman admitted to the Massachusetts Institute of Technology (MIT). She served as first president of the Home Economics Association, which infused women's traditional activities into academia.

Ellen Henrietta Swallow was born in 1842 on a New England farm near the village of Dunstable in northern Massachusetts to Fanny Gould Taylor and Peter Swallow. She was an only child. Her father taught and farmed. In 1859, the family moved to the town of Westford, where her father opened a store. He wanted his daughter to have access to a better education than the small rural town of Dunstable, population 150, could provide.

Ellen Swallow worked for a short time as a teacher before entering Vassar College in 1868. Vassar, a women's college in New York, had opened just a few years before. Until Wellesley and Smith colleges were founded some years later,

Vassar was the only college open to women in New England.

The Massachusetts Institute of Technology (MIT) had begun enrollment in 1865. In 1871, she became the first woman admitted to MIT, or to any academic scientific institution in the United States. In 1872, she discovered a small piece of rare mineral, samarskite. She isolated two insoluble residues, samarium and gadolinium, and published a paper on her findings with the Boston Society of Natural History. In 1873, she completed a bachelor of science degree in chemistry from MIT, becoming its first woman graduate. That same year she completed a master's degree in chemistry from Vassar. In 1875, she married Professor Robert Hallowell Richards, the head of the department of mining and engineering at MIT. She completed her doctoral work in chemistry at MIT but was never awarded the degree, her husband believed, because of her gender.

Richards entered private practice in sanitary chemistry, which examined the purity of water, air, and food. She was an early environmentalist who tested home furnishings, water, and foods for toxic contaminants. Richards also tested wallpapers and fabrics for arsenic content.

Richards was also an inventor who developed safe sewage systems. She developed plumbed water systems and central heating, which she could have been patented, but instead chose not to and so were shared with the general public. Her contributions ranged from testing for lead in plumbing to the development of nutrition education and the school lunch program.

In 1876, she became an instructor in the women's laboratory that, largely through her efforts, had been created at MIT. For the next seven years she worked in this laboratory without salary and donated $1,000 a year to its operations.

In 1877, she devised a method for determining the amount of nickel in various ores. One mining expert called her the "best ore analyst in the United States." In 1879, Richards became the first woman elected to the American Institute of Mining and Metallurgical Engineers.

Ellen Richards, scientist
(From *The Life of Ellen H. Richards* by Caroline L. Hunt. Boston: Whitcomb & Barrows, 1912.)

In 1882, she cofounded the American Association of University Women (AAUW). The organization was founded to challenge the then-popular belief that engaging in higher education was dangerous to women's health.

In 1884, Richards was appointed instructor in sanitary chemistry at MIT, where she taught for almost thirty years, until her death. She introduced biology to MIT's curriculum and founded the oceanographic institute at Woods Hole, where environmentalist RACHEL CARSON would later work.

In 1894, Richards was chosen as a trustee of Vassar. She wrote a number of books during the last decade of her life: *The Cost of Living* was published in 1899; *The Cost of Food* in 1901; *First Lessons in Food and Diet* and *The Art of Right Living* in 1904; *The Cost of Shelter* in 1905; *Sanitation in Daily Life* in 1907; and *The Cost of Cleanliness* and *Industrial Water Analysis* in 1908.

Richards believed that domestic skills, like factory operations, which could be broken down into steps, could be taught with particular steps and standards. Richards was cofounder and first president of the American Home Economics Association in 1908. She also founded and funded the organization's periodical, the *Journal of Home Economics,* which began publication in 1910. That year, Richards was awarded an honorary doctorate from Smith College. She also published *Euthenics* in 1910 and her last book *Conservation by Sanitation* in 1911.

Ellen Richards died on March 30, 1911, in Boston, Massachusetts, at age 68. She is buried in the family cemetery in Gardiner, Maine. Richards is known as the mother of the field of home economics. Her pioneering work on food, air, and water pollution set standards that improved the quality of life throughout the nation.

Further Reading

Cravens, Hamilton. "Establishing the Science of Nutrition at the USDA: Ellen Swallow Richards." *Agricultural History* 64, no. 2 (spring 1990): 122–29.

Hunt, Caroline. *The Life of Ellen H. Richards 1842–1911.* Boston: Whitcomb and Barrows, 1912; anniversary edition, Washington, D.C.: American Home Economic Association, 1958.

ROBINSON, JO ANN GIBSON
(1912–) *Civil Rights Leader*

Jo Ann Robinson was president of the Women's Political Council (WPC), a group that initiated the Montgomery Bus Boycott from 1955 to 1956. The WPC called for a boycott in response to the arrest of ROSA PARKS, who refused to move to the back of a segregated bus. These actions sparked a community-wide protest movement that ended a year later when the U.S. Supreme Court ruled segregation in public transportation to be unconstitutional.

Jo Ann Gibson was born on April 17, 1912, near Culloden, Georgia, the youngest of 12 children. After completing high school at the segregated public school of Macon, Georgia, she attended Fort Valley State College. After completing a B.A., she taught in the public schools in Macon and married Wilbur Robinson. Jo Ann Robinson left Macon for Atlanta after five years of teaching and the death of a child in infancy. She earned her M.A. degree in English at Atlanta University. In 1949, she accepted a position as professor of English at Alabama State College in Montgomery, Alabama.

In Montgomery, Robinson joined the WPC. The group had repeatedly asked city officials to address the abusive treatment African-American patrons received from bus drivers. As president of the WPC, Robinson wrote to the mayor of Montgomery threatening a boycott of city buses by the African-American community.

After the arrest of Rosa Parks in December 1955, Robinson immediately produced pamphlets that called for a boycott of the public buses by the African-American community. Buses throughout the South were racially segregated, and African Americans were expected to sit only in the back. As white passengers boarded the bus and filled the white front section, African Americans were supposed to stand and give up their seats in the African-American back section of the bus to boarding white riders. Rosa Parks was arrested for refusing to give up her seat to a white man. Her arrest and Robinson's organizing efforts the following day galvanized the African-American community to carry out a successful boycott.

The Montgomery Improvement Association (MIA) was formed to lead the boycott efforts. Robinson served on the board of the MIA. However, it was another member, Reverend Martin Luther King Jr., who garnered national media attention. The boycott propelled King into a national leadership position in the civil rights movement. As Robinson recalled the effects of the boycott, "We felt that we were somebody. That somebody had listened to us, that we forced the white man to give what we knew was our citizenship—and if you have never had the feeling that—you are an alien, but that this is your country too, then you don't know what I'm talking about. It is a hilarious feeling that just goes all over you, that makes you feel that America is a great country and we're going to do more to make it better."

In 1961, Robinson moved to Los Angeles, where she resumed teaching English in the public schools until her retirement in 1976. Her memoir, *The Montgomery Bus Boycott and the Women Who Started It,* was published in 1987. Jo Ann Robinson's efforts make her one of the many women who worked behind the scenes, with little public acknowledgment, to change the face of the nation.

Further Reading

Burks, Mary. "Trailblazers: Women in the Montgomery Bus Boycott." In *Women in the Civil Rights Movement,* edited by Vicki Crawford. Brooklyn, N.Y. Carlson Publishing, 1990.

Robinson, Jo Ann. *The Montgomery Bus Boycott and the Women Who Started It.* Knoxville: University of Tennessee Press, 1987.

 ROBINSON, RUBY DORIS SMITH
(1942–1967)   *Civil Rights Leader*

Ruby Doris Smith Robinson was a leader in a preeminent African-American civil rights organization, the Student Nonviolent Coordinating Committee (SNCC). She was a leader in the organization from its founding in 1960 until her early death in 1967. She was the only woman to serve as executive secretary of SNCC. In that short period of time, Robinson and the organization she led changed the way American society thought about race relations.

Ruby Doris Smith was born on April 25, 1942, in Atlanta, Georgia, to Alice Banks Smith and John Thomas Smith. She was the second of seven children raised in Atlanta's African-American Summerhill neighborhood. Her childhood was lived in racial segregation, as most of the South was segregated at that time. She remembered her relation to whites: "I didn't recognize their existence, and they didn't recognize mine." Her mother was a beautician, her father a mover who later became a minister. Ruby's intelligence was apparent at an early age: By age four she was already in first grade. Television coverage of the Montgomery, Alabama, bus boycott when she was 13 sparked her political interests. In high school she was a member of the yearbook staff, the tennis, basketball and track teams, the student government association, the school choir, and the majorettes.

Ruby Smith completed Price High School at age 16 and entered Spelman College in Atlanta in 1959. As a student, she joined the burgeoning sit-in movement that first emerged with a 1960 sit-in at a lunch counter in Greensboro, North Carolina. She was among the group of 200 students selected for the first sit-in demonstration in Atlanta. At sit-ins, African Americans would sit at whites-only restaurants and refuse to leave until they were served.

In 1960, she was one of the founding members of SNCC, a student branch of the Southern Christian Leadership conference (SCLC). Well-known civil rights leader ELLA BAKER served as a mentor to SNCC and to Smith in particular. The students had become frustrated with strategies of the older civil rights groups, which they considered too moderate. Smith's first arrest occurred in Rock Hill, South Carolina, during a 1961 sit-in, and she spent 30 days in jail. This was the first time that civil rights workers employed the tactic of "jail-without-bail," in which the movement did not pay bail for jailed members. The idea was to fill the jails and overburden law enforcement facilities. However, at the end of Smith's sentence she had a stomach ailment that would cause her problems for the rest of her life.

She continued to participate in the pivotal events of the African-American civil rights movement.

In 1961, she participated in the Freedom Ride initiated by the Congress of Racial Equality (CORE). The Freedom Ride set out to challenge the segregation of interstate bus travel by having a Greyhound bus integrated with African-American and white students drive through the South. The riders were attacked by mobs in the South, and the bus was firebombed. Smith was jailed again with the other student riders for the crime of "inflammatory traveling." She served a two-month prison term and again refused bail.

After her release from jail, she joined voter registration projects in Mississippi. Operating under a constant state of fear, some SNCC workers began to question the tactic of nonviolence.

In 1963, Smith became a full-time staff member of SNCC, working as administrative assistant to James Forman. Between 1963 and 1967, she operated as the central administrator of SNCC. As SNCC activist Reginald Robinson recalled, "You got your money from Ruby, you got your orders from Ruby." Still, the SNCC leadership was dominated by men. Some women criticized the male-dominated leadership of SNCC because a majority of the participants were female. Other women in the central office, besides Robinson, were relegated to clerical tasks. The relationship between white and African-American women in the organization was often tense, particularly because some African-American men were attracted to white standards of beauty. As Ruby Smith later recalled, "I spent three years hating white women so much it nearly made me crazy." Nevertheless, when female staff members organized a sit-in at James Forman's office to protest their limited roles and sexism in the organization, she joined them.

In the fall of 1964, she traveled with nine other SNCC members to Africa. On her return to the United States, she urged SNCC to establish connections with Africa. She was one of the first SNCC members to suggest such a step.

In November 1964, she married Clifford Robinson, a veteran. She said her husband was "The only fellow I met . . . stronger than me."

Their son, Kenneth Toure, was named after the president of Guinea, Sékou Touré, whom Robinson had met on her trip to Africa.

In the summer of 1966, Robinson succeeded James Forman as the executive secretary of SNCC. Under her leadership and that of chair Stokely Carmichael, the group moved toward the philosophy of Black Power. Theirs was a more radical approach to changing society that moved beyond legal challenges.

Ruby Doris Smith Robinson died on October 7, 1967, of lymphoma in Atlanta, Georgia. She was only 26 years old. Her funeral was held at West Mitchell Church in Atlanta. She had been married three years at the time of her death, and her son was just two years old. Her papers are still in the possession of her family. Pulitzer Prize–winning novelist Alice Walker used Ruby Robinson as the role model for her protagonist in her 1976 novel, *Meridian*. Walker felt that Robinson was treated "shabbily" by some males in SNCC. A coworker remembered the example Robinson set: "Ruby just stood up to anybody. . . . That's just not the way Blacks acted in the south. As a result, she made you stand taller."

Further Reading

Fleming, Cynthia Griggs. *Soon We Will Not Cry: The Liberation of Ruby Doris Smith Robinson.* New York: Rowman and Littlefield, 1998.

"Ruby Doris Smith Robinson." *Sage* (1988): 3.

Walker, Alice. "Comments on Ruby." *Essence* 7 (July 1976): 3.

ROGERS, EDITH NOURSE
(1881–1960)   *Congressional Representative*

Edith Nourse Rogers was a Republican congressional representative from Massachusetts, the sixth woman to serve in Congress. She is known as the mother of the Women's Army Corps (WAC) because she authored legislation that founded the corps, which allowed women to serve in the U.S. Armed Forces during World War II.

Edith Nourse was born on March 19, 1881, in Saco, Maine, to Edith Frances Riversmith Nourse and Franklin Nourse, both natives of Maine. She was the younger of two children in her family and the only daughter. The family was Episcopalian. Her father was a graduate of Harvard University and manager of a large textile mill.

She graduated from the Rogers Hall School in Lowell, Massachusetts, a small private girls' boarding school, in 1899. She then attended a finishing school, Madame Julien's School, in Paris, France. In 1907, she married John Jacob Rogers, a Harvard law school graduate.

Rogers served with the American Red Cross, from 1917 to 1922, during World War I and beyond. She was appointed to inspect veteran's hospitals beginning in 1922.

Rogers was elected as a Republican to Congress to fill the vacancy caused by the death of her husband, John Jacob Rogers, who died in 1925 from Hodgkin's disease after serving for 12 years. Rogers won her first election by a 72 percent margin and was reelected to congress 18 times, with 72 percent to 100 percent of the vote in each election. She was the first congresswoman from New England.

Rogers supported a 48-hour workweek for women and equal pay for equal work. In 1933, she was one of the first to speak in Congress against Hitler's policies regarding Jews.

During her tenure in Congress she introduced 1,242 bills, more than half of which dealt with veterans and armed services issues. She authored the bill to establish the Women's Army Corps (WAC). The WACs allowed women to be compensated for the work they had formerly done voluntarily during wartime. She coauthored the GI Bill of Rights, which gave returning World War II veterans opportunities for education, employment, and low-interest home loans. She was also the first Republican woman to chair a major committee, Veterans Affairs.

In 1949, at age 67, she was named the romantic partner in the contested divorce case of her long-time staff member and campaign manager, Harold Latta Lawrence, a navy captain. Lawrence continued to manage her campaigns, however. In the 1950s, she supported the House Committee on Un-American Activities and Senator Joseph McCarthy, who instigated a witch hunt for communists in the United States.

She voted with the Republican Party from 60 percent to 92 percent of the time during the early decades of her career in Congress, but by 1960 she voted with the Republican Party, only 33 percent of the time.

Rogers was repeatedly reelected to Congress for 35 years, giving her the longest tenure of any woman in Congress. She served from 1925 until her death on September 10, 1960, in Boston, Massachusetts, from a heart attack. She was buried in Lowell Cemetery in Lowell, Massachusetts. Lawrence inherited her house and served as coexecutor of her estate. A museum dedicated to the WACs in Ft. McClellan, Alabama, was named in her memory. Her papers are housed in the Schlesinger Library at Radcliffe College. Edith Nourse Rogers provided an enterprising political role model to younger women and made significant contributions to veterans and armed services programs.

Further Reading

Biographical Directory of the United States Congress. "Edith Nourse Rogers." Available online. URL: http://bioguide.congress.gov/scripts/biodisplay.pl?index=R000392. Downloaded November 29, 2000.

 ROOSEVELT, ANNA ELEANOR
(1884–1962) *First Lady*

First Lady Eleanor Roosevelt over time became more popular with the public than was her husband, four-term president Franklin D. Roosevelt. When her husband was paralyzed by polio in 1921, Eleanor Roosevelt became more deeply involved in politics through various organizations, including the League of Women Voters, the Women's Trade Union League (WTUL), and the women's division of the Democratic Party. Roosevelt continued to champion the needs of the disadvantaged after she left the White House. She was instrumental in the drafting of the United Nations Declaration of Human Rights.

Anna Eleanor Roosevelt was born on October 11, 1884, in New York City to Anna Hall Roosevelt and Elliott Roosevelt, both descendants of prominent families of Dutch ancestry. She was the oldest of three children. Her father spent some time in a sanitarium for alcoholics during her childhood. Her mother and younger brother died of diphtheria when Roosevelt was eight. Her father fell to his death two years later in an accident related to his alcoholism. Thus, by the time she was 10, both her parents and a younger brother had died. Her maternal grandmother then raised Roosevelt. At age 15 she attended Allenswood, an exclusive girls' school outside London. Roosevelt returned to New York City at age 17.

She developed her lifelong commitment to helping the disadvantaged at an early age. At age 18, she worked in the Rivington Street Settlement House, teaching calisthenics to children. Her mother-in-law had objected to her work in settlement houses because she feared Roosevelt would bring diseases home. She also joined the National Consumers' League, which was headed by FLORENCE KELLEY. As a member of the league, Roosevelt visited factories to inspect working conditions.

She met her cousin Franklin Roosevelt by chance on a train, and the couple became engaged in 1903. They married on March 17, 1905, in New York City. The date was chosen so that her uncle, President Theodore Roosevelt, could give her away—he was in New York to attend a St. Patrick's Day parade.

The first of their six children was born in 1906. Following the death of her third child from influenza just seven months after his birth, Roosevelt experienced a period of depression. At many points in her life she suffered from deep, almost suicidal depressions.

In 1913, President Woodrow Wilson appointed her husband as assistant secretary of the navy, so the family moved to Washington, D.C. Eleanor Roosevelt increasingly dropped out of high society and made more friends through her social reform work. In 1920, Roosevelt became active in the League of Women Voters, though she had opposed suffrage at the time of her marriage, 15 years earlier. She was, in fact, shocked when her husband came out in support of women's suffrage, and she said, "I had never given the question serious thought, for I took it for granted that men were superior creatures, and knew more about politics than women did."

After Roosevelt became aware of her Franklin's affair with her secretary Lucy Mercer, the Roosevelts led increasingly separate lives. To many insiders, their marriage seemed more a partnership and political alliance than a marriage.

In 1921 her husband became disabled after contracting polio, so Roosevelt took over many of his duties with the public. In 1922, she joined the WTUL, a progressive organization that lobbied for maximum-hour and minimum-wage laws for women workers. Roosevelt raised funds and walked picket lines with the WTUL. She formed close friendships with Marian Dickerman and Nancy Cook, both Democratic activists and former suffragists. In 1926, she moved into a specially constructed cottage at her Hyde Park residence, Val-Kill, with the women. The three women had their initials monogrammed on their sheets and towels and jointly managed a furniture crafts factory in an attempt to support employment in the local area.

In 1928, her husband was elected governor of New York and four years later he was elected president of the United States. The Roosevelts moved into the White House during the Great Depression, when one in four Americans were out of work. The press claimed that Roosevelt's influence turned the White House into "Hull House on Pennsylvania Avenue," in a reference to JANE ADDAMS's famous Chicago settlement house. During the depression Roosevelt, Secretary of Labor FRANCES PERKINS, and others held the popular view that married women should leave their jobs to assist in alleviating male unemployment. This view failed to take into account the fact that most jobs were segregated by gender, so most men would not have been able, or willing, to perform most jobs that women held. Roosevelt did not enjoy the public scrutiny that her position as first lady entailed, but she eventually reinvented the role.

During this time, she made a new close friendship with Associated Press reporter Lorena Hickok. Hickok had been assigned to cover Roosevelt during the presidential campaign, and the two became intimate friends for the next 23 years. "Hick," as she was called, gave Roosevelt a sapphire ring. The two took vacation motor trips together. When they were apart, Roosevelt carried Hickok's picture and kissed it. They collaborated on a book entitled *Ladies of Courage* in 1954. Some later scholars have speculated that there may have been some romantic involvement in this relationship. At Hickock's suggestion, Roosevelt began holding the first weekly press conferences given by a first lady, with women reporters, so that papers would be encouraged to employ women. Her intention was to focus on "women's issues."

Roosevelt dictated as many as 100 letters a day. In 1936, she began a syndicated newspaper column called "My Day." The press noted that she was "A cabinet minister without portfolio—the most influential woman of our times."

Roosevelt was more liberal than her husband on several issues. Her stances on civil rights and race were precedent-setting and ahead of her time. At a 1939 meeting of the Southern Conference on Human Welfare in Birmingham, Alabama, Roosevelt refused to sit in racially segregated seating. She arrived with her friend, educational leader MARY MCLEOD BETHUNE, and went to sit on the African-American side of the aisle. Local authorities demanded that she move, so she placed her chair between the two segregated sections.

Eleanor Roosevelt
(National Archives, College Park, MD)

That same year, she resigned from the Daughters of the American Revolution (DAR) after they denied permission to African-American singer Marian Anderson to hold a concert at Constitution Hall in Washington. Roosevelt intervened to arrange for Anderson to perform before a crowd of 75,000 in front of the Lincoln Memorial. Her role in this incident made international headlines, but it was not the first time Roosevelt had taken such a stand. Several years earlier, when a New York women's club refused to admit a Jewish friend, Roosevelt resigned her membership. She also joined the civil rights organization the National Association for the Advancement of Colored

People (NAACP) in 1939. During World War II she made a point of flying with African-American pilots when the army was still questioning their capabilities, and she publicly supported desegregation of the armed forces.

Franklin Roosevelt died of a cerebral hemorrhage in April 1945. After her husband's death, she lived at Val-Kill with her secretary Malvina Thompson, known as "Tommy."

President Harry Truman referred to Roosevelt as the "first lady of the world" and appointed her as a delegate to the United Nations (UN), the only female in the U.S. delegation. She was assigned to work on the humanitarian committee. In her 1958 book, *On My Own,* she recalled her impressions of others' thoughts, "We can't put Mrs. Roosevelt on the political committee. What could she do on the budget committee? Does she know anything about legal questions? Ah, here's the safe spot for her—committee three. She can't do much harm there!"

In 1946, Roosevelt was appointed to head the UN Human Rights Commission and entrusted with drafting a universal declaration of human rights. In 1948, the Universal Declaration of Human Rights was passed by the General Assembly, which then rose and gave her an unprecedented standing ovation. Roosevelt donated the proceeds from one of her lecture tours to the United Jewish Appeal, and she spoke in support of Israel.

Roosevelt spoke out against Senator Joseph McCarthy's hunt for and persecution of suspected communists during the 1950s. She founded and served as an honorary chair of a progressive group called Americans for Democratic Action, which spoke out against McCarthyism. When Dwight Eisenhower was elected president in 1953, Roosevelt resigned from her UN post.

In 1961, President John Kennedy appointed her to chair his commission on the status of women. In 1962, Roosevelt sponsored hearings in Washington, D.C., on abuses that civil rights workers were experiencing in the South. That same year, she testified before Congress in favor of proposed equal pay laws, which mandated that women be paid the same salary as men were paid for the same job. Roosevelt lobbied on behalf of the Equal Rights Amendment, though she had initially opposed it due to her concern that it would nullify protective legislation for women. Protective labor legislation restricted the working conditions and hours of female employees. She hosted a regular television show, *Prospects of Mankind.* Roosevelt's name regularly appeared in the Gallup poll's Most Admired Women list. Roosevelt authored many books, including a three-volume autobiography.

Eleanor Roosevelt died on November 7, 1962, at her home in New York City, from a rare form of tuberculosis of the bone marrow. She was buried beside her husband at Hyde Park, New York. Roosevelt became the first recipient of the UN Human Rights Award, which was awarded posthumously. Her papers are stored at the Franklin Delano Roosevelt Library in Hyde Park. As her friend presidential candidate Adlai Stevenson recalled in his eulogy, "She would rather light a candle than curse the darkness, and her glow has warmed the world." In reflecting on her life, Roosevelt herself once said, "I have spent many years of my life in opposition and I rather like the role."

Further Reading

Black, Allida. *Casting Her Own Shadow: Eleanor Roosevelt and the Shaping of Postwar Liberalism.* New York: Columbia University Press, 1996.

Cook, Blanche Wiesen. *Eleanor Roosevelt, 1884–1933.* New York: Penguin, 1993.

———. *Eleanor Roosevelt. Volume 2, The Defining Years, 1933–1938.* New York: Viking Press, 1999.

Freedman, Russell. *Eleanor Roosevelt: A Life of Discovery.* New York: Clarion Press, 1993.

Goodwin, Doris Kearns. *No Ordinary Time: Franklin and Eleanor Roosevelt: The Home Front in World War II.* New York: Simon and Schuster, 1994.

Roosevelt, Eleanor. *Empty Without You: The Intimate Letters of Eleanor Roosevelt and Lorena Hickok.* New York: Free Press, 1998.

Young, William. *Eleanor Roosevelt: A Personal and Public Life.* New York: Longman, 2000.

ROSE, ERNESTINE LOUISE SIISMONDI POTOWSKI
(1810–1892) *Suffragist*

Suffragist Ernestine Rose was the driving force behind the Married Woman's Property Act passed in 1848 in New York State, one of the first women's rights pieces of legislation in the United States. She campaigned for woman's suffrage, marriage and divorce reform, public education, and suffrage for African Americans. She was one of the few Jewish women active in the predominantly Protestant suffrage movement at the time.

Ernestine Louise Siismondi Potowski was born on January 13, 1810, to Orthodox Jewish parents in Piotrkow, Poland. Her father was a rabbi. Her mother died and left 16-year-old Rose an inheritance. Her father attempted to force Rose into an arranged marriage with an older man. If she had married, all of her inheritance would have passed into her husband's control. But the custom of the time also dictated that a woman's dowry could be given to a rejected bridegroom. Rose successfully pressed her case before the regional tribunal court. Most Jews did not appear in this civil court but took their cases to their communities' religious courts. She represented herself in court and gained a legal document that endorsed her claim to the inheritance her mother left her and freed her from her father's control. After this legal battle in 1827, when she was 17, she gave her inheritance to her father, renounced her faith, and left Poland for Berlin, Germany.

In Germany, she invented a room deodorizer made of chemically treated paper that dispelled unpleasant orders when it was burned. She was able to support herself through sales of her air-freshening device. She left Germany in 1829 and traveled to Holland, Belgium, and France. In 1830, she moved to England, where she taught German and Hebrew while she studied English.

In 1836, she married William Ella Rose, a Protestant jeweler and silversmith. After getting married and learning English, she dropped her surname of Siismondi Potowski, something many immigrants did. The couple left England for the United States when she was 26 years old.

In 1836, she drafted a petition to the legislature of New York State calling for property rights for married women. When women married, any property they owned or inherited automatically came under the control of their husbands. The first year she found only a few women who would sign their names to the petition. As Rose later recalled, "I sent the first petition to the New York legislature to give a married woman the right to hold real estate in her own name. After a good deal of trouble I obtained five signatures." Rose nonetheless carried on an annual petition drive.

In 1840, women's rights activist ELIZABETH CADY STANTON joined her in the petition drive. Rose addressed the state legislature five times on behalf of the Married Woman's Property Act. After

Ernestine Rose, lecturer and orator
(Prints & Photographs Division,
Library of Congress, Washington, D.C.)

her 12 years of activism and a few months before the Women's Rights Convention in Seneca Falls, New York, in April 1848, New York State passed the Married Woman's Property Act, making it the first state in the nation in which a married woman could own property.

Rose also spoke publicly at a time when women customarily did not. She lectured on behalf of abolition, women's rights, and equal educational opportunities. In 1847, she traveled to South Carolina and, when threatened with being tarred and feathered for her abolitionist beliefs, she responded, "Well, Sir, I am an abolitionist in the fullest sense of the word . . . and you are so exceedingly lazy and inactive that it would be an act of charity to give you something to do. . . . You thought that I would be a coward and recant in my sentiments. I tell you, Sir, that if I had never been an abolitionist before, I would have become one here, and you would have helped to make me one."

In 1850, Rose helped organize the first National Woman's Rights Convention, which met in Massachusetts in 1851. Rose wrote the resolution to found the group, and she was a member of the American Equal Rights Association, which pushed for political justice for African-Americans enslaved and women. Rose argued that the Bible should have no place at a woman's rights convention, because the group should be open to all faiths. Women's rights activist Elizabeth Cady Stanton shared Rose's views on religion. As Rose stated, "We require no written authority from Moses or Paul." She was elected president of the National Woman's Rights Convention in 1854 and was a founding officer of the subsequently formed National Woman Suffrage Association (NWSA). Rose became a citizen of the United States in 1869, more than 30 years after immigrating. Some historians wonder why she waited so long to become a U.S. citizen, but she may not have had a strong incentive, as women did not have suffrage.

Her husband died in 1882 while they were visiting in England. In 1887, reflecting on her legacy, Rose stated, "For over fifty years I have endeavored to promote the rights of humanity without distinction of sex, sect, party, country, or color."

Ernestine Rose died on August 4, 1892, at age 83 in Brighton, England. She was buried in Highland Cemetery in London, England, beside her husband. When suffragist SUSAN B. ANTHONY was asked who should be on a women's rights honor roll she responded, "Generally I should say begin with Mary Wollstonecraft as your first great champion, then FRANCES WRIGHT, then Ernestine Rose. They all spoke and demanded suffrage prior to LUCRETIA MOTT, Mrs. Stanton, etc." Rose's lecturing talents were such that she was dubbed "Queen of the Platform." As Rose acknowledged, "I stood on the woman's rights platform before that name was known."

Further Reading

Berkowitz, Sandra. "Debating Anti-Semitism: Ernestine Rose." *Communication Quarterly* 46, no. 4 (1998): 457–72.

Kolmerten, Carol. *The American Life of Ernestine L. Rose.* New York: Syracuse University Press, 1998.

Suhl, Yuri. *Ernestine Rose and the Battle for Human Rights.* New York: Reynal, 1959.

 ROSS, NELLIE DAVIS TAYLOE
(1876–1977)   *Governor*

Nellie Tayloe Ross became the first woman governor of a state when she was elected in 1924 in Wyoming. Wyoming women had gained suffrage in 1869, but federal suffrage did not occur until the Nineteenth Amendment was passed in 1920.

Nellie Davis Tayloe was born on November 29, 1876, in St. Joseph, Missouri, to Elizabeth Blair Green Tayloe and James Wynn Tayloe. Her father was a merchant and farmer. After her mother's death in 1884 when Ross was just seven years old, her father and three older brothers raised her. She graduated from a kindergarten teacher's training school in Omaha in the late 1890s and then taught kindergarten for two years.

While visiting relatives in Tennessee, she met attorney William Bradford Ross, whom she married in 1902 in Omaha, Nebraska. She gave birth to four sons; one died in infancy at the age of 10 months when his crib tipped over and he suffocated. After marriage the couple moved to Cheyenne, Wyoming. The Rosses were supporters of Prohibition and staunch Democrats in a traditionally Republican state.

Her husband died from a ruptured appendix in 1924, just a year after being elected governor of Wyoming. She was then elected to fill the two remaining years of his term. Ross described taking the oath of office as "Something like a birth into a new world." She had not participated in the national suffrage movement but had been a housewife and mother. As she acknowledged, "It does seem passing strange, when one considers the countless women who are well fitted to fill the office of governor, that I should have been the pioneer." She found the scrutiny of the media troubling, particularly its obsession with her physical appearance. As she noted, "Writers described my appearance from the cast of my features to the shape of my foot." Apparently she was judged sufficient in physical assets, since the *Omaha Bee* described her as having a "charmingly feminine personality, with attractive presence, cameo features and a beautiful smile." The physical attributes of male politicians seldom went through the same degree of scrutiny.

Ross was judged favorably in her job performance as well. Within a few months the *Omaha Bee* carried the headline, "Six Months' Trial Proves Governor Nellie Ross Has Met and Defeated Enemies of Women in Office." Ross supported child labor laws and safety regulations to protect coal miners. She pushed for legislation to enforce banking regulations and depositor protections at a time of increasingly common bank failures. The legislature adopted most of her pro-

grams, with the exception of her efforts to criminalize the purchase of liquor. In 1926, her party nominated her for another four-year term, but she lost reelection by a narrow margin.

After her service as governor ended, she remained in politics. Ross was elected to the Wyoming state legislature in 1926. In 1928, she served as vice-chair of the Democratic National Committee. She directed the campaign for women's votes for presidential candidate Franklin Roosevelt. In 1932, President Franklin Roosevelt appointed Ross to serve as director of the U.S. Mint. She was the first woman to serve in this position. Like Secretary of Labor FRANCES PERKINS, Ross served throughout Roosevelt's four terms in office. Ross presided over the largest expansion in mint production in the nation's history. During her tenure, the gold depository at Fort Knox, silver depository at West Point, and the U.S. Mint in San Francisco were erected. Roosevelt's successor, President Harry Truman, retained her as director of the U.S. Mint. She retired after 20 years as director in 1953 when Republican Dwight Eisenhower became president.

Ross was the first U.S. woman to have her image appear on a medal made by the U.S. Mint. She is also recognized on the cornerstone of the famous Fort Knox gold depository. She died November 19, 1977, in Washington, D.C., at age 101. She was buried in Lakeview cemetery in Cheyenne. Ross remains the only female governor of Wyoming to date.

Further Reading

Aslakson, Barbara. "Nellie Tayloe Ross, First Woman Governor." M.A. thesis, University of Wyoming, 1960.

Scharff, Virginia. "Feminism, Femininity, and Power: Nellie Tayloe Ross and the Woman Politician's Dilemma." *Frontiers* 15, no. 3 (1995): 87.

Schmidt, Ann. "The 95 Great Years of Wyoming's Nellie Tayloe Ross." *Empire Magazine* (October 29, 1972): 25–27.

RUFFIN, JOSEPHINE ST. PIERRE
(1842–1924) *Women's Club Leader*

Josephine St. Pierre Ruffin was a suffragist, journalist, and activist in the women's club movement. Josephine St. Pierre was born in 1842 in Boston, Massachusetts, to Eliza Matilda Menhenick St. Pierre and John St. Pierre. She was their sixth child. Her father was of African, French, and Indian ancestry. Her mother was raised in Cornwall, England. St. Pierre was educated in public schools in Salem, Massachusetts, and then a private school in New York City, rather than segregated public schools in Boston. At the age of 16, she married George Lewis Ruffin, a barber from a prominent family, and the couple moved to England in order to escape the degrading racism that permeated the United States at the time.

When the Civil War began, the couple returned to the United States to work for the Union and to help abolish slavery. Ruffin recruited soldiers for the Massachusetts African-American regiment and worked in the U.S. Sanitation Commission during the war. After the war, she became active in the Massachusetts State Federation of Women's Clubs and various charitable causes. Her husband completed a degree from Harvard Law School in 1869. In 1879, she worked with the Boston Kansas Relief Association for African-American migrants, who were leaving the South. Both African-American and white women's clubs were primarily middle-class and Protestant. Many clubs did a great deal of work with scholarships and projects to assist the poor. Her husband became a state legislator, Boston City Councilman, and Boston's first African-American judge in 1883. Ruffin also worked as a journalist for the African-American paper the *Courant* and became a member of the New England Women's Press Association.

In 1886, Ruffin's husband died. In 1893, Ruffin founded the New Era Club, which provided scholarships to African-American women. She served as editor of the club's monthly journal, the *Woman's Era,* which was the first newspaper published by African-American women. She supported anti-lynching and suffrage campaigns.

Ruffin participated in abolitionist and suffragist organizations as well as separate charity-oriented clubs for African-American women. African-American women had begun organizing antislavery and literary clubs since the 1830s.

Ruffin attended the 1900 meeting in Milwaukee, Wisconsin, for the General Federation of Women's Clubs, representing the New Era Club as its president. Only delegates from white clubs were allowed at the Milwaukee meeting, although many predominately white women's clubs were integrated, such as the Young Women's Christian Association (YWCA), Women's Christian Temperance Union (WTCU), and the Massachusetts State Federation of Women's Clubs, of which Ruffin was a member. On principle, Ruffin insisted on being accepted as a delegate from the African-American New Era Club. When the board discovered that all the club's members were African American, they attempted to prevent Ruffin's participation, even going so far as trying to rip her delegate's badge off. Many northern delegates supported Ruffin, but southern delegates used parliamentary procedures to avoid discussion of the issue. (Parliamentary procedures are accepted rules in the government of assemblies. They can be manipulated to reflect the will of the majority.)

Ruffin organized the first national convention of African-American women in 1895, the National Federation of Afro-American Women. The federation merged with the Colored Women's League in 1896 to form the National Association of Colored Women, which elected Ruffin as vice president. The group's motto was "Lifting as We Climb." In 1903, Ruffin founded a Boston branch of the National Association for the Advancement of Colored People.

Josephine Ruffin died of nephritis in 1924 at age 81. She was buried at the Mount Auburn cemetery in Cambridge, Massachusetts. Ruffin worked to alleviate social inequities and racial prejudice. As she stated, "If laws are unjust, they must be continually broken until they are altered."

Further Reading

Hine, Darlene Clark, editor. *Facts On File Encyclopedia of Black Women in America: Religion and Community.* New York: Facts On File, 1997.

Streitmatter, Rodger. *Raising Her Voice.* Lexington: University Press of Kentucky, 1994.

S

◇◇◇◇◇

 SANGER, MARGARET LOUISE HIGGINS
(1883–1966)   *Birth Control Pioneer*

Margaret Sanger waged a 50-year battle to provide legal, safe, and effective birth control options to women. She faced numerous arrests on charges of obscenity for distributing birth control information. She opened the first birth control clinic in the United States and founded the Planned Parenthood Federation, which continues to serve the needs of women and families.

Margaret Louise Higgins was born on September 14, 1883, in Corning, New York, to Irish-Americans Anne Purcell Higgins and Michael Hennessey Higgins. She was the sixth of 11 children and was raised as a Roman Catholic. Sanger would later connect her family's financial insecurity to its high number of children. Her father was an atheist who operated a stone monument shop.

Margaret Higgins worked in the school kitchen to pay her way through Claverack College, a private preparatory school in the Catskill Mountains of New York. After three years at Claverack, she taught first grade in Little Falls, New Jersey, but found herself ill suited to teaching. She then studied nursing in White Plains, New York, even though at the time nursing was considered a more menial job than teaching.

Her mother died of chronic tuberculosis, from which she had suffered for many years, in March 1899 at forty-nine years of age. Margaret Higgins herself had a series of operations for tuberculosis, a condition she most likely contracted while caring for her mother.

She married William Sanger, a Jewish architect in 1902 after a six-month courtship and became pregnant a few months later. She gave birth to three children in seven years, beginning in 1903. Sanger almost died during the difficult birth of her first child, a daughter whom she named Peggy, after her mother.

In 1910, the Sangers were active socialists. Margaret Sanger worked as a nurse on the Lower East Side of New York City. During this time, she was active in the International Workers of the World (IWW), a radical labor organization. In the 1912 Lawrence, Massachusetts, strike Sanger and ELIZABETH GURLEY FLYNN organized an evacuation of the strikers' children. The 1912 strike of 23,000 textile workers in Lawrence, Massachusetts, began when mill owners lowered wages. Police assaulted the women and children strikers on numerous occasions during the two-month-long strike, resulting in numerous deaths and mass arrests. Public outcry forced mill owners to concede wage increases in Lawrence and throughout New England mills.

In 1912, she began publishing articles about female sexuality in the socialist newspaper *The Call.* Her column was called "What Every Girl Should Know." At the time, even leftists ignored the serious health problem that venereal diseases posed. An explicit article about syphilis in a February 1913 issue of *The Call* was censored by the U.S. Post Office under the Comstock Act of 1873. To the general public, contraceptives were perceived as a fitting topic of information only for prostitutes, not for respectable women. Yet, commercial abortionists in the United States had advertised their services as early as the 1830s. Historians have estimated that one in five pregnancies in 1850 was terminated by abortion. Until obscenity statutes were passed in the 1870s, contraception was openly advertised in newspapers, almanacs, and mail-order catalogs. Birthrates had declined up to the 1870s, and the commercial trade in contraception faced little controversy among the general public and no resistance from organized religion. Crusaders against "obscenity" were able to gain passage of a federal statute by Congress in 1873, the Comstock Act. The act criminalized publication, distribution, or possession of information about devices or medications for abortion or contraception. Many doctors (a predominately male group) supported the act due to the competition they faced from midwives, most of whom were female.

A pivotal event in Sanger's decision to become a radical advocate of birth control occurred as the result of the death of one of her clients, Sadie Sachs, from an illegal abortion. Sachs's doctor had refused to give her any contraceptive information. Sanger argued, "No woman can call herself free who does not own and control her own body." Her reaction was to leave "the palliative career of nursing in pursuit of fundamental social change."

In March 1914, Sanger began publication of a militant feminist journal, *The Woman Rebel.* It was Sanger who coined the term *birth control* in 1914. That year, she fled the United States for Europe after being indicted by an all-male jury for mass distribution of a pamphlet on contraceptive techniques.

In Europe Sanger found a different attitude regarding contraception. Midwives freely distributed contraceptive devices, and well-staffed birth control centers were common.

In 1915 while Sanger was still in Europe, Peggy died of pneumonia at age five. Sanger immediately returned to the United States, and within a few months the government dropped its charges against her. The death of her child had raised public sympathy for Sanger and public support of birth control was slowly increasing. Sanger continued her crusade, however, and coined the phrase, "Every child a wanted child."

A $50 donation from a woman who had heard Sanger lecture in California allowed Sanger to open her first birth control clinic, in October 1916 in Brooklyn, New York, with her sister. After 10 days of distributing birth control advice to more than 400 women, the clinic was closed by police. This time, Sanger's 1917 trial and imprisonment for distributing contraceptives garnered national headlines. She was imprisoned for 30 days for "creating a public nuisance." Some members of the press began to write sympathetically of these well-intentioned middle-class women, but not all feminists of the time were supportive of Sanger's efforts. National American Woman Suffrage Association (NAWSA) president CARRIE CHAPMAN CATT criticized Sanger's ideas, because she believed that the sexual liberation of women would lead to their sexual exploitation. Hull House founder JANE ADDAMS and feminist author CHARLOTTE PERKINS GILMAN agreed with Catt's criticisms of Sanger. Sometimes Sanger's views were problematic: for example, she supported eugenicists, who appealed to the need for "racial purity" and advocated the use of birth control among "undesirable" groups.

Margaret Sanger, birth control pioneer
(Prints & Photographs Division,
Library of Congress, Washington, D.C.)

In 1920, Sanger divorced her husband but kept his name. That same year, she published her first book, which argued that dissemination of birth control was a woman's right. She dedicated her book to her mother's memory. In 1921, Sanger organized the American Birth Control League, a national lobbying organization.

In 1922, she married J. Noah Slee, a millionaire in the oil business. Slee agreed that they would maintain separate residences and that Sanger would retain her name. Funds that Slee provided allowed Sanger to smuggle diaphragms from Europe into the United States. Her husband also provided the financial backing to allow Sanger to open a permanent birth control clinic.

In 1923, with the help of a female physician, Sanger opened the Birth Control Clinical Research Bureau in New York City, the first permanent birth control clinic in the United States. Physicians had warned that diaphragms would cause cancer

and madness. The common perception held that interference with "God's will" would result in mental and physical illness. Many churches, particularly the Roman Catholic Church, opposed the use of any form of birth control. However, Sanger's clinic kept careful records of birth control safety and effectiveness. The clinic trained hundreds of physicians in contraceptive techniques, since this was not a part of medical school curriculum. It was not until 1937 that the American Medical Association (AMA) first recognized contraception as a legitimate medical service. By 1938, more than 300 birth control clinics operated in the nation.

Sanger's American Birth Control League evolved into the Planned Parenthood Federation of America in 1942. In 1952, Sanger served as the first president of the International Planned Parenthood Federation. Sanger raised funds for the development of the birth control pill, which was first marketed in 1960. Initially the birth control pill was available only by prescription to married women. It was not until 1965 that a United States Supreme Court ruling, *Griswold v. Connecticut*, guaranteed constitutional protection for the private use of contraceptives.

Margaret Sanger died September 6, 1966, of congestive heart failure following a four-year stay in a Tucson nursing home. She was just a few days shy of her 88th birthday. A service was held at St. Phillips in the Hills Episcopal Church in Tucson, Arizona, where she had lived in retirement.

More than 500 boxes of Sanger's papers are stored at the Library of Congress in Washington, D.C., and at Smith College. The American Birth Control League papers are housed at Houghton Library at Harvard University. Sanger authored numerous books during her lifetime, including two autobiographies that outlined her views. Sanger urged others, "All your life you must have a vital interest in something outside yourself." Sanger stated that she hoped she would be remembered for helping women. Her repeated actions to legalize birth control allowed future generations of women a wider range of choices regarding their health and fertility.

Further Reading

Bachrach, Deborah. *Margaret Sanger.* San Diego, Calif.: Lucent, 1993.

"Margaret Sanger." *Biography* 3, no. 12 (December 1999): 110.

National Women's Hall of Fame. "Margaret Sanger." Available online. URL: http://www.greatwomen.org/sanger. htm. Downloaded November 30, 2000.

Sanger, Margaret. *Margaret Sanger: An Autobiography.* 1938. Reprint. Lanham, Md.: Cooper Square Publishers, 1999.

Steinem, Gloria. "Margaret Sanger." *Time* 151, no. 14 (April 13, 1998): 93–94.

Whitelaw, Nancy. *Margaret Sanger: Every Child a Wanted Child.* New York: Dillon Press, 1994.

 SCHLAFLY, PHYLLIS STEWART
MᴀᴄALPIN
(1924–   ) *Conservative Activist*

Conservative activist Phyllis Schalfly was centrally involved in the defeat of the Equal Rights Amendment (ERA) in the 1970s. She condemned feminism as being destructive to the family and reached out to housewives in particular with her message. Despite her insistence that being a housewife and mother was the most important career a woman could have, Schlafly worked outside the home throughout her life and benefited from the expanded educational and employment opportunities that feminists had struggled to achieve.

Phyllis MacAlpin Stewart was born on August 15, 1924, in St. Louis, Missouri, to Odile Dodge Stewart and John Stewart. She was educated at the Convent of the Sacred Heart and graduated from Washington University in St. Louis in 1944 while working full time at a World War II defense plant. She attended Radcliffe College in Cambridge, Massachusetts, on scholarship, completing a masters' degree in government in 1945.

After graduation, she worked as a researcher for several congressional representatives in Washington, D.C., managed a successful campaign for a Republican congressional representative in St. Louis, and edited a bank newsletter. In 1949, she married John Fred Schlafly, an Alton, Illinois, attorney. Schlafly, a devout Catholic, gave birth to six children and often claimed that the most important career for a woman was raising a family.

Despite her professed sentiments regarding the role of the housewife, Schlafly remained active in politics. She ran unsuccessfully for Congress as a conservative Republican in 1952 and served as a delegate to the Republican National Conventions in 1956, 1960, and 1964. She opposed the Nuclear Test Ban Treaty of 1963 and all arms control agreements with the Soviet Union. According to Schlafly, "The bomb is a marvelous gift that was given to our country by God." Between 1964 and 1978, Schlafly coauthored five books with Rear Admiral Chester Wardon. Her 1964 book, *A Choice Not an Echo,* was an endorsement of conservative Republican presidential candidate Barry Goldwater. She ran unsuccessfully for president of the National Federation of Republican Women in 1967.

Schlafly ran unsuccessfully for Congress a second time in 1970. When Congress passed the ERA in 1972 and sent it to the states for the required ratification, Schlafly began actively organizing against it. The amendment called for equal treatment under the law regardless of gender. Schlafly founded and served as chair of STOP ERA. She was the most visible female antifeminist and anti-ERA spokesperson. She testified against the ERA before 30 state legislatures. Schlafly was covered extensively by the media, who depicted the ERA controversy as a "cat fight" among women. Polls consistently showed that two-thirds of Americans supported the ERA; however, Schlafly served as a lightning rod for popular fears regarding the proposed amendment. She made dire predictions that the ERA would lead to unisex bathrooms, increased homosexuality, destitute housewives, and the downfall of the family. Congressional representative MARTHA GRIFFITHS termed Schlafly's concern regarding coed bathrooms "the potty argument." One point that Schlafly made, which feminists conceded, was that in the event of a draft, both men and women would be called upon to serve in the armed forces if the ERA were ratified. Equal rights amendments existed in other countries throughout the world without the dire consequences Schlafly predicted. Equal rights amendments exist in Australia, Costa Rica, India, Indonesia, Malaysia, and the European Union (Austria, Belgium, Denmark, Finland, France, Germany, Greece, Ireland, Italy, Luxembourg, Netherlands, Portugal, Spain, Sweden and the United Kingdom). Nevertheless, in the United States the ERA fell three states short of ratification and was defeated in 1982.

In 1977, she authored *The Power of a Positive Woman.* In 1978, at age 54 she completed a law degree from Washington University. In 1980, President Ronald Reagan appointed her to his defense policy advisory group.

Schlafly continued her conservative agenda through another organization she founded, the Eagle Forum. Through the Eagle Forum, she campaigned against abortion and pornography. Some feminists agreed with her stance on pornography, but for different reasons. Schlafly's primary concern with pornography was with the obscene and sexually explicit nature of the content. Schlafly thought premarital sex was a sin. Her views on pornography were outlined in her 1987 book *Pornography's Victims.* In the 1990s she toured with *Roe v. Wade* attorney SARAH WEDDINGTON in a debate on abortion. Schlafly remains active in conservative Republican Party politics. The majority of states in the United States have equal rights amendments in their constitutions, but federal passage has yet to be achieved.

Further Reading

Distinguished Women of Past and Present. "Phyllis Schlafly." Available online. URL: http//www.distinguishedwomen.com/biographies/schafly.html. Downloaded December 1, 2000.

Felsenthal, Carol. *The Sweetheart of the Silent Majority: The Biography of Phyllis Schlafly.* New York: Doubleday, 1981.
Schlafly, Phyllis. *A Choice, Not an Echo.* Alton, Ill.: Pere Marquette Press, 1964.

 SCHROEDER, PATRICIA NELL SCOTT
(1940–)   *Congressional Representative*

Patricia Schroeder was elected to the U.S. House of Representatives from Colorado in 1972. She was reelected 11 times, making her the longest-serving woman in Congress. She is a publicly acknowledged feminist and liberal Democrat.

Patricia Nell Scott was born on July 30, 1940, in Portland, Oregon, to Bernice Scott and Lee Combs Scott. She attended public school in Portland. Her mother was a grade school teacher. Her father, an aviation insurance adjuster, told her, "Never frown at your enemies. Smile—it scares the hell out of them." She had learned to fly by the time she was a teen and worked her way through college by assessing damage at crash sites as her father had done. Schroeder graduated magna cum laude from the University of Minnesota in 1961 after only three years of study.

She entered Harvard Law School in 1961, one of 15 women in a class of 530. She remembers male students in her classes who would not sit next to her because she was a "girl." The dean of the Law School told her, "I didn't want any of you here. I don't think you'll ever use this treasured degree that we're going to let you have." She married classmate James White Schroeder in 1962. Schroeder completed a J.D. degree from Harvard in 1964. Harvard had little encouragement for her job prospects, however: "At Harvard, when I was ready to graduate, I went to the personnel office and they said, 'Look, you know nobody wants to hire young women. . . . We only try to put our students out that we feel really have some chance." Schroeder replied, "I have been paying you guys for this degree for three years. What am I supposed to do with it—hang it over the sink! They kind of laughed and said, 'Guess so.'"

After graduation the couple moved to Denver, Colorado. Schroeder was active in Democratic Party politics in Colorado, including serving as a precinct committee chair. From 1964 to 1966, Schroeder served as the field attorney for the National Labor Relations Board. She taught law at the Community College of Denver from 1969 to 1970, the University of Denver in 1969, and Regis College from 1970 to 1972.

In 1970, her husband ran unsuccessfully for a seat in the Colorado state legislature. In 1972, no established politician would agree to run against the incumbent Republican U.S. congressional representative except Schroeder. Schroeder recalled her husband talking her into running for office: "I never saw myself as a candidate. But I was the only person he could talk into it!" Even the Denver Democratic Women caucus did not support her candidacy as they believed it was too early to have a female candidate run for office. She campaigned in support of ending the Vietnam War and increasing environmental protections. She defeated Republican James McKevitt despite a landslide presidential election for Richard Nixon.

When she was first elected there were only 14 women in Congress, all of them in the House, so a woman in Congress was still seen as an oddity. One member of Congress asked Schroeder how she could possibly be "the mother of two small children and a member of Congress at the same time." Schroeder's response was, "I have a brain and a uterus, and I use them both." Even feminist congresswoman BELLA ABZUG expressed concerns about Schroeder's ability to do the job because her children were so young, two and six. Schroeder was an "out" mother. She brought a purse full of diapers to her swearing-in, and her children participated in a sit-in in the House to highlight the need for child care.

Schroeder was the first female to serve on the Armed Services Committee and was a strong advocate for women in the military. Schroeder referred to the military as "the ultimate tree house—no girls allowed." She supported full integration in the armed forces, including allowing gays and lesbians who were "out of the closet" to serve in the military. She also supported arms control and cuts to the military budget. She became Democratic whip in 1978, maintaining discipline and enforcing attendance in Congressional meetings.

Schroeder cofounded and cochaired the Congressional Caucus for Women's Issues. She introduced the Family and Medical Leave Act and sponsored the Violence Against Women Act and the Women's Health Equity Act. On Schroeder's request, the General Accounting Office studied the policies of the National Institutes of Health and found that they routinely excluded women subjects in their medical research. She served as chair of the House Select Committee on Children, Youth, and Families. She was the fourth woman in Congress to chair a committee. It was Schroeder who called President Ronald Reagan the "Teflon president" and defense contractors who overcharged the government "welfare queens."

In 1987, Schroeder raised funds in order to enter the Democratic presidential primary but withdrew from the race because gender was a problem in the campaign. Schroeder acknowledged, "There was a tendency from the very beginning for the press to categorize me as a 'women's candidate'. Would the country see me that way or view me as a presidential candidate who happens to be a woman?" During the campaign Schroeder was criticized for "running as a woman" to which she replied, "Do I have a choice?" The press highlighted the fact that she shed some tears when she announced her decision not to pursue the presidential nomination further.

In 1989, Schroeder published *The Great American Family,* a book that outlined her political agenda and the rationale for it. Senator BARBARA BOXER referred to Schroeder as "the dean of the women of the House." In 1997, Schroeder decided not to run for reelection after serving in Congress for 24 years. She retired from politics to private life.

She has served as president of the Association of American Publishers since her retirement and taught courses at Princeton University. She describes herself as a "recovering politician." In 1999, she published *24 Years of House Work and the Place Is Still a Mess: My Life in Politics,* a book that reflected on her service in Congress. Patricia Schroeder was not afraid of claiming the term *feminist,* and she used her wit and political savvy to create positive change for women and families.

Further Reading

Brinson, Claudia Smith. "Pat Schroeder." *Ms.* (January/February (1997): 56–59.

Newfield, Jack. "An Interview with Pat Schroeder." *Tikkun* 13, no. 5 (September/October 1998): 27–29.

"Pat Schroeder." *Biography Today* 6 (January 1997): 95–106.

"President Pat Schroeder." *Publishers Weekly* 247, no. 4 (January 24, 2000): 170.

Schroeder, Patricia. *The Great American Family.* New York: Random House, 1989.

———. *24 Years of House Work and the Place Is Still a Mess: My Life in Politics.* Kansas City, Mo.: Andrews-McMeel, 1999.

 ## SHAHEEN, JEANNE BOWERS
(1947–)   *Governor*

Jeanne Shaheen became the first female governor of New Hampshire in 1996. A feminist and political scientist, Shaheen honed her political strategy by working on the campaigns of other candidates for 16 years before deciding to run herself.

Jeanne Bowers was born on January 28, 1947, in St. Charles, Missouri, to Belle Bowers and Ivan Bowers. She was the second of three daughters. She completed a bachelor's degree in English from Shippensburg University in Pennsylvania in 1969. While at college, she had complained about the different curfew policies that were mandated for male and female students. A political science pro-

fessor urged her to get involved to change things and her political activism began.

After completing her bachelor's degree, she met her future husband, Bill Shaheen. They eloped three months later. The couple ran a gift shop in York Beach, Maine, and then moved to Mississippi to pursue educational goals. Her husband enrolled in the law school at the University of Mississippi, and Shaheen taught public high school until she saved enough money to begin a master's degree program in political science at the same institution. She earned her master's degree in 1973.

The Shaheens returned to live in New Hampshire in 1973. She gave birth to three children, taught in public schools, and managed political campaigns for 16 years before deciding to run herself. She coordinated the successful presidential campaigns of Jimmy Carter and Gary Hart in her state. She also served as a delegate to the Democratic National Convention.

In 1990, Shaheen was elected to the New Hampshire State Senate, where she served three terms. As a legislator she focused on lowering New Hampshire's electrical rates (then the highest in the nation), health care reform, and education.

She was elected governor of New Hampshire in 1996 with 57 percent of the vote. She was the first Democratic governor of the state in 16 years and the first woman elected to this position. She was reelected in 1998 with 66 percent of the vote. Shaheen is only the fourth governor to be elected to a third term in New Hampshire, a state with a high number of independent voters, to whom Shaheen appealed.

Shaheen made a number of educational reforms. She expanded public kindergarten, began testing first-year teachers, raised teacher recertification standards, placed more computers in schools, and developed report cards on schools so parents could know how their local schools were performing. Her commitment to children led her to create a "Kids Cabinet," in which top New Hampshire meet to coordinate their efforts on behalf of children. Shaheen worked to make New Hampshire the first state to deregulate its electric industry. She remains a popular governor and a high-profile feminist politician.

Further Reading

"Career Paths: Jeanne Shaheen." *Campaigns and Elections* 20, no. 9 (October 1, 1999): 12.

Doyle, Erica. "Into the Breach." *Ms.* (August/September 2000): 17.

Germond, Jack. "Inside Politics—New Hampshire Governor Jeanne Shaheen." *National Journal* 31, no. 43 (1999): 3096–4004.

Maiona, Justin. "On the Scene." *National Review* 49, no. 16 (September 1, 1997): 24.

SHALALA, DONNA
(1941–) *Secretary of Health and Human Services*

Donna Shalala served as secretary of the U.S. Department of Health and Human Services (HHS) during President Bill Clinton's administration, from 1993 to 2001. Shalala was also the first woman to head a Big Ten university, serving as chancellor of the University of Wisconsin, Madison from 1987 to 1993.

Donna Shalala was born on February 14, 1941, in Cleveland, Ohio. After graduating from Western College in 1962 she served two years in Iran with the Peace Corps. She returned to the United States and completed a graduate degree from the Maxwell School of Citizenship and Public Affairs at Syracuse University in New York in 1970. After that, she taught political science at Bernard Baruch College in New York City for two years and then taught politics and education at Columbia University's Teachers College.

In 1975, Shalala left academia to serve as director of the Municipal Assistance Corporation, which helped solve New York city's financial crisis. In 1977, she became an assistant secretary at the Department of Housing and Urban Development (HUD) in Washington, D.C.

Shalala returned to the university environment in 1980 to serve as president of Hunter College in New York City, a position in which she served until 1988. In 1988, she was named chancellor of the University of Wisconsin, Madison. She was named by *Business Week* magazine as one of the five best managers in higher education. Shalala raised more than $400 million for the university.

In 1993, President Clinton appointed her secretary of HHS. HHS administers Medicare, Medicaid, federal welfare, health research institutions, and children's health programs. Shalala undertook five major programs as secretary: revision of health care, expansion of Head Start (an educational program for low-income children), universal childhood immunizations, expansion of AIDS research, and welfare reform. She succeeded in making health insurance available to 2.5 million children through the State Children's Health Insurance program and helped raise child immunization rates to the highest levels in U.S. history. When Shalala took office, some legislators predicted that Medicare would be bankrupt by 1999. At the end of her tenure, the forecast suggested that the Medicare trust fund would remain solvent until the year 2023, the longest projection of solvency since 1974.

Shalala ran HHS with a $387 billion budget and 61,000 employees. Shalala was more liberal in her attitude toward welfare reform than was the Clinton administration. She did not support the welfare reform legislation passed in 1996 by the Republican-controlled Congress. She left office with the election of Republican president George W. Bush. Her foremost regret upon leaving office was "That we didn't put health care for low-income working families, and child care for them, in place before we did welfare reform." President George W. Bush appointed Governor Tommy Thompson of Wisconsin to fill Shalala's position. Shalala accepted a position as president of the University of Miami and left office as the longest-serving secretary of Health and Human Services in U.S. history.

Further Reading

Marshall, Eliot. "Donna Shalala: 'Leaving Footprints' at HHS." *Science* 271 (March 1996): 1225–6.

Toobin, Jeffrey. "The Shalala Strategy." *New Yorker* 69 (April 26, 1993): 59+.

Toner, Robin. "Before Leaving Health Agency Shalala Offers a Little Advice on a Big Job." *New York Times,* January 16, 2001, A16.

U.S. Congress. Senate. Committee on Labor and Human Resources. *Anticipated Nomination of Donna Shalala.* Washington, D.C.: United States Government Printing Office, 1993.

U.S. Department of Health and Human Services. "Donna Shalala." Available online. URL: http://www.os.dhhs. gov/about/bios/dhhssec.html. Downloaded December 2, 2000.

 SHAW, ANNA HOWARD
(1847–1919)   *Suffrage Leader*

Anna Howard Shaw, lecturer and orator
(Still Picture Branch, National Archives, College Park, MD)

Dr. Anna Howard Shaw, the longtime protegée of SUSAN B. ANTHONY, served as president of the National American Woman Suffrage Association (NAWSA) for a decade after Anthony retired. Shaw was known as the best orator of the suffrage movement.

Anna Howard Shaw was born on Valentine's Day, February 14, 1847, in Newcastle, England, to Nicolas Shaw and Thomas Shaw. She was the sixth child in a family of three boys and three girls. (She was called Annie in childhood and did not use the name Anna until 1892, when Susan B. Anthony convinced her it was a more dignified name.) In 1851, her family moved to the United States and settled in Lawrence, Massachusetts, a town of progressive thinking.

The Shaws were Unitarians and abolitionists. Shortly before the Civil War, when Shaw was 12, the family moved to the Michigan frontier, where life was especially harsh for her mother and other pioneer women. Shaw began working as a schoolteacher at age 15 for $2 a week plus board, teaching 14 students. When she was 23, Shaw left home to attend high school in Big Rapids. She excelled in speaking and debating classes but fainted the first time she had to speak publicly. A female Methodist principal, Lucy Foot, encouraged her to pursue public speaking, as Methodist churches were beginning to accept women as ministers.

Shaw prepared for the Methodist ministry and spent 1873 through 1875 at Albion College, a Methodist institution, in Michigan. Shaw completed a degree from the divinity school at Boston University in 1878. She was the only female student in a class with 42 males. Male students were given free dormitory room and board, but Shaw had to live off campus in a small attic room that she rented. She had no heat or running water, cooked over a coal oil lamp, and lived on milk and crackers. After her weight dropped to less than 100 pounds, a superintendent of the Women's Foreign Missionary Society began providing her with $3.50 a week to support her studies.

After managing to complete her studies, Shaw served as a pastor for two churches in East Dennis on Cape Cod—one Methodist and one Congregational—for several years, at a time when women ministers were still controversial. In 1880, she applied for ordination to the Methodist Episcopal Conference. Shaw received the highest grade on her exam, but the bishop refused to ordain her. She transferred to a different Methodist synod and was ordained in 1880.

In 1883, Shaw began working on a medical degree, completing her studies just three years later. She never practiced medicine, however, because once again she changed her career direction. This time, she worked for the cause of suffrage.

Shaw was 39 when she left medicine and the ministry to begin a career as a lecturer, first for temperance and then for suffrage. National president of the Woman's Christian Temperance Union (WCTU) FRANCES WILLARD was the first to recruit Shaw as a lecturer for her organization. Shaw also became a paid lecturer for the Massachusetts Suffrage Association. In 1887, she became a national lecturer for the American Woman Suffrage Association (AWSA). In 1890, Shaw was appointed as a national lecturer for the newly merged National American Women Suffrage Association (NAWSA).

In 1892 Anthony became president and Shaw vice president of NAWSA, a position in which Shaw served from 1892 to 1904. Shaw, a moderate reformer, helped counter the stereotype that suffragists were unreligious and militant. It had been expected that Anthony would promote Shaw to the presidency of the NAWSA when she retired in 1900, but CARRIE CHAPMAN CATT was chosen instead. When Catt resigned in 1904 due to her husband's illness, Shaw became president of the organization. Some criticized her for her lack of administrative and political skills, and annual attempts were made to remove her from office. However, during her tenure, the suffrage movement grew in strength and numbers. The number of states with full suffrage rose from four to 11 and membership of NAWSA grew from 17,000 to 183,000. The organization grew from conducting one campaign every 10 years to conducting five to 10 campaigns annually. Shaw stepped down from the presidency of the NAWSA in 1915. She published her autobiography, *The Story of a Pioneer,* the same year.

Shaw spent the last few months of her life campaigning for the creation of the League of Nations. She traveled tirelessly throughout the country to the point of exhaustion, developing pneumonia in Illinois.

Anna Howard Shaw died on July 2, 1919, at her home in Moylan, Pennsylvania, of pneumonia with inflammation of the liver. She did not live long enough to see the passage of the Nineteenth Amendment, which assured suffrage for women. Carrie Chapman Catt eulogized, "She was of the suffrage struggle its greatest orator, its wit, its humor, its deathless spirit. She staked her whole life on the cause, and death cannot rob her nor us of the victory that was so largely her work."

Further Reading

Linkugel, Wil, and Martha Solomon. *Anna Howard Shaw: A Suffrage Orator and Social Reformer.* Westport, Conn.: Greenwood, 1991.

Shaw, Anna. *The Story of a Pioneer.* New York: Harper, 1915.

 SHRIVER, EUNICE MARY KENNEDY
(1921–   )   *Disability Advocate*

Eunice Kennedy Shriver has devoted her life to working on behalf of the disabled. She began the world-renowned Special Olympics and worked to dispel stereotypes among the general public regarding mental retardation. Her work has changed the way the world views and treats mentally retarded people.

Eunice Mary Kennedy was born on July 10, 1921, in Boston, Massachusetts, to Rose Kennedy

Eunice Kennedy Shriver (center) with President Kennedy and Marshal Tito of Yugoslavia, 1963
(John F. Kennedy Library, Boston, Massachusetts)

and Joseph Kennedy. She was born into one of the most famous families in U.S. political history. She received a B.S. from Stanford in sociology in 1943. In 1953 she married Sargent Shriver, a career public servant who was closely aligned with the administration of President John F. Kennedy, Eunice's brother.

Eunice Shriver's sister Rosemary Kennedy was mentally retarded, but the Kennedy family kept her condition a closely guarded secret. In 1961, President Kennedy allowed her to establish the presidential Committee on Mental Retardation, which developed a legislative program for helping the mentally retarded. The commission's report contained 112 recommendations; 70 percent of these were implemented. Breakthroughs in research and educational programs occurred due to the funding the Kennedy administration pursued. The research findings discovered the importance of early educational efforts, which could raise the IQs of mentally retarded children.

In 1962, Shriver told President Kennedy that she wanted to write an article about their sister Rosemary for the *Saturday Evening Post*. He gave his approval after reading the piece, which was the first public acknowledgment of their "family secret," a secret that many families across the United States shared. Many families still "warehoused" mentally retarded family members in institutions in remote areas and did not speak of their existence. Most families were too embarrassed due to the prejudice and ignorance of the general population regarding mental retardation.

Mentally retarded women often experienced sexual abuse in these institutions and were routinely sterilized without consent so that they might not breed another retarded generation. Initially, Rosemary had been only mildly retarded, but her father, Joseph Kennedy, agreed to a lobotomy for Rosemary, hoping it might result in a medical miracle. After the lobotomy in 1941, however, Rosemary was much worse and remained institutionalized at St. Coletta's Hospital in Jefferson, Wisconsin, for the rest of her life. Until Shriver's article, the Kennedy family had told the public that Rosemary was in a convent. The public reception to the piece was very positive, giving an invisible group, the mentally retarded and their families, public support. In the same year Shriver developed the National Institute for Child Health and Human Development and created the Joseph P. Kennedy Jr. awards in mental retardation for scientific and research breakthroughs.

In 1968, Shriver created the organization for which she is best known, the Special Olympics, which organizes multisport events for the mentally challenged. This event was a precursor of the disability rights movement that would continue to press for integration of mentally challenged people into public life. These Olympics were the first of their kind—an effort to encourage sports training and athletic competition of the mentally retarded. The Special Olympics are now hosted in 130 countries, with 1 million athletes competing in 22 sports. More than 15,000 fund-raising and qualifying events are held annually in preparation for the Special Olympics.

In 1984 President Ronald Reagan awarded Shriver the Presidential Medal of Freedom for her work "on behalf of America's least powerful people, the mentally retarded." Shriver remains active in the cause to which she has devoted her life. She changed the world for the mentally retarded by changing public perceptions of their abilities and achievements.

Further Reading

Leamer, Laurence. "The Toughest Kennedy." *Washingtonian* 29, no. 11 (August 1994): 62.

National Women's Hall of Fame. "Eunice Mary Kennedy Shriver." Available online. URL: http://www.greatwomen.org/shriver.htm. Downloaded December 3, 2000.

"Shriver, Eunice Kennedy." *Current Biography* 57 (July 1996): 48–52.

Shriver, Eunice Kennedy, and Romayne Smith, eds. *Children with Mental Retardation: A Parents' Guide.* Bethesda, Md.: Woodbine House, 1993.

Unsworth, Tim. "Drawn to a Life of Distinguished Service." *National Catholic Reporter* 32, no. 34 (July 12, 1996): 20–21.

Weekly Compilation of Presidential Documents 34, no. 51 (December 21, 1998): 2500–02.

 ## SILKWOOD, KAREN GAY
(1946–1974) *Environmental Activist*

Karen Silkwood, a laboratory technician at a nuclear fuel facility, was a union leader who voiced concerns regarding plant safety. At age 28, she died in a car accident under suspicious conditions near Oklahoma City, Oklahoma, on her way to meet with a *New York Times* reporter and a union official. She allegedly was bringing documents revealing the Kerr-McGee Nuclear Corporation's mishandling of highly dangerous plutonium and Kerr-McGee's coverup of the problem.

Karen Gay Silkwood was born on February 19, 1946, in a small Texas town. She liked science in school. She left college in 1965 to enter a common-law marriage with Bill Meadows, with whom she had three children. Their relationship ended after seven years. Silkwood left Texas in 1973 to work as a chemical technician in Oklahoma. She was employed at Kerr-McGee's plutonium fuel plant in Crescent, Oklahoma, part of one of the largest nuclear energy conglomerates in the United States. Plutonium, used in nuclear bombs and power plants, is one of the most lethal substances on earth, due to its radioactivity. The plant produced fuel rods for a nuclear plant in Hanford, Washington, in order to generate electricity. Kerr-McGee had allegedly not been forthright with the workers about the dangers of plutonium and the cancer risks involved.

Silkwood worked in quality control in the lab and was a member of the Oil, Chemical, and Atomic Worker's Union. A vocal critic regarding plant safety, she was active in her union and was elected to its three-person bargaining committee in the summer of 1974, becoming the first female committee member in Kerr-McGee's history.

Silkwood took her union position seriously and kept a notebook in which she recorded workers' complaints regarding safety violations. In September 1974, she took a trip to the union's national office in Washington, D.C., with a list of complaints. The union wanted to bring charges to the national office of the Atomic Energy Commission, and Silkwood agreed to collect evidence. One of the most serious charges Silkwood made against the company was tampering with quality-control data. It was her job to examine X rays of welds in fuel rods and note the defects. Silkwood found that defective rods that could cause a nuclear explosion were being shipped out after X rays revealing the defects had been retouched.

Silkwood was involved in several unexplained exposures to plutonium. Investigators found high levels of radiation on Silkwood and in her apartment. The reading of radiation levels on her skin was 40 times over the safety limit. Plutonium had contaminated her entire apartment. Men in protective suits removed every piece of furniture, and every one of her possessions was put in 55-gallon barrels to be buried as nuclear waste. Silkwood

thought that someone had planted the plutonium in her home.

Karen Silkwood died on November 13, 1974, in a fatal one-car collision just 10 miles from Crescent. She was on her way to meet *New York Times* reporter David Burnham in Oklahoma City with files of documents on Kerr-McGee's violations. At a union meeting just a few hours before her death, she was seen with the documents. The first highway patrol officer at the accident noted in his report that the documents were in her car, but the papers had disappeared by the next day. Traces of rubber and dents were found on the rear bumper of her car, possibly indicating another car's involvement, but her death was ruled an accident. The circumstances of the accident and her death were suspicious to her union and family. Many believed that her car had been forced off the road. Unions, women, and environmental groups rallied after her death and pursued the issues she had raised.

A 1975 Atomic Energy Commission report upheld Silkwood's allegations about the Kerr-McGee nuclear fuel plant, which closed that year. The circumstances surrounding Silkwood's union work and tragic death were the subject of a popular motion picture in 1983.

In 1976, her family filed a lawsuit against Kerr-McGee for willful negligence and for their lack of safety measures, which led to Silkwood's plutonium exposures. Kerr-McGee publicly charged that Silkwood was a promiscuous drug user who had contaminated herself. During the trial, evidence surfaced that 40 pounds of weapons grade plutonium was missing—enough plutonium to make three nuclear bombs. In 1979, the jury awarded Silkwood's estate $10.5 million for personal injury and punitive damages. However, the Federal Court of Appeals in Denver, Colorado, reduced the award to $5,000 for the personal property she lost during her apartment cleanup.

The lawsuit was being retried in 1986, when an out-of-court settlement of $1.3 million was reached. Her parents had brought the suit hoping to discover who had caused their daughter's death. They had also offered a $10,000 reward to anyone who could provide information about her death, but her accident remains a mystery. Karen Silkwood fought for safe working conditions, and many political activists believe her life was sacrificed to this cause.

Further Reading

Hannam, Joyce. *The Death of Karen Silkwood*. Oxford: Oxford University Press, 1991.

Kohn, Howard. *Who Killed Karen Silkwood?* New York: Summit Books, 1981.

Rashke, Richard. *The Killing of Karen Silkwood: The Story Behind the Kerr-McGee Plutonium Case*. Ithaca, N.Y.: Cornell University Press, 2000.

 ## SMEAL, ELEANOR MARIE CUTRI
(1939–) *National Organization for Women President*

From 1977 to 1982 and 1985 to 1987, Eleanor Smeal served two terms as president of the National Organization for Women (NOW), the largest women's rights group in the United States. She is best known for her role in leading the campaign for passage of the Equal Rights Amendment (ERA), which ultimately failed. She currently serves as president of the Fund for the Feminist Majority (FFM).

Eleanor Marie Cutri was born on July 30, 1939, in Erie, Pennsylvania. The youngest child in her family, she had three older brothers. Her parents were first-generation Catholic Italian Americans. Her activism began in the 1960s with the civil rights movement, when she picketed to integrate Duke University, in Durham, North Carolina, where she was an undergraduate. She considered attending law school but male professors discouraged her. She completed a master's degree in political science in 1963 from the University of Florida, then married Charles Smeal. The couple moved to Pennsylvania, where Smeal served on the board of the local League of Women Voters beginning in 1968. She gave birth

to two children. Wanting to finish her Ph.D. at the University of Pittsburgh, Smeal searched unsuccessfully for day care. This led her to establish the South Hills NOW Day Nursery School in 1971, where she served as administrator.

Smeal and her husband had joined NOW in 1970. She was president of the local Pittsburgh NOW chapter, and her phone number became a NOW hot line where women could call for resources and referrals on health care, education, legal issues, and employment.

In 1972, Smeal became president of the Pennsylvania NOW. In 1975, she began serving as chair of the national NOW board. Two years later, Smeal became the first NOW national president to receive a salary, and she served in this position until 1982.

Two of the most significant campaigns she led during this time were the effort to ratify the ERA and the founding of a NOW political action committee to raise funds for feminist political candidates. She is best remembered for her leadership in the ERA campaign. The deadline for ratifying the ERA was 18 months away when she took office. The ERA ultimately fell three states short of ratification by the 1982 deadline. (A deadline for ratification had never been set on previous amendments.)

After the defeat of the ERA, Smeal took a three-year hiatus from the presidency of NOW, then returned to serve for two more years, from 1985 to 1987. When she returned to a second term, NOW's membership had dropped from 230,000 in 1983 to 150,000 in 1986. During this time, she faced the conservative climate of Ronald Reagan's presidency and the growing religious right. Smeal promised, "I intend to raise a little more hell." Smeal was the first to identify the gender gap, a growing difference in the party affiliation of men and women. She outlined her views in a 1984 book, *How and Why Women Will Elect the Next President*.

In 1984, she authored a resolution at the national NOW conference that demanded a female candidate on the Democratic presidential ticket. Presidential candidate Walter Mondale chose congressional representative GERALDINE FERRARO as his running mate after intensive lobbying by NOW for a female candidate. In 1988, Smeal encouraged NOW to support the presidential candidacy of congressional representative PATRICIA NELL SCOTT SCHROEDER, though Schroeder eventually withdrew from the race.

Smeal led the first national abortion rights march in 1986, which brought a crowd of 100,000 to Washington, D.C. Under Smeal's leadership, 45,000 volunteers who defended clinics against antichoice demonstrators were trained in 47 cities. Clinic defenders were used to escort patients past hostile protestors into clinics. She coauthored and coproduced two award-winning videos on the topic of abortion, *Abortion for Survival* and *Abortion Denied: Shattering Women's Lives*. She was a vocal proponent of U.S. Food and Drug Administration approval for RU-486 (mifepristone), often called the "abortion pill."

After leaving the presidency of NOW in 1987, Smeal cofounded the Feminist Majority Foundation, which worked to increase the number of women running for office. A 1994 U.S. Supreme Court decision finally upheld the use of buffer zones to protect clinics in the landmark case *Madsen v. Women's Health Center*. Smeal was president of the Feminist Majority Foundation, which provided legal counsel to the Aware Woman Center for Choice in the 1994 Madsen case.

Smeal was an early pioneer in promoting use of the Internet as a tool for feminist organizing. When she launched the Feminist Majority Foundation Online in 1995, it was one of the first women's organization sites on the World Wide Web. The site garners some 3 million visits each month.

In 1997, Smeal organized an international movement, Campaign to Stop Gender Apartheid, in Afghanistan. Her campaign was so successful that it led the United States and United Nations to withdraw official recognition of the Taliban government in Afghanistan until women's human rights there were restored. Her strong leadership advanced the feminist cause in the United States and internationally.

Further Reading

Feminist Majority Foundation. "Eleanor Smeal." Available online. URL: http://www.feminist.org/welcome/esbio.html. Downloaded December 4, 2000.

Koppel, Barbara. "Eleanor Smeal." *Progressive* 15 (November 1995): 32–34.

Lader, Lawrence, and Eleanor Smeal. *A Private Matter: RU 486 and the Abortion Crisis.* Amherst, N.Y.: Prometheus Books, 1995.

Smeal, Eleanor. *Why and How Women Will Elect the Next President.* New York: Harper and Row, 1984.

 SMITH, MARGARET MADELINE CHASE
(1897–1995) *Senator*

Margaret Chase Smith was the first woman to be elected to both the U.S. House of Representatives and the Senate. She served more than three decades in Congress, under six different presidents. She was a Republican but an independent thinker who often sided with the Democrats.

Margaret Madeline Chase was born on December 14, 1897, in Skowhegan, Maine, to Carrie Murray Chase and George Emery Chase. She was the oldest of six children. Her mother was a waitress and her father a barber.

She started working at age 12 and worked at a store during high school. After graduating, she could not afford college so instead pursued a career in office work at the local telephone company and a weekly newspaper. She served as president of the Maine Federation of Business and Professional Women's Clubs from 1926 to 1928. In 1930, when she was 34, she married newspaper owner Clyde Smith, a Republican politician who was 21 years her senior. She served on Maine's Republican committee from 1930 to 1936.

Her husband was elected to Congress and Smith served as his secretary. When he suffered a heart attack and died in 1940, Smith became the Republican nominee for his seat. Eight years later, she ran successfully for the U.S. Senate and received the highest percentage of the vote in the history of Maine. She was reelected repeatedly, serving four terms in the Senate. She took one of her first independent stands in Congress when she voted to back President Franklin Roosevelt's policy to intervene in World War II, even though her own party supported isolationism. She supported the policies of Democratic presidents Franklin Roosevelt and Harry Truman more often than any other Republican did. She sponsored legislation that created a women's unit in the Navy and became known as "The Mother of the WAVES." The 1948 Women's Armed Services Integration Act gave women the status of full members, not just volunteers, in all the armed forces. The women's branch in the navy was known as the WAVES.

Smith rose to national prominence when she challenged Senator Joseph McCarthy, the Wisconsin Republican who had launched a "witch hunt" for suspected communists in government and society. She was the first politician to denounce McCarthyism. In 1950, she delivered a speech in the Senate, a "declaration of conscience" in which she denounced McCarthy's practices of "hate and character assassination." Six other Republican senators endorsed the speech. As she stated, "I don't want to see the Republican Party ride to political victory on the four horsemen of calumny—fear, ignorance, bigotry and smear." She later recalled the reign of terror unleashed by McCarthy: "The then junior Senator from Wisconsin had the Senate paralyzed with fear that he would purge any Senator that disagreed with him."

She was a staunch conservative in regard to anticommunism, however. She voted against the nuclear test ban treaty and was rated as the Most Valuable Senator in 1960 by *Newsweek* magazine. Her 1960 reelection campaign was the first campaign in which two women opposed each other. Her opponent was Democratic Maine state legislator Lucia Cormier.

In 1964, Smith sought the Republican Party presidential nomination and won primaries in New Hampshire, Illinois, Massachusetts, Oregon, and Texas. She was the first woman nominee of any major political party. She came in second to Senator Barry Goldwater. When congressional representative MARTHA GRIFFITHS led the campaign to include gender in the Civil Rights Act of 1964, Smith supported the measure in the Senate.

In 1970, Smith issued a second "declaration of conscience" on the 20th anniversary of her original speech. This time she spoke out about her opposition to the polarizing effects of the Vietnam War. She criticized both militant student groups protesting the war and attempts by the Nixon administration to repress the opposition.

Smith undertook a fifth Senate race at age 74 and faced ageist attacks by her opponent Democratic Representative William Hathaway. She was noted for not missing a vote during her tenure in Congress, but she was defeated. Her loss made the U.S. Senate an all-male body again, as it had been when she first took office in

Senator Margaret Chase Smith, 1952
(Prints & Photographs Division,
Library of Congress, Washington, D.C.)

1948. She had served longer in the Senate than any other woman. She stated of her departure, "I hate to leave the Senate when there is no indication another qualified woman is coming in. . . . If I leave and there's a long lapse, the next woman will have to rebuild entirely." She also acknowledged the changing face of campaigning and the increasing importance of fund-raising in politics: "The trouble was I didn't have money for television."

After retiring from public office, Smith worked to establish the Margaret Chase Smith Library Center at the Northwood Institute in Skowhegan, Maine, which was dedicated in 1982. When she visited an elementary school in her hometown that had been named after her, one little boy asked her, "How does it feel to be named after a school?" Smith was awarded the Presidential Medal of Freedom in 1989.

Margaret Chase Smith died on May 29, 1995, in Skowhegan, Maine. Her remains were cremated and the ashes placed in a wing of the Margaret Chase Smith Library, where her papers are also stored. A consummate politician, she will be best remembered for her courageous stand against McCarthyism.

Further Reading

Schmidt, Patricia. *Margaret Chase Smith: Beyond Convention.* Orono: University of Maine Press, 1996.

Sherman, Janann. *No Place for a Woman: A Life of Senator Margaret Chase Smith.* New Brunswick, N.J.: Rutgers University Press, 2000.

Vallin, Marlene Boyd. *Margaret Chase Smith.* Westport, Conn.: Greenwood, 1998.

Wallace, Patricia. *Politics of Conscience: A Biography of Margaret Chase Smith.* Westport, Conn.: Praeger, 1995.

⊠ SNOWE, OLYMPIA JEAN BOUCLES
(1947–) *Senator*

Olympia Snowe was elected as a congressional representative from Maine in 1978 and to the U.S. Senate in 1994. She is the fourth woman in history to be elected to both houses of Congress.

Olympia Jean Boucles was born on February 21, 1947, in Augusta, Maine, to Georgia Goranites Boucles and George Boucles. Her father was a native of Mytilene, Greece. Her maternal grandparents had immigrated to America from Sparta, Greece. After the death of her parents, Snowe was raised by her maternal uncle and his wife. She attended St. Basil's Academy in Garrison, New York, in 1962. She graduated from Edward Little High School in Auburn, Maine, in 1965, and completed a bachelors's degree in political science from the University of Maine, Orono, in 1969. She then worked in the office of a congressional representative. She married Peter Snowe, who was later elected to the state house of representatives. When he died in an automobile accident, Snowe was elected to the Maine House of Representatives in 1973 to fill his seat. She served in this position until 1976, when she was elected to the state senate.

In 1978, Snowe was elected to the U.S. House of Representatives and served for 16 years. At age 31, she was the youngest Republican woman and the first Greek-American woman elected to Congress. She was reelected for eight terms and served as cochair of the Congressional Caucus on Women's Issues for 10 years. In 1989, she married Maine governor John McKernan after a 10-year courtship.

She was elected to the U.S. Senate in 1994 with more than 60 percent of the vote. Snowe defeated Democrat Thomas Andrews in the race to replace the retiring Senate Majority Leader, Democrat George Mitchell. She was reelected in 2000. She was the second woman senator from Maine; her predecessor was Senator MARGARET CHASE SMITH, who served from 1949 to 1973. Snowe is the fourth woman in history to be elected to both houses of Congress. She has won more federal elections in the state of Maine than any other person since World War II. She served as deputy whip and in 1997 became counsel to the assistant majority leader. In 1997, her appointment to the Senate Armed Services Committee made her fourth woman ever to serve on this position. In 1999, she became the first woman senator to chair the Subcommittee on

Seapower, which oversees the navy and marine corps. She also chairs the Subcommittee on Oceans and Fisheries of the Senate Committee on Commerce, Science and Transportation, which oversees U.S. fisheries and the U.S. Coast Guard.

Snowe is viewed as a moderate and is pro-choice. In 1999, she was recognized by *Congressional Quarterly* for her centrist leadership. She worked with Senator John Breaux, Democrat of Louisiana, to form the Senate Centrist Coalition in order to build communication between Senate Democrats and Republicans. Olympia Snowe's bipartisan leadership is respected by both Democrats and Republicans in Congress.

Further Reading

Biographical Directory of the United States Congress. "Olympia Jean Snowe." Available online. URL: http://bioguide.congress.gov/scripts/biodisplay.pl?index=S000663. Downloaded December 5, 2000.

Congressional Quarterly Weekly Report. "Olympia Snowe." 53, no. 1 (January 7, 1995): 107.

Congressional Quarterly Weekly Report. "Olympia Snowe." 57, no. 42 (October 30, 1999): 58–59.

Congressional Quarterly Weekly Report. "Olympia Snowe, R-Maine." 52, no. 44 (November 12, 1994): 13.

Current Biography. "Snowe, Olympia." 56 (May 1995): 51–55.

"That's 'Senator Seapower' to You." *Defense Week* (January 4, 1999): 1A.

Whitney, Catherine. *Nine and Counting: The Women of the Senate.* New York: Perennial, 2001.

 ## STANTON, ELIZABETH CADY
(1815–1902) *Suffragist*

Elizabeth Cady Stanton was a leader in the women's rights movement several years before her lifetime friend SUSAN B. ANTHONY got involved in the cause. Stanton was the primary author of the Declaration of the Rights of Women, an early feminist manifesto penned at one of the first women's rights conventions in the United States, at Seneca Falls, New York, in 1848. Stanton had organized the event.

Elizabeth Cady was born on November 12, 1815, in Johnstown, New York. Her father, a judge, mourned her brother, his only son, who had died young, and Elizabeth was raised as a "replacement" for her brother. Her father use to tell her, "I wish you were a boy." She would later trace her activism to seeing the unequal treatment her father's female legal clients experienced. Her father did not approve of her later activism, however, and for a brief period of time disinherited her.

She studied Greek and Latin in books that had been bought for her brother. She attended Emma Willard's Troy Female Seminary in 1832, before colleges were opened to women. Her immediate family thought the issue of abolition was too radical, but her extended family members were abolitionists. She met abolitionist Henry Stanton, a liberal journalist 10 years her senior, and married him in 1840. At 24, she was older than most brides of her era, but she had spent her courting years emotionally involved with her unhappily married brother-in-law. In her wedding ceremony, she had the word *obey* deleted from the vows and continued to use her maiden name (in conjunction with his). On their honeymoon, the couple traveled to London for the World Anti-Slavery Convention. Stanton, women's rights leader LUCRETIA MOTT, and other women in attendance were excluded from the proceedings because of their gender. Angered by this treatment, they decided to organize a woman's rights convention on their return to the United States.

Her husband became an attorney, and the family lived for a short time in Boston before settling in Seneca Falls, New York. Beginning in 1842, Stanton gave birth to seven children in 17 years. Her myriad responsibilities led to recurrent bouts of severe depression throughout her life. Often pregnant and nursing, Stanton relied on writing as a form of activism while her friend Susan B. Anthony, who had no children, was able to travel and speak more easily.

Mott and Stanton organized a women's rights convention to be held in Seneca Falls in 1848. It would be the first national conference for women's rights. Stanton drafted the famous Declaration of the Rights of Women using the Declaration of Independence and the language of President Thomas Jefferson as a guide. Stanton compared the oppression of women by men to the tyranny of the English king over American colonists and argued for the need for radical change. Stanton stated in the declaration, "The history of mankind is a history of repeated injuries and usurpation's on the part of man toward woman, having in direct object the establishment of absolute tyranny over her."

When Stanton began her activism, women were prevented from attending college, serving on juries, voting, testifying in court, signing contracts, keeping their earnings, working in most professions, maintaining custody of their children, and preaching as ministers. As Stanton stated, "They tax our property to build colleges, then pass a special law prohibiting any woman to enter there. A married woman has no legal existence; she has no more absolute rights than a slave on a southern plantation. She takes the name of her master, holds nothing, owns nothing, can bring no action in her own name; and the principle on which she and the slave are educated is the same."

Stanton called for female suffrage at the Seneca Falls conference, a move that was seen as too radical by many in attendance, including Mott. Stanton was one of the first to publicly articulate the issue of suffrage for women. She felt that in order to change unjust laws, women needed the vote. Stanton was often at the vanguard of issues rather than in the mainstream.

In an 1852 meeting of the Woman's State Temperance Society, Stanton pushed another controversial issue, the right to divorce drunken and abusive husbands, a scandalous idea at that time. Stanton asserted, "Man marrying gives up no right, but a woman, every right."

In 1860, the women's rights movement achieved some of its aims when the New York State legislature passed a bill giving married women rights to their property, wages, and custody of their children.

When the Civil War began, the Stanton family moved to New York City, where Stanton resided for the rest of her life. Anthony and Stanton founded the National Woman's Loyal League in 1861 in order to collect hundreds of thousands of petitions for a constitutional amendment to end slavery.

Always one to push the limits, Stanton ran for Congress in 1866, when women were still ineligible to vote. Of the 12,000 men who voted in that Congressional election, only 24 cast their ballot for Stanton.

In 1868, Anthony and Stanton began publishing a journal for the National Women's Suffrage Association (NWSA), the *Revolution*. Its motto was blunt: "Men, their rights, and nothing more; women, their rights, and nothing less!" Stanton did most of the writing for the journal and continued writing on topics that others had not begun to address, such as prostitution and the exclusion of women from jury duty. Stanton refused to accept advertising for unsound medical practitioners and "cures," which created financial difficulties for the *Revolution*. The paper went into bankruptcy in 1869.

A separation in the women's rights movement occurred when the Fifteenth Amendment was passed, extending suffrage to African-American men but not to any women. The American Woman Suffrage Association (AWSA) accepted the exclusion of women from the amendment and supported the enfranchisement of African-American men. Some later feminists and historians have critiqued Stanton's argument as having racist undertones. She insisted that educated white women were more deserving of the vote than were ex-slaves.

Stanton and Anthony formed a separate organization, the National Woman Suffrage Association (NWSA) in 1869. NWSA was open to male membership, but men could not hold office. NWSA was one of the first organizations to mandate such a policy. Stanton served as president of the organization for most of its 21-year history, with Anthony as her vice president. The NWSA statement of purpose was visionary: "The woman question is more than a demand for suffrage. . . . It is a question covering a whole range of women's needs and demands. . . . including her work, her wages, her property, her education, her physical training, her social status, her political equalization, her marriage and her divorce."

Stanton spent the 1880s working on three volumes of the *History of Woman Suffrage,* which she coauthored with Anthony and Matilda Joslyn Gage. Stanton's husband died in 1887.

By 1890, the two suffrage groups had merged and Stanton served as president of the newly formed National American Woman Suffrage Association (NAWSA) from its founding in 1890 until 1892. The suffrage movement and Anthony grew more moderate in approach, while Stanton continued to put forth radical proposals. As Stanton viewed it, "Miss Anthony has one idea and she has no patience with anyone who has two. . . . I cannot sing suffrage evermore: I am deeply interested in all the questions of the day." Stanton noted in her diary a growing gap between herself and Anthony: "I get more radical as I grow older, while [Anthony] seems to grow more conservative." When black abolitionist Frederick Douglass married a white woman, Stanton penned a statement of support for the interracial marriage, but Anthony was against it.

In 1895, Stanton published *The Woman's Bible,* a feminist analysis of the Old and New Testaments and a denouncement of them, "For their degrading teaching with regard to women." The public found such proclamations abhorrent, and the suffrage movement was divided. Suffrage leader ANNA HOWARD SHAW and others passed a resolution from NAWSA in 1896 condemning *The Woman's Bible.* The condemnation seemed to have little effect, since Stanton published a second volume of *The Woman's Bible* in 1898. She published her autobiography, *Eighty Years and More,* that same year.

Elizabeth Cady Stanton, suffragist
(Still Picture Branch, National Archives, College Park, MD)

Suffrage leaders increasingly excluded issues other than suffrage from their agenda, while Stanton continued to push many issues, among them dress reform, divorce, education, and the damage she believed Christianity inflicted on women. Stanton advocated for social change, not just legal change.

Elizabeth Cady Stanton was enfeebled and blind at the end of her life. She died on October 26, 1902, at age 83. Her obituary was written by an atheist and published in a secular magazine. The family held a private funeral with Susan B. Anthony one of the few guests in attendance. Anthony, the more moderate leader, received public honors during her lifetime, while Stanton was largely forgotten by later generations.

Two of her children published her diary and other writings in 1922. She was not the subject of a biography until 1940. Her papers are stored at the Library of Congress, Vassar, Radcliffe, and Smith Colleges. Her restored home in Seneca Falls is open to visitors. She is best remembered as a radical visionary who devoted her life to creating changes that later generations continue to build upon.

Further Reading

Burns, Ken. "Our Big Time." *American Heritage* 50, no. 7 (November 1999): 98–100.

Rutgers, The State University of New Jersey. Department of History. "Elizabeth Cady Stanton and Susan B. Anthony Papers Project Online." Available online. URL: http://ecssba.rutgers.edu/. Downloaded July 27, 2001.

Stanton, Elizabeth Cady. *Eighty Years and More: Reminiscences 1815–1897.* Boston, Mass.: Northeastern University Press, 1993.

———. *The Woman's Bible.* Boston, Mass.: Northeastern University Press, 1993.

Strange, Lisa. "Elizabeth Cady Stanton's Women's Bible and the Roots of Feminist Theology." *Gender Issues* 17, no. 4 (fall 1999): 15–36.

Ward, Geoffrey. *Not For Ourselves Alone: The Story of Elizabeth Cady Stanton and Susan B. Anthony: An Illustrated History.* New York: Knopf, 1999.

⊠ STEINEM, GLORIA
(1934–) *Founder of* Ms. *Magazine*

Gloria Steinem founded *Ms.,* the world's first mass-market feminist magazine. The premiere issue appeared in 1972, and within a year *Ms.* had 1.4 million readers. The publication brought feminism out of the limited world of academia and radical politics and into larger society. Steinem established *Ms.* as a "how-to" magazine: "Not how to make jelly, but how to seize control of your life."

Gloria Steinem was born on March 25, 1934, in Toledo, Ohio, the younger of two daughters of Ruth Nuneviller Steinem and Leo Steinem. Her father was Jewish, her mother Protestant. Her mother held a master's degree in history and had worked as a journalist before starting a family. She suffered a nervous breakdown just before Steinem's birth and battled depression for the rest of her life. Steinem's grandmother had been president of the Ohio Women's Suffrage Association.

Her father was a traveling salesman, and he often left Steinem and her mother without money or heat in the home. When her parents divorced, Steinem continued to be the primary caretaker for her mother, who suffered from depression and agoraphobia. Her mother sold the family's Toledo home in order to finance Steinem's college education.

Steinem received a scholarship from and attended Smith College, one of the best women's colleges in the nation, located in Northampton, Massachusetts. Steinem completed a bachelor's degree in political science from Smith, graduating magna cum laude in 1956. After graduation, she received a Charles Bowles Asian Fellowship to pursue graduate work at the University of Delhi and the University of Calcutta in India in 1957 and 1958. After returning to the United States she worked as a freelance writer. Steinem received her first byline in 1962 from *Esquire* magazine. She was a contributing editor of *Glamour* magazine from 1962 to 1969.

In 1963, Steinem went undercover for a month to write an exposé of life as a Playboy bunny. Her article, "A Bunny's Tale," garnered national attention and was made into a movie. It highlighted the sexism women encountered while working as scantily clad waitresses in Playboy clubs instead of stressing the glamorous images of the bunnies that the Playboy corporation promoted.

When *New York* magazine was founded in 1968, Steinem served as contributing editor and wrote a regular column called "The City Politic." In 1968, she attended a meeting of the Redstockings, a New York City radical feminist group, in order to research an article on them but found she sympathized with the issues they discussed.

Her commitment to feminism also surfaced when she attended abortion law hearings in New York City in 1968, "I will never forget that night as long as I live, because I heard women stand up and tell the truth in public for the first time in my life." Steinem went public with the story of an abortion she had undergone at age 22. (Abortion was illegal and therefore unsafe until the 1973 U.S. Supreme Court decision *Roe v. Wade* decriminalized it.)

In 1970, she won the Penney-Missouri Award for her article on the Black Power movement. Steinem was increasingly drawn to women's groups. In 1970 she marched in the Women's Strike for Equality, a nationwide protest organized by the National Organization For Women that occurred on the 50th anniversary of women's gaining suffrage. She cofounded the Women's Action Alliance in 1970, which developed programs and services for women. Some women from the alliance, including Steinem, developed a plan for a national magazine on feminism. They decided to call it *Ms.*, a term coined by the women's movement for liberated women to use without identifying themselves by marital status, as the use at Miss and Mrs. did.

Steinem was cofounder of the National Women's Political Caucus with congressional representatives BELLA ABZUG, SHIRLEY CHISHOLM, and PATSY MINK in 1971.

Steinem was named woman of the year by *McCall's* magazine in 1972, the same year that the first issue of *Ms.* magazine appeared. The publication was an immediate success; the first press run, 300,000 copies, sold out in eight days. Steinem served as editor of *Ms.* for 15 years. Later, the magazine decided not to accept advertising from liquor and tobacco companies. The financial hardship created by this decision led the journal to switch from a monthly to a quarterly publication schedule.

Steinem was also a cofounder of the Coalition of Labor Union Women in 1974. In 1983, a collection of her essays entitled *Outrageous Acts and Everyday Rebellions* became a best-seller. She had another best-seller with her study of Marilyn Monroe, entitled *Marilyn: Norma Jean,* published in 1986. In the 1980s, she served as contributing editor of the *Today* television program. In 1989 she underwent successful treatment for breast cancer. In 1990, Steinem and new editor-in-chief Robin Morgan changed *Ms.* into a subscriber-supported, advertising-free magazine.

Gloria Steinem, journalist
(Still Picture Branch, National Archives, College Park, MD)

Her 1992 book *Revolution from Within: A Book of Self-Esteem* was criticized for its emphasis on self-help advice rather than political analysis. In December 1998, Liberty Media for Women, a newly formed group of feminists, purchased *Ms.* Steinem continues to serve as a consulting editor for the magazine.

Steinem defines feminism as "equality for all females—a transformation of society." She summarized the achievements of feminism in a speech at Yale University: "We have become the men we wanted to marry." Another statement of Steinem's, "A woman needs a man like a fish needs a bicycle," gave the impression that she was dismissive of marriage. Some were surprised when she married South African David Bale in September 2000. Steinem saw no contradiction, however, noting that "feminism is about the ability to choose what's right at each time of our lives." Steinem has worked to broaden the range of choices that are available to women.

Further Reading

Finn, Robin. "Single No More, and Still Wedded to the Cause." *New York Times,* Wednesday, May 21, 2001, 1.

Heilbrun, Carolyn. *The Education of a Woman: The Life of Gloria Steinem.* New York: Ballantine Books, 1995.

Steinem, Gloria. *Outrageous Acts and Everyday Rebellions.* New York: Henry Holt, 1983.

———. *Marilyn: Norma Jean.* New York: Henry Holt, 1986.

———. *Moving Beyond Words.* New York: Simon and Schuster, 1994.

———. *Revolution from Within: A Book of Self-Esteem.* Boston: Little, Brown, 1992.

STONE, LUCY
(1818–1893) *Suffragist, Women's Rights Leader, Abolitionist*

Lucy Stone was an abolitionist and women's rights activist. She organized early women's rights conventions and founded the American Woman Suffrage Association (AWSA) in 1869.

Lucy Stone was born on August 13, 1818, on a farm just outside of West Brookfield, Massachusetts, to Hannah Matthews Stone and Francis Stone. She was the eighth of nine children, seven of whom survived childhood. Because she was female, her father would not pay for her college education. When she was 16, she began teaching and spent nine years saving money so she could finance her college education.

She attended Oberlin College and graduated with honors in 1847. Oberlin was a station on the Underground Railroad, a system of safe hiding places for slaves escaping north to freedom. In college, Stone taught fugitive slaves but found they were unhappy being taught by a woman. She began working as a lecturer for the New England Anti-Slavery Society, where she was often confronted by angry mobs. Her lectures often drew crowds of 2,000 to 3,000 people. From the beginning, however, she was also committed to gender equality. She wrote to her mother, "Especially do I mean to Labor for the Elevation of My Sex."

Stone recalled that her initial interest in political activism was inspired by the antislavery writings of ANGELINA and Sarah GRIMKÉ. In 1850, Stone organized one of the first women's rights conventions, which was held in Worcester, Massachusetts.

In 1855, Stone married abolitionist Henry Blackwell, the brother of medical doctors Elizabeth and Emily Blackwell. Stone was one of the first married women to retain her maiden name as a statement of her own identity. In a letter to her husband, Stone wrote, "A wife should no more take her husband's name than he should her's. My name is my identity and must not be lost." Other women who followed her example were called "Lucy Stoners." At the wedding, the couple read what they termed a marriage protest: "This act on our part implies no sanction of, no promise of voluntary obedience to such . . . laws of marriage, as refuse to recognize the wife as an independent, rational being, while they confer upon the husband an injurious and unnatural superiority."

In 1858, Stone's property was seized because she refused to pay taxes to a government in which her gender, and thus herself, was not represented.

A division occurred in the suffrage movement in 1869 over the issue of the Fifteenth Amendment, which granted the franchise to African-American men but not to any women. Suffragists who supported the amendment joined the American Woman Suffrage Association, which Stone founded in 1869. The other faction, which opposed the amendment for its exclusion of women from suffrage, was led by ELIZABETH CADY STANTON and SUSAN B. ANTHONY, and they formed the National Woman Suffrage Association. The two groups would reunite at the turn of the 20th century to form the National American Woman Suffrage Association. In 1870, Stone founded the *Woman's Journal,* and served as its editor, a position she held until her death. The publi-

Lucy Stone, suffragist
(Prints & Photographs Division,
Library of Congress, Washington, D.C.)

cation was a weekly chronicle of the women's rights movement, both in the United States and abroad. After her death in 1893, the publication continued for another 40 years.

Lucy Stone died on October 18, 1893, in Boston, Massachusetts. Her papers are stored at the Library of Congress in Washington, D.C. One of her most famous speeches, delivered in 1855, expressed her disappointment with the institution of marriage: "I have been a disappointed woman. . . . In education, in marriage, in religion, in everything, disappointment is the lot of woman. It shall be the business of my life to deepen this disappointment in every woman's heart until she bows down to it no longer."

Further Reading

Kerr, Andrea Moore. *Lucy Stone: Speaking Out for Equality.* New Brunswick, N.J.: Rutgers University Press, 1992.

National Women's Hall of Fame. "Lucy Stone." Available online. URL: http://www.greatwomen.org/wotmc.html. Downloaded December 5, 2000.

Stone, Lucy. *Friends and Sisters: Letters Between Lucy Stone and Antoinette Brown Blackwell, 1846–93.* Champaign: University of Illinois Press, 1987.

✦ SZOLD, CHAYELEH (Henrietta Szold)
(1860–1945)   *Founder of Hadassah*

Chayeleh Szold, known as Henrietta, was a Zionist leader and founder of the Hadassah women's organization. She is best known for her work in bringing thousands of Jewish children from Germany to Palestine during World War II.

Chayeleh Szold was born on December 21, 1860, in Baltimore, Maryland, to Sophia Schaar Szold and Benjamin Szold. She was named Chayeleh after her grandmother but called Henrietta. Her parents had moved to Baltimore from a town in Hungary near the German border just one year before Szold was born. Her father was a rabbi of the Oheb Shalom congregation. In 1877, she graduated first in her class from Baltimore Western Female High School, where she had been the only Jewish student. She was fluent in English, German, French, and Hebrew.

For 15 years, Szold taught French, German, and mathematics at an exclusive Baltimore school for girls, Misses Adams' School. During that time she also taught religious classes at her father's synagogue. She began to write essays for the *Jewish Messenger,* a newspaper printed in New York and Baltimore.

In 1889, Szold organized night classes to teach English to new immigrants. Many of her students in the night school had fled pogroms (massacres of Jews) in Russia and Poland. The Baltimore city government took over her program when it became too large for her to handle, and it became the first official night school in the United States. Her model was copied in cities throughout the nation.

Concerning the Jews in Europe she wrote, "I am more than ever convinced that if not Zionism, then nothing, only death for the Jew." Zionism is a nationalist movement that supported a Jewish state in Palestine, the ancient homeland of the Jews. It originated in Europe in the 19th century as a response to continued anti-Semitism. In 1893, Szold joined Hebras Zion, the first Zionist society in the United States. She also became the editorial secretary of the Jewish Publication Society during that time. Szold translated books into English and edited *The Jewish Encyclopedia.* She remained in her editorial position for 23 years.

In 1903, Szold moved to New York City and enrolled in the Jewish Theological Seminary of America. She was allowed to attend classes only with the understanding that she could not become a rabbi.

In 1907, Szold joined the Hadassah Study Circle, a group that studied Jewish history and the philosophy of Zionism. After traveling to Palestine in 1909, Szold was convinced that a Jewish homeland should be re-created there. In 1910, she became secretary of the Federation of American Zionists. In 1912, with other women from the Hadassah Study Circle, she established the Jewish women's voluntary organization Hadassah, which would become the largest Zionist organization in the world. Szold was elected its first president.

U.S. Supreme Court Justice Louis Brandeis and others believed so strongly in the work Szold was doing that they provided her with a lifetime income. She was able to continue her work without having to worry about earning a living. With a guaranteed income, Szold was able to resign from the Jewish Publication Society in 1916 at the age of 56. In 1918, Szold was named director of the education department of the national Zionist Organization of America.

Szold returned to Palestine in 1920 after her mother's death. There she served on the executive committee of the American Zionist Medical Unit. While in Palestine she also founded Histadrut Nashim Ivriot (the League of Jewish Women), a

collective of women's organizations. She was the group's first president.

Szold returned to the United States in 1923 and worked for Hadassah. In 1927, she was named as one of three members of the Palestine Zionist executive committee of the World Zionist Organization, the first woman to hold such a position.

In 1927, she returned to Palestine again and spent the remainder of her life there, except for occasional trips to the United States. Szold was elected to the executive committee of the Knesset Israel, the Palestinian Jewish National Assembly and served from 1931 to 1933. She was one of several prominent Zionists who supported a dual Jewish-Arab national identity for Palestine.

Szold helped 30,000 Jewish children escape from Nazi Germany and settle in Palestine between 1934 and 1948. She became a "mother" to thousands of young refugees from Nazi Germany. On her 80th birthday, in 1940, she founded the Szold Foundation, a child welfare and research institution.

Henrietta Szold died on February 13, 1945, in the Hadassah-Hebrew University hospital in Jerusalem. Thousands of her refugee children came to her funeral. The *New York Times* called her "the grand old lady of Palestine." The *Baltimore Sun* recognized her as "the foremost Jewish woman of modern time." Numerous Israeli children called her mother. She was buried in the cemetery at the Mount of Olives. During the Six-Day War in 1967, Arabs built roads through the cemetery that destroyed many grave markers, including Szold's. In 1968, Israel erected a new stone to mark her grave, placed next to the road in the cemetery. In Baltimore, a street was named after her, and her portrait was hung on a wall at the University of Maryland. A street was also named after her on New York City's Lower East Side.

As of 2001, nearly 400,000 members of Hadassah continue to raise money for hospitals and schools. Szold's legacy continues in the descendants of the 30,000 children she rescued.

Further Reading

Gidal, Tim. *Henrietta Szold: Documentation in Photos and Text.* Hewlett, N.Y.: Gefen Books, 1997.

Krantz, Hazel. *Daughter of My People: Henrietta Szold and Hadassah.* Northvale, N.J.: Jason Aronson, 1998.

Kustanowitz, Shulamit. *Henrietta Szold: Israel's Helping Hand.* New York: Viking, 1990.

Szold, Henrietta. *Henrietta Szold and Youth Aliyah: Family Letters, 1934–1944.* New York: Herzl Press, 1986.

T

TARBELL, IDA
(1857–1944) *Journalist*

Ida Tarbell, a journalist at *McClure's Magazine,* wrote a series of articles exposing the ruthless and monopolistic business practices of John D. Rockefeller and his Standard Oil Company. The work of Tarbell and other muckraking investigative journalists led to antitrust legislation in the Progressive era.

Ida Tarbell was born on November 5, 1857, in a log cabin in Erie County, Pennsylvania, to Esther Ann McCullough Tarbell and Franklin Sumner Tarbell. Her father supported Prohibition, and her mother supported women's rights. Her father worked as a teacher, river pilot, and joiner. He invented a wooden tank that held a hundred or more barrels of oil and became an independent oilman. When Tarbell was three years old, her family moved to Cherry Run, Pennsylvania.

Tarbell entered Allegheny College in Meadville, Pennsylvania, just before her 19th birthday. She was the only woman in her class. Tarbell served as editor of the college newspaper and completed a degree in biology in 1879. After graduation she worked as a teacher in Poland, Ohio, for a salary of $500 a year. Discovering that she did not like teaching, she quit in 1882. She also turned down a post teaching French and German at Allegheny College.

In 1883, at age 26 Tarbell became an editor of the monthly magazine of the Chautauqua movement, *The Chautauqua Assembly Herald.* The Chautauqua movement began as a training school for Sunday school teachers after the Civil War. It was named after the school's location at Chautauqua Lake in New York. By 1900 the Chautauqua school had expanded to 400 locations and featured a lecture circuit of speakers. It served as a form of adult education and entertainment. Its popularity declined by 1924 with the growth of movie theaters. Tarbell had never meant to be a journalist, however. She wrote at the time, "I had no inclination toward writing or toward editorial work. This was a stop-gap—nothing more." She translated articles from French literary magazines for U.S. publication. The *Assembly Herald* had a feminist tone, and its initial circulation of 15,000 grew to 50,000 under Tarbell's direction. After eight years in that position, Tarbell went to Paris to study at the Sorbonne.

She supported her studies in Paris by publishing articles in U.S. newspapers. "I had heard of newspaper syndicates, and it occurred to me that I might write articles in Paris and syndicate them. I hadn't the faintest idea of how to go about it. . . . I did persuade half a dozen editors to take articles from me at six dollars an article." She began writing from Paris for *McClure's Magazine,* a popular progressive journal known for its investigations into corporate and political corruption.

When she returned to the United States in 1894, Tarbell became an editor at *McClure's.* Her writings on Napoleon were published first as a series of articles in *McClure's* and then as a book in 1895. That was followed by a book based on her investigation of the role women played in the French Revolution, *Life of Madame Roland,* in 1896. Tarbell's articles on Abraham Lincoln from *McClure's* were published in book form in 1900.

Tarbell's most famous work was her exposé on John D. Rockefeller and the Standard Oil Company. Tarbell began her research on Rockefeller with an open mind. Her interest in the subject was encouraged by her own family history, since her father had been forced to mortgage the family home as a result of Standard Oil's consolidation of oil companies. (From 1870 to 1911, the Standard Oil Company controlled 95 percent of all oil production.) Her articles appeared serially in 16 issues of *McClure's,* beginning in 1902, and were published in the two-volume *History of the Standard Oil Company* in 1904. The book was an instant success. Her investigative journalism on the ruthless and monopolistic practices led to the Sherman Anti-Trust Act, the establishment by Congress of the Department of Commerce and the Bureau of Corporations. The subsequent government investigation led to the breakup of Standard Oil Company. In 1906 the federal government brought suit against Standard Oil under the Sherman Anti-Trust Act. In 1911 Standard Oil was ordered to divest 33 of the companies in its monopoly.

Tarbell left *McClure's* two years after her exposé on Standard Oil and in 1906 cofounded *American Magazine,* where she worked as coeditor until 1915.

Though she had published numerous pieces on the history of feminism in the United States and the exploitation of female workers in factories, as she aged Tarbell become more conservative and opposed suffrage for women. She worked with suffrage leaders in the burgeoning peace movement that accompanied World War I, however.

Her autobiography *All in the Day's Work* was published in 1939. She suffered from Parkinson's disease toward the end of her life.

Ida Tarbell died on January 6, 1944, in Bridgeport, Connecticut, of pneumonia. *The History of the Standard Oil Company* was ranked number five in a list of the top works of journalism in the 20th century by the *New York Times.* Her investigations of corporate misdeeds set a standard for journalists who followed in her footsteps.

Ida Tarbell, journalist, 1922
(Prints & Photographs Division,
Library of Congress, Washington, D.C.)

Further Reading

Brady, Kathleen. *Ida Tarbell: Portrait of a Muckraker.* Pittsburgh, Pa.: University of Pittsburgh Press, 1989.

Kochersberger, Robert Ed. *More Than a Muckraker: Ida Tarbell's Lifetime in Journalism.* Knoxville: University of Tennessee Press, 1996.

Tarbell, Ida. *History of the Standard Oil Company.* Temecula, Calif.: Reprint Services Corporation, 2001.

 ## TEMPLE, SHIRLEY

See BLACK, SHIRLEY JANE TEMPLE.

 ## TENAYUCA, EMMA
(1916–1999)   *Labor Leader*

Emma Tenayuca helped organize Mexican-American workers during the Great Depression in Texas. Her involvement in leftist politics informed her activism, although she was persecuted for those beliefs.

Emma Tenayuca was born on December 21, 1916, in San Antonio, Texas. Her mother's family name was Zepeda; she was descended from one of the original Spanish families in San Antonio. Her father was a South Texas Indian. She had little contact with her father's side of the family and in an interview claimed not to know much about their tribal ancestry. (Her father's family name was spelled Teneyuca but a mistake in spelling was made during baptism and so all her records used a spelling with the letter *a* instead of *e*.) Her parents had 11 children, and Emma lived with her grandparents to help ease their financial burdens.

In high school, Tenayuca was arrested when she joined picket lines in a labor strike at the Finck Cigar Company in 1932. She began reading works by socialist economist Karl Marx and Russian novelist Leo Tolstoy at this time. She graduated from Brackenride High School in 1934 and then worked as an elevator operator.

In 1934, Tenayuca helped organize two branches of the International Ladies' Garment Workers' Union and organized a group of unemployed people into the Workers Alliance. The Workers Alliance served as an extension of the Communist Party, staging demonstrations that demanded jobs for Spanish-speaking people. Tenayuca served as secretary to the 11 chapters in the San Antonio area and as the national organization's executive secretary. Under Tenayuca's leadership, the Workers Alliance protested deportations and harassment of immigrant workers by the border patrol. She joined the Communist Party in December of 1937 and remained a member for a year and a half.

San Antonio was the pecan capital of the United States. Pecan shellers, who were predominantly Mexican-American women, earned five cents a day. When management cut their wages to three cents a day, Tenayuca led the 12,000 workers in a strike in 1938. Tenayuca served as the strike representative until union officials from the United Cannery, Agricultural, Packing and Allied Workers of America removed her because of her Communist Party affiliation. For several months, 6,000 to 8,000 female workers continued to strike even though they were harassed and tear gassed, and 1,000 strikers were arrested. As Tenayuca recalled, "What started out as an organization for equal wages turned into a mass movement against starvation, for civil rights, for a minimum-wage law, and it changed the character of West Side San Antonio." The governor intervened, and wages were raised to prestrike levels.

In 1938, she married the leader of the Texas Communist Party and one-time gubernatorial candidate Homer Brooks. Her marriage lasted only a few years. In 1939, Tenayuca became the chair of the Texas Communist Party. In 1939, a small meeting of the Communist Party was scheduled at the San Antonio Municipal Auditorium. The group was attacked by a mob of 5,000. On that night, the Ku Klux Klan also tried to kill the mayor of San Antonio (and his family), who had issued the permit to allow the communists to meet in the auditorium. Tenayuca was hounded with death threats afterward and was blacklisted.

Unable to find work in San Antonio, Tenayuca moved briefly to Houston, Texas, and then to San

Francisco, California. During World War II, Tenayuca attempted to enlist in the Women's Army Corps but was rejected for unspecified reasons, more than likely because of her past Communist Party affiliation. She completed her teacher certification in 1952 and graduated magna cum laude from San Francisco State College. She gave birth to a son but never married again.

Tenayuca returned to Texas to teach elementary school in San Antonio in the late 1960s. She earned a master's degree in education from Our Lady of the Lake University in 1974. Tenayuca retired in 1982.

Emma Tenayuca died on July 23, 1999. A poem read at her funeral mass honored Tenayuca's contributions, "Because she was our heart,—defendiendo a los pobres (defender of the poor), speaking out at a time when neither Mexicans nor women were expected to speak at all."

Further Reading

Salas, Lesley. "El Corrido de Emma Tenayuca." *The Texas Observer* 87, no. 10 (May 19, 1995): 20.

Vargas, Zaragosa. "Tejana Radical: Emma Tenayuca and the San Antonio Labor Movement During the Great Depression." *Pacific Historical Review* 66, no. 4 (1997): 553–81.

 TERRELL, MARY ELIZABETH CHURCH (Mollie Church)
(1863–1954) *Founder of the National Association of Colored Women*

Mary Church Terrell was the founding president of the National Association of Colored Women. She continued to organize against racism and segregation into her 80s.

Mary Elizabeth Church (called Mollie) was born on September 23, 1863, in Memphis, Tennessee, to former slaves Louisa Ayres Church and Robert Reed Church. She had one younger brother. Her mother had been a house slave before emancipation and afterward started a very successful beauty shop in Memphis. Her father, the son of a white man, Captain Charles Church, worked on his father's Mississippi River boats and then opened a saloon in Memphis. During race riots in Memphis in 1866 her father was shot in the head but survived. He was a shrewd businessman who bought land after a yellow fever epidemic drove prices down. By the 1880s, he was one of the South's first African-American millionaires.

After her parents' divorce, she attended a boarding school at Antioch College in Yellow Springs, Ohio, for two years. She graduated from high school in Oberlin, Ohio, in 1879, then enrolled in the four-year classical curriculum rather than the two-year "ladies course" at Oberlin College. Founded by abolitionists, Oberlin was one of the few integrated institutions in the United States. She was often the only woman and the only African American in her classes. She completed her bachelor's degree in 1884 and her master's degree in 1885 from Oberlin, making her one of the best-educated African-American women in the nation.

After graduating from Oberlin in 1884 she returned to Memphis. Her father forbade her to work but she thought differently and accepted a teaching position at Wilberforce University in Xenia, Ohio. She taught Latin at the M Street High School in Washington, D.C., in 1887, then spent two years traveling in Europe from 1888 to 1890. She considered living overseas permanently because of the absence of racial barriers them compared to the United States.

She married Harvard-educated attorney Robert Heberton Terrell, a supervisor from the M Street High School, in 1891. Her skin was so light that she was often mistaken for white. Her marriage ended her teaching career, since women were not allowed to continue teaching after marriage. Terrell suffered three miscarriages before giving birth in 1898 to a daughter, whom she named after early African-American poet Phillis Wheatley. She also raised a niece. In 1901, Theodore Roosevelt appointed her husband as the only African-American federal judge, a position he held until his death in 1925.

For 11 years, beginning in 1895, Terrell served as a member of the District of Columbia Board of

Education, the first African-American woman to serve in such a position.

In 1896, Terrell become president of the National Association of Colored Women, a self-help organization. She served three terms. The group established kindergartens and day care for African-American working mothers.

She spoke at the 1898 National American Woman Suffrage Association (NAWSA) convention. In her speech she spoke of the double burden of prejudice that African-American women faced. "A white woman has only one handicap to overcome—a great one, true, her sex; a colored woman faces two—her sex and her race. A colored man has only one—that of race."

In 1908, she delivered speeches for NAWSA during its celebration of the 60th anniversary of the Seneca Falls Women's Rights Convention. She was a member of the National Association for the

Mary Church Terrell, civil rights leader
(Still Picture Branch, National Archives, College Park, MD)

Advancement of Colored People (NAACP) and lectured on the topic of lynching. She usually sided with the radical views of civil rights leader W. E. B. DuBois in debates within the NAACP.

Terrell joined the National Woman's Party suffrage picket of the White House in 1919 and served on the executive committee of the Women's International League for Peace and Freedom, founded in the wake of World War I.

She published her autobiography *A Colored Woman in a White World*, in 1940. She was the leader of the Enforcement of the District of Columbia Anti-discrimination Laws Coordinating Committee and undertook several actions in this capacity. At age 85, she successfully sued the American Association of University Women (AAUW) over the group's segregation policies. In 1950, she joined picket lines and sit-ins that were attempting to desegregate Washington, D.C., restaurants. When she was 89, she sued in *District of Columbia v. John Thompson* under 1870s Reconstruction-era laws that had never been repealed. To see if the antidiscrimination laws were being enforced, she and three others—two black, one white—requested service at Thompson's Restaurant. All three blacks were denied service, and they filed affidavits against the restaurant. She got involved in other cases of discrimination during the time of the court case. For instance, she began picketing and boycotting Hecht's department store, and thousands became aware of inequalities through banners and leaflets. She also got wide support from civic and social organizations. During the whole two-month-long Thompson trial she was harassed with derogatory letters and threatening phone calls. Her case achieved success and in 1953 the U.S. Supreme Court banned discrimination in public accommodations in the District of Columbia.

Two months before her 91st birthday, Mary Church Terrell died of cancer on July 24, 1954, in Annapolis, Maryland. Her funeral was held at the Lincoln Temple Congregational Church. She is buried at Lincoln Memorial Cemetery in Suitland, Maryland. Her papers are stored at the Library of

Congress and in the Moorland-Spingarn Collection at Howard University in Washington, D.C. A Washington, D.C., school was named in her honor. She summarized her life philosophy: "I will not shrink from undertaking what seems wise and good because I labor under the double handicap of race and sex, but, striving to preserve a calm mind with a courageous and cheerful spirit, barring bitterness from my heart, I will struggle all the more earnestly to reach the goal."

Further Reading

Jones, Beverly Washington. *Quest for Equality: The Life and Writings of Mary Church Terrell*. Brooklyn, N.Y.: Carlson Publishers, 1990.

Terrell, Mary Church. *Colored Woman in a White World*. 1940. Reprint, New York: G. K. Hall, 1996.

 THORPE, GRACE (No Ten O Quah, "Wind Woman")
(1921–   )   *Sac and Fox Red Power Movement and Environmental Activist*

Grace Thorpe, a member of the Sac and Fox tribes, rose to national prominence as an American Indian leader during the late 1960s Red Power movement of young urban Indians. She continued her activism into the 1990s as a leader of the Native American environmental movement. Thorpe was descended from Chief Black Hawk, a leader in the 1832 Black Hawk War. Her father, Jim Thorpe, won the decathlon and pentathlon in the 1912 Olympic games. Her father's medals were confiscated by the Olympic committee a year after his victory for a technical transgression regarding his brief involvement with semiprofessional baseball prior to the Olympics. Many suspected he had been targeted because he was Indian.

The youngest of three daughters, Grace Thorpe was born in Yale, Oklahoma, to Jim and Iva Thorpe in 1921. She went to the same Indian boarding school that her father had attended in Carlisle, Pennsylvania. Later, during World War II, she joined the Women's Army Corps (WACs).

Thorpe was a U.S. corporal stationed in New Guinea and Japan at the end of the war, and she served on the staff of General Douglas MacArthur. She was married to Fred Seeley for a brief time while in Japan. With two children, her daughter, Dagmar, and son, Thorpe, she returned to the United States to live in Pearl River, New York, in the 1950s. In Pearl River, she worked selling Yellow Pages ads to businesses.

Thorpe moved to California and began her activism with the 1969 American Indian occupation on Alcatraz Island. The goal of the occupation was to draw attention to the plight of American Indians and to gain title to the abandoned land. The 19-month occupation of the island, which began in November 1969 and ended in June 1971, garnered national and international coverage and became the spark that ignited the Red Power movement. As Thorpe recalled, "Alcatraz made me put my furniture into storage and spend my life savings." Many historians incorrectly state that the American Indian Movement (AIM), formed in Minneapolis in 1968, led the occupation. Although young Indians from throughout the country, including some members of AIM, traveled to Alcatraz, the occupation was led by young, urban American Indian students from California campuses. They occupied the island, and bay area community members provided the necessary support from the mainland. The support from community members on the mainland was crucial, because Alcatraz, formerly a federal prison, had been shut down for several years and had no running water or electricity—living conditions similar to those found on many reservations, as the occupiers pointed out. Every necessity, including water and food, had to be brought in by supporters past a U.S. Coast Guard blockade.

Thorpe was 48 years old at the time of the Alcatraz occupation, an elder compared to the student occupiers. She negotiated with the federal government for a power generator, water barge, and ambulance service for the island. The ambulance service was in great demand, since numerous injuries occurred due to the crumbling building. She also coordinated publicity for the occupation, handling press releases and arranging visits by sympathetic Hollywood stars such as Jane Fonda, Marlon Brando, Anthony Quinn, and Candice Bergen. The Alcatraz protest was the longest continuous occupation by American Indians, though it did not achieve the occupiers' goal of ownership of the island. American Indians recognized the significance of the occupation, which helped to end the government policy of Termination (which attempted to end official recognition, or terminate, various tribes), and marches by Indian groups still use Alcatraz as their starting point.

Seventy-four shorter occupations by American Indians followed Alcatraz. Thorpe continued her activism by serving as a press liaison for the March 1970 occupation at Fort Lawton, Washington, which was successful in securing land for the Daybreak Star Cultural Center. She also served as press liaison for an occupation of the old, 640-acre Nike missile base near Davis, California, in November 1970. That occupation resulted in the building of an Indian university, an objective the earlier occupiers on Alcatraz had tried to achieve. The Davis occupation successfully secured the site of Deganawidah-Quetzalcoatl (DQ) University by April 1971, the first university for American Indian and Chicano students.

While residing in California, Thorpe also participated in the struggle of Pit River Indians to hold their sacred land in northern California against the wishes of the federal government and the Pacific Gas and Electric Company, a large energy corporation. Reportedly, in one confrontation with police, nearly a dozen officers were needed to carry Thorpe off the property. Pit River Indians had refused a $29.1 million settlement by the government for their traditional lands. In 1972, a settlement was reached that included partial land restoration and a monetary payment.

Thorpe left California to work as a lobbyist for the National Congress of American Indians (NCAI), the largest American Indian civil rights organization in the nation. In that position she tried to persuade factories to locate on reservations in order to provide more jobs for Indians, allowing families to remain on the land. In 1971, she cofounded the National Indian Women's Action Corps. In 1974, the U.S. Senate Subcommittee on Indian Affairs hired her as its legislative assistant. She later served for two years in the U.S. House of Representatives on the American Indian Policy Review Board. During this time she also furthered her education, receiving a paralegal certificate in 1974 from the Antioch School of Law, and a bachelor's degree in 1980 from the University of Tennessee, Knoxville.

Thorpe returned to the Sac and Fox Reservation in Oklahoma in 1980 and served as a district court judge for the Five Tribes of Oklahoma and also as a health commissioner.

Thorpe served as vice president of the Jim Thorpe Foundation and, with her sister Charlotte, lobbied for restoration of her father's Olympic medals. In 1983, 30 years after her father's death, the International Olympic Committee annulled its previous decree and presented gold medals to the Thorpe family.

In her 60s, with income only from her social security checks, she started a fight against what she called "radioactive racism" when her own tribal government considered storing nuclear waste on their land. The federal government and private industry were exerting pressure and offering money to numerous tribes, trying to persuade them to store nuclear waste on their reservations. Thorpe and other community members convinced their tribal council to withdraw its application for consideration of a nuclear waste repository on reservation land, though it could have brought millions of dollars a year to the reservation.

In 1993, she founded the National Environmental Coalition of Native Americans (NECONA), which urged tribes to establish nuclear-free zones on their reservations. Thorpe's organization was so successful that by 1998 only two tribes, the Ft. McDermitt Paiutes and Skull Valley Goshutes, were still considering nuclear waste storage.

Grace Thorpe built on the proud heritage of her father's accomplishments and changed environmental policy across the nation. She has remained an activist throughout her life.

Further Reading

Berman, Susan. "Working for My People: Thorpe's Daughter Indian Activist." *Akwesasne Notes* 3 (March 1971): 27.

National Environmental Coalition of Native Americans. Available online. URL: http://oraibi.alphacdc.com/ necona. Downloaded December 6, 2000.

Thorpe, Grace. "The Jim Thorpe Family History: From Wisconsin to Indian Territory." Part I. *Chronicles of Oklahoma* 59 (spring 1981): 91–105.

Weaver, Jace. *Defending Mother Earth: Native American Perspective on Environment Justice.* Maryknoll, N.Y.: Orbis Books, 1996.

 TRUTH, SOJOURNER (Isabella Baumfree) (1797–1883)   *Abolitionist, Supporter of Women's Suffrage and Temperance*

Sojourner Truth lectured on abolition, woman suffrage, and temperance. She was a renowned orator whose speeches continue to inspire new generations of feminists.

Isabella Baumfree was born in 1797 in Hurley, New York. At that time African-Americans composed 15 percent of the New York population. Her parents were enslaved and were simply known as Elizabeth and James. She was the 11th of 13 children. Her family ate and slept in the cellar of the house, and when it rained, their floor became a pool of mud. When her father became too old to work, his master sent him to a cabin in the woods, where he starved to death in the winter.

As a child Isabella was sold four times. She was sold away from her family when she was nine. Her first language was Dutch, which she spoke until she was 10. When she was sold to an English-speaking family, the Nealys, they interpreted her inability to follow orders as stubbornness. Mr. Nealy heated metal rods over red-hot coals and beat her with the rods until her back was covered in blood. She later said that working for the Nealy family was like being in a war. She carried the physical scars from her treatment as a slave for the rest of her life.

She next worked for John Dumont in 1810. When she was 14 years old, Isabella was married to another of Dumont's slaves, an older man named Thomas. Thomas had been married twice before but both his other wives had been sold. Marriage was often forced upon slaves in order to encourage the reproduction of offspring who could then be sold. The couple had five children. One of their children died early and others were sold into slavery.

She took her daughter and ran away from Dumont in 1827. She went to work for a Quaker couple, Maria and Isaac Van Wagener, who purchased her and her daughter's freedom for $25 (Quakers were members of the Society at Friends religious denomination, which was strongly antislavery.) For a short time she used their last name. Of her enslavement she would later state, "All the gold in California, all the wealth of this nation could not restore to me what the white people have taken from me."

In 1828, she filed a lawsuit for the freedom of her son, who had been sold (illegally, under New York law) when he was five years old to a buyer in Alabama. Isabella went to court in Kingston, New York, and successfully sued for his return.

She supported herself as a domestic worker in New York City from 1828 to 1843. She began to preach at camp meetings held around the city. She joined the John Street Methodist Church in New York City. As she stated, "I like the Quakers, but they wouldn't let me sing, so I joined the Methodists." She worked in the Magdalene Society, a mission to prostitutes.

In 1843, she became an itinerant preacher after having a series of visions. It was at this time that she changed her name to Sojourner Truth and began 40 years of preaching. Regarding her name change, she said, "The Lord gave me Sojourner because I was to travel up and down the land, showing people their sins, and being a sign unto them." She took the last name of Truth because it was the name God was called in the Bible. She completed much of her travel on foot, because African Americans were not allowed on public coaches or trains.

In 1846, she began to speak for the abolitionist cause. After hearing American antislavery leader William Lloyd Garrison speak, she decided that

Sojourner Truth, abolitionist
(Prints & Photographs Division,
Library of Congress, Washington, D.C.)

if it were delivered in a southern dialect, but it is doubtful that this was Truth's actual speech pattern, since she was raised in upstate New York and her first language was Dutch. Truth responded to comments made by a clergyman that women did not deserve the same rights as men because they were weaker. "That man over there says that women need to be helped into carriages, and lifted over ditches, and to have the best place everywhere. . . . Nobody ever helps me into carriages, or over mud puddles, or gives me any best place, and aren't I a woman? Look at me! Look at my arm! I have plowed, and planted, and gathered into barns, and no man could heed me—an aren't I a woman? I could work as much and eat as much as a man, when I could get it, and bear the lash as well—and aren't I a woman?" When another minister made the mistake of arguing that women were inferior because God had made Jesus a man, Truth retorted, "Where did your Christ come from? From God and a woman. Man had nothing to do with him."

Truth moved to Battle Creek, Michigan, in 1856 after Henry Willis, a Quaker, brought her to speak there. In 1858, a man in an audience challenged her gender and demanded that she prove she was a woman. She bared her breast in public to a shamed audience.

In 1863, Truth went to Washington, D.C., to assist African-American refugees fleeing the Civil War in the South. Thousands of African Americans fled to the capital during the war, thinking they would be safe and free there. In 1864, the National Freedman's Relief Association hired her to counsel freed slaves. The National Freedman's Relief Association was part of the Freedmen's Aid Society, which grew out of the Freedman's Bureau Agency. The government had founded the Freedmen's Bureau Agency to help former slaves find jobs and homes.

After a conductor dislocated her shoulder while trying to evict her from a streetcar, Truth filed a lawsuit in Washington, D.C., in 1865 that successfully affirmed the right of African Americans to use public transportation. In 1867, she initiated a job

God wanted her also to speak against slavery. Speeches were a popular form of entertainment before movies were invented. Attending them did not cost much, and many people looked forward to hearing speakers, just as many people today look forward to the opening of new movies.

In 1850, Truth dictated her autobiography, *The Narrative of Sojourner Truth.* Slave narratives gained sympathy for the abolitionist cause and dispelled widely touted myths that slaves were content with their condition and well cared for by their masters.

The most famous speech Truth made was before a woman's rights convention in Akron, Ohio, in 1851. Newspaper reporters recorded it as placement effort for the freed refugees. Truth drafted a petition to Congress to demand that western land be set aside for freed slaves. She gathered signatures for her petition for two years but nothing ever came from it. However, scores of African American southerners migrated to the free state of Kansas spontaneously. Truth traveled extensively for two years, from New England to as far west as Kansas, campaigning for the western lands. Her efforts failed to get Congress to act. By the end of the decade, however, waves of blacks known as the Exodusters left the South in search of opportunity and freedom in the West, and to escape racial prejudice and violence. Approximately 20,000 came to Kansas. There may be a casual relationship between the efforts of Truth, and others, and the Kansas migration.

After the Civil War, ELIZABETH CADY STANTON recruited Truth to lecture for the woman's suffrage movement. When the Fifteenth Amendment gave suffrage to African American males but not to women, Truth objected, "There is a great stir about colored men getting their rights, but not a word about the colored women and if colored men get their rights, and not colored women theirs, you see the colored men will be masters over the women, and it will be just as bad as it was before."

In 1872, she attempted to vote in a local election, nearly 50 years before women achieved suffrage. She was turned away at the polling booth in Grand Rapids, Michigan.

A few years before her death she began to have problems with leg ulcers, which she tried to fix by using medicine made for horses. The horse medicine caused terrible fevers to rack her body. Of her illness, Truth said, "I'm not going to die, honey; I'm going home like a shooting star." During her lifetime she liked to claim to be older than she really was because she thought old age earned her more respect.

Sojourner Truth died on November 26, 1883, in Battle Creek, Michigan, at age 86. Some 1,000 people attended her funeral service. She was buried at Oak Hill Cemetery in Battle Creek. The question "Is God Dead?" is inscribed on her tombstone; she

had asked this question of Frederick Douglass when he was despondent. The public made donations to erect a marker at her graveside in 1891, which deteriorated and was replaced with a second marker in 1916, followed by a third in 1946. The Sojourner Truth Association placed a historical marker at her grave in 1961. A section of Michigan's North Highway 66 was named in her honor, and in 1986 a U.S. postage stamp was issued in her honor as part of the Black Heritage series.

Her famous "Aren't I a Woman" speech remains a powerful statement to today's feminists, 150 years after it was delivered.

Further Reading

Fitch, Suzanne Pullon, and Roseann Mandziuk. *Sojourner Truth as Orator, Wit, Story and Song.* London: Greenwood Press, 1997.

Mabee, Carleton, and Susan Mabee Newhouse. *Sojourner Truth Slave, Prophet, Legend.* New York: New York University Press, 1993.

Painter, Nell Irvin. *Sojourner Truth: A Life, a Symbol.* New York: Norton, 1996.

Samra, Matthew. "Shadow and Substance: The Two Narratives of Sojourner Truth." *Midwest Quarterly* 38 (winter 1997): 158–71.

Stetson, Erlene, and Linda David. *Glorying in Tribulation: The Lifework of Sojourner Truth.* East Lansing: Michigan State University Press, 1994.

Truth, Sojourner. *Narrative of Sojourner Truth: A Bondswoman of Olden Time, With a History of Her Labors and Correspondence Drawn from Her "Book of Life."* Reprint. New York: Penguin, 1998.

 TUBMAN, HARRIET ARAMINTA GREENE
(1820–1913)   *Abolitionist, Underground Railroad Conductor*

Harriet Tubman served as a scout, spy, and nurse during the Civil War. After escaping to freedom in the North, she returned to the South to free hundreds of enslaved African Americans, earning herself the name "Moses" among her people. She also supported women's suffrage.

Araminta Greene was born in 1820 in Dorchester County, Maryland, to Harriet Greene and

Benjamin Ross Greene, both slaves. Her master named her Araminta at birth, but she later took her mother's name. She was one of 11 children. When she was 13, an angry overseer fractured her skull. As a result of the injury, she suffered spells of narcoleptic seizures throughout her life, sometimes several each day.

In 1844, when she was 24 years old, she married John Tubman, a free African American. When her master died she discovered plans to sell her, so she escaped by herself to Philadelphia in 1849, supporting herself as a domestic.

The Underground Railroad was a system of routes, safe houses, and supporters in the northern states before the Civil War, who helped enslaved African Americans escape to live in the U.S. North or in Canada. As a conductor on the Underground Railroad, over a 10-year period Tubman made 19 return trips to the South at great personal risk to rescue others who were enslaved. She donned a variety of disguises to escape detection. In one case she appeared as an apparently mentally impaired homeless man, and another time she showed up as an old woman chasing hens down the street. She often chose Saturday night for a rescue, because an extra day would elapse before a notice about the runaways could appear in the papers. Tubman carried a sedative to silence crying babies and a gun to prevent those having second thoughts from trying to return. She often took her passengers on the Underground Railroad as far as Canada to ensure their freedom. The North Star was used as a point for navigation along their route to freedom. Tubman never lost a passenger. She allegedly freed nearly 300 slaves, including many in her family, although her husband never joined her in the North. Maryland slaveholders offered a $40,000 reward for her capture.

When the Civil War began, Tubman volunteered for the Union army. She served with distinction, becoming the only woman in American history to plan and execute an armed expedition. One of her most famous raids occurred in 1863 at the Combahee River in South Carolina, where she commanded soldiers on a raiding expedition that freed 700 slaves. She crossed Confederate lines to obtain vital information from southern African Americans who, as servants, were often in positions to overhear their white owners' conversations. She served as a nurse without pay during the war and afterward in a Virginia hospital set up to care for newly freed slaves.

Tubman founded the Harriet Tubman Home to care for African-American orphans and the elderly. After her husband's death in 1867, she married a Civil War veteran and former slave, Nelson Davis, in 1869. Following the Civil War, Tubman dictated her story to a friend who wrote her biography, *Scenes in the Life of Harriet Tubman,* in 1869.

When the suffrage movement split over the Fifteenth Amendment, which granted suffrage to African-American males but not to any women,

Harriet Tubman in a picture by
Bernardo Bryson, 1934
(Prints & Photographs Division, Library of Congress,
Washington, D.C.)

Tubman sided with ELIZABETH CADY STANTON and SUSAN B. ANTHONY, who objected to the Fifteenth Amendment.

Tubman helped establish the National Association of Colored Women. She was denied payment by Congress for her wartime services, but after the death of her second husband she was granted a pension of $20 a month as a veteran's widow.

Harriet Tubman died of pneumonia on March 10, 1913, in Auburn, New York. She received full military honors at her funeral. In 1974, the Department of Interior made the Harriet Tubman Home a national historic landmark. In 1978, the U.S. Postal Service issued its first stamp in the Black Heritage USA Series, which bore Tubman's image. In 1990, Congress passed Senate Joint Resolution 257 in observance of Harriet Tubman Day on the 77th anniversary of her death. A bill was introduced in Congress in the summer of 2000 to recognize Tubman's heroic Civil War service.

A bronze plaque on her Auburn home reads, "On my Underground Railroad I never ran my train off the track. And I never lost a passenger."

Further Reading

"Bill Introduced in Congress to Recognize Harriet Tubman's Civil War Heroics." *Jet* 98 no. 11 (August 21, 2000): 24–25.

Bisson, Terry. *Harriet Tubman.* New York: Chelsea House, 1990.

Bradford, Sarah Elizabeth. *Harriet Tubman the Moses of Her People.* Magnolia, Me: Peter Smith Publishing, 1961.

McMullan, Kate. *The Story of Harriet Tubman: Conductor of the Underground Railroad.* New York: Dell, 1991.

 VAID, URVASHI
(1958–)   *Political Activist, Writer*

As executive director of the National Gay and Lesbian Task Force (NGLTF), Urvashi Vaid attracted increased media coverage to the burgeoning gay and lesbian civil rights movement.

Urvashi Vaid was born on October 8, 1958, in New Delhi, India. When she was eight, her family moved to the United States after her father, a novelist, accepted a teaching position at the State University of New York at Potsdam.

Vaid was politically astute at an early age. One of her first political protests occurred when she participated in an antiwar demonstration when she was 11 years old. She recalled that her immigrant status marked her as an outsider in childhood. "I was a very awkward young girl. I spoke with an Indian accent. I had these very thick glasses. I had long hair, very thick, straight hair, Indian hair, down to my waist. . . . I lived a lot in my head."

Vaid attended Vassar College on a scholarship, where she became involved in feminist groups. In 1979, she interned on a women's prison project. She completed a bachelor's degree in English and political science in 1979. After graduation she worked as a legal secretary in Boston until entering Northeastern University School of Law in Boston in 1980. In 1982, she cofounded the Boston Lesbian/Gay Political Alliance, a group that evaluated and endorsed political candidates. She completed a law degree in 1983 and found employment as a staff attorney at the American Civil Liberties Union (ACLU).

Vaid worked on the National Prison Project for the ACLU in Washington, D.C. Her work brought class action civil rights lawsuits to change injustices in the prison system. In 1984, she began working with prisoners who suffered from AIDS in efforts to protect their civil rights.

Vaid first became involved with the NGLTF, one of the nation's oldest and largest lesbian gay civil rights organizations, in 1985 when she began serving on its board of directors. She had valuable insights to offer the group. "As a woman who is a lesbian, who's out, and who's a woman of color—it's not possible for me to divorce the prejudice I experience one from the other," she said. In the following year she became director of public information for the NGLTF and served in that position for three years. Vaid increased the group's visibility in the media by "making sure that gay issues were going to be . . . in the media's face, and [we] hatched a lot of plots to do that."

In 1989, Vaid became the executive director of NGLTF. Under her tenure the group's budget increased threefold from $700,000 to $2 million. She was a supporter of direct-action protests advocated by radical gay lesbian civil rights groups. Frustrated with the lack of progress on public policy regarding AIDS during Republican administrations, Vaid interrupted President George H. W. Bush's first speech on AIDS in 1990 by holding up a sign that read, "Talk Is Cheap, AIDS Funding Is Not." Police escorted her out of the room. In 1991, she was arrested while protesting against the U.S. Supreme Court *Webster v. Reproductive Health Services* decision, which restricted abortion laws.

She cofounded the first national gay and lesbian political conference, the NGLTF Creating Change conference, and moved the organization to a more active presence in the 1988 and 1992 presidential campaigns. Her vision was expansive: "As a lesbian of color, I can't help but bring more than one identity and more than one issue to the table, and try to lead our movement not just on this narrow issue called homosexuality but on this larger thing called oppression."

In 1992, Vaid left NGLTF to move to Provincetown, Massachusetts, and begin work on a book. Her articles have appeared in the *Nation,* the *Advocate,* and the *New Republic.* Her book *Virtual Equality: The Mainstreaming of Gay and Lesbian Liberation* was published in 1995. In summarizing the difference her work has made, Vaid stated, "We've made huge progress, I don't mean to put a negative spin on all this—there's been a tremendous momentum that's been built up today—but we really have a long way to go." That distance has been made somewhat shorter by the work of Urvashi Vaid.

Further Reading

Cusac, Anne-Marie. "Urvashi Vaid." *Progressive* 60 (March 1996): 34–38.

Schulman, Sarah, and Urvashi Vaid. *My American History: Lesbian and Gay Life During the Reagan/Bush Years.* New York: Routledge, 1994.

Torregrosa, Luisita Lopez. "The Gay Nineties." *Vanity Fair* (May 1993): 124–29.

Vaid, Urvashi. *Virtual Equality: The Mainstreaming of Gay and Lesbian Liberation.* New York: Doubleday Books, 1996.

W

 WARD, NANCY (Nanye-Hi, "One Who Goes About," Tsistunga-gis-ke, "Wild Rose")
(ca. 1738–ca. 1822)   *Cherokee Tribal Leader*

Nancy Ward was the last Ghigau, or "Beloved Woman," an honorary leadership position in the Cherokee Nation.

Nanye-Hi was born in 1738 in Echota, called variously the sacred capital, peace town, or "Mother Town" of the Cherokee. Her mother was Tame Deer; her father, Fivekiller, was part Lenni Lenape, or Delaware. Her nickname was Tsistunga-gis-ke ("Wild Rose") because her skin color was a delicate pink. She was a member of the Wolf Clan and niece of Chief Attakullakulla, or Little Carpenter. The Cherokee Nation was one of the largest American Indian tribes in population and geographical size, covering territory in what are now the states of Kentucky, Tennessee, Virginia, North Carolina, South Carolina, Alabama, and Georgia.

Nanye-Hi married another Cherokee, Kingfisher, while in her teens, and had two children.

She accompanied her husband to battle and prepared firearms at his side. In 1755, she accompanied her husband in a group of 500 warriors to the Battle of Taliwa against Muskogean Creek in northern Georgia. When her husband was killed, 18-year-old Nanye-Hi picked up his weapon and led a charge against the enemy. The Cherokee viewed her brave leadership as the determining factor in their victory. In recognition she was named Beloved Woman, an institutionalized leadership position for women in the tribe. It was believed that the Great Spirit used the voice of the Beloved Woman to speak to the Cherokee.

The Cherokee were matrilineal, and Cherokee women had a great deal more status and power than European-American women of the same period. Americans referred to the Cherokee system as a "petticoat government" because of the prominent role women had in civil and war councils. The position of Beloved Woman was a lifetime distinction and the highest office to which a Cherokee woman might be selected. As a Beloved Woman, Nanye-Hi held a voting position on the General Council, led the Women's

Council, had decision-making rights regarding the fate of prisoners, and served as the tribe's ambassador and negotiator. She spoke for her nation in negotiations with the U.S. government and counseled against land cessions and removal to the West.

When militant Cherokee prepared to attack a white settlement on the Watauga River, she warned several settlers so that they could escape. One of the captives taken in this battle, Mrs. Bean, had her life spared by Nanye-Hi. It was reported that the Beloved Woman stated, "No woman shall be tortured or burned at the stake while I am honored woman." Mrs. Bean taught Nanye-Hi how to weave and prepare dairy foods, two skills that allowed the Cherokee to be less dependent on traders.

When she entered peace talks in 1781 at Little Pigeon River in Tennessee with state representatives, she asked the officials to take the treaty back to their women for ratification. The white men were upset that a woman had been sent to negotiate with them; she was disappointed that they had not brought their women to the meeting. Among the Cherokee, women had veto and ratification power regarding decisions of war and peace. She stated further, "This peace must last forever. Let your women's sons be ours; our sons be yours. Let your women hear our words." She negotiated the first treaty the Cherokee made with the new U.S. government in 1785, the Treaty of Hopewell.

In 1808, under her leadership, the women's council made a statement protesting the sale of tribal lands and instructing the men to keep their "hands off white man's paper talks." She protested proposed removals to the West. In an 1817 document she sent to the general council, she wrote, "We do not wish to go to an unknown country, which we have understood some of our children wish to go over the Mississippi, but this act of our children would be like destroying your mothers." Several years after Kingfisher's death, she married Irish-Scots trader Bryant Ward, and

the couple had one child. They ran an inn near Echota on the Ocowee River, in eastern Tennessee, and eventually separated. Ward returned to live in Chota in 1824 and was cared for in her old age by her son.

According to some sources, Nancy Ward died on November 19, 1822. Her grave is located in Polk County near Benton, Tennessee. Her father, Fivekiller, was buried nearby. Ward died before her people were removed to western lands in the present-day state of Oklahoma, in 1838, on a forced march called the Trail of Tears during which one in four Cherokee died.

In 1915, a chapter of the Daughters of the American Revolution (DAR) named their society in her honor. In 1923, this DAR chapter placed a pyramid of quartz fieldstones and a bronze tablet over her grave. The story of Nancy Ward's position of leadership in her nation provides a stark contrast to the status of European American women of the same time period.

Further Reading

Alderman, Pat. *Nancy Ward.* Johnson City, Tenn.: Overmountain Press, 1978.

A Celebration of Women. "Nancy Ward." Available online. URL: http://pages.ancientsites.com/~Neenah Amaru/Nancy.html. Downloaded on December 8, 2000.

Cherokee Nation. "Nancy Ward." Available online. URL: http://www.suite101.com/article.cfm/cherokee nation/32053. Downloaded on December 8, 2000.

Sonneborn, Liz. *A to Z of Native American Women.* New York: Facts On File, 1998.

WATERS, MAXINE MOORE
(1938–)   *Congressional Representative*

Maxine Waters was elected to the U.S. House of Representatives in 1990, representing south central Los Angeles. A forthright manner and liberal disposition are her trademarks.

Maxine Moore was born on August 15, 1938, in St. Louis, Missouri, to Velma Lee Carr Moore and Remus Moore. The fifth of 13 children, she was raised in a housing project. Her parents divorced when she was two years old, and her mother remarried. Maxine began working at age 13 at a segregated restaurant. She participated in music, track, and swimming in high school. Her high school yearbook predicted that she would serve as Speaker of the House one day.

After graduating from high school in 1956, she married her high school sweetheart, Edward Waters, had two children, and worked in factories. The family moved to Los Angeles, California, in 1961 where Waters worked in a garment factory and for the telephone company.

After the 1965 riots in the Watts section at Los Angeles, Waters worked as an assistant teacher in Head Start, a national program that provided early schooling to children from poor families. She completed her degree in sociology at California State University, Los Angeles, in 1972. She divorced her husband in 1972, and five years later she married Sidney Williams, a former Cleveland Browns football player who was U.S. ambassador to the Bahamas. Her mother had been active in local politics, and Waters became involved with local politics as well. She served as chief deputy to Los Angeles city council member David Cunningham from 1973 to 1976.

Waters first campaigned for the California state assembly in 1976. She planned a campaign that reached out to African-American women. Waters recalled, "They would say, 'Well, honey, you may as well run, the men haven't done anything, you know.'" In 1976, Waters was elected to the California state assembly from south central Los Angeles. She served in this position for 14 years.

As a state legislator, she authored a bill to divest California state pension funds from South African businesses because of that nation's apartheid policies. She sponsored legislation to prevent law enforcement officers from conducting strip searches on persons arrested for misdemeanors. She also sponsored the first child abuse prevention training program in the nation. *Essence* magazine noted her effectiveness as a legislator and wrote, "If

Maxine Waters maneuvers as easily among the makers and shapers of public policy on Capitol Hill as she does among the welfare mothers, blue-collar workers and street toughs in Watts, it's because she knows, firsthand, what it's like at both ends of the spectrum."

For Waters one of the greatest experiences of her life was attending the National Women's Conference in Houston, Texas, in 1977. When Waters entered the state assembly, she immediately challenged the way female representatives were addressed as "assemblyman." Some saw her feminist stances as threatening. She was quoted as saying, "Oh, I got raked through the coals. Some people even said I was trying to neuter the men."

In 1980, at the Democratic National Convention, she seconded the nomination of Senator Edward Kennedy for president. In 1981, Waters became majority whip. She was the first woman in California to be elected chair of the Democratic Caucus, the fourth-highest leadership position in the state. In 1984, she was a cofounder of the National Political Congress of Black Women, a group formed to promote the political participation of African-American women. In 1984 and 1988, she seconded the nomination of Reverend Jesse Jackson for president at the Democratic National Convention.

Waters was elected in 1990 to the U.S. House of Representatives with 80 percent of the vote. She joined the only other African-American female in Congress at the time, CARDISS COLLINS of Chicago. Waters's constituency was largely African-American and Latino, in a district that included south central Los Angles, Inglewood, Hawthorne, and Gardena. One of the most liberal members of Congress, Waters pushed passage of legislation to create a center for women veterans within the Department of Veterans Affairs.

In 1992, during Water's first term in Congress, riots broke out in Watts following the acquittal of four white police officers who had been charged with beating an African-American motorist, Rodney King. The beating was captured on videotape and broadcast repeatedly on national TV. Waters's office was burned, along with other sections of the community. After the riot, she worked tirelessly to bring resources and stability to the community. At one point she invited herself to a White House meeting of the Bush administration on Watts, because she thought a person of color needed to be there. In response to the riots she stated, "Listen up America! If there is no justice, there will be no peace."

Waters once told a male congressman to shut up, telling him, "The day is over when men can intimidate and badger women." She reflected on her political style in a speech at the 1992 Democratic National Convention, "I'm a member of the House of Representatives of the U.S. Congress and I take my job seriously. I'm not known as one who vacillates, or hesitates. I know what I'm doing and I know why I'm doing it."

In 1993, she garnered $50 million in appropriations for her Youth Fair Chance program to provide job skills to unemployed youth. She was a founder of the Free South Africa movement, and she was arrested in protest against their apartheid practices. In 1994, she attended the inauguration of Nelson Mandela as president of a free South Africa, helping others celebrate the end of apartheid. Waters reflected on her generation's activism in a *Ms.* magazine article: "It's different these days. There's no war, no civil rights movement. Young people are more mobile than ever, lured from community to community by big-paying corporate jobs with stock options."

From 1996 to 1998, she served two terms as president of the Congressional Black Caucus, a position that only twice before had been held by a woman. In 1998, Waters was reelected to the House with 89 percent of the vote. On January 6, 2001, Waters offered a speech on the floor of the House of Representatives objecting to the electoral vote count of the state of Florida, on the basis of which the Supreme Court declared President George W. Bush the winner.

Waters is not afraid to challenge the Republican Party or leadership within the Democratic Party. In the 2000 presidential campaign she challenged the voting record of Democratic vice presidential candidate Joseph Lieberman regarding his support to end affirmative action. Waters led democratic reforms by supporting former mayor of Atlanta Maynard Jackson to head the Democratic National Committee. Jackson was not ultimately successful, but Waters had made her point about the need to "give stage and voice to one of the most loyal elements of the Democratic base, the African American component." In February 2001 she introduced bills to provide debt relief to poor countries in Africa and to eliminate mandatory penalties on crack cocaine offenses in the hope of introducing a "common sense" approach to the governments "war on drugs."

She now serves as chief deputy whip of the Democratic Party. Maxine Waters offers a wise and empowered role model to women throughout the United States.

Further Reading

Collier, Aldore. "Maxine Waters Elected." *Ebony* 46 (January 1991): 105+.

Hughes, Bill. "Waters: One of a Kind." *Oakland Post,* (February 11, 2001): B1.

Krikorian, Greg. "Representative Waters Holds Back Support." *Los Angeles Times,* August 15, 2000, U3.

Liebert, Larry. "Maxine Waters in Washington." *California Journal* 23, no. 8 (August 1992): 18–20.

Milloy, Marilyn. "Just Add Waters." *Ms.* 10, no. 5 (August/September 2000): 14–19.

Mills, Kay. "Maxine Waters." *Progressive* 57 (December 1993): 32–34.

Thro, Ellen. *Twentieth-Century Women Politicians.* New York: Facts On File, 1998.

 ## WATTLETON, ALYCE FAYE
(1943–)   *Planned Parenthood President*

Faye Wattleton worked to protect the reproductive rights of American women and served as president of the Planned Parenthood Federation of America (PPFA) from 1978 to 1992.

Alyce Faye Wattleton was born on July 8, 1943, in St. Louis, Missouri, to Ozie Garrett

Wattleton and George Wattleton. She was an only child. Her mother was a minister in the Church of God and a seamstress; her father was a factory worker. She completed high school at age 16 and entered Ohio State University Nursing School, because her mother had encouraged her to become a missionary nurse. In 1964, Wattleton completed her college degree, the first in her family to do so.

After graduation, she worked for two years as a maternity nursing instructor at the Miami Valley Hospital School of Nursing in Dayton, Ohio. In this position she saw firsthand the consequences of illegal abortions on women's health and lives.

In 1966, Wattleton entered a master's degree program at Columbia University in New York City. During this time, she interned at Harlem Hospital, where she continued to see the effects of illegal abortions on poor women's lives. Wattleton recalled one case in particular, saying, "One of the cases I remember in Harlem was a really beautiful 17-year-old-girl. She and her mother had decided to induce an abortion by inserting a Lysol douche into her uterus. It killed her." She completed an M.S. degree in maternal and infant health care with certification as a nurse-midwife in 1967.

Wattleton returned to Dayton to work as an assistant director of Public Health Nursing Services in the Ohio Public Health Department. She worked with several groups, including teen mothers. Wattleton began to work as a volunteer for Planned Parenthood. She served on the board of directors for two years before accepting a position in 1970 as executive director, a position in which she served for seven years. Under her leadership, the number of women served by the organization tripled and the budget rose from just under $400,000 to nearly $1 million a year. In 1973, she married Franklin Gordon, a social worker. They would divorce in 1981.

Two years later, while pregnant with her daughter, Wattleton was elected to chair the national executive director's council of the PPFA. She was in labor with her daughter when she won the election to this position. Three years later she was elected president of PPFA, becoming the first woman, the first African American, and, at 35, the youngest person ever to serve in this position. PPFA was the largest voluntary health agency in the country and the largest pro-choice organization. Some journalists commented on her fashionable dress; others admired her combination of calm repose and sharp articulation skills.

Wattleton headed PPFA during the time when the religious right had begun to organize against reproductive choice in earnest. Planned Parenthood clinics in Minnesota, Nebraska, Ohio, Vermont, and Virginia were firebombed. Most of the patients at Planned Parenthood were poor or working-class people, and they were severely affected when the Hyde Amendment passed in 1977, cutting federal funding for abortions for women on Medicaid. Abortion had been legalized with the 1973 U.S. Supreme Court decision in *Roe v. Wade,* but equal access to the procedure was often denied. Wattleton said, "If they really cared about equity and fairness in life they would say that as long as abortion is legal in this country, poor people should have the same access as the rich."

As an advocate of sex education as a prevention for teen pregnancy, Wattleton coauthored the book *How to Talk to Your Child About Sex* (1986), which sold 30,000 copies. By 1989, however, Wattleton noted, "No major network would accept contraceptive advertising and only 17 states and the District of Columbia required sex education in their school systems."

In 1989, the U.S. Supreme Court decision in *Webster v. Reproductive Health Services,* access to abortion was further restricted. Wattleton's response to the decision was, "My commitment and my determination is in no way diminished. I am furious as can be."

Wattleton resigned from her position at Planned Parenthood in 1992. She published a best-selling autobiography in 1995 called *Life on the Line.* Wattleton believed that continued activism was necessary, "We must act. If we are to stem the forces that continue to resist women's progress, feminism must be unequivocal and redoubled."

Wattleton remains hopeful that younger generations will build upon the gains that her generation achieved for women. Expressing her views on leadership, she says: "Leadership is not exclusive to those who occupy a national platform. We have to accept responsibility for change. You have the power within yourself to create beneficial change for yourself and for others."

A chapter in her autobiography, written as a letter to her daughter, speaks to all young women: "When I look at your life, I see a world of choices that I could not have imagined when I was your age. I think of the rights that you take for granted—rights that would not exist if not for the grit and determination of all those women who resisted oppression. And at the close of the twentieth century, I think about how your rights are being seriously threatened. I wonder whether you fully appreciate how important it is to accept the responsibility of protecting your freedom. I pray that you will never forget that you are the beneficiary of the struggles and sacrifices of others, and that your children in turn will reap the investment you make in their future." Faye Wattleton's leadership led to improved health choices for women and families.

Further Reading

"Faye Wattleton Preaches to the Choir." *Time* 148, no. 17 (1996): 99.

Wattleton, Faye. "A Champion for Choice." *Ms.* 7 (September/October 1996): 44–53.

———. *Life on the Line.* New York: Ballantine Books, 1998.

 **WEDDINGTON, SARAH RAGLE**
(1945–)   *Attorney*

Sarah Weddington successfully argued *Roe v. Wade* before the U.S. Supreme Court in 1973, and the decision in that case legalized abortion.

Weddington was 28 years old at the time and just out of law school when she achieved this legal victory for women.

Sarah Ragle was born on February 2, 1945, in Abilene, Texas, to Lena Ragle and Herbert Ragle. Her father was a Methodist minister, and Sarah served as an officer in the Methodist Youth Fellowship. In high school she served as president of Future Homemakers of America (FHA). She completed high school two years early, then attended McMurry College in Abilene, Texas. In 1965, she graduated magna cum laude with a bachelor's degree in English.

She attended law school at the University of Texas. The dean of her college had discouraged her from applying to law school, stating: "Well, no woman from this college has ever gone on to law school. It would be too tough." She was one of five women in a class of 125 law students. In 1967, at age 22, while in law school, she had an unplanned and unwanted pregnancy with Ron Weddington, the man she would later marry in 1968. The couple went to a clinic across the border in Mexico so Sarah could obtain an abortion. Though the procedure was conducted without problems, Weddington had feared that she might die and that her family might find out. During the 1960s, more than 1 million illegal abortions were performed every year. Although abortions were illegal, women nevertheless sought the procedure under dangerous, unsafe conditions.

In 1967, she completed her J.D. degree from the University of Texas, Austin. She had graduated in the top quarter of her class, but no law firm would hire her. In retrospect, she noted with irony that it was a good thing no one would hire her, since she would not then have had time to devote to the abortion issue.

Weddington became active in women's consciousness-raising groups in Austin. In October 1969, an abortion referral group, the Women's Liberation Birth Control Information Center, approached her seeking legal counsel. Weddington discovered during her research that abortion had not been illegal in the United States until the

Sarah Weddington, attorney, 2000
(Courtesy of Sarah Weddington)

protect her identity. Weddington and Coffee also found a married couple who sought an abortion on the grounds that the woman's pregnancy complicated her medical condition, endangering her life. Weddington filed a class-action suit, and the case was first heard in May 1970 at the Dallas Federal Courthouse. The judges found in the plaintiffs' favor that current abortion laws in Texas were unconstitutional.

The state of Texas appealed the decision and so the case then proceeded to the U.S. Supreme Court and immediately garnered national attention. At that time Weddington had finally found employment as an assistant city attorney in Fort Worth, Texas. After the Supreme Court announced its decision, her supervisor called her into his office and handed her a note that read, "No more women's lib. No more abortion." Weddington left the job and returned to Austin to open a private practice with her husband.

The Supreme Court received thousands of cases that year for review. In May 1971, the Supreme Court decided that it would hear *Roe v. Wade.* Weddington was just 26 years old, and few women had argued cases before the court. When Weddington appeared before the Supreme Court, there was no women's restroom in the lawyers' lounge, although one has been added since. One of the precedents that Weddington built upon was the 1965 U.S. Supreme Court decision in *Griswold v. Connecticut,* which legalized the sale of contraceptives to women, based on the right to privacy. She further argued that many national laws did not recognize an embryo as a child: tax deductions were deferred until the year the child was born, and pregnant women did not get a passport for two people.

In the months that followed her appearance before the Supreme Court, while waiting to hear the Court's decision Weddington began her campaign for the Texas House of Representatives. Future Texas governor ANN RICHARDS was her campaign manager. Then the Supreme Court requested a second argument on the case, which occurred in October 1972.

1850s, when the male-dominated medical profession lobbied to restrict the work of midwives, which included abortion. By 1900, abortion had been driven underground, and as a result abortion became more dangerous to women's health.

Weddington had never even appeared in court when she filed a federal lawsuit challenging the constitutionality of the Texas statute on abortion. Her former law school classmate Linda Coffee joined the legal team. Seeking a plaintiff to challenge the statute, they found Norma McCorvey, who had an unwanted pregnancy and had previously had two children taken away from her on the grounds that she was an unfit mother. In the suit, she was called "Jane Roe" to

Weeks after the second argument, Weddington won election as the first woman from her district in Austin to serve in the Texas House of Representatives. She was one of five women in the state legislature. One of her first actions as a legislator was to author a bill altering the state abortion laws. She helped reform Texas rape statutes and passed an equal credit bill for women. Her legal and legislative work was often spurred on by personal experience. Regarding the need for equal credit, she remembered being denied credit even though she was the one working to put her husband through school at the time.

In January 1973, Weddington heard from a *New York Times* reporter that she had won her case in the Supreme Court in a 7-2 decision. The Court ruled that the decision to terminate a pregnancy in the first trimester was solely the decision of the woman and her physician.

Anti-abortion groups began to organize intense opposition. Immediately after the decision, however, access to abortion was still limited, since few physicians had the training or equipment to perform the procedure. Even fewer hospitals were willing to offer care in this area. The Hyde Amendment in 1977 cut federal funding for abortion, thus restricting access for poor women. Further restrictions on abortion occurred in later Supreme Court decisions such as *Webster v. Reproductive Health Services* and (1989) *Planned Parenthood of Southeastern Pennsylvania v. Casey,* (1992) in which the Court upheld mandatory waiting periods and parental consent.

Weddington divorced in 1974. She served three terms in the Texas House of Representatives, then accepted a position in President Jimmy Carter's administration. From 1978 to 1981, Weddington led White House efforts to extend the time for ratification of the national Equal Rights Amendment (ERA) but was unsuccessful. She has lectured at the University of Texas at Austin since 1986. In 1992, she published a best-selling account of her life, *A Question of Choice.*

Public opinion polls continue to show that the majority of Americans support abortion rights, but Weddington worries that *Roe v. Wade* will be overturned. Recent votes on abortion cases in the U.S. Supreme Court have split 5-4. Weddington has evaluated the current makeup of the Court; she feels it is composed of three members who want to overturn *Roe v. Wade* (William Rehnquist, Antonin Scalia, and Clarence Thomas), three who would support it (John Paul Stevens, RUTH BADER GINSBURG, and Stephen Breyer) and three who are prepared to weaken it (David Souter, Sandra Day O'Connor, and Anthony Kennedy). Weddington remains passionate about women's right to reproductive health services. Reflecting on the role she has played in history, Weddington commented, "I've been very, very fortunate to be able to have a key role in something I cared about."

Women who have been able to enjoy better reproductive health services are indebted to her work.

Further Reading

Bennetts, Leslie. "A Woman's Choice." *Vanity Fair* 55 (September 1992): 148.

Godwin, Michelle Gerise. "Sarah Weddington." *Progressive* 644, no. 8 (August 2000): 33–37.

Mangan, Katherine. "The Lawyer Who Won *Roe v. Wade* Brings Its Lessons to the Classroom." *Chronicle of Higher Education* 39 (December 2, 1992): A17+.

Taylor-McGhee, Belle. "One on One: An Interview with Sarah Weddington." *NARAL News* 27, no. 3 (1997) 1+.

Weddington, Sarah. *A Question of Choice.* New York: Penguin, 1993.

 WELLS-BARNETT, IDA BELL
(1862–1931) *Journalist*

Ida Wells-Barnett was the most famous African-American female journalist in the nation during her lifetime. She broke the silence on the issue of lynching of African Americans in the United States.

Ida Wells was born on July 16, 1862, in Holly Springs, Mississippi, to Lizzie Bell Warrenton

Wells and James Wells. Both her parents had been enslaved, and Wells, born during the Civil War, was enslaved until she was three years old. Her father was the son of his master. Her parents met when her mother came to cook on the plantation where her father was employed. After the Emancipation Proclamation in 1863, the family remained in Holly Springs and continued to work for their former master. Wells was the oldest of eight children. She was educated in a local freedmen's school, one of several established after emancipation to offer schooling to African Americans. Her mother often accompanied the children to school so she also could learn to read and write. Under slavery in the South, attending school or even learning to read had been illegal.

In 1878, when she was 14, both her parents and her nine-month-old brother died of yellow fever. Her father's local Masonic group wanted to send the remaining children to live in different homes, but Wells worked to keep them together. Wells was a student at Shaw University in Raleigh, North Carolina, when her parents died. Her training there allowed her to pass the teacher's exam for county schools. She lied about her age and wore long skirts and upswept hair to look older in order to find a job as a teacher, which would allow her to support her remaining five siblings. She taught at a school six miles from her home for $25 a month. The following year she relocated to Memphis, Tennessee, to earn a higher salary in the Shelby County school district.

In 1884, while traveling from Memphis to Woodstock, Tennessee in the ladies' car of the Chesapeake and Ohio Railroad, Wells was forcibly removed from the first-class car because of her race. The 16-year-old Wells hired a white attorney to press her case in the courts. The circuit court decided in her favor with a settlement of $500, and the case made headlines. One, in the *Memphis Daily Appeal,* read, "A Darky Damsel Obtains a Verdict for Damages Against the Chesapeake and Ohio Railroad—What It Can Cost to Put a Colored School Teacher in a Smoking Car." In 1887, the Tennessee Supreme Court reversed the ruling and found in favor of the railroad. Wells had to pay court costs and return the $500. She wrote an article about her experience and thus began her career writing for African-American newspapers.

She began writing a weekly column under the pen name of Iola. Her articles challenged the loss of rights that local African Americans experienced under Reconstruction, the period following the Civil War when traditional Southern politicians, often racist, returned to power in the South. The pieces appeared in local and national publications such as the *New York Age* and *Chicago Conservator.* In 1889, she purchased one-third ownership in the *Memphis Free Speech and Headlight* and became its editor. When she wrote about the poor conditions in local schools that African-American children attended, however, her teaching contract was not renewed by the white school board.

In 1892, three African-American male acquaintances of Wells were lynched. Lynching had grown in the years following Reconstruction in the South. The three men were owners of a successful grocery store, much to the chagrin of a competing white store owner. The three men were jailed on a bogus charge of starting a riot and then removed by a mob that shot and hanged them. Most Americans at this time believed that lynching happened in response to sexual assaults. Wells herself thought this, but as she knew the three men in this situation, it was apparent that the only crime they had committed was one of economic success.

In her editorial on the lynching, Wells urged African Americans in Memphis to "save our money and leave a town which will neither protect our lives and property nor give us a fair trial in the courts, but takes us out and murders us in cold blood."

Six thousand African Americans fled Memphis to Oklahoma, which had been admitted to the Union just three years earlier. Their flight from Memphis created an economic crisis for white business owners. Foreshadowing civil rights leaders such as Martin Luther King Jr., who led boycotts to change Jim Crow laws, which legalized segregation in the South, half a century later, Wells had urged African Americans to boycott the city's streetcars until those responsible for the lynchings were brought to justice. Wells argued further, "Nobody believes the old threadbare lies that Negro men rape white women. If white men are not careful . . . a conclusion will be reached which will be very damaging to the moral reputations of their women." When her editorial was published she was on her way to a conference in Philadelphia, Pennsylvania. Her life was threatened should she return to Memphis, and her *Free Speech* office was destroyed. White patrols watched for disembarking train passengers in case she attempted to return, and she was hanged in effigy in front of the courthouse.

Wells could not return to Memphis, so she moved to New York City and began working for the *New York Age.* She continued her investigations of lynching. Her research and writings on the topic led to a speaking tour and a national audience. Her column "Ida B. Wells Abroad" was carried in papers throughout the United States and in Great Britain.

She published two books on lynching. The first, *Southern Horrors,* appeared in 1892. In that volume, she critiqued the myth of the black rapist and spoke openly of the pervasive sexual abuse of African-American women by white men. In 1895, her three-year statistical study of lynching was published in a second book, *A Red Record.*

In 1895, when she was 33, Wells moved to Chicago and married Ferdinand Barnett, a lawyer and owner of the *Chicago Conservator.* She retained her maiden name and took over the editorship of the *Conservator* while her husband devoted himself to his law practice. Barnett was a widower with two children, and the couple had four children of their own.

In 1909, Wells was one of two African-American women who helped found the National Association for the Advancement of Colored People. She soon came to view the organization as too moderate in its approach, however.

Ida B. Wells
(Prints & Photographs Division,
Library of Congress, Washington, D.C.)

Wells believed that the African-American community could empower itself by using the vote. The Fifteenth Amendment (ratified 1870) had enfranchised African-American men, but all women were still disenfranchised until the Nineteenth Amendment was passed in 1920. In 1913, Wells formed the Alpha Suffrage Club, the first African-American female suffrage club in Illinois. The club studied political issues and voting. It sent Wells as its delegate to a National American Woman Suffrage Association (NAWSA) parade in Washington, D.C. Illinois suffragists at the march asked Wells to march at the back of the procession. She refused, stating, "If the Illinois women do not take a stand now in this great democratic parade then the colored women are lost." Some white allies supported Wells, but the parade organizers directed her to march in the back. Wells remained undeterred, saying, "I shall not march at all unless I can march under the Illinois banner." As marchers began to parade down Pennsylvania Avenue, Wells stepped from the crowd of spectators and took her place in the Illinois state contingent. In one quick action, she had integrated the suffrage movement.

In 1920, the Nineteenth Amendment passed, giving women the right to vote. In 1930, Wells ran unsuccessfully for the Illinois senate as an independent candidate. She was a supporter of black nationalist leader Marcus Garvey and often an opponent of moderate Booker T. Washington. Wells was the most famous African-American female journalist in the country.

Ida B. Wells-Barnett died at 69 on March 25, 1931, in Chicago, Illinois, of uremia, a kidney disease. In 1941, the Chicago Housing Authority named a housing project after her and encased her diary in the cornerstone of the building. Her daughter edited her autobiography, *Crusade for Justice,* which was published posthumously in 1970, some four decades after her death. A U.S. postage stamp was issued in 1990 for the Black Heritage Series in her honor. In her autobiography she stated, "I felt that one had better die fighting against injustice than die like a rat in a trap."

Further Reading

Freedman, Suzanne. *Ida B. Wells-Barnett and the Anti-Lynching Crusade.* Brookfield, Conn.: Millbrook Press, 1994.

McMurray, Linda. *To Keep the Waters Troubled: The Life of Ida B. Wells.* New York: Oxford University Press, 1998.

Thompson, Mildred. *Ida B. Wells-Barnett: An Exploratory Study of an American Black Woman, 1893–1930.* Brooklyn, N.Y.: Carlson Publishing, 1990.

Wells, Ida B. *Crusade for Justice: The Autobiography of Ida B. Wells.* 1970. Reprint. Chicago, Ill.: University of Chicago Press, 1991.

———. *The Memphis Diary of Ida B. Wells.* Boston, Mass.: Beacon Press, 1995.

 WHITMAN, CHRISTINE TODD
(1947–) *Administrator of the Environmental Protection Agency, Governor*

Christine Todd Whitman was elected as the first female governor of New Jersey in 1993. She kept her campaign pledge to cut taxes and reduced tax rates by 15 percent in her first year in office. She was a moderate Republican who supported abortion rights. In 2001, she was appointed by President George W. Bush to serve as administrator of the Environmental Protection Agency (EPA).

Christine Todd was born on September 26, 1946, in New York City to an upper-class family. Her father, Webster Todd, was a Republican state chairman, and her mother, Eleanor Schley Todd, was vice-chair of the Republican National Committee. Christine earned a bachelor's degree in government from Wheaton College in Massachusetts in 1968. She asked her future husband, John Whitman, out on their first date because she needed an escort to the Nixon inauguration. She married Whitman, a financial consultant, in 1974, and had two children. The family moved to Somerset, New Jersey, in 1982.

Before running for governor of New Jersey, her only previous political experience was election to and service on the Somerset County board, from 1982 to 1988. She was appointed to the New Jersey board of public utilities, where she served until 1990.

The first statewide public office Whitman sought was as U.S. Senator in 1990. She had been a virtual unknown before coming within 2 percentage points of unseating incumbent Democratic senator Bill Bradley. She next ran for governor of New Jersey in 1993. She received 47 percent of the vote in a three-person race against Democratic incumbent governor Jim Florio and popular Democratic senator Bill Bradley. For her campaign she hired controversial media consultant Larry

McCarthy, who had been responsible for producing the infamous "Willie Horton" advertisement, part of an ad campaign criticized for having racist implications, during President George H. W. Bush's campaign against Michael Dukakis. Whitman won the 1993 election by 26,000 votes, becoming the 50th governor of the state. She was the first person in New Jersey history to defeat an incumbent governor in a general election. Scandal occurred after her election when her campaign manager, Ed Rollins, who had run President Ronald Reagan's campaign, told a *Time* magazine reporter that the Whitman team had won by suppressing the African-American vote, specifically by paying African-American ministers not to encourage voter turnout. Rollins apologized for his comments and stated that they had no basis in fact. An investigation found no proof to substantiate Rollins's original claims.

Whitman's goal was to see state income taxes reduced by 30 percent in her first three years in office. She reached that goal in two years by implementing 38 tax cuts, which saved $11 billion in taxes. Some $1 billion was returned annually in property tax rebates that were phased in over a five-year period. She also implemented Megan's Law, to protect children from sexual offenders, a law that was copied nationwide. She supported legislation to mandate trigger locks on all new handguns sold in New Jersey.

Whitman supported improvements in education by expanding preschool education for all three- and four-year-olds in the poorest school districts. She also implemented the most extensive plans for school construction of any state in the nation. Whitman used female state troopers among the bodyguards who protected her.

People magazine named Whitman one of its 25 most intriguing people of 1994. In 1995, she was the first governor ever chosen by the Republicans to give their televised party response to President Clinton's State of the Union address. She made clear her difference with the conservative wing of her party by strongly endorsing affirmative action programs in 1995.

Whitman was considered as a potential vice presidential candidate in 1996 by candidate Bob Dole, but she took herself out of the running. In 1996 she was also mentioned as a possible presidential candidate in 2000. She narrowly defeated a relatively unknown Democrat, James McGreevey, the mayor of Woodbridge, New Jersey, in her reelection campaign.

In 1997, her decision to veto state legislation that would have banned late-term abortions angered many conservatives. The Republican-controlled New Jersey State Assembly overrode her veto. In 1998 anti-abortion protestors followed her appearances including at interfaith prayer services. Whitman, however, believed that the Republican Party was ready to nominate a woman who supported abortion rights for president or vice president.

In 2001, President George W. Bush appointed Whitman as administrator of the EPA. Coal and utility industries have felt more comfortable with the work of Vice President Dick Cheney's task force, which released a report on energy policy that supported drilling for oil in the Arctic National Wildlife Refuge despite Whitman's previous announcement, which suggested otherwise. Whitman serves on the Cheney task force. When President Bush reversed a pledge to reduce carbon dioxide emission by power plants, Whitman defended his actions. Whitman also ordered the withdrawal of a safe level standard of arsenic in drinking water that had been enacted by President Bill Clinton. Environmental groups criticized this decision, citing a National Academy of Sciences study that found that arsenic in drinking water could cause cancer of the lungs, bladder, and skin. In a memo to President Bush, Whitman had recommended that the United States not oppose the Kyoto treaty on global warming, but it did anyway and was criticized domestically and abroad. She has also defended a 6 percent cut in the EPA budget. By summer 2001, some environmental groups, including Friends of the Earth, had already begun pressing for the resignation of Whitman, arguing that her defense of decisions made by the Bush administration have cost her credibility as a moderate on environmental issues. Her reputation seemed to be rebounding in late 2001, despite the reservations of some environmental groups, as the EPA ordered General Electric to dredge or pay for the dredging of 40 miles of the upper Hudson River. She also found funding for Brownfields cleanup projects, which return abandoned industrial sites to productive use, and praised Congress for passing Brownfields legislation in December 2001. However, on January 10, 2002, a conflict of interests charge was filed by the ombudsperson of the EPA against Whitman after she allegedly punished his department by stripping it of its independence in the wake of a Superfund case settlement that limits Citigroup's liability to a fraction of the cleanup costs at a nuclear waste site.

Christine Todd Whitman is one of the most visible leaders in the Republican Party.

Further Reading

Beard, Patricia. *Growing Up Republican: Christie Whitman, The Politics of Character.* New York: HarperCollins, 1996.

Cohen, Adam. "Jersey's Falling Star." *Time* 150 (October 27, 1997): 48.

Duke, Lynne. "On the Inside Looking Out: EPA Chief Christie Whitman's Agenda." *Washington Post,* April 23, 2001, C1.

Henneberger, Melinda. "Despite Appearances, Whitman Says She and Bush Agree on Environment." *New York Times,* April 17, 2001, A12–13.

Jehl, Douglas. "Whitman Calls for Patience on Environmental Policies." *New York Times,* April 7, 2001, A 16.

McClure, Sandy. *Christie Whitman for the People: A Political Biography.* New York: Prometheus Books, 1996.

Weissman, Art. *Christine Todd Whitman: The Making of a National Political Player.* New York: Carol Publishing Group, 1996.

⊠ WILLARD, FRANCES ELIZABETH CAROLINE

(1839–1898) *Women's Christian Temperance Union President*

Frances Willard was an American reformer who served as president of the national Woman's Christian Temperance Union (WCTU), which crusaded for prohibition.

Frances Elizabeth Caroline Willard was born on September 28, 1839, in Churchville, New York, to Mary Willard and Frances Willard. The family were Methodists. Her father was a full-time student at Oberlin College and her mother was a part-time student when Willard was just a few years old.

In 1845, the family moved to a homestead in Wisconsin. Her father became a state legislator. Willard was schooled at home until a school in their area was finally opened when she was 15. At 17 she attended the Milwaukee Female College. Later, she studied at Northwestern Female College, graduating in 1859.

During the Civil War, Willard taught in Illinois and Pennsylvania secondary schools. She then spent a year teaching at a female seminary in western New York. She left teaching to accompany a wealthy friend on a two-year European tour from 1868 to 1870.

When she returned to the United States, Willard became president of the Evanston College for Ladies, a new school founded in 1871. It was absorbed into Northwestern University in 1873. At Northwestern, she served as dean of women. She was one of the first female administrators to hold a high position at a coeducational university. In 1873, she cofounded and was elected vice president of the Association for the Advancement of Women.

Willard left her career in college administration due to burn-out in 1874 to serve as secretary of the Woman's Christian Temperance Union (WCTU), the largest women's group of the time. In Chicago she founded Illinois Women's Christian Temperance Union and was a delegate at the founding conference of the national body. She also edited WCTU's publications. Willard was successful at mobilizing white middle-class women.

In 1879, five years after joining the organization, Willard was elected to the presidency of the WCTU at age 40. She held the position for the rest of her life. In 1883, she published *Women and Temperance.*

The WCTU was a much larger organization than women's suffrage groups of the same time

Frances Willard, temperance advocate
(Prints & Photographs Division,
Library of Congress, Washington, D.C.)

period. At the beginning of Willard's tenure there were only 27,000 members. In 1890 there were 150,000 members in the WCTU, compared with 13,000 in the National American Woman Suffrage Association (NAWSA). Willard grew more progressive than most WCTU members did as the years passed. She was a longtime supporter of suffrage for women. She identified as a Fabian socialist and began arguing that alcoholism was the result of poverty. The popular view at the time was that alcoholism was the cause of poverty. She came to support economic reform more than prohibition.

In 1889, her autobiography, *Glimpses of Fifty Years,* became a best-seller. In an 1890 interview, Willard expressed sympathy for Southerners and argued that they were wronged when a restriction was not placed on the African-American male vote. Some interpreted her comments as a sign of support for lynching. Willard was challenged on her views regarding race by antilynching reformer and journalist IDA B. WELLS regarding the comments.

Frances Willard died on February 17, 1898, in New York City. She had led the largest organiza-tion of women in the nation. Her support of suffrage for women led the issue into the mainstream of American society.

Further Reading

Leeman, Richard. *"Do Everything" Reform: The Oratory of Frances E. Willard.* Westport, Conn.: Greenwood Press, 1992.

Marilley, Suzanne. "Frances Willard and the Feminism of Fear." *Feminist Studies* 19, no. 1 (spring 1993): 123–46.

Tyrrell, Ian. *Frances Willard and Temperance.* Westport, Conn.: Greenwood Press, 1992.

Willard, Frances. *A Wheel Within a Wheel: How I Learned to Ride the Bicycle.* Bedford, Mass.: Applewood Books, 1997.

———. *Writing Out My Heart: Selections from the Journal of Frances Willard, 1855–96.* Champaign: University of Illinois Press, 1995.

 **WINNEMUCCA, SARAH HOPKINS
(Thoc-me-tony, "Shell Flower")
(1844–1891)** *Northern Paiute Activist*

Sarah Winnemucca served as an intrepreter and negotiator for the Northern Paiute (Numa) nation. Her lecture tour inspired others to support American Indian issues.

Sarah Winnemucca was born in 1844 at Humboldt Sink in what later became the state of Nevada. Her birth name, Thoc-me-tony, translates as "Shell Flower." She was the fourth of nine children. Her father was chief of the Paiute. Her grandfather Winnemucca had escorted Captain John Fremont across the Sierra Nevada to California in 1845.

In 1860, at age 16, Winnemucca was sent to convent school in San Jose, California. Her schooldays ended abruptly after three weeks when white parents complained about the presence of an Indian student, and the nuns sent her home. After her brief attendance at the convent school, she converted to Christianity and took the name Sarah. She was fluent in several languages, including English, Spanish, and three American Indian languages.

In 1865, when some white men's cattle were stolen, soldiers massacred the Paiute, including Winnemucca's mother, sister, and a baby brother.

Winnemucca worked as an interpreter at a U.S. Army base, Camp McDermitt, in Nevada from 1868 to 1871 and later at the Malheur Agency in Oregon. In 1871, she married Lieutenant E. C. Bartlet but left him because of his alcoholism. She later married an Indian man but left him shortly afterward because he abused her.

In 1872, a new reservation in southeastern Oregon was established for the Paiute. Winnemucca accompanied her tribe to the Malheur Reservation, where she worked as an interpreter and taught at the agency school. She became the personal interpreter and guide for General Oliver Howard during the Bannock War in 1878, after which the Paiute who had remained largely peaceful during the conflict were forced to move to the Yakima Reservation in Washington State in the dead of winter, along with hostile tribes.

In January 1880, she traveled to Washington, D.C., on behalf of her tribe. She met with President Rutherford Hayes and Secretary of the Interior Carl Schurz because the tribe had lost their lands and been forced to relocate twice. Secretary Schurz promised Winnemucca that the Paiute would be allowed to return to the Malheur Reservation, but the Indian agent at the Yakima Reservation refused to allow them to leave. The next year, the federal government opened Malheur Reservation lands to white settlement, ending Paiute hopes to return.

In 1881, she taught for a year in Vancouver, Washington, where she met and married Lieutenant L. H. Hopkins. Her husband accompanied her on lecture tours in which she sought support for the retention of tribal lands. She spoke in cities throughout New England and the East Coast.

Her lectures led to the 1883 publication of a book that was part autobiography, part tribal history, and part political activism, entitled *Life Among the Piutes.* The first volume written in English by an American Indian woman, it concluded with a petition that readers could sign and send to Congress. She continued touring and collecting thousands of signatures on petitions she sent to Congress asking that the government fulfill its

promised land allotment to the Paiute. Congress passed a bill ordering this action in 1884, but the secretary of the interior refused to sign it.

In 1886, she taught at government-run schools for Paiute students in Nevada for three years. Contrary to the established white-centered curriculum, Winnemucca taught Indian history, culture, and language. Her husband died of tuberculosis in 1886. Winnemucca retired to her sister's home in Monida, Montana.

Sarah Winnemucca died on October 16, 1891, in Monida of tuberculosis when she was 48. She was buried with Paiute rites, and her obituary appeared on the front page of the *New York Times.* She had been the most famous American Indian woman of her time, although the cause to which she devoted her life, reclamation of her tribal lands, was never achieved.

Further Reading

Canfield, Gae Whitney. *Sarah Winnemucca of the Northern Piutes.* Norman: University of Oklahoma Press, 1988.

Lape, Noreen Groover. "'I Would Rather Be With My People, But Not to Live With Them as They Live'; "Cultural Liminality and Double Consciousness in Sarah Winnemucca Hopkins' *Life Among the Piutes: Their Wrongs and Claims.*" *American Indian Quarterly* 22, no. 3 (summer 1998): 259–79.

Morrison, Dorothy. *Chief Sarah: Sarah Winnemucca's Fight for Indian Rights.* Portland: Oregon Historical Society Press, 1990.

Winnemucca, Sarah. *Life Among the Piutes: Their Wrongs and Claims.* 1883. Reprint. Reno.: University of Nevada Press, 1994.

Zanjani, Sally. *Sarah Winnemucca.* Lincoln: University of Nebraska Press, 2001.

 ## WOODHULL, VICTORIA CLAFLIN
(1838–1927)   *Presidential Candidate, Women's Rights Leader*

Victoria Woodhull led an eventful life. She was the first woman to run for the U.S. presidency, the first woman to address Congress regarding women's suffrage, the first female stockbroker, the first female to open a bank on Wall Street, and the first woman to establish a newspaper, *Woodhull & Claflin's Weekly*. She rose from humble beginnings to open new avenues for women.

Victoria Claflin was born on September 23, 1838, in Homer, Ohio, to Roxana Hummel Claflin and Reuben Buckman Claflin. She was the sixth of 10 children.

Spiritualism (the belief that mediums can communicate with the dead) swept the nation in the 1840s. Woodhull claimed that her spiritual visions had begun at age three. During her childhood, her father, a con artist, used Woodhull and a younger sister as psychic healers in a traveling medicine show. Woodhull was familiar with many spiritualistic practices and for the rest of her life she claimed that her actions were guided by psychic insights. She received little formal education—only three years of elementary school between the ages of eight and 11.

In 1853, two months before her 15th birthday, she married Canning Woodhull. The couple lived in California, where Woodhull worked as a cigar girl and seamstress to help support the family. They remained married for 11 years and had two children. After being deserted by her alcoholic husband, Woodhull left her mentally retarded son with family members and took her daughter, Zula Maud, to join her sister Tennessee Claflin. They lived for a brief time in Cincinnati, Ohio, where Woodhull abandoned healing and concentrated on clairvoyance. The sisters conducted a tour throughout the midwestern and southern states. They were charged with prostitution, blackmail, and other criminal offenses in several towns. A common solution to law enforcement problems was to run offenders out of town, so Woodhull did not serve serious jail time.

In 1864, she obtained a divorce and entered into an open common-law marriage with Colonel James Blood, who had served in a Missouri regiment during the Civil War, but she did not use his name. In 1868, the sisters moved to New York City after Demonsthenes, her guiding spirit, reportedly told Woodhull to move to a house on Great Jones Street. She took an early interest in women's rights and traveled to Washington, D.C., to attend the first national female suffrage convention in 1869.

Multimillionaire Cornelius Vanderbilt became interested in spiritualism after his wife's death, and he met with the sisters because of their reputation as spiritualists. With Vanderbilt's financial backing, the sisters became successful investors in both real estate and the stock market. In 1870, they opened their own successful brokerage firm, Woodhull, Claflin & Company. They made a profit of $700,000 in their first six weeks of operation. The press referred to them as the "bewitching brokers," because they wore tailored jackets and brightly colored neckties but no jewelry. Woodhull, recognizing the importance of being the first woman to become a broker, said, "While others argued the equality of woman with man, I proved it by successfully engaging in business; while others wanted to show that there was no valid reason why women should be treated, socially and politically, as being inferior to man, I boldly entered the arena of business and exercised the rights I already possessed."

In 1870, when women did not have suffrage, Woodhull declared herself a presidential candidate of the Equal Rights Party. That party's convention was the largest third-party convention in the 1872 election, but the press treated her candidacy as a novelty. She chose abolitionist leader Frederick Douglass as her vice presidential running mate, ignoring the fact that he did not accept the nomination.

She addressed the Judiciary Committee of the U.S. House of Representatives in 1871 on the topic of suffrage. Woodhull read a manifesto she had written that called for a sixteenth amendment to the Constitution, giving women the right to vote. Her document included legal and constitutional precedents. She claimed that spirits had given the document to her while in a trance. One of her arguments was that the Fourteenth Amendment had already conferred the right of suffrage for women. She was the first suffragist to gain a hearing before Congress. Some suffrage leaders, such as ELIZABETH CADY STANTON and SUSAN B. ANTHONY, supported her

Victoria Woodhull reading her argument in favor of women's suffrage to the House of Representatives Judiciary Committee in Washington, D.C.
(Still Picture Branch, National Archives, College Park, MD)

at the time. Woodhull held views that many suffragists would have condemned, however, since she endorsed legalized prostitution and free love.

From 1870 to 1876, Woodhull and her sister Tennessee Claflin published *Woodhull & Claflin's Weekly*. They became the first women in the United States to found a newspaper. The purpose of the paper was to present Woodhull's campaign platform, but it also addressed a number of issues, including birth control and free love, and conducted investigative reporting. It was the first U.S. paper to print a translation of Karl Marx's *Communist Manifesto*.

In 1872, Woodhull and her sister were indicated for mailing obscene material after their publication carried an accusation of adultery against well-known clergyman Henry Ward Beecher. (Her sister also wrote an article on a New York stockbro-

ker who boasted of seducing young schoolgirls.) The *Weekly* sold out and scarce copies of the 10-cent paper were being sold at prices inflated up to $40. Presidential candidate Woodhull spent election day in jail. The sisters paid more than $60,000 in bail money for a misdemeanor. They had been indicated specifically for a phrase they used in the stockbroker article that also appeared in the Bible and in two larger newspapers that carried their article. They were ultimately acquitted of the obscenity charge in 1873, but their public careers were ruined. The following year they were also found not guilty of libel in the stockbroker article. Woodhull had run the exposé because Beecher had publicly criticized her philosphy of free love, which he secretly practiced.

In 1877, the sisters moved to England and both married wealthy businessmen. Woodhull, who had always felt a mystical tie to Queen Victoria, started wearing royal purple. In 1883, Woodhull married British banker and nobleman John Martin. Soon after marriage Woodhull began a conservative publication, the *Humanitarian,* in which she denounced free love and many of her former views.

She supported eugenics and spoke on "the scientific propagation of the human race," which endorsed breeding of special races for "aristocracy of the blood." She still continued to write about the economic inequality between men and women, however, and she continued to speak for women's rights. She began an autobiography, and the first chapter appeared in pamphlet form, but the book was never finished. She visited the United States a few times and twice spoke about the possibility of running for president. When her husband died of pneumonia in 1897, Woodhull was left with a sizable fortune.

Victoria Woodhull died in Tewkesbury, England, on June 10, 1927, at age 88. Only six mourners attended her funeral. She was cremated and her ashes scattered at sea. Her daughter, Zula Maud, inherited her fortune. Victoria Woodhull was ahead of her time in some respects and suffered persecution because of it.

Further Reading

Gabriel, Mary. *Notorious Victoria: The Life of Victoria Woodhull, Uncensored.* Chapel Hill, N.C.: Algonquin Books, 1998.

Goldsmith, Barbara. *Other Powers: The Age of Suffrage, Spiritualism, and the Scandalous Victoria Woodhull.* New York: Harperperennial Library, 1998.

Underhill, Lois Beachy. *The Woman Who Ran for President: The Many Lives of Victoria Woodhull.* New York: Penguin, 1996.

 ## WRIGHT, FRANCES
(1795–1852) *Abolitionist, Women's Rights Leader, Public Education Advocate*

Frances Wright was one of the first American women to lecture in public, an activity that was viewed as inappropriate for "ladies" at the time. She was an abolitionist, women's rights leader, and advocate of public education.

Frances Wright was born on September 6, 1795, in Dundee, Scotland, to Camilla Campbell Wright and James Wright. She was the second of three children. Her father was a graduate of Trinity College in Dublin, Ireland, and a linen merchant. He admired American patriots such as Thomas Paine. Her parents died when she was two years old, and relatives raised Wright, the heiress to a large fortune. At the age of 21, she lived for a year with a great-uncle who was a professor at Glasgow College. During this time, she had access to the college library.

In 1819, Wright traveled to the United States. During her visit, her play *Altorf,* which covered the Swiss struggle for independence, was produced in New York. The play closed after three performances. Her travel memoir *Views of Society and Manners in America* published in 1821, was a success and preceded a similar work by Frenchman Alexis de Tocqueville by more than a decade. She remained a permanent resident of the United States. Wright next published *A Few Days in Athens,* a historical novel with a utopian message, in 1822. Wright began speaking in public in the 1820s and ANGELINA and Sarah GRIMKÉ followed in the 1830s. After the 1848 Seneca Falls women's rights convention, a few more women began speaking publicly.

Wright abhorred slavery. In 1825, she published *A Plan for the Gradual Abolition of Slavery in the United States Without Danger of Loss to the Citizens of the South.* Wright's work proposed that the government allow those who were enslaved to work on public lands in order to earn the necessary funds to purchase their freedom. In 1825, she took action to implement her plan by purchasing 640 acres in western Tennessee near Memphis. The colony, called *Nashoba,* a Chickasaw word for "wolf," was the only secular commune founded by a woman in 19th-century America. Its purpose was to show how a transition to emancipation could occur. She assumed that owners would donate the first group of 50 slaves to her and that each could work off his or her debt within five years. Only one family was donated, and Wright could afford to buy only eight other slaves. The group living at the colony managed to clear 100 acres, but few residents had adequate agricultural experience to make the experiment economically viable. The group garnered harmful publicity when a journal of the overseer, who advocated free love, was published in an abolitionist newspaper. The project was disbanded in 1828. Wright agreed with those in the colonization movement who felt that once African Americans were no longer enslaved, they could be sent to colonies in Africa. Wright took the 30 African-American residents of her commune to Haiti in 1830. The experiment had cost her half her fortune.

Wright then moved to New Harmony, Indiana, to serve as editor of the *New Harmony Gazette,* a publication of the Robert Owen utopian community. (Robert Owen owned a textile mill. He was born in Wales but moved to the United States and tried to establish a utopian community for workers.) Wright then moved to New York City and copublished the socialist paper *Free Enquirer.*

Wright advocated changes in marriage laws, female education, birth control, suffrage, equal rights for women, and interracial relationships. She also spoke out against capital punishment and racially segregated schools. At a time when only half the children in New York City attended school, Wright called for a national system of free state schools financed by graduated property taxes. She was very critical of organized religion. She outlined her views in another book, *Address on the State of the Public Mind,* in 1829. She married an older French physician, William Darusmont, in 1831. They had one daughter. Her book *England, the Civilizer,* published in 1848, offered her vision of a global government. Wright read from her works in public, much to the consternation of clergymen and others who felt women had no right to speak in public. Wright and her husband divorced in 1850. He retained custody of their daughter. Wright fell on ice and never recovered from the complications of the broken hip she suffered.

Frances Wright died on December 13, 1852, in Cincinnati, Ohio, at age 57. She was buried in Spring Grove Cemetery in Cincinnati. Her gifts as an orator were supported by her work to achieve practical applications of her visions.

Further Reading

Morris, Celia. *Fanny Wright: Rebel in America.* Champaign: University of Illinois Press, 1992.

Travis, Molly Abel. "Frances Wright: The Other Woman of Early American Feminism." *Women's Studies* 22, no. 3 (1993): 389–97.

RECOMMENDED SOURCES ON AMERICAN WOMEN LEADERS AND ACTIVISTS

Andersen, Kristi. *After Suffrage: Women in Partisan and Electoral Politics Before the New Deal.* Chicago: University of Chicago, 1996.

Anderson, Karen. *Changing Woman: A History of Racial Ethnic Women in Modern America.* New York: Oxford University Press, 1996.

Antler, Joyce. *The Journey Home: How Jewish Women Shaped Modern America.* New York: Schocken, 1998.

Apple, Rima, and Janet Golden, eds. *Mothers and Motherhood: Readings in American History.* Columbus: Ohio State University Press, 1997.

Berkin, Carol, and Leslie Horowitz, eds. *Women's Voices, Women's Lives: Documents in Early American History.* Boston: Northeastern University Press, 1998.

Berry, Mary Frances. *Why ERA Failed: Politics, Women's Rights, and the Amending Process of the Constitution.* Bloomington: Indiana University Press, 1988.

Berkeley, Kathleen. *The Women's Liberation Movement in America.* Westport, Conn.: Greenwood, 1999.

Bingham, Clara. *Women on the Hill: Culture of Congress.* New York: Random House, 1997.

Boxer, Barbara. *Strangers in the Senate: Politics and the New Revolution of Women in America.* Washington, D.C.: National Press Books, 1993.

Boyd, Melba Joyce. *Discarded Legacy: Politics and Poetics in the Life of Frances W. W. Harper, 1825–1911.* Detroit: Wayne State University Press, 1994.

Buhle, Mari Jo. *Women and American Socialism, 1870–1920.* Urbana: University of Illinois Press, 1981.

Burell, Barbara. *A Woman's Place Is in the House: Campaigning for Congress in the Feminist Era.* Ann Arbor: University of Michigan Press, 1996.

Clinton, Catherine. *The Other Civil War: American Women in the Nineteenth Century.* New York: Hill and Wang, 1999.

Cohen, Cathy, Kathleen Jones, and Joan Tronto, eds. *Women Transforming Politics: An Alternative Reader.* New York: New York University Press, 1997.

Cott, Nancy. *Root of Bitterness: Documents of the Social History of American Women.* Boston: Northeastern University Press, 1996.

Crawford, Vicki, Jacqueline Anne Rouse, and Barbara Woods, eds. *Women In the Civil Rights Movement: Trailblazers and Torchbearers, 1941–1965.* Bloomington: Indiana University Press, 1993.

Dasgupta, Shamita Das, ed. *Patchwork Shawl; Chronicles of South Asian Women in America.* New Brunswick, N.J.: Rutgers University Press, 1998.

Davis, Flora. *Moving the Mountain: The Women's Movement in America Since 1960.* Champaign: University of Illinois Press, 1999.

Dinkin, Robert. *Before Equal Suffrage: Women in Partisan Politics from Colonial Times to 1920.* Westport, Conn.: Greenwood Publishing Group, 1995.

DuBois, Ellen Carol. *Woman Suffrage and Women's Rights.* New York: New York University Press, 1998.

DuBois, Ellen, and Vicki L. Ruiz, eds. *Unequal Sisters: A Multicultural Reader in U.S. Women's History.* New York: Routledge, 1994.

Earnshaw, Doris, and Maria Raymond, eds. *American Women Speak: Voices of American Women in Public Life.* Davis, Calif.: Alta Vista Press, 1996.

Echols, Alice. *Daring to Be Bad: Radical Feminism in America, 1967–75.* Minneapolis: University of Minnesota, 1989.

Eckart, Celia Morris. *Fanny Wright: Rebel in America.* Cambridge, Mass.: Harvard University Press, 1984.

Eldridge, Larry, ed. *Women and Freedom in Early America.* New York: New York University Press, 1997.

Faderman, Lillian. *To Believe in Women: What Lesbians Have Done for America—A History.* Boston: Houghton Mifflin, 1999.

Fedler, Deborah. *A Century of Women: The Most Influential Events in Twentieth-Century Women's History.* Secaucus, N.J.: Carol, 1999.

Flammang, Janet. *Women's Political Voice: How Women are Transforming the Practice and Study of Politics.* Philadelphia: Temple University Press, 1997.

Flexner, Eleanor. *Century of Struggle: The Woman's Rights Movement in the United States.* Cambridge, Mass.: Belknap Press, 1996.

Foerstel, Karen, and Herbert Foerstel. *Climbing the Hill: Gender Conflict in Congress.* Westport, Conn.: Greenwood, 1996.

Forbes, Ella. *African American Women During the Civil War.* New York: Garland, 1998.

Fowler, Robert Booth. *Carrie Catt: Feminist Politician.* Boston: Northeastern University Press, 1988.

Fox, Richard. *Gender Dynamics in Congressional Elections.* Thousand Oaks, Calif.: Sage Publications, 1996.

Garcia, Alma, and Mario Garcia, eds. *Chicana Feminist Thought: The Basic Historical Writings.* New York: Routledge, 1997.

Gavin, Lettie. *American Women in World War I: They Also Served.* Niwot: University Press of Colorado, 1997.

Gertzog, Irwin. *Congressional Women: Their Recruitment, Integration, and Behavior.* Westport, Conn.: Greenwood, 1995.

Giddings, Paula. *When and Where I Enter: The Impact of Black Women on Race and Sex in America.* New York: Harper Trade, 1996.

Gill, Laverne. *African American Women in Congress.* New Brunswick, N.J.: Rutgers University Press, 1997.

Gordon, Ann. *African American Women and the Vote, 1837–1965.* Amherst: University of Massachusetts Press, 1997.

Green, Elna. *Southern Strategies: Southern Women and the Woman Suffrage.* Chapel Hill: University of North Carolina Press, 1997.

Griffith, Elisabeth. *In Her Own Right: The Life of Elizabeth Cady Stanton.* New York: Oxford University Press, 1985.

Gustafson, Melanie, Kristie Miller, and Elisabeth Perry, eds. *We Have Come to Stay: American Women and Political Parties, 1880–1960.* Albuquerque: University of New Mexico Press, 1999.

Hardy, Gayle. *American Women Civil Rights Activists: Bibliographies of 68 Leaders, 1825–1992.* Jefferson, N.C.: McFarland, 1993.

Harvey, Anna. *Votes Without Leverage: Women in American Electoral Politics, 1920–1970.* New York: Cambridge University Press, 1998.

Hine, Darlene Clark, ed. *Black Women in America: An Historical Encyclopedia.* Bloomington: Indiana University Press, 1994.

———. *Hine Sight: Black Women and the Re-Construction of American History.* Brooklyn, N.Y.: Carlson, 1994.

Hine, Darlene Clark, and Kathleen Thompson. *A Shining Thread of Hope: History of Black Women in America.* New York: Broadway Books, 1998.

hooks, bell. *Ain't I a Woman: Black Women and Feminism.* Boston: South End Press, 1981.

Huls, Mary Ellen. *United States Government Documents on Women, 1800–1990: A Comprehensive Bibliography.* Westport, Conn.: Greenwood, 1993.

Isenber, Nancy. *Sex and Citizenship in Antebellum America.* Chapel Hill: University of North Carolina Press, 1998.

James, Joy. *Shadowboxing: Representations of Black Feminist Politics.* New York: St. Martin's, 1999.

Jeansonne, Glen. *Women of the Far Right: The Mother's Movement and World War II* Chicago: University of Chicago Press, 1996.

Jeffrey, Julie Roy. *The Great Silent Army of Abolitionism: Ordinary Women in the Antislavery Movement.* Chapel Hill: University of North Carolina Press, 1998.

Jeffreys-Jones, Rhodri. *Changing Differences: Women and the Shaping of American Foreign Policy, 1917–1994.* New Brunswick, N.J.: Rutgers University Press, 1997.

Jones, Jacqueline. *Labor of Love, Labor of Sorrow: Black Women, Work, and the Family from Slavery to the Present.* New York: Random House, 1986.

Kahn, Kim. *The Political Consequences of Being a Woman: How Stereotypes Influence the Conduct and Consequences of Political Campaigns.* New York: Columbia University Press, 1996.

Kann, Mark. *The Gendering of American Politics: Founding Mothers, Founding Fathers, and Political Patriarchy.* Westport, Conn.: Greenwood Publishing Group, Inc., 1999.

Kerber, Linda, Alice Kessler-Harris, and Kathryn Kish Sklar, eds. *U.S. History As Women's History: Knowledge, Power and State Formation.* Chapel Hill: University of North Carolina Press, 1995.

Kerber, Linda, and Jane De Hart-Mathews, eds. *Women's America: Refocusing the Past.* New York: Oxford University Press, 1999.

Kierner, Cynthia. *Women's Place in the Early South, 1700–1835.* Ithaca, N.Y.: Cornell University Press, 1998.

Klein, Laura, and Lillian Ackerman. *Women and Power in Native North America.* Norman: University of Oklahoma Press, 1995.

Kleinberg, S. J. *Women in the United States, 1830–1945.* New Brunswick, N.J.: Rutgers University Press, 1999.

Kuhlman, Erika. *Petticoats and White Feathers: Gender Conformity, Race, The Progressive Peace Movement and the Debate Over War, 1895–1919.* Westport, Conn.: Greenwood, 1997.

Langley, Winston, and Vivian Fox, eds. *Women's Rights in America: A Documentary History.* Westport, Conn.: Greenwood, 1994.

Leonard, Elizabeth. *Yankee Women: Gender Battles in the Civil War.* New York: W. W. Norton, 1995.

Ling, Huping. *Surviving on the Gold Mountain: A History of Chinese American Women and Their Lives.* Albany: State University of New York Press, 1998.

Logan, Shirley. *We Are Coming: The Persuasive Discourse of Nineteenth-Century Black Women.* Carbondale: Southern Illinois University Press, 1999.

Lopez, Antoninette Sedillo, ed. *Latina Issues: Fragments of Historia.* New York: Garland, 1995.

Magill, Frank, ed. *Great Lives From History. American Women Series.* Pasadena, Calif.: Salem Press, 1995.

Mankiller, Wilma, ed. *The Readers's Companion to U.S. Women's History.* Boston: Houghton Mifflin, 1998.

Marilley, Suzanne. *Woman Suffrage and the Origins of Liberal Feminism in the United States, 1820–1920.* Cambridge Mass.: Harvard University Press, 1996.

Marshall, Susan. *Splintered Sisterhood: Gender and Class in the Campaign Against Woman Suffrage.* Madison: University of Wisconsin Press, 1997.

Martin, Mart. *Almanac of Women and Minorities in American Politics.* Boulder, Colo.: Westview, 1998.

Morgan, Robin, ed. *Sisterhood Is Powerful: An Anthology of Writings from the Women's Liberation Movement.* New York: Vintage Books, 1970.

Morton, Patricia, ed. *Discovering the Women in Slavery: Emancipating Perspectives on the American Past.* Athens: University of Georgia Press, 1996.

Moynihan, Ruth. *Rebel for Rights: Abigail Scott Duniway.* New Haven, Conn.: Yale University Press, 1985.

Niethammer, Carolyn. *Daughters of the Earth: The Lives and Legends of American Indian Women.* New York: Macmillan, 1977.

O'Farrell, Brigid, and Joyce Kornbluh, eds. *Rocking the Boat: Women, Unions and Change, 1915–1975.* New Brunswick, N.J.: Rutgers University Press, 1996.

Orleck, Annalise. *Common Sense and a Little Fire: Women and Working-Class Politics in the United States, 1900–1965.* Chapel Hill: University of North Carolina Press, 1995.

Perdue, Theda. *Cherokee Women: Gender and Culture Change, 1700–1835.* Lincoln: University of Nebraska Press, 1998.

Perex, Emma. *The Decolonial Imaginary: Writing Chicanas into History.* Bloomington: Indiana University Press, 1999.

Robnett, Belinda. *How Long? How Long?: African-American Women in the Struggle for Freedom and Justice.* New York: Oxford University Press, 1998.

Rose, Kenneth. *American Women and the Repeal of Prohibition.* New York: New York University Press, 1995.

Ruiz, Vicki. *From Out of the Shadows: Mexican Women in Twentieth-Century America.* New York: Oxford University Press, 1998.

Schultz, Jeffrey, and George Kurian. *Encyclopedia of Women in American Politics.* Phoenix, Ariz.: Oryx, 1998.

Solinger, Rickie, ed. *Abortion Wars: A Half Century of Struggle, 1950–2000.* Berkeley: University of California Press, 1998.

Sonneborn, Liz. *A to Z of Native American Women.* New York: Facts On File, 1998.

Springer, Kimberly, ed. *Still Lifting, Still Climbing: Contemporary African-American Women's Activism.* New York: New York University Press, 1999.

Stanton, Elizabeth Cady, and Susan B. Anthony. *Elizabeth Cady Stanton, Susan B. Anthony Reader: Correspondence, Writings, Speeches.* Boston: Northeastern University Press, 1992.

Sterling, Dorothy. *We Are Your Sisters: Black Women in the Nineteenth Century.* New York: W. W. Norton, 1997.

Terborg-Penn, Rosalyn. *African American Women in the Struggle for the Vote, 1850–1920.* Bloomington: Indiana University Press, 1998.

Thom, Mary. *Inside* Ms.: *25 Years of the Magazine and the Feminist Movement.* New York: Henry Holt, 1997.

Treckel, Paula. *To Comfort the Heart: Women in Seventeenth-Century America.* New York: Macmillan, 1996.

Weatherford, Doris. *Milestones: A Chronology of American Women's History.* New York: Facts On File, 1997.

Woloch, Nancy, ed. *Early American Women: A Documentary History, 1600–1900.* New York: McGraw-Hill, 1996.

Yee, Shirley. *Black Women Abolitionists: A Study in Activism, 1828–1860.* Knoxville: University of Tennessee Press, 1992.

Zepatos, Thalia, and Elizabeth Kaufman. *Women for a Change: A Grassroots Guide to Activism and Politics.* New York: Facts On File, 1995.

Zinn, Maxine, and Bonnie Thorton Dill, eds. *Women of Color in U.S. Society.* Philadelphia: Temple University Press, 1993.

ENTRIES BY AREA OF ACTIVITY

Abolitionist

Craft, Ellen Smith
Grimké, Angelina Emily
Harper, Frances Ellen
    Watkins
Haviland, Laura Smith
Mott, Lucretia Coffin
Stone, Lucy
Truth, Sojourner
Tubman, Harriet Araminta
    Greene
Wright, Frances

American Indian Advocate

Jackson, Helen Maria Fiske
    Hunt

American Indian Leader

Deer, Ada
LaDuke, Winona
LaFlesche Picotte, Susan
Mankiller, Wilma Pearl
McCloud, Janet Reneecker
Thorpe, Grace
Ward, Nancy
Winnemucca, Sarah
    Hopkins

Attorney

Berry, Mary Frances
Eastman, Crystal

Edelman, Marian Wright
Ginsburg, Ruth Joan Bader
Hernandez, Antonia
Kennedy, Florence Rae
MacKinnon, Catharine
    Alice
Murray, Anna Pauline
Reno, Janet
Weddington, Sarah Ragle

Birth Control Advocate

Sanger, Margaret Louise
    Higgins
Wattleton, Alyce Faye

Civil Rights Leader

Baker, Ella Josephine
Bates, Daisy Lee Gatson
Clark, Septima Poinsette
Cotera, Martha Castanos
Hamer, Fannie Lou
    Townsend
Hernandez, Antonia
Hernandez, Maria Latigo
Heumann, Judy
Parks, Rosa Louise
    McCauley
Robinson, Jo Ann Gibson
Robinson, Ruby Doris
    Smith

Terrell, Mary Elizabeth
    Church
Vaid, Urvashi

Disability Advocate

Heumann, Judy
Keller, Helen Adams
Shriver, Eunice Mary
    Kennedy

Educational Reformer

Bethune, Mary McLeod
Butler, Selena Sloan
Cooper, Anna Julia
    Haywood
Wright, Frances

Entrepreneur

Mason, Bridget

Environmental Activist

Bari, Judith Beatrice
Carson, Rachel Louise
LaDuke, Winona
Silkwood, Karen Gay
Thorpe, Grace

Feminist Activist

Anthony, Susan Brownell
Dorr, Rheta Childe

Eastman, Crystal
Friedan, Elizabeth Naomi
   Goldstein
Fuller, Margaret
Gilman, Charlotte Anna
   Perkins Stetson
Grimké, Angelina
Kennedy, Florence Rae
MacKinnon, Catharine
Millett, Katherine Murray
Morgan, Robin
Murray, Anna Pauline
Paul, Alice Stokes
Rose, Ernestine
Smeal, Eleanor Marie Cutri
Stanton, Elizabeth Cady
Stone, Lucy
Wattleton, Faye

Health Reform Advocate

Barton, Clarissa Harlowe
Dix, Dorothea Lynde
Hamilton, Alice
Sanger, Margaret
Wattleton, Faye Alyce

Journalist

Bryant, Louise Moran
Day, Dorothy
Dorr, Rheta Louise Childe
Fuller, Sarah Margaret
Morgan, Robin
Steinem, Gloria
Tarbell, Ida
Wells-Barnett, Ida Bell

Labor Activist

Flynn, Elizabeth Gurley
Kelley, Florence Molthrop
Silkwood, Karen Gay

Labor Leader

Chavez-Thompson, Linda
Huerta, Dolores Fernandez

Jones, Mary Harris
Parsons, Lucy Gonzalez
Tenayuca, Emma

Lesbian and Gay Rights Activist

Vaid, Urvashi

Lecturers and Orator

Anthony, Susan Brownell
Fuller, Margaret
Gilman, Charlotte Anna
   Perkins Stetson
Goldman, Emma
Harper, Frances
Rose, Ernestine
Shaw, Anna Howard
Stanton, Elizabeth Cady
Truth, Sojourner
Tubman, Harriet
Wells-Barnett, Ida Bell
Wright, Frances

Peace Advocate

Addams, Laura Jane
Baez, Joan Chandos
Balch, Emily Greene
Catt, Carrie Clinton
   Champman
Eastman, Catherine Crystal
Hughan, Jessie Wallace
Rankin, Jeannette Pickering

Political Figure

Adviser and Appointee
Albright, Madeleine Korbel
Berry, Mary Frances
Chavez, Linda
Deer, Ada
Dole, Mary Elizabeth
   Alexander Hanford
Ginsburg, Ruth Joan Bader
Harris, Patricia Roberts
Herman, Alexis

Heumann, Judy
Hobby, Oveta Culp
Kirkpatrick, Jeanne Jordan
Lathrop, Julia Clifford
Novello, Antonia Coello
Perkins, Frances Coralie
Reno, Janet
Shalala, Donna
Whitman, Christine Todd

Ambassador
Black, Shirley Jane Temple
Bloch, Julia Chang
Luce, Ann Clare Boothe

Congressional Representative
Abzug, Bella Savitsky
Chisholm, Shirley Anita
   St. Hill
Collins, Cardiss Robertson
Ferraro, Geraldine
Griffiths, Martha Wright
Jordan, Barbara Charline
Luce, Ann Clare Boothe
Mikulski, Barbara Ann
Mink, Patsy Takemoto
Norton, Eleanor Holmes
Rankin, Jeannette Pickering
Rogers, Edith Nourse
Schroeder, Patricia Nell
   Scott
Waters, Maxine Moore

Elected Official
Molina, Gloria

First Lady
Adams, Abigail Smith
Clinton, Hillary Rodham
Roosevelt, Anna Eleanor

Governor
Grasso, Ella Rosa Giovanni
   Oliva Tambussi
Ray, Dixy Lee
Richards, Dorothy Ann
   Willis

Ross, Nellie Davis Tayloe
Shaheen, Jeanne Bowers
Whitman, Christine Todd

Senator

Boxer, Barbara Levy
Clinton, Hillary Rodham
Feinstein, Dianne
Felton, Rebecca Ann
    Latimer
Hutchison, Kay Bailey
Kassebaum, Nancy
    Josephine Landon
Mikulski, Barbara Ann
Moseley-Braun, Carol
Murray, Patty Johns
Smith, Margaret Madeline
    Chase
Snowe, Olympia Jean
    Boucles

Scientist

Hamilton, Alice
Richards, Ellen Henrietta
    Swallow

Settlement House Leader

Addams, Laura Jane
Kelley, Florence Molthrop
Lathrop, Julia Clifford

Social and Civic Reform Leader

Castillo, Sylvia
Cervantes, Magdalena

Hale, Clara
Harper, Frances
Height, Dorothy Irene
Kuhn, Margaret Eliza
Low, Juliette Magill Kinzie
    Gordon
Roosevelt, Anna Eleanor
Schlafly, Phyllis Stewart
    MacAlpin
Szold, Chayeleh
Vaid, Urvashi

Socialist and Radical

Balch, Emily Greene
Bryant, Louise Moran
Davis, Angela
Day, Dorothy
Flynn, Elizabeth Gurley
Goldman, Emma
Hutchinson, Anne Marbury
Jones, Mary Harris
Kelley, Florence Molthrop
O'Hare, Carrie Kathleen
    Richards Cunningham
Parsons, Lucy
Sanger, Margaret
Tenayuca, Emma
Willard, Frances Elizabeth
    Caroline
Woodhull, Victoria Claflin
Wright, Frances

Suffragist

Anthony, Susan Brownell

Catt, Carrie Clinton Lane
    Chapman
Dorr, Rheta Childe
Duniway, Abigail Jane Scott
Eastman, Catherine
    Crystal
Mott, Lucretia Coffin
Paul, Alice Stokes
Rose, Ernestine Louise
    Siismondi Potowski
Shaw, Anna Howard
Stanton, Elizabeth Cady
Stone, Lucy
Terrell, Mary Elizabeth
    Church
Truth, Sojourner
Tubman, Harriet
Wells-Barnett, Ida Bell
Willard, Frances Elizabeth
    Caroline
Woodhull, Victoria Claflin
Wright, Frances

Temperance Advocate

Harper, Frances
Nation, Carry Amelia
    Moore Gloyd
Willard, Frances Elizabeth
    Caroline

Women's Club Leader

Harper, Frances
Height, Dorothy Irene
Ruffin, Josephine St. Pierre
Wells-Barnett, Ida Bell

ENTRIES BY YEAR OF BIRTH

1500–1600s

Hutchinson, Anne Marbury

1700–1749

Adams, Abigail Smith
Ward, Nancy

1750–1799

Mott, Lucretia Coffin
Truth, Sojourner
Wright, Frances

1800–1829

Anthony, Susan Brownell
Barton, Clarissa Harlowe
Craft, Ellen Smith
Dix, Dorothea Lynde
Fuller, Sarah Margaret
Grimké, Angelina Emily
Harper, Frances Ellen
    Watkins
Haviland, Laura Smith
Mason, Bridget
Rose, Ernestine Louise
    Siismondi Potowski
Stanton, Elizabeth Cady
Stone, Lucy
Tubman, Harriet Araminta
    Greene

1830–1859

Catt, Carrie Clinton Lane
    Chapman
Cooper, Anna Julia
    Haywood
Duniway, Abigail Jane
    Scott
Felton, Rebecca Ann
    Latimer
Jackson, Helen Maria Fiske
    Hunt
Jones, Mary Harris
Kelley, Florence Molthrop
Lathrop, Julia Clifford
Nation, Carry Amelia
    Moore Gloyd
Parsons, Lucy
Richards, Ellen Henrietta
    Swallow
Ruffin, Josephine St. Pierre
Shaw, Anna Howard
Tarbell, Ida
Willard, Frances Elizabeth
    Caroline
Winnemucca, Sarah
    Hopkins
Woodhull, Victoria Claflin

1860–1879

Addams, Laura Jane

Balch, Emily Greene
Bethune, Mary McLeod
Butler, Selena Sloan
Dorr, Rheta Louise Childe
Gilman, Charlotte Anna
    Perkins Stetson
Goldman, Emma
Hamilton, Alice
Hughan, Jessie Wallace
LaFlesche Picotte, Susan
Low, Juliette Magill Kinzie
    Gordon
O'Hare, Carrie Kathleen
    Richards Cunningham
Ross, Nellie Davis Tayloe
Szold, Chayeleh
Terrell, Mary Elizabeth
    Church
Wells-Barnett, Ida Bell

1880–1899

Bryant, Louise Moran
Clark, Septima Poinsette
Day, Dorothy
Eastman, Catherine Crystal
Flynn, Elizabeth Gurley
Hernandez, Maria Latigo
Keller, Helen Adams
Paul, Alice Stokes
Perkins, Frances Coralie

266

Rankin, Jeannette Pickering
Rogers, Edith Nourse
Roosevelt, Anna Eleanor
Sanger, Margaret Louise
    Higgins
Smith, Margaret Madeline
    Chase

1900–1919

Baker, Ella Josephine
Carson, Rachel Louise
Grasso, Ella Rosa Giovanni
    Oliva Tambussi
Griffiths, Martha Wright
Hale, Clara
Hamer, Fannie Lou
    Townsend
Height, Dorothy Irene
Hobby, Oveta Culp
Kennedy, Florence Rae
Kuhn, Margaret Eliza
Luce, Ann Clare Boothe
Murray, Anna Pauline
Parks, Rosa Louise
    McCauley
Ray, Dixy Lee
Robinson, Jo Ann Gibson
Tenayuca, Emma

1920–1939

Abzug, Bella Savitsky
Albright, Madeleine Korbel
Bates, Daisy Lee Gatson
Berry, Mary Frances
Black, Shirley Jane Temple
Chisholm, Shirley Anita
    St. Hill

Collins, Cardiss Robertson
Cotera, Martha Castanos
Deer, Ada
Dole, Mary Elizabeth
    Alexander Hanford
Edelman, Marian Wright
Feinstein, Dianne
Ferraro, Geraldine
Friedan, Elizabeth Naomi
    Goldstein
Ginsburg, Ruth Joan Bader
Harris, Patricia Roberts
Huerta, Dolores Fernandez
Jordan, Barbara Charline
Kassebaum, Nancy
    Josephine Landon
Kirkpatrick, Jeanne Jordan
McCloud, Janet Reneecker
Mikulski, Barbara Ann
Millett, Katherine Murray
Mink, Patsy Takemoto
Norton, Eleanor Holmes
Reno, Janet
Richards, Dorothy Ann
    Willis
Schlafly, Phyllis Stewart
    Macalpin
Shriver, Eunice Mary
    Kennedy
Smeal, Eleanor Marie Cutri
Steinem, Gloria
Thorpe, Grace
Waters, Maxine Moore

1940–1949

Baez, Joan Chandos
Bari, Judith Beatrice

Bloch, Julia Chang
Boxer, Barbara Levy
Chavez, Linda
Chavez-Thompson, Linda
Clinton, Hillary Rodham
Davis, Angela
Herman, Alexis
Hernandez, Antonia
Heumann, Judy
Hutchison, Kay Bailey
MacKinnon, Catharine
    Alice
Mankiller, Wilma Pearl
Molina, Gloria
Morgan, Robin
Moseley-Braun, Carole
Novello, Antonia Coello
Robinson, Ruby Doris
    Smith
Schroeder, Patricia Nell
    Scott
Shaheen, Jeanne Bowers
Shalala, Donna
Silkwood, Karen Gay
Snowe, Olympia Jean
    Boucles
Wattleton, Alyce Faye
Weddington, Sarah Ragle
Whitman, Christine
    Todd

1950–1959

Castillo, Sylvia
Cervantes, Magdalena
LaDuke, Winona
Murray, Patty Johns
Vaid, Urvashi

INDEX

◇ ◇ ◇ ◇ ◇

Page numbers in **boldface** indicate main entries.
Page numbers in *italics* indicate illustrations and photographs.